BEHIND THE MASK

BEHIND THE MASK

The Life of Vita Sackville-West

Matthew Dennison

WILLIAM COLLINS

William Collins
An imprint of HarperCollins*Publishers*
77–85 Fulham Palace Road,
Hammersmith, London W6 8JB
WilliamCollinsBooks.com

Published by William Collins in 2014

1

A catalogue record for this book
is available from the British Library

ISBN 978-0-00-748696-0

Typeset in Bell MT by Palimpsest Book Production Ltd, Falkirk, Stirlingshire

Printed and bound in Great Britain by Clays Ltd, St Ives plc

MIX
Paper from
responsible sources
FSC
www.fsc.org   FSC™ C007454

FSC™ is a non-profit international organisation established to promote
the responsible management of the world's forests. Products carrying the
FSC label are independently certified to assure consumers that they come
from forests that are managed to meet the social, economic and
ecological needs of present and future generations,
and other controlled sources.

Find out more about HarperCollins and the environment at
www.harpercollins.co.uk/green

For Gráinne, with all love

'. . . he told her that he could find no words to praise her;
yet instantly bethought him how she was like the spring
and green grass and rushing waters.'

(*Orlando*, Virginia Woolf)

'All the coherence of her life belonged to Condaford; she had a passion for the place . . . After all she had been born there . . . Every Condaford beast, bird and tree, even the flowers she was plucking, were a part of her, just as were the simple folk around her in their thatched cottages, and the Early-English church, where she attended without belief to speak of, and the grey Condaford dawns which she seldom saw, the moonlit, owl-haunted nights, the long sunlight over the stubble, and the scents and sounds and feel of the air.'

John Galsworthy, *Maid in Waiting* (1931)

'. . . we write, not with the fingers, but with the whole person. The nerve which controls the pen winds itself about every fibre of our being, threads the heart, pierces the liver.'

Virginia Woolf, *Orlando* (1928)

CONTENTS

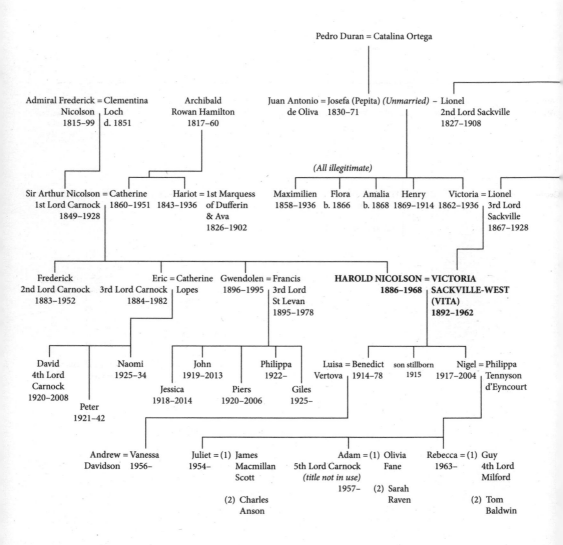

The Family Trees of the
Sackville-Wests and the Nicolsons

Pedro Duran = Catalina Ortega

Admiral Frederick = Clementina
Nicolson   Loch
1815–99   d. 1851

Archibald
Rowan Hamilton
1817–60

Juan Antonio = Josefa (Pepita) *(Unmarried)* – Lionel
de Oliva   1830–71   2nd Lord Sackville
                                          1827–1908

(All illegitimate)

Sir Arthur Nicolson = Catherine
1st Lord Carnock   1860–1951
1849–1928

Hariot = 1st Marquess
1843–1936 of Dufferin
            & Ava
            1826–1902

Maximilien   Flora   Amalia   Henry   Victoria = Lionel
1858–1936   b. 1866 b. 1868 1869–1914 1862–1936 3rd Lord
                                                    Sackville
                                                    1867–1928

Frederick
2nd Lord Carnock
1883–1952

Eric = Catherine
3rd Lord Carnock Lopes
1884–1982

Gwendolen = Francis
1896–1995   3rd Lord
            St Levan
            1895–1978

HAROLD NICOLSON = VICTORIA
1886–1968   SACKVILLE-WEST
                (VITA)
                1892–1962

David
4th Lord
Carnock
1920–2008

Naomi
1925–34

John
1919–2013

Jessica
1918–2014

Philippa
1922–

Piers
1920–2006

Giles
1925–

Luisa = Benedict
Vertova 1914–78

son stillborn
1915

Nigel = Philippa
1917–2004 Tennyson
           d'Eyncourt

Peter
1921–42

Andrew = Vanessa
Davidson 1956–

Juliet = (1) James
1954–   Macmillan
           Scott

        (2) Charles
            Anson

Adam = (1) Olivia
5th Lord Carnock Fane
(title not in use)
1957–   (2) Sarah
             Raven

Rebecca = (1) Guy
1963–   4th Lord
           Milford

        (2) Tom
            Baldwin

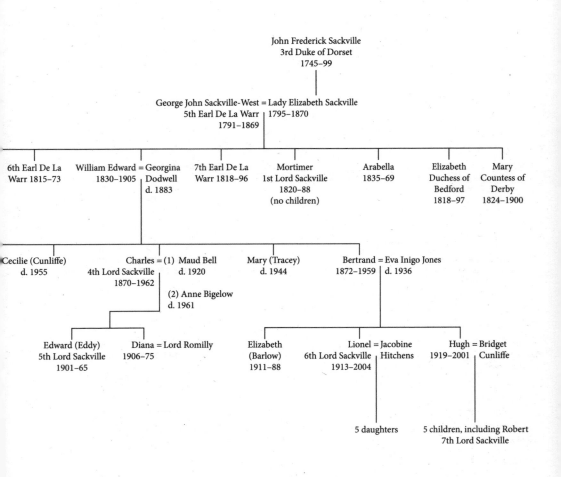

John Frederick Sackville
3rd Duke of Dorset
1745–99

George John Sackville-West = Lady Elizabeth Sackville
5th Earl De La Warr | 1795–1870
1791–1869

| 6th Earl De La Warr 1815–73 | William Edward = Georgina 1830–1905 | Dodwell d. 1883 | 7th Earl De La Warr 1818–96 | Mortimer 1st Lord Sackville 1820–88 (no children) | Arabella 1835–69 | Elizabeth Duchess of Bedford 1818–97 | Mary Countess of Derby 1824–1900 |

Cecilie (Cunliffe)
d. 1955

Charles = (1) Maud Bell
4th Lord Sackville | d. 1920
1870–1962

(2) Anne Bigelow
d. 1961

Mary (Tracey)
d. 1944

Bertrand = Eva Inigo Jones
1872–1959 | d. 1936

Edward (Eddy)
5th Lord Sackville
1901–65

Diana = Lord Romilly
1906–75

Elizabeth
(Barlow)
1911–88

Lionel = Jacobine
6th Lord Sackville | Hitchens
1913–2004

Hugh = Bridget
1919–2001 | Cunliffe

5 daughters

5 children, including Robert
7th Lord Sackville

List of Illustrations

Plate section 1

Page 1: Vita by Philip Alexius de László, oil on canvas, 1910 (© *National Trust Images/John Hammond*)

Page 2: Vita with her mother; Vita with her father

Page 3: Knole; King's Bedroom, Knole (© *English Heritage*)

Page 4: Harold, Vita, Rosamund Grosvenor and Lionel Sackville on their way to court; Vita and her parents (*Photo by Hulton Archive/Getty Images*)

Page 5: Vita as Portia by Clare Atwood, oil on canvas, 1910 (© *National Trust Images*)

Page 6: Vita and Mrs Walter Rubens (© *Illustrated London News Ltd/Mary Evans*); Vita (© *Illustrated London News Ltd/Mary Evans*)

Page 7: Sir Harold Nicholson, *c.*1920 (© *Private Collection/ Bridgeman Images*); Vita at Ascot with Lord Lascelles (*Photo by Hulton Archive/Getty Images*)

Page 8: Violet Keppel by Sir John Lavery, oil on canvas, 1919 (© *National Trust Images*)

Plate section 2

Page 1: Vita and her two sons (*Photo by Hulton Archive/Getty Images*)

Page 2: *View of Long Barn, Kent, in Winter* by Mary Margaret Garman Campbell, oil on paper, *c*.1927–8 (© *National Trust/ Charles Thomas*)

Page 3: Vita at the BBC (© *BBC/Corbis*); Vita in sitting room at Long Barn with her sons (© *Hulton-Deutsch Collection/ CORBIS*)

Page 4: Vita (© *Mary Evans/Everett Collection*)

Page 5: Dorothy Wellesley by Madame Yevonde (© *The Yevonde Portrait Archive*); Virginia Woolf (*Photo by Mondadori Portfolio via Getty Images*); Hilda Matheson by Howard Coster (© *National Portrait Gallery, London*)

Page 6: Sissinghurst Tower (© *Niek Goossen/Shutterstock*); White Garden at Sissinghurst (© *Eric Crichton/CORBIS*)

Page 7: Vita by John Gay, 1948 (© *National Portrait Gallery, London*); Vita in the Sissinghurst Tower by John Hedgecoe, 1958 (© *2006 John Hedgecoe/Topham/The Image Works*)

Page 8: Vita's desk by Edwin Smith, 1962 (© *Edwin Smith/ RIBA Library Photographs Collection*)

Preface

VITA SACKVILLE-WEST ONCE described herself as someone
who loved 'books and flowers and poetry and travel and trees
and dragons and the wind and the sea and generous hearts
and spacious ideals and little children'.[1] Later she added that
she loved 'literature, and peace, and a secluded life'.[2]

There is no reason to doubt her. 'Books and flowers and
poetry' became the outward purpose of her life: at the time of
her death she was famous twice over, as a writer and a gardener.
She never lost the taste for travel that began during her enor-
mously privileged childhood; at home, she balanced curiosity
and wanderlust with a powerful need for solitude ('peace, and
a secluded life'). Her love of nature – 'trees and . . . the wind
and the sea' – is among her defining attributes as a poet and
a novelist. It also shaped her understanding of the role of the
landowning aristocracy to which she belonged, and in particular of her own role as a dispossessed aristocrat in the twentieth
century. I interpret those 'dragons' symbolically. Vita was an
extravagant dreamer. Her self-perception was shaped by myths

and fairy tales. Intensely imaginative, like many artists she realised early in her life the subjectivity both of reality and realism. She valued intensity of feeling. She once described the ideal approach to life as 'the ardour that [lights] the whole,/ Not expectation of that or this'.[3] And she admired – and inclined to – lavishness. 'I like generosity wherever I find it.'[4]

As in most lives, Vita defined 'spacious ideals' to suit herself. So too, although with greater particularity, 'generous hearts'. These are the qualities which overwhelm Vita's posthumous reputation. Since publication more than forty years ago of her confessional autobiography, written in 1920, in which she described her passionate affair with her childhood friend Violet Keppel, Vita's literary achievements and the plantsmanship of her garden at Sissinghurst Castle have played second fiddle to her role as lesbian icon. Vita's affair with Violet Keppel, described in *Portrait of a Marriage*, changed her life; it altered the course of what has become one of the best-known marriages of the last century, to diplomat, politician and writer Harold Nicolson, himself predominantly homosexual.

I suggest that this affair defines Vita as a person only to the extent that it demonstrates her determination to realise in her life the fullest possible understanding of the terms 'spacious ideals' and 'generous hearts'. In arriving at working definitions of those terms, Vita hurt herself and others too, including her husband and her own 'little children', Ben and Nigel Nicolson. She was occasionally selfish, occasionally cruel. Jilted lovers threatened physical violence and legal action; on one occasion, Vita was forced to wrestle a pistol out of a lover's grip; amorous entanglements forced Vita to deception and concealment. Neither her selfishness nor her cruelty was deliberate; blind to the small scale, she was without pettiness. 'To hope for Paradise is to live in Paradise, a very different thing from actually getting there,' she once wrote.[5] She was a lifelong romantic, who understood herself well enough to recognise the slipperiness of her grasp on happiness. Her quest was for 'beauty and comprehension, those two smothered elements which hide in all souls and are so seldom allowed to find their way to the surface'.[6]

We should not lose sight of the 'irresistible charm', remembered by those closest to her, her 'nobility and grandeur . . . largeness and generosity in everything she did or said or felt' – but must set against it the vehemence of her need for privacy and her obsessive secrecy.[7] Even her immediate family sometimes had no idea of Vita's current literary project.

Vita consistently legitimised her peccadilloes in her writing. Internal debates, the need for secrecy among them, were played out in black and white on the printed page, albeit in the case of her sexuality in necessarily disguised form. Of the heroine of her best novel, *All Passion Spent*, Vita wrote in 1930, 'Pleasure to her was entirely a private matter, a secret joke, intense, redolent, but as easily bruised as the petals of a gardenia.'[8] It was Vita's own mission statement as faithless wife and lover. Through concealment, she achieved the compartmentalisation of her life that was essential to her. She rationalised it unapologetically as 'carry[ing] one's life inside oneself'.[9]

The equation of pleasure and privacy was fundamental to Vita. She rebelled behind closed doors or within the safety of a small circle of friends gathered frequently from her own elite background. She did not advertise her transgressions, but maintained her 'secluded life'. She once described the literary hostess Lady Ottoline Morrell as 'a very queer personality . . . with masses of purple hair, a deep voice, teeth like a piano keyboard and the most extraordinary assortment of clothes, hung with barbaric necklaces . . . a born bohemian by nature'.[10] Vita never imagined herself 'a born bohemian'. Her identity as daughter of Knole, the great Sackville house in Kent, overruled all other personae.

On 27 June 1890, less than two years before Vita's birth, her mother Victoria Sackville-West wrote in her diary, 'What a heavenly husband I have and how different our love and union is from that of other couples.'[11] In time – and repeatedly – Vita would say something similar; Harold told her that 'our love is something which only two people in the world can understand' and that 'the thought of you is a little hot water bottle of happiness which I hug in this cold world'.[12] There is a variant on these statements for every happy marriage.

Vita claimed that hers was not an intellectual background, but she was mistaken when she insisted that analysis did not intrude upon her parents' lives. Her mother's diary contradicts her. Happily the trait, like many in Vita's makeup, was inherited. The result is that Vita's was a thoughtful and thought-provoking life, even if, surprisingly, she excluded the bulk of her questioning from her diary or, in some cases, her letters, choosing instead to resolve her conflicts in her poetry and prose (unpublished as well as published). She was a consistently autobiographical author, even in her nonfiction; in the best of her writing this autobiographical element was skilfully handled and subtly nuanced. Through role-play scenarios in her writing, Vita expanded and explained her sense of herself. I suggest that it was these varied roles, recognised and understood by those nearest to her, which provided this shy but uncompromising woman with the masks she needed to live the several lives she almost succeeded in uniting.

In her introduction to the diary of her redoubtable seventeenth-century kinswoman Lady Anne Clifford, Vita stated, 'Few tasks of the historian or biographer can be more misleading than the reconstruction of a forgotten character from the desultory evidence at his disposal.'[13] She indicated the danger of posthumous judgements based on 'a patchwork of letters, preserved by chance, independent of their context'. That argument is a truism of all biography. In revisiting Vita's own life story, I have supported the evidence of letters and her diary with the textual evidence of so much of her writing: poetry, novels, plays, short stories, travel books, books of literary criticism, biography and journalism. The sections of this book are named after Vita's own novels and poems (or, in the case of Part Four, a book written about Vita during her lifetime by Virginia Woolf, who knew her well and loved her). Such recourse, I recognise, is a commonplace of literary biography; it is particularly apt in Vita's case. 'Few things are more distasteful than veiled hints,' Vita wrote once, addressing head on rumours of lesbianism on the part of the Spanish saint, Teresa of Avila.[14] I believe that her writing is full of hints – sometimes veiled, sometimes otherwise – indicative of her state of mind, her emotional dilemmas, the nature of her engagement with herself and the world around her. I have used these 'hints' to support more conventional evidence in order to reach the fullest possible picture of this remarkable woman. As Vita herself concluded about St Teresa, 'every point concerning so complex a character and so truly extraordinary a make-up is of interest as possibly throwing a little extra light on subsequent behaviour'.[15]

Vita never fully succeeded in explaining herself to herself. In one of her poems she imagined staring at her reflection in a mountain pool: 'seen there my own image/ As an upturned mask that floated/ Just under the surface, within reach, beyond reach'.[16] I hope that the present account, which does not attempt a blow-by-blow chronology of her life, helps to bring reflections of Vita closer within reach.

PROLOGUE

Heritage

'Those brief ten years we call Edwardian . . . were a gay and yet
an earnest time . . . Money nobly flowed. Ideals changed . . .
"Respectability", that good old word, . . . sank into discredit . . .
Among most of the wealthy, most of the titled, most of the gay
and extravagant classes, a wider liberty grew.'

Rose Macaulay, *Told by an Idiot*, 1923

THE SUM OF money at stake was impressively large. At his
death on 17 January 1912, Sir John Murray Scott, sixty-five-
year-old great-grandson of Nelson's captain of the fleet Sir
George Murray, left estate valued at £1.18 million (the equivalent, at today's values, of around £80 million).[1] The challenge
to Sir John's will brought by his family the following year was
heard in a packed courtroom. An eight-day trial conducted by
England's foremost barristers, it made headlines on both sides
of the Atlantic. It transformed its plaintiffs – a family notable
for reserve and taciturnity – into reluctant celebrities. In the
process, it exposed the deceits and compromises of Edwardian

morality, stripping away the veneer of well-mannered discretion to reveal a cynical culture of avarice and lust, a preference for appearances over truth.

Like many rich men, Sir John had enjoyed playing a cat-and-mouse game with family and friends over the contents of his will, which extended to numerous bequests. Principal legatees were his brothers and sisters – middle-aged, unmarried, over-weight: the sober-minded offspring of a Scottish doctor. Collectively they inherited £410,000 and the family's London home in Connaught Place plus contents. Further legacies, to the tune of £223,000, benefited a series of recipients. A single large legacy provided the bone of contention. In addition to furniture and works of art valued at the enormous total of £350,000, childless bachelor Sir John left £150,000 in cash to the woman he described as 'ma chère petite amie'.

Victoria Sackville-West was fifty years old. Of mixed English and Spanish parentage, she had the wide-eyed gaze of a languorous fawn, a complexion which, with care, had retained its lustre into middle age and an ample bosom ideally suited to the role of Edwardian grande dame. In her youth, she claimed she had received twenty-five proposals of marriage before accepting her husband, who was also her first cousin and heir to one of the greatest houses in England; she was a vain and fanciful woman. At twelve stone, her height five feet seven inches, she may no longer have been as 'petite' as formerly: undimmed were her powers of persuasion and her theatricality. She was also prone to an unpredictable Latin exactingness. This trait appears to have had an invigorating rather than an alienating effect on admirers including the American millionaire banker John Pierpont Morgan, hero of the Sudan, Lord Kitchener, and Observer editor J. L. Garvin. Rudyard Kipling described Victoria as 'on mature reflection the most wonderful person I have ever met'; throughout her life she attracted rich

and powerful men.[2] Even less sympathetic onlookers acknowledged her distinctive allure. 'In her too fleshy face, classical
features sought to escape from the encroaching fat. An admi-
rable mouth, of a pure and cruel design, held good. It was
obvious that she had been beautiful.'[3] Counsel for the prosecution described her damningly as possessing all 'the fascinations
of an accomplished woman'.[4] Unspoken accusations of immo-
rality added a tang to the courtroom proceedings.

In fact the 'affair' of Sir John Murray Scott and Victoria
Sackville-West was a sentimental friendship of rare intensity,
a compromise at which the latter excelled. Their relationship
was almost certainly unconsummated. In her diary Victoria
claimed to be 'much too fond of [her] husband to flirt with
anybody';[5] the frisky baby talk of her letters to Scott suggests
otherwise. Bachelor Sir John may have been over-fastidious in
the matter of sex.

Victoria's past was romantic and picaresque. She was illegitimate, Catholic, the daughter of a small-town Spanish
dancer Josefa Durán, known as Pepita, 'the Star of Andalusia'.
Pepita had become the mistress of an English nobleman. She
bore him seven children, including Victoria. In a bid for respectability, she reinvented herself as Countess West and enlisted
kings and princes as godparents to her illegitimate children.
At her lover's request, she set up home on the French coast
southwest of Bordeaux, away from the eyes of the world.

Like Sir John, Victoria had lived part of her life in Paris.
Until her absent father reappeared to rescue her, she had been
educated for a governess at the Convent of St Joseph on rue
Monceau. In 1890 she became chatelaine of Knole in Kent. She
described it with simple pride – and truthfully – as 'bigger
than Hampton Court'. The vast house was the ancestral home
of her husband, Lionel Sackville-West. Victoria learned swiftly
that the income which supported it was less splendid. That

Victoria's husband was also her first cousin was a curious twist worthy of Victorian popular fiction: the English nobleman, Pepita's lover, was the 2nd Baron Sackville, not only Victoria's father but her husband's uncle. Pepita died in 1871, her lover, Lord Sackville, in 1908. In the absence of legitimate offspring the latter's title passed to his nephew.

After 'ten perfect years of the most complete happiness and passionate love', Lionel and Victoria's marriage had turned sour.[6] In the summer of 1913, the couple had a single child, their daughter Vita, who had lately celebrated her twenty-first birthday. Given her sex, the Sackville title would again descend collaterally. Meanwhile, out of love with his wife, Lionel took a series of mistresses: Lady Camden, Lady Constance Hatch, called Connie, an opera singer called Olive Rubens. Like miscreants on a saucy seaside postcard, Lionel and Lady Connie played a lot of golf.

Sir John Murray Scott had been a giant of a man. Measuring more than five feet around the waist and tall too, he weighed in excess of twenty-five stone. He died of a heart attack. The fortune he left behind him derived neither from his family nor his own entrepreneurialism. Instead, in 1897, he had inherited £1 million from his employer, a former shop girl who had caught the eye of Sir Richard Wallace, first as his mistress and afterwards his wife. Wallace was the illegitimate son of the 4th Marquess of Hertford. Lord Hertford left him estates in Ireland, a Parisian apartment of legendary magnificence at 2 rue Laffitte and the chateau de Bagatelle, a charming neoclassical *maison de plaisance* built by Louis XVI's brother, the comte d'Artois, and surrounded by sixty acres of the Bois de Boulogne to the west of Paris. To this splendid inheritance Wallace had added a lease on Hertford House in London, today home of The Wallace Collection, which is named after him. All these glittering prizes Lady Wallace willed to John Murray Scott. For three decades he had served the Wallaces as their devoted secretary. No conditions restricted the bequest. He was free to act as he wished, which is exactly what he did.

What Sir John wished was to help his *chère petite amie*. In a letter delivered to Victoria after his death, he had written, 'It will be found that I have left you in my Will . . . a sum of money which I hope will make you comfortable for life and cause all anxiety as to your future ways and means to cease.'[7] Gratitude inspired his generosity: 'You did everything to make my broken life, and my last words to you are: "I am very grateful."'[8] Victoria had ensured that Sir John, or 'Seery' as the Sackvilles called him, was fully aware of the contrast between his own wealth and the relatively modest income generated by the Sackville estates (a sum of £13,000 a year, recently estimated at 'perhaps a third of what was needed to support an establishment such as Knole'[9]). As an added sweetener to his £500,000 bequest, he left Victoria a diamond necklace that had once belonged to Queen Catherine Parr, a pocket book of Marie Antoinette's and, from Connaught Place, a bust by eighteenth-century French sculptor Houdon and a chandelier. Together, chandelier and sculpture were worth a further £50,000: Sir John intended them for Knole. For good measure, he left a second diamond necklace to Victoria's daughter Vita and a valuable pearl necklace, which became his posthumous twenty-first birthday present to her.

A fly on the wall in Connaught Place would have known the way the wind was blowing long before writs were issued. Even during Sir John's lifetime, his siblings had referred to Lionel and Victoria as 'the Locusts'. Sir John had made Victoria a number of 'gifts' in the dozen years of their friendship. Beginning with a modest single payment of £42 8s 6d, these ultimately amounted to a figure close to £84,000. In several instances the purpose of these gifts was understood to be expenses relating to Knole or the settlement of Sackville debts and mortgages (a handout of £38,600, for example, begun as a loan for this purpose, was subsequently written off). The real recipients were not Victoria but Lionel and Knole. In addition, at a cost of £17,000, Sir John had provided Victoria with a handsome London townhouse at 34 Hill Street in Mayfair. With little regard for the feelings of his unmarried sisters, who nominally kept house for him, Victoria chose to divide much of her time between Hill Street and Connaught Place. There she rearranged the furniture, instructed the servants, commandeered Sir John's carriage and hosted dinner parties from which she excluded his sisters Miss Alicia and Miss Mary. She dismissed them both as irredeemably drab. Sir John did not object. To rub salt into the wound, he presented Victoria with a handsome and valuable red lacquer cabinet, which he had bought for his sisters' boudoir. By the summer of 1913, in the eyes of her opponents, Victoria's offences were manifold.

The case that began on 26 June concerned Victoria's exercise of 'undue influence' over Sir John's will. As *The New York Times* explained to American readers, F. E. Smith, counsel for the prosecution, 'in concluding his nine hours' [opening] speech, said the question was whether the testator at a vital and critical moment was in a position to give free play to his own wishes or whether he was so under the influence of Lady Sackville that the decisions he took were not his, but hers'.[10] Sir John's siblings were clear on the matter. So, too, was Victoria. Dressed with colourful and costly panache, she gave a bravura performance in the witness box. In one of several early, unpublished novels, Vita reimagined her mother's triumph: 'Her evidence was miraculous in its elusiveness; she held the court's attention, charmed the judge, took the jury into her confidence, routed the opposing counsel, wept at some moments, looked beautiful and distressed . . .'[11] The jury needed only twelve minutes to reach their judgement. Victoria emerged victorious and just about exonerated. The judge, Sir Samuel Evans, acclaimed her as a woman of 'very high mettle indeed'; afterwards Victoria made a friend of him. The *Pall Mall Gazette* reached a less partial assessment: 'Sir John was ready to give, and Lady Sackville scrupled not to receive.' In acknowledgement of her gratitude, Victoria afterwards invited all twelve jurymen to her daughter's wedding.

As long ago as 17 June 1904, Victoria had confided to her diary 'I hate gossiping'.[12] Later she wrote, 'People may do what they like but it ought to be either sacred or absolutely private. It is nobody's business to know our private life. The less said about it, the better . . .'[13] It was fear of exposure which added a frisson to Edwardian misbehaviour. 'The code was rigid,' Vita later wrote in a novel about the period. 'Within the closed circle of their own set, anybody might do as they pleased, but no scandal must leak out to the uninitiated. Appearances must be respected, though morals might be neglected.'[14]

Swayed by such feelings, and in an attempt to shield her husband and her daughter from scandal, Victoria had written to the Scotts' counsel on the eve of the trial, '*Do Spare Them*, and attack *me* as much as you like.'[15] Her plea fell on deaf ears. Her victory involved the very public airing of family secrets she had hoped to conceal; even Lady Connie was called on to give evidence. Among unwelcome revelations were those concerning the Sackville finances, aspersions on Victoria's own morality and rapacity, and an exposé of Lionel's relationship with Lady Connie, with all the associated inferences to be drawn about the Sackvilles' marriage. In Leicester Square, the Alhambra Theatre, home of popular music-hall entertainment, staged a musical revue based on the trial. One of Victoria's maxims confided to Vita was, 'One must always tell the truth, darling, if one can, but not *all* the truth; *toute verité n'est pas bonne à dire.*[16] With hindsight, it sounded like closing the stable door when the horse had already bolted. The public display of the Sackvilles' dirty linen offended every stricture of aristocratic Edwardian conduct: it would mark them for the remainder of their lives. Both Lionel and Victoria paid a high price for the latter's hard-fought riches. As Vita wrote afterwards, they would realise 'that innocence was no shield against the pointed fingers of the crowd'.[17]

Yet rich Victoria undoubtedly was. Disregarding Sir John's unspoken wish that she transfer the contents of the rue Laffitte apartment to Knole, Victoria sold them *en bloc* to French antiques dealer Jacques Seligmann for £270,000. They were dispersed across the globe, the memory of their rich assembly confined to a short story, *Thirty Clocks Strike the Hour*, which Vita published in 1932. 'There were silence and silken walls, and a faint musty smell, and the shining golden floors, and the dimness of mirrors, and the curve of furniture, and the arabesques of the dull gilding on the ivory boiseries.'[18]

Extravagant as she was covetous, Victoria settled down to living off the interest on the sum of £150,000. The capital itself became part of the Sackville Trust, in accordance with the terms of her marriage settlement. Only Vita emerged from the courtroom unscathed. Jurymen and journalists had discovered that Sir John had called her by the pet name 'Kidlet'. Harmless enough, the label stuck.

In her diary for 7 July, Vita wrote briefly in Italian: 'Triumphant day! All finished!'[19] She invested the short word 'all' with considerable feeling. Her mother's 'triumph' concluded what threatened to be costly legal action with a magnificent windfall. It also brought to an end a troubling five-year period in which the Sackvilles had been continuously involved in, or threatened with, court proceedings.

Three years earlier, in February 1910, Victoria had found

herself with Lionel and, briefly, Vita, in London's High Court. In order to defend her husband's inheritance of the Sackville estates and title in preference to her brother, Pepita's son Henry, Victoria was forced publicly to attest her own illegitimacy and that of her siblings. The *Daily Mail* called the case 'The Romance of the Sackville Peerage'. It was anything but a romantic interlude for Victoria. Proud and spoilt, she habitually masked deep embarrassment about the circumstances of her birth behind ferocious snobbery. Had it not been for her greedy possessiveness towards Knole, she would have found it a more painful experience. Her mother and father were dead, her husband unfaithful and indifferent to her. In the cold light of the High Court she battled the treachery of her brother Henry and her spiteful, disaffected sisters Amalia and Flora. Only one of Pepita's surviving children, Victoria's brother Max, kept clear of the fray. As in the Scott case, Victoria and Lionel won. Knole remained theirs. They retained too the Sackville title, which assured the illegitimate Victoria the respect and deference she craved. In Sevenoaks, their victory was celebrated with a public holiday. They returned to Knole in a carriage drawn by men of the local fire brigade. Bouquets covered the seats. Defeated and deeply in debt, Henry subsequently committed suicide. Expenses associated with the case cost the Sackvilles the enormous sum of £40,000.

In a poem called 'Heredity', written in 1928, Vita Sackville-West asked: 'What is this thing, this strain,/ Persistent, what this shape/ That cuts us from our birth,/ And seals without escape?' To her cousin Eddy she would write: 'You and I have got a jolly sort of heredity to fight against.'[20] Dark shadows clouded Vita's adolescence. On two occasions, crises in the life of her family became public spectacles, she herself – as 'Kidlet' – an unwitting heroine of the illustrated papers. Exposed to public gawping were the sexual foibles of her parents and her grandparents, and a world in which love, sex, money and rank coexisted in a greedy system of barter and plunder. Set against this was the feudal loyalty of Sevenoaks locals, the splendour of life in the rue Laffitte, where Seery entertained European royalty, and the majesty and mystery of Knole itself. It was, for Vita, a varied but not a straightforward existence: courtroom exposure of its flaws increased a tendency to regard herself as distinct and apart, which began in her childhood. Ultimately she longed to retreat from view. Inheritance became a vexed issue for Vita, and one that dominated chapters of her life and facets of her mind. Over time she regarded heredity as immutable and inescapable, but unreliable. This in turn coloured her sense of identity: an element of bravado underpinned her stubborn pride. She did not struggle to escape. Her understanding of her inheritance – temperamental, physical, material – shaped the person she became.

PART I

The Edwardians

'While he was still an infant John learned not to touch glass cases and to be careful with petit-point chairs. His was a lonely but sumptuous childhood, nourished by tales and traditions, with occasional appearances by a beautiful lady dispensing refusals and permissions . . .'

Violet Trefusis, *Broderie Anglaise*, 1935

'IN LIFE,' WROTE Vita Sackville-West in her best-known novel, *The Edwardians*, 'there is only one beginning and only one ending': birth and death.[1] So let it be in this retelling of Vita's own life.

Imagine her as a newborn baby, as she herself suggested, 'lying in a bassinette – having just been deposited for the first time in it . . . surrounded by grown-ups . . . whose lives are already complicated'.[2] The bassinette stands temporarily in her mother's bedroom. The grown-ups are Mrs Patterson the nurse and Vita's mother and father, Victoria and Lionel Sackville-West. We have already seen something of the complications: more will reveal themselves by stages.

In the early hours of 9 March 1892, the grey and green courtyards of Knole were not, as Vita later described them, 'quiet as a college'.[3] Howling and shrieking attended her birth. Outside the great Tudor house, once the palace of the Archbishop of Canterbury, once a royal palace and expansive as a village with its six acres of roof, seven courtyards, more than fifty staircases and reputedly a room for every day of the year, darkness hung heavy, 'deepening the mystery of the park, shrouding the recesses of the garden';[4] the Virginia creeper that each year crimsoned the walls of the Green Court clung stripped of its glowing leaves. Inside, a night of turmoil dragged towards dawn. Dizzy with her husband's affection, less than two years into their marriage, Vita's mother confessed to having 'drunk deep at the cup of real love till I felt absolutely intoxicated':[5] not so intoxicated that the experience of childbirth was anything but terrible. Its horrors astonished Victoria Sackville-West. She wept and she yelled. She begged to be killed. She demanded that Lionel administer doses of chloroform. It was all a hundred times worse than this charming egotist had anticipated. Lionel could not open the chloroform bottle; Mrs Patterson was powerless to prevent extensive, extremely painful tearing. And then, within three quarters of an hour of giving birth, she succumbed to 'intense happiness'. Elation displaced agony. She was dazzled by 'such a miracle, such an incredible marvel': 'one's own little baby'. She was no stranger to lightning changes of mood.

Her 'own little baby' was presented to Victoria Sackville-West by her doting husband. Like a precious stone or a piece of jewellery, Vita lay upon a cushion. Her tiny hands, her miniature yawning, entranced her mother. So, too, her licks and tufts of dark hair. Throughout her pregnancy Victoria had been certain that her unborn child would be a daughter. Long before she was born, Victoria and Lionel had taken to calling her Vita (they could not refer to her as 'Baby' since 'Baby' was Victoria's name for Lionel's penis); her wriggling in the womb had kept Victoria awake at night. On the day of Vita's birth, Victoria headed her diary entry 'VITA': bold capitals indicate that she considered the name settled, inarguable. It was, of course, a contraction of Victoria's own name, just as the daughter who bore it must expect to become her own small doppelgänger. For good measure Victoria christened her baby Victoria Mary. Mary was a sot to the Catholicism of her youth. It was also a tribute to Mary, Countess of Derby, Lord Sackville's sister, who had once taken under her wing Pepita's bastards when first Lord Sackville brought Victoria and her sisters to England. Vita was the only name she would use. Either way, the identities of mother and child were interwoven. Even-tempered and still infatuated, Lionel consented.

And so, at five o'clock in the morning, in her comfortable Green Court bedroom with its many mirrors and elegant four-poster bed reaching right up to the ceiling, Victoria Sackville-West welcomed with open arms the baby she regarded for the moment as a prize chattel. 'I had the deepest gratitude to Lionel, who I was deeply in love with, for giving me such a gift as that darling baby,' she remembered many years later.[6] She omitted to mention the lack of mother's milk which prevented her from feeding Vita: her thoughts were not of her shortcomings but her sufferings. 'I was not at all comfy,' she recorded with simple pique. She was ever self-indulgent. The combination of intense love, possessiveness and an assertive sort of self-absorption imprinted itself on Vita's childhood. In different measure, those same characteristics would re-emerge throughout her life.

In the aftermath of Vita's birth, Lionel Sackville-West retreated to his study to write letters. He may or may not have been disappointed in the sex of his child, for which Victoria, with a kind of sixth sense, had done her best to prepare him. On 9 March, he conveyed news of his new daughter to no fewer than thirty-eight correspondents. The habit of entrusting intense emotions to the page and ordering those emotions through the written word would similarly form part of Vita's make-up. As would his daughter, Lionel wrote quickly but with care. Later he shared with her his advice on how to write well.

When Lionel was not writing he read. In the fortnight up to 27 March, he offered his French-educated bride an introduction to the works of Victorian novelist William Makepeace Thackeray. Beginning with *The Book of Snobs*, he progressed, via *Vanity Fair*, to *The History of Henry Esmond*. Appropriately it was Becky Sharpe, self-seeking heroine of *Vanity Fair*, 'a wicked woman, a heartless mother and a false wife', who captured Victoria's interest. The women shared coquetry, worldliness, allure. In time Victoria would indeed prove herself capable of falsity, heartlessness and something very like wickedness. But it was the story of Henry Esmond that ought to have resonated most powerfully for Lionel and his family.

Victoria's diary does not suggest that either husband or wife drew parallels between the novel and their own circumstances. Those are for us to identify. As the illegitimate son of an English nobleman, Henry Esmond is unable to inherit the estate of his father, Viscount Castlewood, and ineligible as a suitor for his proud but beautiful cousin Beatrix: the paths to happiness, riches, respectability and title are liberally strewn with thorns. As we have seen, the legal and social ramifications of illegitimacy would for a period dominate the married life of Lionel and Victoria Sackville-West: their affection did not survive the struggle. In turn, Vita's own life would be shaped, indeed distorted, by her inability as a daughter to inherit her father's title and estates. In the early hours of 9 March 1892, wind buffeted the beeches of Knole's park, 'dying in dim cool cloisters of the woods' where deer huddled in the darkness;[7] the grey walls of the house, which later reminded Vita of a medieval village, stood impassive. All was not, as Vita wrote glibly in the fictional account of Knole she placed at the centre of *The Edwardians*, 'warmth and security, leisure and continuity':[8] in her own life it seldom would be. There were very real threats to the security of her infant world. In addition, it was 'continuity' that demanded the perpetuation of that system of male primogeniture which was to cause her such lasting unhappiness. She once claimed for Knole 'all the quality of peace and permanence; of mellow age; of stateliness and tradition. It is gentle and venerable.'[9] But that statement was for public consumption. On and off, what Vita expressed publicly and what she felt most strongly failed to overlap. She was born at Knole, but died elsewhere. She would struggle to reconcile that quirk of fate.

In the short term, within days of her birth, baby Vita's left eye gave cause for concern. Boracic lotion cleared up the problem and Victoria Sackville-West complacently committed to her diary the similarity between the blue of her daughter's eyes and those of her great-uncle by marriage, Lord Derby. A smoking chimney in Vita's bedroom resulted in her being moved back into her mother's room. It was a temporary solution. Victoria's diary frequently omits any mention of her daughter, even in the first ecstatic days which she celebrated afterwards as more wonderful than anything else in the world. Her thoughts were of herself, of Lionel, of how much she loved him. Most of all she recorded the extent of his love for her. It would be more than a month before she witnessed for the first time Mrs Patterson giving Vita her bath, a sight that nevertheless delighted her. In the meantime she rested, cocooned and apparently safe in her husband's adoration.

These were happy days, as winter gave way to spring and Vita made her first sorties outdoors. She was accompanied on these excursions by Mrs Patterson, by her father or her grand-father, Lord Sackville. As the little convoy passed, clouds of white pigeons fluttered on to the roof, startled by the opening and closing of doors. 'You have to look twice before you are sure whether they are pigeons or magnolias,' Vita remem-bered.[10] March faded into April and 'underfoot the blossom was/ Like scattered snow upon the grass';[11] in the Wilderness, close to Knole's garden front, daffodils and bluebells carpeted the artful expanse of oak, beech and rhododendron. Sometimes, indoors, Vita was placed on her mother's bed, with its hang-ings embroidered with improbably flowering trees, 'and I watched her for hours, lying or sitting on my lap. Her little sneezes or yawning were so comic. I hugged her till she screamed.' At other times, husband and wife lay next to one another with their baby between them. When Vita cried, Lionel walked up and down Victoria's bedroom, cradling her in his arms. In time, when Vita had learnt to talk, 'she used to look at each of us in turn and nod her head, saying "Dada – Mama – ". This went on for hours and used to delight us.'[12]

These are common enough pictures, albeit the surroundings were uncommonly sumptuous. The air was densely perfumed with a mix of Victoria's scent (white heliotrope, from a shop off the rue St Honoré in Paris), potted jasmine and gardenias that stood about on every surface, apple logs in the grate and, on window ledges and tables, 'bowls of lavender and dried rose leaves, . . . a sort of dusty fragrance sweeter in the under layers': the famous Knole potpourri, made since the reign of George I to a recipe devised by Lady Betty Germain, a Sackville cousin and former lady-in-waiting to Queen Anne.[13] Such conventional domesticity – husband, wife and baby happy together – is unusual in this chronicle of fragmented emotions. 'She loved me when I was a baby,' Vita wrote of her mother in the private autobiography that was published posthumously as *Portrait of a Marriage.*[14] In her diary, which she kept in French, Victoria described her baby daughter as *'charmant'*, *'adorable'*, *'si drôle'*: *'toujours de si bonne humour'* (always so good humoured). On 17 June, she and Vita were photographed together by Mr Essenhigh Corke of Sevenoaks. But it was Lionel's name, 'Dada', that Vita uttered first. It was 4 September. She was six months old.

Victoria's diary charts Vita's growth and progress. Some of it is standard stuff. There are tantalising glimpses of the future too. On 19 April 1892, Victoria opened a post office savings account for her daughter. Her first deposit of £12 was partly made up of gifts to Vita from Lionel and Lord Sackville. The sum represented the equivalent of nearly a year's wages for one of Knole's junior servants, a scullery maid or stable boy. Until her death in 1936, Victoria would continuously play a decisive role in Vita's finances: her contributions enabled Vita to perpetuate a lifestyle of Edwardian comfort. Later the same year, Victoria introduced her baby daughter to a group of women at Knole. Vita's reaction surprised her mother. Confronted by new faces, she behaved 'wildly' and struggled to get away. It is tempting to witness in her response first flickers of what the adult Vita labelled 'the family failing of unsociability'.[15] In Vita's case, that Sackville 'unsociability' would amount to virtual reclusiveness.

The faces little Vita loved unhesitatingly belonged to her dolls. Shortly after her first birthday, Victoria made an inventory of her daughter's dolls. It included those which she herself had bought at bazaars, a French soldier and 'a Negress' given to Vita by Victoria's unmarried sister Amalia, as well as Scottish and Welsh dolls. 'Vita adores dolls,' Victoria wrote. In the 'Given Away' column of her list of expenses at the end of her diary for 1896, she included 'Doll for Vita', for which she paid five shillings. It is the only present Victoria mentions for her four-year-old daughter and contrasts with the many gifts she bestowed on her friends, her expenditure on clothing and the sums she set aside for tipping servants. Happily Vita could not have known of this imbalance. The following year she was photographed on a sturdy wooden seat with three of her dolls, Boysy, Dorothy and 'Mary of New York'. Wide-eyed, Vita gazes uncertainly at the viewer. She is wearing a froufrou bonnet reminiscent of illustrations in novels by E. Nesbit; her ankles are neatly crossed in black stockings and buttoned pumps. She was two months short of her fifth birthday then and had ceased to ask her mother when she would bring her a little brother;[16] she was still too young to be told of Victoria's fixed resolve that she would rather drown herself than endure childbirth for a second time. Vita's dolls had become her playmates and surrogate siblings. She had quickly grown accustomed to being alone: eventually solitude would be her besetting vice. For the moment her favourite doll was tiny and made of wool: Vita called him Clown Archie. He was as unlike 'Mary of New York', with her flaxen curls and rosebud mouth, as Vita herself, though there was nothing clown-like about the serious, dark-haired child. There never would be.

By the age of two, Vita was a confident walker. Earlier her grandfather had described to Victoria watching her faltering progress across one of Knole's courtyards. On that occasion a footman attended the staggering toddler. In the beginning, Vita's world embraced privilege and pomp. 'My childhood [was] very much like that of other children,' she afterwards asserted, itemising memories of children's games, dressing up and pets.[17] She was mistaken. Granted, there were universal aspects to Vita's formative years: her love for her dogs and her rabbits; her fear of falling off her pony; her disappointment at the age of five, on witnessing Queen Victoria's Diamond Jubilee procession from the windows of a grand house in Piccadilly, that the Queen was not wearing her crown; her frustration at her parents' strictures; even the ugly, homemade Christmas presents she embroidered for Victoria in pink and mauve. Too often her childhood lacked a run-of-the-mill quality. Hers was a distinctive upbringing, even among her peers. Its atypical aspects shaped her as a person and a writer; shaped too her feelings about herself, her family and her sex; shaped her outlook and her sympathies, her moral compass, her emotional requirements.

The trouble lay mostly with her mother. At thirty, recovering at her leisure from her confinement, Victoria Sackville-West remained beguilingly contrary; she had not yet been wholly spoiled. On the one hand she was capricious and snobbish (she described Queen Victoria as looking 'very common and red-faced'[18]); on the other she was passionate and romantic, still the same eager, loving young woman who had confided to her diary with cosy delight, 'Every day the same thing, walking . . . reading, playing the piano, making love'; still capable of enchantment.[19] With her hooded dark eyes and hair that tumbled almost to her knees, she was lovely to look at. In the right mood, she was exhilarating company. Like Juliet Quarles in Vita's novel *The Easter Party*, 'she was irresponsible, unstable, intemperate, and a silly chatterer – but . . . under all these things she possessed a warm heart'.[20] In time the combination of beauty, wealth and position encouraged less attractive facets to her character, but this illegitimate daughter of a poor Spanish dancer had yet to forget her good fortune in marrying her cousin. Hers was the zeal of a convert, leavened at this stage with apparently boundless *joie de vivre*: she embraced with gusto the life of an aristocratic chatelaine that had come to her like the happy ending to a fairy tale. As she herself repeated with justification, '*Quel roman est ma vie!*' (My life is just like a novel). No one ever persuaded her to relinquish the heroine's role.

Victoria's year consisted of entertaining at Knole, country house visits and extended Continental holidays; her favourite days were those she spent alone with Lionel. These were leisurely days of flirtation and passionate lovemaking, of arranging and rearranging the many rooms she thrilled to call her own. She papered one room entirely with used postage stamps and made a screen to match. She installed bathrooms, the first for Lord Sackville, one for herself and another for Vita, close to the nursery. Along the garden front of the house, she rearranged furniture in the Colonnade Room to complete its transformation into an elegant if draughty sitting room. Its walls were painted in grisaille with grand architectural trompe l'oeil; seventeenth-century looking glasses and silver sconces threw light on to deep sofas. There Vita's fifth birthday was celebrated with a Punch and Judy show; Vita dressed on that occasion with appropriate smartness in 'an embroidered dress with Valenciennes insertion over [a] blue silk slip', the sort of dress Victoria herself might have worn.[21] As would her daughter, Victoria Sackville-West exulted in her splendid home. 'Everybody says that I made Knole the most comfortable large house in England, uniting the beauties of Windsor Castle with the comforts of The Ritz, and I never spoilt the real character of Knole,' she claimed for herself.[22] Knole became her passion and filled her with a pride that was essentially vanity; she delighted in her 'improvements' to its vast canvas. 'No one knew how, when the day was over and the workmen had gone home, she would lay her cheek against the panelling, marked like watered silk, and softer to her than any lips,' imagined one of her observers.[23] She had no intention of allowing mother-hood to unsettle a routine that suited her so admirably. Inevitably, her manner of life affected her daughter.

Vita's first Christmas was spent in Genoa. It was a family party of Victoria, Lionel, Lord Sackville, Vita, and Vita's nurse, Mrs Brown. After Christmas, Mrs Brown took Vita to the South of France to stay with Victoria's former chaperone,

Mademoiselle Louet, known as Bonny; Lionel and Victoria continued on to Rome. Vita's parents did not cut short their travels in order to celebrate her first birthday in March 1893: they were more than 1,600 miles from their baby daughter, in Cairo. In subsequent years they exchanged Cairo for Monte Carlo, their destination for Vita's third, fourth and sixth birthdays. On those occasions Vita remained at Knole. On 9 March 1896, Victoria enumerated in her diary her losses and winnings, and those of Lionel, at the Casino: only as a parting shot did she note 'Vita is four today.' She did not suggest that she missed her daughter or regretted their separation; on the same day two years later, she admitted: 'I think so much of my Vita today.'[24] Every year there were visits to nearby London and a trip to Paris in the spring, 'with the chestnut trees coming out and the spring sunshine sparkling on the river'.[25]

Accommodated within this routine, Vita's childhood was by turns permissive and repressive. From infancy she was frequently left alone at Knole with her shy and silent grandfather. Lord Sackville believed in fairies. Morose and uncommunicative in adult company, he enjoyed the companionship of a tame French partridge and a pair of ornamental cranes called Romeo and Juliet, who accompanied him on his walks outdoors. His presence in Vita's early years was benign if detached. Together they played draughts in the hour after nursery tea: as time passed, a shared antipathy to parties and smart society types sharpened their bond. Vita endeavoured to please her grandfather: 'She is very busy gardening and cultivates mostly salad and vegetables for her Grand Papa,' noted Victoria when Vita was eleven.[26] Nurses and governesses oversaw Vita's days; they were overseen in turn by Victoria, whose volatility ensured that none remained long at their post and that each dismissal could be traumatic and painful for Vita. When Vita was five, 'Nannie' was dismissed for theft. The truth was somewhat different. After the unexplained disappearance of three dozen quail, ordered for a dinner party, Victoria decided that Nannie had secretly consumed the entire order and acted accordingly.

With her parents abroad, as soon as she could walk Vita was free to lose herself in the self-contained fastness of Knole. She remembered '[splashing] my way in laughter/ Through drifts of leaves, where underfoot the beech-nuts/ Split with crisp crackle to my great rejoicing'.[27] She climbed trees and stole birds' eggs. She ran wild in 'wooded gardens with mysterious glooms' and on one occasion she fell into a wishing well. Indoors, even the frayed and faded curtains of Knole's state rooms possessed a peculiar power of enchantment over her. After nightfall, beginning as a small child, she wandered through the rooms with only a single candle to hold fear at bay. Hers was a playground like few others.

The company of her mother, 'maddening and irresistible by turns',[28] was predictably more stringent. Victoria's sharp tongue was quick to wound, particularly on the subject of Vita's looks, which proved an ongoing source of disappointment. 'Mother used to hurt my feelings and say she couldn't bear to look at me because I was so ugly':[29] it was Vita's hair, with its stubborn resistance to curling, that exercised Victoria above all. She may have spoken more from pique than conviction – on 20 February 1903 she recorded in her diary, 'The drawing of Vita by Mr Stock is finished and is quite pretty, but the child is much prettier and has far more depth and animation in her face;'[30] it was all the same to Vita. Vita subsequently categorised her mother 'more as a restraint than anything else in my existence',[31] but as a small child she delighted her with her quick affection and her loving nature. 'She is always putting her little arm round my neck and saying I am the best Mama in the world,' Victoria wrote on 1 August 1897.[32] Vita grew up to regard her mother as compelling but incomprehensible: she dreaded her unpredictability and her ability to humiliate with a look or word. 'She wounded and dazzled and fascinated and charmed me by turns.'[33] Mutual misunderstanding coloured their relationship almost from the first: Vita was probably thinking of her mother when, in an essay about art composed in her late teens, she wrote, 'It is possible, and indeed common, to possess personality allied to a mediocre soul.'[34] In one letter, written in a round, childish hand, Vita implored Victoria to 'forgive me. Punish me, I deserve it, but forgive me if you can and please don't say you are sorry to have me and go on loving me.'[35] Vita learned from Victoria that so-called loving relationships could embrace indifference, pain and even hatred, and that equality was not assured between partners in love. As she wrote in 1934 of one particularly mismatched couple in her novel *The Dark Island*, 'She liked him, yet she hated him. She was surprised to find how instantly she could like and yet hate a person, at first sight.'[36] For Vita that model of loving and hating existed in the first instance not in stories but her family life. It was a dangerous lesson.

It was Victoria, not Lionel, who administered punishments, and Victoria who ordered Vita's life. When Vita was five, Victoria forced her to eat dinner upstairs: 'she is always eating raw chestnuts and they are so bad for her'.[37] Instead she insisted on simple food typical of nursery regimes of the period; Vita's particular hatred was for rice pudding. The following year, Vita was again punished by dining upstairs: the six-year-old tomboy with the post office savings account had escaped her nursemaid in Sevenoaks in order to buy herself a ball and a balloon. Accustomed to extravagant flattery and naturally autocratic in all her relationships, Victoria inclined to high-handedness: where Vita was concerned she expected obedience. As it happened, her treatment of her daughter hardly differed from her behaviour towards her husband or her father. In each case she preferred to jeopardise affection rather than yield control.

Until Vita was four, Knole was home not only to her parents and her grandfather, but also her Aunt Amalia, 'very Spanish and very charming' in one estimate,[38] remembered by Vita only as 'a vinegary spinster . . . [who] annoyed Mother by giving me preserved cherries when Mother asked her not to'.[39] (She annoyed Victoria more with her constant requests for money. The women were temperamentally incompatible and 'endless rows and quarrels' made both miserable.[40]) Also in the great house, hugger-mugger within its far-flung walls and 'rich confusion of staircases and rooms',[41] lived Vita's other families: four centuries of Sackville forebears, 'heavy-lidded, splenetic',[42] preserved in heraldic flourishes and the rows of portraits in which Vita would glimpse 'our faces cut/ All in the same sad feature';[43] and Knole's servants and retainers. All influenced the small girl in their midst.

From the outset of her marriage, Victoria Sackville-West had set about rationalising Knole's running costs. By 1907, she would successfully reduce the annual household expenditure by a third to £2,000.[44] She did so while retaining a staff of sixty, including twenty gardeners; their combined wage bill cost her father and afterwards her husband a further £3,500.[45] Few of these servants were known personally to Victoria, Lionel or Lord Sackville, or even recognised by them by sight. To Vita, free to explore regions of the house her parents seldom visited, they formed an extended kinship.

'As a mere child, I was privileged. I could patter about, between the housekeeper's room and the servants' hall,' Vita recalled in an article written for *Vogue* in 1931. 'The Edwardians Below Stairs' examines the elaborate staff hierarchies of her childhood. It also demonstrates how much of Vita's time was spent among Knole's servants, whom she knew by name, who shared her games and who omitted to lower their voices or silence their gossip in front of the dark-haired little girl who moved among them so easily. 'I could help to stir the jam in the still-room or to turn the mangle in the laundry; I could beg a cake in the kitchen or a bottle of cider in the pantry; I could watch the gamekeeper skinning a deer or the painter mixing a pot of paint; my comings and goings remained unnoticed; conversation and comment were allowed to fall uncensored on my childish ears.'[46] As Vita wrote of Sebastian and Viola in *The Edwardians*, 'As children in the house, they had of course been on terms of familiarity with the servants, particularly when their mother was away.'[47] So it was in her own case.

On the surface Vita's childhood world was one of order and stability. Foresters cut timber and sawmen sawed logs – different lengths for different fires. Melons, grapes and peaches ripened in hothouses. Victoria's guests enjoyed clean linen sheets daily; the flowers in their rooms were rearranged with similar frequency. Extravagance was endemic, splendid in its excess – as Vita remembered it in *The Edwardians*, 'the impression of waste and extravagance . . . assailed one the moment one entered the doors of the house'.[48] It contributed the necessary note of magnificence to this feudal environment of fixed places and shared loyalties. For Knole and its denizens, the world of 1892 appeared to differ from that of 1592 only in refinement and ease: given the estate's modest income, it was a gorgeous charade. On the shell of Victoria's pet tortoise, as it shuffled between sitting rooms, glittered her monogram, a liquid swirl of diamonds. It was a fantastical detail, afterwards appropriated by Evelyn Waugh in the lushest of his novels, *Brideshead Revisited*.

That the childish Vita should take for granted these insubstantial cornerstones of her parents' existence is inevitable. Her memories indicate something more, a window on to Vita's position as Knole's only child: at home upstairs and downstairs, nowhere fully at home, everywhere proprietorial, keenly aware of her connection to the house and its history – as she herself offered, 'Small wonder that my games were played alone; . . ./ I slept beside the canopied and shaded/ Beds of forgotten kings./ I wandered shoeless in the galleries . . .'[49] Knole dominates all Vita's memories of her childhood. She regarded it as her own munificent present and disdained to share it; later she would claim that a house was 'a very private thing'.[50] It was also an irresistible compulsion and seeped into so many of her thoughts. 'At the centre of all was always the house,' she wrote in an early story: 'the house was at the heart of all things.'[51] It occupied voids left by the absence of more conventional emotional outlets. That she learned early on that one day she must relinquish it, that as a girl she was prevented from inheriting what she already considered her own, served only to quicken those feelings which transcended ordinary love, feelings which went too deep to be put into words, so deep that throughout her life she hardly dared examine them.

A journalist in Vita's lifetime described Knole as 'too homely to be called a palace, too palatial to be called a home'[52] – an outsider's view. For Vita, even as a child, Knole was more than either home or palace. It was a living organism, 'to others dormant but to me awake':[53] she lavished upon it the quick affection children usually reserve for their parents. 'God knows I gave you all my love,' she wrote later, 'Scarcely a stone of you I had not kissed.'[54] 'So I have loved thee, as a lonely child/ Might love the kind and venerable sire/ With whom he lived,' she claimed in a poem she dedicated to Knole.[55]

Finding her way through passages and galleries, crossing courtyards, peeping into workshops and domestic offices, what was Vita looking for and what did she see? Why did she give over her days to wandering and exploring, save for the pleasure of escaping her nursemaid or eluding her mother? At times, the connection she forged with Knole was the strongest bond of her life: to strengthen her conviction of reciprocity she endowed the house and its park with human attributes. 'I knew thy soul, benign and grave and kind/ To me, a morsel of mortality,' she wrote self-consciously, the night before she left Knole as a married woman for a new home of her own;[56] in a later unpublished poem she went a step further and claimed that she was Knole's soul. From a precociously young age, she was nourished and sustained by Knole's accumulated memories: swaggering, picturesque, tragic or simply humdrum. The history she learned she read in its tapestries and portraits. In the first instance it was companionship Vita sought in the cavernous house: the romantic distraction of the past came next. 'I knew all the housemaids by name . . . [and] was on intimate terms with the hall-boy . . . The hall-boy and I used to play cricket together.'[57] They also indulged in wrestling bouts, for which Vita was punished by being made to keep her diary in French. But the hall-boy's name is lost and we question the intimacy of those terms.

Day by day Vita absorbed an inflated, erroneous sense of Knole's importance. Its place in British life – the prestige of her own family – overwhelmed her imagination. That sense persisted. A novel written when she was fourteen included the question, from father to son, 'And you can bear that name, the name of Sackville, and yet commit a disgraceful action?'[58] In fact, in the 850 years since Herbrand de Sackville had journeyed from Normandy with William the Conqueror, the Sackville achievement had been middling. Knole suggested otherwise, and it was Knole's version of her family history that the young Vita unquestioningly imbibed and the mature Vita avoided revising.

As a child events conspired to delude her. In 1896, after Lord Sackville had persuaded the prime minister, Lord Salisbury, to make Lionel a temporary honorary attaché to the British embassy in Moscow, Lionel and Victoria set off from Knole to the coronation of Nicholas II of Russia; on the eve of departure their neighbours flocked to admire Victoria's dresses and her jewels laid out for display like wedding presents. Two years later, the Prince and Princess of Wales lunched at Knole, in a party that included the Duke and Duchess of Sparta, heirs to the throne of Greece. Photographs show Vita and the Princess of Wales holding hands, an intimacy few six-year-olds could rival; they had stood side by side at the inevitable tree-planting ceremony. In his thank-you letter written afterwards, the prince admired Knole as 'so beautifully kept', a state he attributed to 'the tender care *"de la charmante Chatelaine!"'*.[59] In the summer of 1897, Victoria had recorded in her diary the visit to Knole of 'Thomas the Bond Street jeweller'. She had summoned him to examine the silver. 'He said that we had not the largest, but the *best* collection of silver in England.'[60] Her life at Knole turned Victoria's head. Knole turned Vita's head too. In Vita's case she knew no alternative.

The child shaped by parental absenteeism, maternal whim and her extraordinary surroundings was all angles and corners, 'all knobs and knuckles', 'with long black hair and long black legs, and very short frocks, and very dirty nails and torn clothes'.[61] She regarded her mother – indeed everyone outside the closed Knole–Sackville circle – with unavoidable hesitancy. Like the Godavarys in her later novella, *The Death of Noble Godavary,* she mistrusted any alien element within the family circle. From an early age, she took on her grandfather's role of showing the house to visitors: the task exacerbated a tendency to unsociability. Although by modern standards Knole's visitor numbers were low – on a 'busy' August day in 1901, the tally reached twenty-seven[62] – Vita's guide work stimulated her sense of possessiveness towards the house that would never be hers, and a rigid, atavistic pride in its glories. Showing the house was an exercise in showing off. Even as a teenager, travelling through Warwickshire en route to Scotland, Vita measured everything she saw against Knole's yardstick. Of Anne Hathaway's cottage she noted only its 'very small, low rooms', and she poured scorn on the idea that ruined Kenilworth Castle, covering three acres, had any claim to be considered 'enormous': 'Knole covers between four and five acres.'[63]

The 'tours' she led even as quite a young child sealed the imaginative pact Vita made with Knole. She was reluctant and unskilled at making friends, sullen and shy confronted by unknown visitors, hostile and bullying to local children to the extent that 'none of [them] would come to tea with me except those who . . . acted as my allies and lieutenants'.[64] Knole super-seded Clown Archie as her childhood love; perhaps it precluded – or prevented – other intimacies. 'Vita belonged to Knole,' Violet Keppel remembered; 'to the courtyards, gables, galleries; to the prancing sculptured leopards, to the traditions, rites, and splendours. It was a considerable burden for one so young.'[65]

Unsurprisingly, given her surrounds, while her social instincts faltered, her imagination blossomed: her taste was for adventure. Vita was a scruffy, despotic, busy child. Her inclinations were starkly at odds with late-Victorian ideas about little girls. Victoria did her best. She commissioned elaborate fancy dress costumes, including a tinsel fairy dress, a May queen dress complete with a maypole made from wild flowers, and a flower-encrusted frock intended to transform Vita into a basket of wisteria (Victoria herself had been '*very* much admired' when she wore a dress of similar design, with added diamonds, to a costume ball in 1897[66]). It was not enough. Neither in appearance or character would Vita achieve conventional prettiness and all that it implied; Victoria's diary does not suggest she always troubled to sympa-thise with the daughter whose nature and instincts were so different from her own. Of a seaside holiday in August 1898, her mother recorded simply: 'Vita was much impressed by seeing a runaway horse smashing a butcher's cart.'[67] Victoria and Lionel's presents to Vita that year included a costly tricycle and a balloon. Even Vita's greedy passion for chocolates and bonbons challenged Victoria's ideas of appropriate behaviour. Concerned for her daughter's complexion, and the figure she would later cut in the marriage market, Victoria 'put away mercilessly what I thought was bad for her'.[68]

Although she was not aware of it, Vita learnt cruelty from her mother. It was not simply that isolation bred introspection or that Knole itself made Vita a dreamer, uninterested in those outside her gilded cage. Victoria's exactingness threatened to deprive those closest to her both of autonomy and their sense of themselves. Her unconditional love for her daughter, whose birth she had regarded as a 'miracle', an 'incredible marvel', ceased with Vita's babyhood. In time Vita learned to fear the mother whose love was so contrary, 'so it was really a great relief when she went away'[69]: she never stopped loving her mother extravagantly. The family name for Victoria, 'BM' (*Bonne Mama*), contained no deliberate irony. 'I love thee, mother, but thou pain'st me so!/ Thou dost not understand me; it is sad/ When those we love most, understand us least,' Vita's Chatterton exclaims in the verse drama she wrote about the doomed poet in 1909.[70] Vita wrote the part of Chatterton for herself. Like many who are bullied, she responded by becoming herself a bully. Children invited to Knole to play with Vita were left in little doubt of the value she placed on their companionship.

Vita contributed a less-than-flattering anecdote to a volume of childhood reminiscences published at the height of her literary fame in 1932. It concerned the children of neighbours called Battiscombe, four girls and a boy, and happened at the beginning of the Second Boer War in 1899. Vita befriended the boy, Ralph. 'The four girls were our victims', forced to impersonate Boers. Together Vita and Ralph Battiscombe tied the girls to trees, thrashed their legs with nettles and blocked their nostrils with putty.[71] Vita dressed for this activity in a khaki suit in which she masqueraded as Sir Redvers Buller, a popular military commander in South Africa and winner of the Victoria Cross. At her mother's insistence, and much to Vita's irritation, the suit had a skirt in place of trousers. The girls, she insisted in 1932, enjoyed their ordeal 'masochistically'. She was equally clear about the sadistic pleasure she derived from her own part in this horseplay. For her seventh birthday that year, according to Victoria's diary, Vita had received only presents of model soldiers. Within a year her toy box included guns, swords, a bow and arrow, armour and a fort for the soldiers. Seery bought her a cricket set. It ranked alongside her football among her prized possessions. 'I made a great deal of being hardy, and as like a boy as possible,' she wrote in 1920.[72] She described a Dutch museum full of 'all kinds of odds and ends: instruments of torture . . . old carriages' as 'a place where one could spend hours'.[73] Forgotten were Clown Archie and his fellows. She composed a single poem about a doll. It was written in French in 1909 and called simply 'La Poupée'. She invested more of herself in her subsequent biography of Joan of Arc. Like Vita, the tomboyish French saint fought her battles in armour and men's clothing: brave, zealous, uncompromising. 'One wonders what her feelings were, when for the first time she surveyed her cropped head and moved her legs unencumbered by her red skirt,' Vita mused.[74]

Throughout her life Vita would appear easy with the inevitability of inflicting pain. There was a thoughtlessness to much of her cruelty, just as there was to Victoria's. From Victoria, Vita had learnt that pain and suffering were implicit in the complicated experience of love. 'Pain holds beauty in a fiery ring/ Much as the wheelwright fits the hissing tyre/ White-hot to wooden wheel,' she wrote later.[75] In a short poem, 'The Owl', she admired a similar combination: 'Such beauty and such cruelty were hers,/ Such silent beauty, taloned with a knife.'[76] All the principal relationships of Vita's life – with her mother, with her husband Harold Nicolson, with Violet Keppel and a host of subsequent lovers, as well as with Knole – included this negotiation between positive and negative. The surprise is that she herself remained highly sensitive and easily wounded.

In keeping with her cruelty and her sensitivity, Vita also retained the habit, learnt in childhood, of secrecy. 'Secrecy was my passion,' she confessed.[77] She later suggested that the passion for secrecy was the natural state of childhood.[78] She avoided punishment as a small child by hiding under the pulpit in Knole's Chapel, which lay within easy reach of her bedroom; as a teenager she resorted to code for those parts of her diary she meant to be private; later, in order to foil her mother, she wrote her diary entirely in Italian. Secrecy was Vita's retreat: it inspired neither guilt nor reflection. Instead she excused it on grounds of heredity: 'it's a trait I inherit from my family. So I won't blame myself excessively for it.'[79] But while the family she referred to meant Lionel and the Sackvilles, the secretive impulse she developed as a child arose in response to the non-Sackville aspect of her upbringing, Vita's under-standing of her mother's uncontrolled, unmannerly 'Spanish' emotionalism, which frightened and, over time, alienated her and forced her to keep her own counsel. For all her unwitting cruelty, Vita was seldom histrionic. The instinct for conceal-ment, her dislike of 'scenes', were legacies of her childhood. As one future lover would remember, 'She did demand peace and quiet . . . no rows. Certainly no inquisitiveness . . .'[80]

It seems surprising that Vita claimed subsequently that her memories of her childhood were hazy. As early as February 1912, weeks short of her twentieth birthday, she wrote to her future husband Harold Nicolson a selective description of her growing up that excluded more than it confided. It revealed what we know already, that like all children of her class, Harold included, Vita had led a double life: that of her parents' daughter and that of the girl entrusted to a shifting cast of nurses and governesses. In addition, in Vita's case, was the interior life of an only child who, inspired by her home and by loneliness, absented herself into daydreams and make-believe. As she grew older, while her parents travelled, Vita mastered time travel. She spirited herself into moments of Knole's past, at one with the portraits and historic artefacts which surrounded her: the silver furniture made for James I in the King's Room; the paintings by Holbein, Frans Hals, Van Dyck and Gainsborough; the heraldic leopards which prompted her to verse ('Leopards on the gable ends, Leopards on the painted stair'); the white-painted rocking horse belonging to the 4th Duke of Dorset, an object doubly endowed in Vita's eyes since the duke's tragic early death in the hunting field had resulted in Knole's inheritance by his sisters, a period of female ownership spanning half a century. Her spirited reveries excluded her parents. Often she dressed up, as in those Boer War games with the Battiscombes, fought in trenches among the rhododendrons; actually and metaphorically she would go on dressing up for much of her life. At the outset, the performance was for herself, Vita as player and Vita as audience.

As a writer, Vita seldom dwelt on the subject of childhood. Even the stories she wrote as a child focused on adults. Her poetic description of 'children taken unawares', 'Arcady in England', is an outdoor scene as much concerned with the lushness of an idealised autumn day as the particular nature of the children who catch the poet's eye. For Vita's upbringing was one in which, unusually alone, she learnt above all to observe; she forged few childish relationships, even within her

family. Some things she saw clearly: the wonders of the great
house that captivated her from infancy, ghosts of the past, the
power of genius loci. Others she struggled to discern with any
clarity throughout her life, among them her mother's oscilla-
tion between absence and presence, affection withheld and
affection lavishly bestowed, spite and charm. As in every childhood, happiness was balanced with unhappiness for Vita. As
an adult she quoted one of her favourite forebears, Lady Anne
Clifford: 'the marble pillars of Knole in Kent . . . were to me
oftentimes but the gay arbours of anguish'.[81]

Vita's response to her dilemma was creative: she mythologised
an existence she only partly understood. It was her own version
of her mother's '*Quel roman est ma vie!*', but lacked the unqualified
exuberance of Victoria's joyful exclamation. For Vita, she and
Knole and its whole population of relatives and servants became
characters in a fable. She described her grandfather as 'rather
like an old goblin'. Contemptuously she listened to her mother
'making up legends about the place, quite unwarrantable and
unnecessary', but acknowledged that 'no ordinary mother could
introduce such fairy tales into life'.[82] Stalwartly and in silence,
she worshipped her long-suffering father whom she imagined
not as an individual but a type, 'a pleasing man'[83] – as Virginia
Woolf described him, 'the figure of an English nobleman, decayed,
dignified, smoothed, effete'.[84] Even the buildings themselves had
an unreal quality, like a theatrical backcloth: 'my little court [is]
so lovely in the moonlight. With its gabled windows it looks like
a court on a stage, till I half expect to see a light spring up in
one window and the play begin.'[85] When at length Vita devised
a role for herself, she existed in a mythical tower, part heroine,
part observer. At Sissinghurst thirty years on, she made good
that pretence. Her sense of life as a performance – theatrical and
containing elements of make-believe – began much earlier.

Victoria rejoiced in a reality that surpassed any romantic novel:

Vita transformed the reality of her unsatisfactory childhood into a personal fiction. It was one way of placing herself centre stage and making sense of her fellow actors; the process also implied distance. These impulses of mythomania and detachment would remain part of Vita's psyche until death. Early on, albeit subconsciously, she resorted to fiction to clarify the business of living: later she recycled her own reality as the principal element of her fiction, and all her novels contain fragments of autobiography. Despite this, Vita was an honest child and naturally affectionate. For the most part, those traits too would endure.

Vita Sackville-West described the childhood of the Spanish saint, Teresa of Avila, in *The Eagle and the Dove*, published in 1943. Identifying Teresa's favourite childhood pastime as 'tales of adventure', she warmed to her theme. Throughout her youth, Vita wrote, Teresa, along with her brother Rodrigo, 'could think of nothing but honour and heroism, knights and giants and distressed ladies, defeated evil and conquering virtue; they even collaborated in composing a story of their own, modelled on these lines'.[86]

Vita's was a life of storytelling. Aspects of her poetry, the fiction she wrote in order to make money, her nonfiction and much of her journalism have a strong narrative content; ditto her diary, in which events, appointments and people take the place of analysis or self-searching. Honour, heroism and conquest – sometimes metaphorical, sometimes reimagined – all find a place within the stories Vita spun; invariably she projects herself into the person of her hero. She glimpsed an echo of these vigorous heroics in the youthful St Teresa, a fiery and imaginative aristocratic teenager sent to the Convent of Santa Maria de Gracia after suspicions of a lesbian affair. It was this swashbuckling quality that endeared Teresa to her: similar feelings coloured Vita's interpretation of seventeenth-century

writer Aphra Behn and French saint Joan of Arc, whose biographies she also wrote. Vita's juvenilia, written in her teens,
includes 'tales of adventure': so too the more fanciful of her
mature fiction, for example, *Gottfried Künstler* and *The Dark
Island*. The greatest adventure was writing itself. It would
remain so. 'I do get so frightfully, frenziedly excited writing
poetry,' she once admitted. 'It is the only thing that makes me
truly and completely happy.'[87] Predictably her happiness was
shared by neither of her parents, both of whom disapproved.

At Knole, Vita wrote at a small wooden table in a summer-
house shaded by tall hedges. It overlooked the Mirror Pond
and the sunken garden. Previously, it had served as her school-
room. She did her lessons there: by the time she was ten, essays
written in English, French and German on geography and
history (Norway and Sweden, 'L'Amérique du Nord',
Charlemagne, Charles I, William and Mary, Trafalgar), as well
as exercises in creative writing ('Un jour de la vie d'un petit
Chien'). Vita cannot have enjoyed these lessons unreservedly:
she remembered at moments of boredom or revolt gouging the
table's wooden surface with the blade of her pocketknife.

Initially she wrote what she subsequently described as 'historical novels, pretentious, quite uninteresting, pedantic'.[88] She
wrote plays, too, inspired by history or by plays she had seen
or read and particularly enjoyed. She wrote at speed. Fully
bilingual until her late teens, she was as comfortable in French
as in English; she worked with an easy facility, as if writing
were for her the most natural thing imaginable. Inspiration
never failed her: 'the day after one [book] was finished another
would be begun'.[89] In 1927 she quoted a contemporary assessment of Aphra Behn: 'her muse was never subject to the curse
of bringing forth with pain, for she always writ with the greatest
ease in the world'.[90] So it was, at the outset of her career, for
Vita. Rapidly, the pile of lined Murray's exercise books and

foolscap ledgers mounted. All were neatly written in the clear, unselfconscious, undecorated handwriting that scarcely changed until her death. She dated her efforts, noting the days she began and ended. Sometimes a comment recurs in the margin: V. E. – 'my private sign, meaning Very Easy; in other words, "It has gone well today."'[91] From the outset Vita's manuscripts were remarkable for their tidiness and the absence of large-scale corrections and alterations. She claimed that she began writing at the age of twelve and 'never stopped writing after that'.[92] She identified as a catalyst Edmond Rostand's *Cyrano de Bergerac*.

When Vita first encountered it, Rostand's play was relatively new: it was written in 1897. By her twelfth birthday seven years later, she knew all five acts by heart. It was a work custom-made for this proud, fierce, boyish but still, on occasion, sentimental young woman of gnawing insecurities, a story of a nobly born soldier-poet, swashbuckling by nature but crippled by self-doubt on account of his enormous nose: 'My mother even could not find me fair . . . and, when a grown man, I feared the mistress who would mock at me.' The play is set in seventeenth-century France. The teenage Vita followed Rostand's lead and repeatedly returned to the *grand siècle*: in *Richelieu*, a 368-page historical novel she began in French in October 1907; *Jean Baptiste Poquelin*, a one-act comedy about Molière, also written in French the same year; and *Le Masque de Fer*, a five-act French drama about Richelieu and Louis XIII, written, like *Cyrano*, in a poetic form resembling alexandrines. At the time Vita's favourite writers were historical novelists Walter Scott and Alexandre Dumas: their shadows loomed large.

A portrait of Scott hung in Knole's Poets' Parlour, the room used by Lionel and Victoria as their family dining room. Vita's early writing could never be anything but self-conscious. 'She allowed her readings of . . . heroic romances to . . . flavour her interpretation of her hero with an air of classic chivalry,' the mature Vita wrote of Aphra Behn's story of thwarted love and racial prejudice, *Oroonoko*. 'Oroonoko resembles those seventeenth-century paintings of negroes in plumes and satins, rather than an actual slave on a practical plantation.'[93] It was a criticism she might have levelled at her younger self. The teenage Vita admired heroism, grand gestures, the dramatic (and the melodramatic) impulse. 'In our adolescence, I suppose we have all thought Ludwig [II of Bavaria] a misunderstood figure of extravagant romance,' she reflected later; 'in the sobriety of later years we see him to have been only an exaggerated egoist . . . who happened also to be a king.'[94] Twice as a young woman she wrote about Napoleon, a suitably leviathan figure – in a novel, *The Dark Days of Thermidor*, and a verse drama, *Le roi d'Elbe*, both written in 1908. Both are exercises in historic romanticism.

In the beginning Vita approached her writing in a spirit of earnestness and painful sincerity: she described her adolescent self as 'plain, priggish, studious (oh, very!)'.[95] Her teenage notebooks include historical jottings, scene-by-scene breakdowns of her plays, and chapter summaries for novels. Heavily she puzzled over the nature of literature, the qualities necessary to write well and the purpose and requirements of art; essays from this time include 'The difference between genius and talent', and 'The outburst of lyric poetry under Elizabeth'. 'Sincerity is the only possible basis for great art,' she offered sententiously;[96] certainly her output lacked humour. Vita's submergence in her self-appointed task was complete. She revelled in losing herself in an imaginary past; she was dizzy with the thrill of creation: here was an occupation to match her loneliness. Her adult self likened the experience to drunkenness. It was especially heady on those occasions when she turned her attention to family history.

Vita wrote her first 'Sackville' novel in 1906. *The Tale of a Cavalier* was inspired by Edward Sackville, 4th Earl of Dorset, for Vita 'the embodiment of Cavalier romance'. His portrait by

Van Dyck, in breastplate and striped vermilion doublet, hung in Knole's Great Hall, constantly before her. The following year she wrote *The King's Secret.* Its subject was Charles Sackville, 6th Earl of Dorset, minor poet, rake, lover of Nell Gwyn, latter-day patron of Dryden and friend of Charles II (Victoria described it as Vita's 'Charles II book'). The 6th Earl was largely responsible for the appearance of the Poets' Parlour in Vita's childhood. In addition to Scott, its panelled walls were crowded with portraits of Chaucer, Shakespeare, Milton and Dr Johnson, alongside Sackville's friends and contemporaries Dryden, Addison, Congreve, Wycherley and Pope. Such an illustrious visual compendium provided a powerful spur to Vita's sense of vocation.

The King's Secret included a self-portrait: 'a boy muffled up in a blue scarf . . . scribbling something in a ponderous book . . . His pen flowed rapidly over the paper . . . He wrote from morning till evening.'[97] She called her alter ego Cranfield Sackville, the first of numerous masculine fictional self-representations. He wrote 'in a little arbour situated in the garden at Knole'.[98] As she worked, Vita remembered, 'the past mingled with the present in constant reminder',[99] the former as tangible as the latter, she herself in her own words a fragment of an age gone by.[100] Victoria queried Vita's self-portrait: Cranfield she considered 'more open, less reserved' than Vita. Plaintively she confided to her diary the wish that her daughter could 'change and become warmer-hearted'.[101] By chance, a visit to Dover Castle on 18 July, midway through *The King's Secret,* brought Vita to the last meeting place of Charles II and his sister Henrietta. 'This is interesting to me, as I am just writing about their meeting!' she noted.[102] Her earliest approaches to fiction were the literary equivalent of method acting.

But it was from a less picturesque source that Vita drew her first literary income. In July 1907, she was one of five winners of an *Onlooker* competition to complete a limerick. Her prize was

a cheque for £1. In her diary, fifteen-year-old Vita put a characteristically heroic spin on events: 'This morning I received the
£1 I had won in the "Onlooker" verse competition. This is the
first money I have got through writing; I hope as I am to restore
the fortunes of the family that it will not be the last.'[103] She
resorted to code to record her intention of restoring the family
fortunes. A fitting ambition for this ardent Sackville scion, it was
not one she intended to expose to her mother's watchful gaze.

Predictably, opposition came from close to home: Vita's parents.
Lionel was too conventional to embrace the idea of a daughter
whose writing was more than a diversion. Like the majority of
upper-class Englishmen of the time he mistrusted intellectualism,
particularly in women: Vita described life at Knole as 'completely
unintellectual . . . analysis wasn't the fashion'.[104] Lionel had sown
his wild oats in marrying his illegitimate cousin; in the short
term, there would be no further public transgressions. Even the
eventual breakdown of his marriage was managed with relative
decorum on Lionel's part. In her diary Victoria noted the physical resemblance between father and daughter and Lionel's pride
in Vita; his only plan for her was marriage into a family like his
own, preferably to an eldest son. More than anything he longed
for her to embrace 'normal and ordinary things', among which
he did not count writing.[105]

On the surface, Victoria showed more sympathy. Victoria was
Vita's chosen reader. 'How marvellously well she writes!' she
admitted later. 'Reading her calm descriptions fills me with
admiration . . . No one can beat her at her wonderful descriptions of Nature, or analysing a difficult character.'[106] But Victoria
too mistrusted the intensity of Vita's involvement with her
writing. Pepita's daughter was too parvenu to condone such
evident disregard for the conventional preoccupations of the
society she had married into. (Vita afterwards condemned these
preoccupations as limited to parties and investments, pâté de

foie gras and the novels of E. F. Benson.) Two years earlier Victoria had confided to her diary her relief that Vita was 'getting a little more coquette and tidy', suggesting a growing interest in clothes and appearances to match her own; it was a chimera. On 16 July 1907, while she continued to work on *The King's Secret*, Vita's parents finally made their feelings plain: 'Mama scolded me this morning because she said I write too much, and Dada said he did not approve of my writing . . . Mother does not know how much I love my writing.'

Vita was mistaken. Both her parents saw the extent of her passionate engagement with her writing. They noted, for example, that the majority of her thirteenth birthday presents were books: as a counterbalance, their own present consisted of sumptuous squirrel furs.[107] Yet, despite their disapproval, they did little to redirect Vita's energies. By 1907, confronted by overwhelming evidence of Lord Sackville's mismanagement, they had embarked on a course of unwelcome financial retrenchment which only the Scott bequest would resolve; Victoria's troublesome siblings continued their carping demands for money and title which afterwards erupted into the succession case of 1910. Above all, Victoria and Lionel knew now that their marriage was broken beyond repair. If Lionel's response was one of courteous indifference, Victoria's emphatically was not. She was angry, hurt, uncomprehending. There would be no resolution. Their days of acting in unison were running out. For her twenty-first birthday, Victoria presented Vita with the Italian desk which remains today in her writing room at Sissinghurst.

On 8 April 1908, an ebullient Vita recorded in her diary, 'We had the results of the exams at Miss Woolff's. I am first in French literature, French grammar, English literature and geography, and I won the prize essay. Brilliant performance!' Later that year she consolidated her position. 'Prize essay day at Miss Woolff's,' she wrote on 16 December: 'I won it ("Reminiscences of an Oak Tree"). I was also first in mythology!' She won the same prize for the third time on 5 April 1909. The title on that occasion played to bookish Vita's strengths: 'Thoughts in a Library'.

By 1909, Vita was in her fourth and final year at Helen Woolff's School for Girls in London's South Audley Street. She had first attended classes there at the age of thirteen and pursued her studies thereafter during the autumn and Easter terms. At the same time, until July 1905, Victoria retained the services of Vita's French governess of 'such an uneven temper', Hermine Hall.[108] Vita continued to write outside school: her earliest surviving poems, along with fragments of poems, date from this period. Like *Cyrano de Bergerac*, Miss Woolff's school was a catalyst in Vita's life: it represented her first sustained participation in the world of her contemporaries outside Knole. Neither the curriculum studied nor Miss Woolff herself impacted significantly on her intellectual growth or her development as a writer. Nor did she much relish the company of her peers, dismissing in her diary 'the average run of English girls' as dull and stupid.[109] Meanwhile Victoria oversaw her cultural education: on 13 February 1909, Vita attended a matinée of *The Mikado*; on 16 February she went to an organ recital in Westminster Abbey given by Master of the King's Musick, Sir Walter Parratt; on the following day she was present at 'a most interesting lecture on Madame Récamier'.

More compelling than anything Miss Woolff or Victoria offered was Vita's unquenchable thirst for her writing. 'There is writing, always writing,' she remembered of this period:[110] her best days resembled those of Cranfield Sackville, at work undisturbed in his garden arbour. Vita was an autodidact. In every area she prized most highly, from poetry to gardening, she was partly self-taught. Writing had the added attraction of temporarily screening Vita from her parents' world of acrimony and threats of litigation: she excluded from her first fictions anything unheroic in her Sackville heredity. In *Orlando*, her fictional 'biography' of Vita, Virginia Woolf describes Orlando's hope 'that all the turbulence of his youth . . . proved that he himself belonged to the sacred race rather than the noble – was by birth a writer rather than an aristocrat'.[111] Throughout her life, Vita thirsted for just such an acknowledgement. She was never brave enough to separate her two identities. At first an aristocrat who wrote, she became a writer whose work affirmed her own ideal of aristocracy. It was one of several conflicts in her nature.

Vita considered that she had worked hard at Miss Woolff's. 'I set myself to triumph at that school, and I did triumph. I beat everybody there sooner or later, and in the end-of-term exams, I thought I had done badly if I didn't carry off at least six out of eight first prizes.'[112] Her triumph transcended examinations. She did indeed earn the reputation for cleverness she had deliberately cultivated. It went some way towards softening the blow of her unpopularity, which she attributed to her moroseness, pedantry, priggishness and savagery, as well as an appearance of aloofness that she was at a loss to explain. There were other discoveries too. Among her fellow pupils were girls who fell in love with Vita.

As an adult, Vita seldom loved singly and was always, as one of her sons remembered, in love.[113] Her childhood had been poor preparation for intimacy. Neither Victoria nor Lionel consistently gave her grounds to suppose herself the exclusive object of their affections. Victoria's love was erratic, Lionel's mostly implied. As Vita wrote of Shirin le Breton in *The Dark Island*, 'It was not a particularly united family, and indeed was held together, as is the case in many families, less by the ties of affection than by those of convenience and convention.'[114] Vita loved Knole and believed that Knole returned her love. Her attitude refuted that of Leonard Anquetil in *The Edwardians*: 'Chevron [Knole] is really a despot of the most sinister sort: it disguises its tyranny under the mask of love.'[115] Yet the house could not wholly replace more conventional relationships. When she was older, Vita wrote in one of the unpublished private poems she called diary poems: 'The horrible loneliness of the soul makes one crave for some contact.'[116] 'Contact' was not love, nor limited to a single donor or recipient. During her teenage years at Miss Woolff's, Vita inspired, and partly reciprocated, the love of two classmates: Rosamund Grosvenor and Violet Keppel.

She had known them both before. Rosamund Grosvenor was an old familiar, Vita's first friend, a relation of the Duke of Westminster. They were ten and six respectively when Rosamund first visited Vita at Knole in 1899. In his capacity as commander of the West Kent Yeomanry, Lionel had departed for South Africa and the Boer War, and Victoria worried that Vita would be lonely. Rosamund stayed for three days: Vita remembered only that her neatness and cleanliness contrasted with her own grubbiness. Until 1908, when her family moved away from Sevenoaks, Rosamund shared Vita's morning lessons at Knole. Initially, theirs was a milk-and-water relationship. Vita complained in private of Rosamund's ordinariness and lack of personality; Rosamund fell under the combined spell of Vita and Knole. Despite her four years' seniority, Rosamund learned to adopt the role of supplicant. It may have come naturally to her or she may have realised that the Vita who prided herself on her hardiness and her resemblance to a boy could only be conquered by weakness. Fortunately for Rosamund, who by her late teens was deeply in love, she had good looks on her side. Her soft, creamy curvaceousness earned her the nickname 'the Rubens lady'. Eventually it was Rosamund's body, not her mind, which provoked a response in Vita. In her diary for 17 July 1905, she noted that Rosamund had gone swimming, noted too her appearance in a bathing costume 'on the skimpy side'. Vita was thirteen, Rosamund seventeen. When their relationship progressed beyond girlish friendship, Vita was clear that, as far as she was concerned, its root was physical attraction: Rosamund was fatally uninterested in books.

Hero worship, and a tendency she could not resist to regard Vita as the living incarnation of centuries of Sackville swank, characterised Rosamund's love. She revelled too in Vita's Spanish blood, an association of exotic glamour which Vita herself exploited. Vita provoked a similar response in Violet Keppel: 'All this, and a gipsy too! My romantic heart overflowed.'[117] Rosamund addressed Vita as 'Princess'; for Violet, Vita was her 'Rosenkavalier'.[118] Both names imply status, desirability, a prize.

Violet's novel *Broderie Anglaise* offers a version of her relationship with Vita, whom she reimagines as a youthful peer, John Shorne. There is 'a languid grace' about Shorne, 'a latent fire'. Like Vita, he bears a strong resemblance to his family portraits. His 'face recalled so many others seen in frames and surrounded by a ruff, a jabot or a stock, a face that had been a type since 1500 . . . a hereditary face which had come, eternally bored through five centuries'.[119] Like Rosamund, Violet romanticised Vita. Yet while Rosamund's affection had the puppyishness of first love, Violet's, even as a child, was characterised by an obsessive decisiveness. It was not, Vita insisted, 'the kind of rather hysterical friendship one conceives in adolescence':[120] there was nothing exploratory about Violet's feelings. Her emotional precocity was matched only by her determination. If Rosamund's love for Vita resembled the blushing passions of a girls' school story, Violet's possessed from the beginning a more adult quality. Her decision that Vita was her destiny was virtually instantaneous and never rescinded. Decades later she underlined in her copy of *The Unquiet Grave* Cyril Connolly's statement that 'We only love once, for once only are we perfectly equipped for loving.'[121] She had not needed a book to tell her that. Even at the end of her life, fragile and lonely in the Villa Ombrellino in Florence, Violet spoke of Vita in adulatory tones. When it happened, she became Vita's lover through force of will. Vita was a mostly willing participant, but it was Violet who contrived their collision.

Their first meeting took place on a winter afternoon: Mayfair, 1905, a tea party of sorts for a girl friend with a broken leg, who remained in her bed. The only fellow guest Violet noticed at the bedside was Vita. Vita was thirteen, tall for her age, ungainly and unmannerly (Lionel had recently complained of her abruptness and her roughness). Violet was two years younger. Vita rebuffed her conversational gambits, Violet inwardly criticised Vita's dress. Both were evidently curious. Violet persuaded her mother to invite Vita to tea; Vita's mother was delighted and Vita went. Again their conversation was at cross purposes. Violet described Paris while Vita enlarged on her rabbits. They found common ground in inventorying aloud lists of their ancestors: as Vita explained later, in upper-class Edwardian society 'genealogies and family connections . . . formed almost part of a moral code'.[122] On Vita's departure, Violet kissed her. At home Vita congratulated herself on having made a friend – this was so unusual that she sang about it in the bath – while Violet embarked on what would become a lengthy and at times inflammatory sequence of letters. Vita responded with more news of her rabbits and also her dogs: an Aberdeen terrier called Pickles and an Irish terrier predictably known as Pat. Nothing daunted, Violet poured out what Vita labelled 'precocious letters on every topic in a variety of tongues, imaginative exceedingly, copiously illustrated, bursting occasionally into erratic and illegible verse'.[123]

Between letters Vita visited Violet at her parents' house in Portman Square; Violet was invited to Knole. Portman Square, where Violet's mother, Alice Keppel, played host to Edward VII as his mistress, suggested sex at its most discreet and profitable; Knole, with its whispering galleries of Sackville history, imparted romance, a thrill of derring-do glittering in dust motes. Vita's shortcomings as a correspondent notwithstanding, for Violet it was a perfect combination. 'I fell in love with John when I was eleven and a half – I swear that's the truth – and for eight years I never stopped thinking about him,' she wrote of Vita–John in *Broderie Anglaise*.[124] In another novel, *Hunt the Slipper*, she suggested that 'one never loves more passionately than at the age of ten'.[125]

Vita and Violet shared dancing and Italian lessons. In the spring of 1906 they were in Paris at the same time. In the apartment in the rue Laffitte, in front of an audience of Lionel and Victoria and Sir John Murray Scott's French servants, they staged Vita's play about the reign of Louis XIII, *Le Masque de Fer*. Vita took the part of the Man in the Iron Mask and was delighted when Seery's cook burst into tears. Less competent a French speaker than Vita (she did not have the benefit of a French-convent-educated mother), Violet took French lessons. They began to talk to one another in French. There was a special excitement to the intimacy of addressing each other as '*tu*'. That sense of intimacy grew. In the spring of 1908, Violet told Vita she loved her, 'and I,' wrote Vita, 'finding myself expected to rise to the occasion, stumbled out an unfamiliar "darling"'.[126] Violet sought to make a pact of the exchange by presenting Vita with a ring when next they met. The ring had been a reluctant present to Violet from the Bond Street art dealer Sir Joseph Duveen when Violet was six. It was carved from red lava with the image of a woman's head and had belonged to a Venetian Doge of the early Renaissance. The sixteen-year-old Vita composed a special entry in her diary and kept the ring lifelong.

Vita's relationship with Violet Keppel changed the course of her life: she was slow to respond fully to overtures which, on Violet's part, contained a sexual dimension almost from the start. This was not, Vita would claim, because she mistook Violet's intentions. Violet was always unique among Vita's friends: colourful and sophisticated; her 'erratic' friend, as she introduced Violet to Harold Nicolson; 'this brilliant, this extraordinary, this almost unearthly creature', as Vita described her at the height of their affair in 1920;[127] the friend whose love she argued she had recognised immediately. She said that she had understood Violet's early feelings for her as she had understood those of Rosamund, whom she had admitted she loved by the time she was fifteen. Her mother's diary challenges such assertions of sexual maturity. 'Vita and I had begun together *The Woman in White*,' Victoria wrote on 21 September 1904; 'I dropped it as the child's mind is still too young and I am careful to keep her very pure-minded.' She had confiscated *The Count of Monte Cristo* for the same reasons.

If Vita was aware of the nature of Rosamund and Violet's feelings, she ought to have recognised that they were rivals. In the event she admitted no need to arbitrate between them. In this way, at the outset of her romantic career, she established a pattern which would continue, juggling multiple lovers with no apparent sense of conflict or disloyalty. 'All love is a weakness . . . in so far as it destroys some part of our independence,' says Sebastian in *The Edwardians*.[128] For Vita, invariably more loved than loving, love would seldom compromise her independence. She exercised freedom of choice both romantically and sexually, countering Silas's statement to Nan in her early novel *The Dragon in Shallow Waters* that 'freedom goes when the heart goes'.[129] Invariably she retained a clear conscience, and she did not often lose her heart.

Vita did not return to Miss Woolff's school in the autumn of 1909. Instead she went abroad with her mother and Sir John. Her extended visit to the Continent took in Germany, Austria, Poland and Russia. At Antoniny in the Ukraine, Vita experienced a last gasp of the *ancien régime*, staying with Count Joseph Potocki, 'riding, dancing, laughing; living at a fantastic rate in that fantastic oasis of extravagance and feudalism, ten thousand horses on the estate, eighty English hunters, and a pack of English hounds; a park full of dromedaries; . . . Tokay handed round by a giant; cigarettes handed round by dwarfs in eighteenth-century costumes'.[130] Potocki's estate covered a hundred miles. Dazzled by splendour, aware of the poverty endured by all bar her host, Vita recognised an alternative, and disturbing, version of the tale of inheritance she had imbibed as Knole's child. The inequalities shocked her. 'That experience was really like going back to France before 1789,' she wrote in 1944. 'It was horrible; it was revealing.' The travellers wound up in October in Paris, where Victoria ordered dresses for Vita at Worth. As her eighteenth birthday approached, her mother had different plans for Vita, who that year had begun her reluctant career as a debutante. 'Party in the evening at Lady Jane Coombe's,' Vita had written laconically in her diary on 25 January: 'Hated it.' For Lionel and Victoria, whose ambitions for Vita's marriage were considerable, it was an ominous beginning to her first season. Vita would discover, as she had predicted leaving Russia, a stultifying sense of confinement about the life that was now expected of her at home: 'How shall I ever be able to live in this restricted island! I want expanse.'[131] In the short term she did not rebel. She wrote out her protest in a new novel. In *Behind the Mask*, a story of modern marriage set in France, she dismissed 'the whole business' of the marriage market as 'coarse and vulgar'.[132]

On 5 October 1905, Victoria Sackville-West had decided to make a new will. She had visited the family solicitor, Mr Pemberton of Meynell & Pemberton, back in March 1897, in order to formalise her intention of leaving 'everything to Lionel in trust for Vita, till she marries with his consent; then he will give her the income of the capital'.[133] On that occasion Vita was days short of her fifth birthday. By the time Victoria returned to the fray, her daughter was thirteen. Victoria explained her motives: 'Now . . . I do not think I shall have another child, after all the precautions Lionel and I have taken.'[134]

Sexual intercourse ceased for Lionel and Victoria Sackville-West in 1904. Once it had formed the bedrock of this mismatched couple's relationship. The decision was Victoria's, her justification the weakness of her nervous system, as explained to her by her obliging physician Dr Ferrier. From now on, iron tablets rather than Lionel would be her medicine. Her husband was thirty-seven years old, active and highly sexed: previously Victoria had described him as 'a stallion', their lovemaking 'delirium'. Lionel, for his part, had once thought Victoria 'the very incarnation of passionate love': 'Her breasts are too delicious for words – round firm and soft with two darling little buttons which I adore kissing. She has the most magnificent hips and legs with the most ravishing little lock of hair between them which is as silky and soft as possible.'[135] During the early years of their marriage, Victoria's diary is full of sex: when, where and how often. In the beginning, the naughtiness of 'Baby' (Lionel's penis) is a constant refrain. Sex forced the couple to miss morning appointments; it inconvenienced the servants; it kept Victoria awake at night; it bound them together.

Childbirth brought about the change. For Victoria, desire gave way to fear. Uppermost in her mind was the spectre of another unendurable confinement. In the aftermath of Vita's birth, she claimed she would do anything to make Lionel happy, 'even if it meant undergoing the horrors of childbirth'.[136] Then she persuaded him to adopt the rudimentary contraceptive practices of the time and did her best to avoid that very contingency.

If abstinence appeared to reassure Victoria, its effect on Lionel was quite different. Victoria was volatile. In all her relationships she lacked self-control. In her marriage she positively embraced the *Sturm und Drang* of lovers' quarrels. By contrast Lionel was peaceable, uncommunicative, too polite for histrionics: the more

Victoria railed, the further Lionel retreated behind a carapace of good manners and watery dislike, and so on and on. Like Evelyn Jarrold in need of reassurance from Miles Vane-Merrick in *Family History*, 'the more she saw that she was making herself a nuisance, the more of a nuisance she made herself'.[137] Despite their close blood relationship, the Sackville-Wests were remarkably ill-suited. For ten years, beginning around 1899, they no longer scrupled to disguise their differences. Vita witnessed this breakdown. She absorbed a highly distorted idea of marriage at a time when she was insufficiently emotionally mature to set it in context or to recognise the unusual starkness of her parents' incompatibility. Instead she struggled to reach a solution through writing. In *Behind the Mask*, written between November 1909 and March 1910, her heroine renounces the man she loves in order to avoid the coruscating effects of marriage: 'It is better for us to live apart and love each other all our lives, than to marry and quarrel after a few months.'[138] The extremes in her parents' behaviour suggested to Vita an oversimplified equation of Englishness and equanimity on Lionel's part and Victoria's Spanish blood and emotional misrule, as well as a model of marriage in which love was doomed to fail. Increasingly she would choose to blame Victoria. As one of her later fictional heroines states, 'I hate lack of control . . . I hate people who let themselves go.'[139]

The collapse of her parents' marriage was one factor which convinced Vita of her own 'duality': that her nature combined conflicting elements or 'sides', the English and the Spanish, which both demanded satisfaction. She imagined those elements as opposites and therefore irreconcilable: propriety pitched against protest, conformity against self, kindness against cruelty, 'a free spirit or a prisoner';[140] or, as Violet Keppel explained it to Vita, purity and gravity on the one hand, dominance, sensuousness and brutality on the other. An inward struggle along these lines is often part of the experience of growing up. Vita never fully outgrew it because she regarded it as a quirk of her heredity rather than a passing phase; it further complicated her transition from childhood to adulthood. In her first published novel, *Heritage*, of 1919, she investigated the same dichotomy in the character of Ruth, a version of herself. Ruth is 'cursed with a dual nature, the one coarse and unbridled, the other delicate, conventional, practical, motherly, refined . . .'.[141] Another of her heroines likens such polarities to the two halves of an apple: 'Was it impossible ever to keep the apple whole?' she asks herself, 'a globe to hold entire in the hand?'[142] For Vita, the 'coarse and unbridled' side of her nature was every bit as appealing as its more refined opposite. On the eve of her first visit to Spain in 1913, a journey that took her from Madrid south to Granada, she wrote to her friend Irene Lawley: 'I am going to SPAIN . . . If I write about it, my hand begins to shake, and my hair piles itself up on the top, like under a mantilla, with a comb, all of its own accord. So I won't say any more.'[143] A kind of coarseness could excite Vita.

Instead of steering a middle course, or choosing one way over the other, Vita indulged both inclinations separately. 'My whole curse has been a duality with which I was too weak and too self-indulgent to struggle,' as she explained in 1920.[144] 'Nothing is foreordained./ I hold my liberty/ Unstained and unconstrained,' Vita would write in her poem 'Heredity'. In the event, the 'stain' of her parents' marriage proved ineradicable. The desire to satisfy in full both facets of her make-up would shape key moments in her life.

Lionel and Victoria had in common their devotion to Knole and to Vita: even that was at variance, different in origin, form and expression. A selfish and romantically uncomplicated man, Lionel was incapable of interpreting Victoria's sexual withdrawal other than as a corresponding emotional withdrawal, so he sought satisfaction elsewhere. In transferring his desire he ended up transferring his affection. Victoria expended her energy on Knole and, with increasing frequency, on scenes of the sort guaranteed to drive Lionel further away. Unwitting it may have been, but Victoria's first blind steps along the road to bitterness and disillusion were taken deliberately.

Vita watched her and saw what she regarded as her mother's 'mistake'. It did not occur to her that Victoria's behaviour was a *cri de coeur*. She had not read in her mother's diary her desperate desire for warmth; she suspected nothing then of her frustration at the coldness first of Lord Sackville, then Lionel and even Vita herself, with her tendency to keep her feelings secret and resist confidences. Vita's solution, explored through fiction, was a world in which partners simply deceived one another, concealing their true emotions beneath a smiling veneer, their motives self-protection and survival, the result a semblance of marriage in appearance only: legitimate mendacity in the interests of the greater happiness. *Behind the Mask* is among the most aptly titled of her books. 'Is there anyone without the mask?' she asks.[145] It was a pragmatic, cynical approach, and undesirable in a girl of eighteen on the brink of adulthood. She saw it very clearly: she was never wholly disabused of her theory. 'Men have two natures,' she wrote later, 'and one of them they keep concealed.'[146] At another level, her conviction that each of us presents to the world a mask which conceals as much as it reveals explained the impossibility of ever fully knowing anyone but ourselves, another theme she would explore in her fiction. 'When you see a person, a body, marvellous casket and mask of secrets, what do you think?' she asked in *Heritage*.[147]

Unsurprisingly, Victoria proved incapable of wearing any sort of mask. As her relationship with Lionel worsened, she took up with Seery instead. As an added distraction, she opened a shop on South Audley Street, selling lampshades, waste-paper baskets, boxes, blotters and ashtrays decorated with epigrams and mottoes, including her favourite: 'A camel can go for nine days without water, but who wants to be a camel?' She called the shop Spealls, an anagram of the name of its first manageress, and harried Vita to think up similar mottoes and short verses; Vita failed. Spealls enabled Victoria to visit London frequently. Her relationship with Seery grew closer; it was peppered with rows and reconciliations. Seery resented Spealls and its call on Victoria's time; the shop provided further grounds for differences. Then, sporadically, Seery threatened to cut Victoria out of his will. To both of them this constant negotiation and renegotiation of the terms of their relationship was the breath of life. Even as a teenager, such tempestuousness appalled Vita. After witnessing a particularly acrimonious quarrel between Seery and her mother on 22 March 1910, Vita wrote: 'I thought they would quarrel for good, but he became apologetic and they have half patched it up, though it can't ever be as before. It was all very unpleasant, and they called each other names and I hated it.'[148]

For Victoria, such incidents were a game, a form of self-affirmation. They proved her continuing ability to dominate a man completely. With Seery in the role of *cavaliere servente*, there was no unwelcome complication of sex. Vita's own self-affirmation would take different forms, though, like Victoria, her 'Spanish' side revelled in the world of feelings: like the narrator of *Heritage*, 'Spanish' Vita believed that 'the vitality of human beings is to be judged . . . by the force of their emotion'.[149] In the decades to come, her own emotions, alongside her attitude to sex, would give rise to numberless complications.

PART II

Challenge

'Oh, what an awful word!' said Juliet, her spirits suddenly re-
asserting themselves. 'Wedlock! It makes me feel as though I
had chains round my wrists and ankles, and a great dragging
load of wood. Wed-lock! Locked-in!'
                              V. Sackville-West, *The Easter Party*, 1953

'I SHALL NEVER forget it,' Vita recorded of *The Masque of
Shakespeare*, staged in the park at Knole on the afternoon of 2
July 1910. In a costume loaned to her by Ellen Terry, Vita
took the part of Portia from *The Merchant of Venice*. Terry
herself had worn the costume in 1875, voluminous robes of
red velvet. It was Portia's disguise as the 'young doctor of
Rome', a celebrated instance of Shakespearean cross-dressing.
    Vita was photographed and painted in her borrowed robes.
She was eighteen and had grown into a beauty. 'The knobs
and knuckles had disappeared. She was tall and graceful. The
profound hereditary Sackville eyes were as pools from which
the morning mist had lifted. A peach might have envied her

complexion.'[1] Victoria drew attention to the loveliness of Vita's skin and her eyes, 'with their double curtain of long lashes'.[2] Shyness appeared as aloofness: with 'her sleek brown head, her glowing skin, her disdainful poise', she resembled Ruth Pennistan in *Heritage*.[3] Thanks to the Sackville succession case in February, Vita also possessed, in attractive measure, a degree of notoriety; newspaper reports had emphasised her connection to Knole, which possessed a glamour of its own. With her schooldays at Miss Woolff's behind her, Vita would find that she had graduated from inspiring schoolgirl crushes to provoking a similar response in the young men she encountered. At eighteen, there was a soft and gentle quality to Vita's beauty. Later this softness gave way to something more florid: a harder, bolder, more masculine appearance, 'all rather heroic and over life-size; all on a big scale; no feminine charm at all', as she herself described one of her fictional alter egos.[4] The shift would reflect a change in her attitudes. For the moment, youthful curiosity had yet to be overwhelmed by the certainties of middle age.

Clare Atwood's portrait of Vita as Portia, which today hangs in Ellen Terry's former home of Smallhythe Place, suggests androgyny: Vita as a romantic Italian youth. Set against a medieval cityscape, she appears as she would have wished: as she described herself three years later, 'essentially primitive; and not 1913, but 1470; and not "modern"'.[5] For all its self-consciousness, it is a picture of a sitter without vanity, as if she disregarded her own looks. Victoria considered that a true assessment: she claimed that Vita was not in the least conceited. Unlike her mother, Vita at eighteen was not interested in feminine wiles; her interests lay elsewhere. Two years previously, in *Le Masque de Fer*, she had dressed up as the Man in the Iron Mask; a year ago, in her verse drama about doomed poet Thomas Chatterton, she was Chatterton himself, forger and Romantic hero, martyr to the written word. She wore a costume of breeches, white stockings, buckled shoes and a white shirt, which her maid Emily made for her in secret. Each time she played the part, learnt by heart and performed in an attic at Knole to an audience of abandoned trunks and cast-off furnishings, she reduced herself to tears: 'Earth has been my hell,/ Another world must surely be my heaven.'[6] Even at their most vulnerable, the men Vita chose for her alter egos were heroic. Her posturing arose from other impulses than vanity, but the element of self-association was potent. 'Each time I burnt Chatterton's manuscripts in the candle I felt I was burning my own,' she remembered; 'each time I died most uncomfortably on the oak settle, it was not only Chatterton but I myself who died.'[7]

On a rainy July day in 1910, in the guise of Portia masquerading as a lawyer in order to contrive her own happy ending, Vita continued that narrative of heroism and wish fulfilment she had begun in childhood – as Sir Redvers Buller, bold in khaki amid Knole's flowerbeds, and as Cranfield Sackville in *The King's Secret*, writing, always writing. This was Vita's other life, the life of her imagination. In imagination, every Sackville was a conquering hero and each, as she described them in 1922, 'the prototype of his age';[8] Vita was their latest incarnation. Her life would retain this element of fantasy. Repeatedly in her fiction she celebrated a male version of herself, because she associated maleness with control, possession, inheritance, fulfilment and love – as she invested 'the bull' in her poem of the same name, the ability to 'stand four-square and lordly scan/ His grass, his calves, his willing cows,/ Male, arrogant, alone'.[9] She is Julian in *Challenge*, buoyant with love for Eve; Peregrine Chase in *The Heir*, inheriting, and refusing to give up, the Tudor manor house of Blackboys; Sebastian in *The Edwardians*, handsome, fêted, secretive, heir to a fictional Knole; Nicholas

Lambarde in her unpublished story 'The Poet', certain of his writer's vocation, author of 'a contemplative poem on solitude' as Vita would be: 'The only important thing in the world to him was poetry.'[10] Most of all, and most revealingly, she is aspects of Miles Vane-Merrick in *Family History*. His house is a castle in Kent, based on Vita's future home of Sissinghurst; his interests include poetry, farming and philosophy; his emotional requirements are specific and unyielding: 'He wanted to retain his individuality, his activity, his time-table. He wanted to lead his own life, parallel with the life of love, separate, independent.'[11] For Miles, everything has its allotted place. His life is docketed, divided into compartments, but he relinquishes nothing. From early in her romantic career, the same idea appealed to Vita. She would prove herself mostly skilful at maintaining her independence, her 'separateness' from the life of love. Like Julian in *Challenge*, she learned to put things – people – aside until she wanted them: 'not forgotten, not faded . . . but merely put aside, laid away like winter garments in summer weather'.[12]

In the neverlands of her fiction and drama, Vita changed her sex as a means of taking control and a preliminary to action. It was a simple conceit. She continually rewrote her own history and, in swapping her sex, perfected what she regarded as imperfections. It enabled her for an instant to bypass those impediments to inheriting Knole which she could never overcome; it enabled her to love as she wished, unconstrained by social expectation; as Cranfield, Chatterton and Portia, using language with a lawyer's skill, she staked her claim to be a writer in the face of parental resistance. The Vita of her books was never dispossessed and never without love: always the cynosure, never the pariah; always autonomous. In *Seducers in Ecuador*, the unreliable Miss Whitaker shares Vita's fantasy: 'her own stories were marvellously coming true.

Indeed, to her, they were always true; what else was worthwhile? But that the truth of fact should corroborate the truth of imagination! Her heart beat.'[13]

In fiction, imagination and reality merged: it was a mission statement for Vita. Even Shakespeare forced her into men's clothing. She did not resist. Her desire to share in all the possibilities and perquisites of a man's life shaped her. If, as she suggested, her role, like her forebears', was to be the 'prototype' of the age, it is appropriate that this woman who was born into the smug certainties of aristocratic Victorian England, and who witnessed their collapse in the aftermath of the First World War, should in her life embrace areas of confusion and uncertainty. Added to which, she enjoyed dressing up. Events like the *Masque*, which included several of her friends, were a high point in that debutante life she decried as 'distasteful and unsuccessful'. Deep down Vita's real reservation, as at Miss Woolff's, arose from her fear of not being liked.

The *Masque* was a fundraising exercise. A theatrical performance showcasing many of Shakespeare's best-known characters, it was intended, as the programme notes explained, to benefit 'the Shakespeare Memorial National Theatre Fund, which is established to promote the erection and endowment of a Tercentenary Memorial to Shakespeare to take the form of a National Repository Theatre'. Vita had attended her first rehearsal at Apsley House on 10 June. Also taking part were Rosamund Grosvenor and Vita's friend Irene Lawley, along with Lionel's current mistress Olive Rubens, as well as professionals including Ellen Terry. A London performance on 30 June was abandoned midway because of rain. Three days later it rained at Knole, too, 'torrents, but cleared up and we were able to finish it'.[14]

In her diary, Vita makes no comment on her role. She lists rehearsal times and weather conditions for the outdoor performances; she records the loan of Terry's costume. She does not reflect on Portia's emotional dilemma – or her own. In Shakespeare's Venetian comedy, Portia is the wealthy young woman whom suitors squabble over. Her father has set a riddle to determine the choice; her own choice is set on Bassanio. 'The lottery of my destiny/ Bars me the right of voluntary choosing,' Portia tells the Prince of Morocco. In the summer of 1910, Vita's case appeared quite different. She was surrounded by choices. She understood her parents' hopes for her, but estimated correctly that they would allow her to make up her own mind. To Victoria, Lionel wrote, 'I see that it's no good trying to force her.'[15] To Vita, when the time came to choose between suitors, he made it 'clear he had other dreams'. Even in his disappointment, Vita wrote, he was 'sweet'.[16]

Rosamund Grosvenor was still in love with Vita; only Vita's engagement would painfully sever their tie. There was Violet Keppel, too, who had symbolically bound Vita to her with the gift of the Doge's ring. At the end of October, departing for Ceylon with her mother in the aftermath of the death of Edward VII, Violet kissed Vita goodbye with all the (considerable) passion she could muster; Vita was disturbed by her passion and by her urgency. Violet wrote her love letters: 'I love you, Vita, because you never gave me back my ring.'[17] Later Violet wrote asking Vita not to get married before her return.

Her letter was prescient. On 29 June, only four days before the *Masque*, Vita met the man she would marry. The occasion was a dinner party before a trip to Conan Doyle's *The Speckled Band* at the Adelphi Theatre. The young man was subsequently invited to Knole for the *Masque*. With Rosamund and a small party, he stayed for the weekend. Victoria took the chance to show him over the house. Vita felt a degree of curiosity, no more. On 29 June, the first words she had heard the young man utter were 'What fun!'. She liked at once 'his irrepressible brown curls, his laughing eyes, his charming smile':[18] these were not necessarily lover-like attributes. He appeared boyish and light-hearted. These, too, were not lover-like traits but they appealed to Vita – even as they contrasted with the vigorous, troubadour quality that distinguished the men she herself impersonated in her writing and her daydreams. It was not love at first sight when Vita met Harold Nicolson, though she would later recycle the scene in *Family History*: 'Miles came to fetch [Evelyn]. He was especially gay. What fun, he said in his most boyish way.'[19]

In fact, Vita wrote, it was not until three years later, in the spring of 1913, that 'something snapped, and I loved Harold from that day on'.[20] In her diary, she contradicts herself: she decided that she loved Harold as soon as he had kissed her. That was September 1912. Harold's kiss took him more than two years. In his defence, he was away for much of that period: in Madrid until September 1911, thereafter in Constantinople, where he served as a secretary at the British embassy. In the meantime for Vita there was Rosamund; a Florentine marquess called Orazio Pucci, who had fallen in love with her in Italy in 1909 and the following year trailed her halfway across Europe, even to Knole; and, in Pucci's footsteps, a nameless artist encountered on a boat trip on Lake Como, whom Vita rejected lightly as 'second *coup de foudre*!!!'.[21] With beauty came the brittleness and casual unkindness of one growing rapidly accustomed to being pursued. On and off during that summer of 1910, Harold and Vita met, often at Victoria's invitation at Knole. In November, in her first surviving letter to Harold, Vita asked him to accompany her to dinner and then a dance. Her letter was deliberately light in tone. She told Harold that she was not alone: Rosamund was with her, and one of Harold's colleagues from the Foreign Office. Harold could not dance and disliked it as a pastime. He would learn that Vita was a poor dancer too.

Clearly, unlike Portia, Vita's 'destiny' would not deny her 'voluntary choosing'. Nevertheless, there were similarities as well as differences between the women's predicaments. Like Portia, Vita too was squabbled over. Her own actions served to complicate rather than to simplify those squabbles and, at times, as we shall see, she actively encouraged jealousies among her lovers. The child who had spent so much time on her own, uncertain of her parents' love, grew up to crave close, intense, intimate connections and, often, to need more than one person's love at a time. Her parents intended Vita to make 'a great match with a great title'. Vita balked; but her interlude as a debutante was a busy one, with four balls a week and lunch parties daily.

The young men Vita met did not attract her. She dismissed them disparagingly as 'little dancing things in ballrooms', 'the little silly pink and whites'.[22] Even dancing frequently left her unmoved: 'All the dance tunes sounded much the same . . . Faintly lascivious, faintly cacophonous; a young man's arm round one, a young man's body surprisingly close, his breath on one's hair, and yet a disharmony between oneself and him, or, at most, a fictitious temporary closeness which tumbled to pieces as soon as the music stopped.'[23] She made an exception for the clever Patrick Shaw-Stewart (and he was '*so* ugly' that she dressed him up in her mind 'in Louis XI clothes'[24] but omitted to think of him romantically) and for Lady Desborough's tall son Julian Grenfell. Grenfell was 'a Soul', part of a pre-war set of thoughtful, poetic, politically minded aristocrats, and Vita liked Souls: 'They are amusing and easy and not heavy to talk to.'[25]

Given Vita's literary aspirations, Lionel considered it a distinct, if troubling, possibility that she would marry a Soul. (Handsome Edward Horner, another Soul, was also attentive.) In the event Julian Grenfell may have been put off by his mother;

Lady Desborough's ambivalence is clear in a letter she wrote after Vita's marriage to Harold. She reported that Vita had become 'so *charming*, so *pretty* and so clean! and quite tidy, and not a bit of a prig or a bore'.[26] Her tone of surprise indicates her previous assessment. For her part, Vita explained simply that, until she married Harold, she had 'scarcely understood the meaning of being young'.[27] Grenfell himself, like several of Vita's would-be suitors including Edward Horner and Patrick Shaw-Stewart, died in the First World War. Before that he was caught in a downstairs cloakroom with Violet Keppel.

Yet even as Vita failed to feel any quickening of the pulse in the company of her most notable suitors – Lord Granby, heir to the Duke of Rutland, 'a curious rather morose person',[28] and Lord Lascelles, future Earl of Harewood, whom she considered 'rather dull' – she realised she would have to marry someone. She never seriously considered the possibility of an unmarried life, or a life restricted to female admiration of the sort Rosamund and Violet offered her. Meeting Harold Nicolson did not persuade her to give up such admiration, however. Harold's on-and-off, three-year courtship of Vita was conducted against a background of Rosamund's constant companionship; constrained by his work, Harold himself was more often absent than present. From the summer of 1911, Rosamund had her own bedroom at Knole. It was next door to Vita's, overlooking the Pheasants' Court. Vita described the two of them as 'inseparable'. She also claimed that they were 'living on terms of the greatest possible intimacy'.[29] A letter written by Rosamund during a separation from Vita appears to corroborate that statement: 'I do miss you, darling, and I want to feel your soft cool face coming out of that mass of pussy hair.'[30] Vita, however, denied that they made love: she admitted only that she was so overwhelmingly in love with Rosamund, that 'passion . . . used to make my head swim sometimes'.[31]

Also asserting her claim on Vita's heart long distance was Violet Keppel, who travelled from Ceylon to Italy and Germany. 'You won't tell me you love me, because you fear (wrongly, most of the time) that I will not make the same declaration to you at the same moment!' she wrote from Bavaria.[32] Since Vita's side of their correspondence has not survived, we do not know exactly what she said or did to inspire such an outburst. Having been sustained by the thought of Vita through her 'exile' in Ceylon, Violet had decided already on the course of their relationship. In the end, as in all her relationships, it was Vita who would make the crucial decision. If Vita was slow to fall in love with Harold, and untouched by the attentions of men like Granby, Lascelles, Grenfell, Horner and Shaw-Stewart, it was because her heart was otherwise occupied, her physical appetites fully stimulated and mostly satisfied.

Harold's recommendation to Vita was unusual. She regarded him as an ideal companion, a *'playmate'* (her own italics) and someone with whom she could 'talk about anything without minding, quite brutally'.[33] He corresponded exactly to her description of the hero of *Behind the Mask*, which Vita began that year: 'a playmate, clever and gay, with whom she feels an effortless affinity';[34] in another unpublished novel, *Marian Strangways*, of 1913, Vita described feelings of 'companionable love . . . half-friendship, half-playfellowship'.[35] Harold would remain all of these things for half a century; these commendations survived the crises in their marriage. Vita did not base her choice on sexual attraction. Portia tells Bassanio, 'In terms of choice I am not solely led/ By nice direction of a maiden's eyes.' The same was true for Vita. Physical attraction characterised her relationship with Rosamund Grosvenor, whom she first admired in her bathing costume when she was thirteen; her relationship with Violet Keppel subsequently represented a more intense infatuation. Vita knew already that these feelings were different from those which men inspired in her; she admitted that she did not think of men 'in what is called "that way"'.[36] Where men were concerned she remained as she was at eleven, when a farmer's son in Scotland 'told [her] a great many things he oughtn't to have told [her]' about sex: she was 'neither excited nor interested' by his revelations.[37] His subsequent demonstration of the physical differences between boys and girls provoked a more dramatic response. Deeply shocked, Vita fled.[38]

For all his boyishness and his bright eyes, the curly-haired young man invited to Knole for the *Masque of Shakespeare* failed to excite Vita physically. At no point in his undemonstrative courtship would he do so. Afterwards, Vita stated that it was Harold's own fault. He was too 'over-respectful'; his behaviour convinced her (correctly, in the event) that he was not 'the lover-type of man'.[39] Until Harold's kiss in September 1912, Vita's response to him was like that of Gottfried Künstler, in her novella of the same name. As Gottfried grew closer to Anna Roche, we read, nevertheless 'it never entered his head to fall in love with her'.[40] Unlike Vita, Gottfried did not blame Anna for his conduct. Her protest has a hollow ring to it. She later claimed of the period before Harold's proposal, 'People began to tell me he was in love with me, which I didn't believe was true, but wished that I could believe it.' Significantly she adds: 'I wasn't in love with him then.'[41] Yet for reasons of her own — insecurity and confusion uppermost — she needed to believe that Harold loved her.

Harold almost certainly did fall in love with Vita, albeit his affection, like hers, lacked physical ardour. It was a conundrum rich in irony. At eighteen, Vita had yet to realise the implications of her feelings of arousal or non-arousal: she did not regard her 'intimacy' with Rosamund as any sort of disqualification from marriage or, more surprisingly, disloyalty to

Harold. 'It never struck me as wrong that I should be more or less engaged to Harold, and at the same time very much in love with Rosamund,' she confessed in her autobiography.[42] To Harold she wrote: 'I love the Rubens lady [Rosamund], and somewhere in the world there is you.'[43] She did not think of herself as gay. Like the majority of women of her generation, she considered her long-term sexual choices as marriage or abstinence. Lesbianism, as understood today, did not exist as an option for Vita; the word itself had yet to enter common parlance. Later she told Harold that she had known nothing then of homosexuality. It was, anyway, a label she would have rejected. Rosamund provided affection, distraction and physical excitement during Harold's lengthy absences. There was virtually no intellectual companionship between the women. In time, Vita would come to consider them temperamentally mismatched: 'She is a stupid little thing, and her conventionality drives me mad.'[44] Regardless of her sexual feelings for Rosamund – or Rosamund's apparently deeper feelings for her – Vita would shortly decide to marry Harold. Rosamund's destiny, like Julian's winter garments in *Challenge*, was to be 'put aside'.

Six years her senior and a man, Harold was less naïve than Vita. He was aware that, despite his love for her, his sexual inclinations were predominantly homosexual and could not be satisfied by a wife. As recently as September 1911, he had been forced to leave Madrid under a cloud after contracting gonorrhoea from an unidentified partner. (Unaware of the nature of his illness, Vita described him sympathetically as 'rather a pathetic figure wrapped up in an ulster'.[45]) But he was not deterred. Throughout his life Harold treated his affairs lightly. They provided physical pleasure, they were divertissements, but they did not, in his own eyes, define him as a person. With few exceptions, they never overwhelmed him emotionally in the way that Vita was repeatedly consumed by her affairs.

Intermittently Harold craved sex with another man: he avoided acknowledging any need for the larger commitments – and rewards – of a full-scale relationship. Marriage was still a conventional expectation in early-twentieth-century England: Harold Nicolson was a man of conventional background. He had chosen a conventional career and would pursue it with more or less conventional success until Vita's intransigence knocked the wheels off the cart. In 1910, male homosexuality was a criminal offence. The need for secrecy in relation to this central aspect of his life surely shaped Harold's behaviour in the summer he met Vita; the fact of his homosexuality partly accounted for the nature of his polite but dilatory courtship. As it happened, his chosen wife was every bit as secretive as he was. She allowed Harold to believe that her love for Rosamund was no more than an intensely loving friendship, while reciprocating Rosamund's devotion and, up to a point, her desires. The courtship of this young man and woman already skilled in concealment, uncertain or dishonest about the nature of their sexual appetites and their emotional needs, was inevitably bound for choppy waters.

In the eyes of Vita's mother, Harold's parents Sir Arthur and Lady Nicolson were 'very ugly and very small and very unsmart looking'.[46] From the beginning, Vita and her parents discounted Harold's family. (Fifty years later, Vita forbad Harold to be buried alongside her in the family vault at Withyham on the grounds that he was not a Sackville.) They discounted Sir Arthur's achievements as ambassador to Russia; they discounted Lady Nicolson's Anglo-Irish connections and her sister's marriage to the Viceroy, Lord Dufferin and Ava. (Lord Dufferin was an eminent Victorian whose record as a diplomat and public servant eclipsed that of any Sackville since the end of the sixteenth century, when Thomas Sackville served his cousin Elizabeth I as Lord High Treasurer of England. Lord Dufferin had an Irish estate at Clandeboye – the Sackvilles discounted that too.) After Lionel had failed his Foreign Office examinations in 1890 and given up on the idea of a career, the Sackvilles discounted the world of work entirely. Referring to Harold's position as a junior diplomat in Constantinople, Sackville family gossip labelled him 'a penniless Third Secretary'. Harold did not deny it. With a salary of £250 a year, he described himself as 'supremely ineligible';[47] he categorised his family background as that of a 'landless tribe' lacking 'hereditary soil'.[48] There was the rub. For though the Nicolson baronetcy originated in the first half of the seventeenth century, and Sir Arthur would be created Baron Carnock in 1916, the Nicolsons were members of a service class which the Sackvilles had forgotten and forsaken. They could not lay claim to a Knole. Rather they lived at 53 Cadogan Gardens, supported only by Sir Arthur's salary. Harold's own salary contrasted poorly with that of his wealthiest competitors for Vita's hand: the annual income of Lord Granby's father, the Duke of Rutland, was somewhere in the region of £100,000,[49] while Lord Lascelles told Victoria that his father's income was '£31,000 a year from his land alone, plus plenty of cash'.[50] With uncharacteristic understatement, Victoria wrote in her diary about the prospect of an engagement between Vita and Harold: 'It is not at present a good marriage.'[51]

Vita was as conscious as her parents of the discrepancy, however slight, between her own claim to elite status and Harold's. It was a claim which counted for more then than now. Brought up as a child of the diplomatic aristocracy, Harold's childhood memories included vignettes of the royal courts of Bulgaria, Spain and Russia, of the British embassy in Paris, with its powdered footmen and gilded opulence, and of the Anglo-Irish ascendancy life of his mother's family and his Uncle Dufferin. He confessed a sense of 'effortless superiority'.[52] It was an attitude of mind. That he chose to articulate this feeling at all suggests a degree of self-conscious-ness incompatible with effortlessness. Vita's social outlook was more straightforward. Hers were the assumptions of an age-old landed caste; later in life she adopted a tag of Victoria's about her attitudes having been formed before the French Revolution. Virginia Woolf would describe her as 'very splendid': 'all about her is . . . patrician'. An upbringing at Knole, latterly smoothed by Seery's generous handouts, had done little to cultivate 'ordi-nary' instincts in Vita. Only in middle age did she acknowledge that the Sackville glory days were long past: she never made such an admission to Harold. She 'ought to be a *grande dame*, very rich', Victoria wrote, 'where she could do what she likes and not have to do anything against the grain'.[53] To Harold, Vita wrote: 'I like having things done for me.' It bored her to do things for other people.[54] She never learned to cook and, until her death, relied on servants in most areas of her domestic life. As a debutante she preferred 'a very fine ball . . . with powdered footmen announcing duchesses' to 'those scrimmages at the Ritz'.[55] There was an opulence to Vita that was mostly uncontrived.

As Vita herself was aware, her own background was closer to that of the early suitors she rejected – Lord Granby and Lord Lascelles – than to Harold's family, with its steady accum-ulation of diligent public service. On 6 June 1912, Vita attended a '100-years-ago' ball at the Royal Albert Hall. She was dressed as a figure from one of the Hoppner portraits at Knole, in the very costume worn by the sitter, with 'two tall grey feathers and a white turban'.[56] Walking round the hall in company with the heirs to dukedoms, she told Harold, 'I could see *"How suitable!"* in people's eyes as we went by.'[57] Her motive in writing in this vein was partly ironic; she may also have intended to rouse Harold to jealousy. In her complacency she overlooked Harold's previous unofficial engagement – to Lady

Eileen Wellesley, herself a duke's daughter (as well as one of Vita's fellow cast members in the Shakespeare *Masque*). If the Nicolsons lacked élan, they were not, as all acknowledged, what the Sackvilles termed 'bedint': middle class, vulgar or worse. Despite Vita's family pride, the marriage of Harold Nicolson to Vita Sackville-West was no *mésalliance*.

Her sense of social superiority notwithstanding, Vita was ripe to fall in love. Remembering in 1920, she disparaged Rosamund's intellectual limitations (in *Challenge*, where Rosamund appears loosely fictionalised as Fru Thyregod, Vita dismisses her conversation as a 'babble of coy platitudes'[58]); their liaison undoubtedly made Vita happier than otherwise. It stimulated that streak of romance which inspired her to write; the same impulse affected the nature of her writing and some, but not all, of her relationships. It would never leave her. In 1913, in a poem called 'Early Love', she described a relish for 'those fond days when every spoken word/ [Is] sweet, and all the fleeting things unspoken/ Yet sweeter . . .'.[59] She told Harold: 'There is no fun equal to being *quite* at the beginning of things.'[60] A part of Vita was in love with the idea of love and would remain so.

Two centuries earlier, in his poem 'Dorinda's Sparkling Wit and Eyes', Charles Sackville had written: 'Love is a calm and tender joy,/ Kind are his looks and soft his pace.' Vita had seen little of the calmness and tenderness, the kindness or softness of love. Calmness was so seldom a feature of Victoria's relationships; and kindliness had long ceased to play a central part in Lionel and Victoria's marriage. As a child, Vita had frequently lacked the easy reassurance of her parents' love. Of those other adults in her life, Lord Sackville was costive in his emotional reticence and few of Vita's governesses enjoyed more than a fleeting tenure. The departure of Miss Bennett, known as 'Bentie', when Vita was ten, caused her real distress. Vita admired her father and convinced herself (correctly) of the depth of their mostly unspoken bond: 'You and I are so alike and are not always able to show these things,' he would write to her later.[61] Indeed, she minded so much about her father's good opinion that she prevented him from reading any of her early novels and plays. According to Victoria, Seery also thought of Vita as 'like a daughter';[62] along with Bentie, Ralph Battiscombe and her parents, he was a legatee in a will Vita compiled aged nine. The bequests to Seery included 'my minia-ture, my claret jug, my whip', in addition to the khaki suit in which Vita played at being Sir Redvers Buller. She was not troubled by the discrepancy in size between her nine-year-old self and twenty-five-stone Sir John: she regarded him, she would write, as 'a mass of good humour and kindliness'.[63]

By the time she met Harold Nicolson, Vita had limited but vexed experience of male libido. Her first sexual encounter occurred when she was eleven. It happened in Scotland, at Sluie, the Aberdeenshire estate overlooking the lower Grampians which Seery rented annually. Afterwards Vita remembered the place with something close to rapture: 'those lovely, lovely hills, those blazing sunsets, those runnels of icy water where I used to make water-wheels, those lovely summer evenings'.[64] At Sluie, rules were relaxed: 'I had a kilt and a blue jersey, and I don't suppose I was ever tidy once, even on Sundays.'[65] Vita spent her days with the gillies; she accompanied Seery shooting, helping him over stiles and stone walls; she ran through beech trees, silver birches and pines, foraged in the heather and the bracken and the loch behind the house; she played with the children of the local farmer. It was a paradise for this tomboy with a taste for fresh air and disdain for conventional girlish pastimes; her time outdoors was enlivened by that element of easy companionship missing from so much of her childhood. In her diary for 29 August 1907, shortly after arriving at Sluie, she recorded her first meeting that year with the farmer's children: 'I think Jack and Phemie were pleased to see me.'[66] Four years previously, the same Jack had told Vita he loved her. He told her so again when Vita was thirteen.

It happened the first time in the shadow of the gillie's hut. Despite what Vita described as his crippling awareness of the social gulf that existed between himself and the object of his affections, Jack took it upon himself to suit the deed to the word. His intention, Vita concluded years later, was to rape her: only 'his inborn respect, his sense of class' prevented him.[67] Instead he sought relief in masturbation, a hand on Vita's thigh. At the same time he forced Vita 'to take hold of his dog's penis and work it backwards and forwards until "the dog reached the point where he came and squirted his semen all over my shoes, and I was alarmed by this manifestation"'.[68] That 'alarmed' sounds an understatement. With hindsight Vita sought to minimise the oddness of this encounter by explaining her lack of childish squeamishness about sex: she was a country child, with a country child's knowledge of birds and bees. She denied that either Jack's masturbation or his dog's ejaculation had troubled her.

More distasteful were the unwelcome attentions of her god-father. The Hon. Kenneth Hallyburton Campbell, stockbroker son of Lord Stratheden and Campbell, was twenty-one years Vita's senior, a friend of Seery's, called by Victoria 'Kenito'. This affectionate diminutive proved misleading. Campbell first tried to rape Vita when she was sixteen, in her bedroom at Knole. On that occasion only the appearance of a housemaid carrying hot water saved her. 'Frequently after that' he renewed his attempt.[69] Campbell's position of trust exacerbated the gravity of his offences, which Vita grew practised at evading. Later, like Jack, he told Vita he loved her. In her diary she confided her sense of horror. Later still, when his marriage to

Rosalinda Oppenheim turned out badly, Campbell complained to Vita of his unhappiness.

Vita's upbringing had taught her the egotism of love. She learned too an idea of the selfishness of sexual gratification, particularly male sexual gratification. Jack could be excused on grounds of his youth. Not so Campbell. Within Vita's family circle were examples of men behaving badly. The Sackville succession case had inevitably drawn attention to the different consequences for Vita's grandfather and Pepita of their illicit love. Lord Sackville, as part-time lover, received unlimited sexual access and devotion: in provincial nineteenth-century Spain, Pepita forfeited respectability and her dancing career. She made herself ridiculous by adopting the title 'Countess West', and she died giving birth to the seventh of Lord Sackville's children. Despite her best efforts, she failed to shield those children from the implications of their illegitimacy. In the case of Vita's parents, Lionel does not appear to have worried over explanations for Victoria's sexual withdrawal; forgotten were the ecstasy of first infatuation, her exclamations of delirium, his tender lover's, 'Was it nice, Vicky?'[70] Instead Lionel sought consolation elsewhere. To Victoria's evident distress, he allowed his emotions to keep pace with his libido. In time Lionel and Victoria's physical separation eroded their relationship entirely.

Vita was young when she discovered that Knole could never belong to her. A male entail promised house and estate instead to her cousin Eddy, son of Lionel's brother Charles. Nine years younger than Vita and a gifted pianist from an early age, Eddy was in every way her inferior in fighting and war games and cricket and boyish bluster. If Vita was hardy and masculine, Eddy was soft and girlish (and afterwards homosexual). The cruelty of this reversal was not lost on Vita. 'I used to hate

Eddy when he was a baby and I wasn't much more, because he would have Knole,' she explained to Harold in 1912.[71] Gender was an accident of birth, but maleness — even Eddy's unconvincing, panstick-and-rouged, velvet-clad maleness — was rewarded. 'Knole is denied to me for ever, through a "technical fault over which we have no control", as they say on the radio,' she wrote.[72]

As with inheritance, Vita decided that in relationships the male role was that of taking, not giving: an unthinking assumption of the upper hand. It was a role she herself would play. In her novel *All Passion Spent*, Vita's octogenarian heroine Lady Slane questions a life that has been devoted to her husband: 'She was, after all, a woman . . . Was there, after all, some foundation for the prevalent belief that woman should minister to man? . . . Was there something beautiful, something active, something creative even, in her apparent submission to Henry?'[73] Certainly Vita thought at length on the contrasting roles of men and women. For the most part she was clear about her answers to such questions: she was incapable of discerning the beauty of submission. She devised a solution to suit herself. As with much in her life, her 'feminism' was self-serving. It consisted of a refusal to compromise anything touching her self-identity. That identity, as we have seen, embraced both masculine and feminine.

Sackville history included examples of formidable women, independent-minded and financially independent. Chief among them was the seventeenth-century matriarch Lady Anne Clifford. In 1923, Vita edited Lady Anne's diary for publication. Occasionally she likened herself to her indomitable forebear. Among other things, Lady Anne shared Vita's taste for solitude: 'though I kept my chamber altogether yet methinks the time is not so tedious to me as when I used to be abroad'.[74] But the forebears who appealed to Vita as a child were not women like

Lady Anne; rather, they were associated with tales of cavalier adventure and derring-do. In the history Vita loved, it was men who played the hero's part. Unconsciously or otherwise, she determined to take the same part, and Vita was often selfish in her relationships, not only with her lovers but within her family too. She excused it as her 'happy-go-lucky . . . everything-will-turn-out-right-if-you-don't-fuss-about-it' nature: in practice it meant she left the fussing – and the fallout – to other people.[75] Her life in retrospect is a wholesale rejection of the idea that sexual gratification exists as a masculine prerogative. Twice she turned down proposals of marriage from a young man who wooed her with a Christmas present of a bear cub; 'He has the worst temper of anyone I know. He is cruel,' she wrote of Ivan Hay.[76] Correctly she estimated the unlikelihood of his indulging her need for dominance. In a rare instance of humour she christened the bear cub 'Ivan the Terrible'. With Rosamund she was photographed for an illustrated paper, walking baby Ivan in the gardens at Knole. The paper captioned its photograph 'Beauty and the Bear'.[77] Irritated by Vita's debutante success, from which she felt herself excluded, and laconic in her sarcasm, Violet Keppel commented that 'bears had taken the place of rabbits'.[78]

A century ago, Vita's rejection of conventional gender roles in sex was more controversial than it is today. Like much in her life, she attempted to resolve the issue through writing. She created male protagonists who deliberately deny their sexual instincts and in this way forfeit the aggressor's role, or, like Calladine in *Grey Wethers*, have their sex stripped from them by the author: 'Mr Calladine was a gentleman, – she couldn't call him a man, no, but a gentleman he certainly was, and she was even a little overawed by his gentility.'[79] The private life of Sir Walter Mortibois in *The Easter Party* for example, is dominated by his suppression of his sexual appetite and his determination that his marriage to Rose remains platonic, uncompromised by love or desire. 'A man isn't born with wife and children, and if he acquires them he has only himself to blame,' Arthur Lomax tells readers of *Seducers in Ecuador*. Explaining the particular outlook of Lester Dale in *Grand Canyon*, Vita wrote: 'As for women . . . I took myself off whenever they threatened to interfere with me. If a woman began to attract me, even if the poor soul remained quite unaware of it, it constituted interference. It was all part of my settled policy.'[80] The men in question are guilty of misogyny, but it is they, not the women associated with them, who in Vita's narratives are the ultimate victims.

Although Vita arrived at this philosophy over time – she may have been influenced by Otto Weininger's equation of excessive intellectualism in men with insincerity, which she read in 1918 – there were implications for Harold Nicolson from the outset. In 1910, her homosexuality prevented her from thinking of Harold in 'that way'. Harold's apparent lack of vigorous physical desire for her, alongside her conviction that marriage was unavoidable, were factors that eventually recommended him to her. It soothed the wounds this daughter of Knole sustained as a result of her sex; it suggested a husband who was foremost a 'playmate' and a 'companion'. 'You and I are not grown-up,' she wrote to Harold in 1912. 'Nor ever will be.'[81] This 'childishness', with its implied sexlessness, was the very prescription that would preserve their marriage long term. They were child-like together: they would pursue more 'adult' diversions separately, in time by mutual consent.

The Masque of Shakespeare is one of numerous instances of role play which characterised for Vita the years preceding her marriage. She dressed up; she wrote herself into novels and plays; she sat for painters and photographers. She was not always aware of her motivation. She was experimenting with self-discovery, trying on and taking off a series of masks, adopting personae, as she would for decades to come. Implicit in her fantasy life was a rejection of that powerlessness which she saw as part and parcel of a woman's conventional existence. She craved Knole; she would become a writer. Both were 'masculine' impulses, just as the writers she admired, and those Sackville heroes, were male. In its uncompromisingness, the act of self-creation was equally male.

On 13 February 1910, Vita noted in her diary the first of seven sittings with fashionable Hungarian-born society portraitist, Philip de László. Today that portrait hangs in the Library at Sissinghurst Castle. Vita wears a large hat and furs. In this instance it was her mother's idea. Artist and sitter had met before: at lunch with Seery in the rue Laffitte in May of the previous year, and in October 1908, when de László visited Knole to paint from photographs a portrait of the recently deceased Lord Sackville. Vita recorded then: 'I showed him the show rooms and he made me strike attitudes! saying that he would like to paint me in a Velasquez style!'[82] Victoria had other ideas. The costume she chose for Vita consisted of a high-necked white blouse with a waterfall of ruffles and a black hat decorated with a large brooch. It was presumably not her intention that Vita should suggest a feminine Edwardian version of those portraits of Sackville cavaliers which lined Knole's walls; she was equally unaware of the resemblance to Vita's Chatterton costume. The palette of black, white and red emphasised the connection between de László's image and family portraits by Larkin and Cornelius de Neve. Apparently this visual affinity was lost on Vita too. She wrote simply that 'the picture is finished and, I think, good: anyway it is magnificently painted'.[83] She changed her mind when she inherited the portrait after Victoria's death. In the altered climate of the 1930s, she regarded it as 'too smart' and banished it to one of

Sissinghurst's attics.[84] By then Vita had achieved sufficient sexual autonomy no longer to require this glossy objectification as limpid-eyed ingénue.

De László's Vita is a young woman at a crossroads. Her clothes suggest the riches and excess of upper-class Edwardian England, but look backwards to a history of boisterous swagger that is bloodier, fiercer, less languorous. Her expression combines pride and wistfulness, conviction and uncertainty. The heaviness of her coat and hat, the lack of colour, the absence of ornaments save the red amber necklace, serve to throw into relief her slender femininity. Victoria surely intended Vita's portrait, painted in the year of her first season, as a statement of her marriageability. Unsurprisingly, her daughter appears as if she is play-acting.

Vita described the pneumonia she contracted that summer as 'heaven sent'.[85] With Victoria she retreated to the South of France, to a large white villa, the château Malet, near Monte Carlo, where she remained from November until April the following year. Ever the social opportunist, Victoria took her for tea with Napoleon III's widow, the Empress Eugénie. Among guests at château Malet during Vita's convalescence were Rosamund Grosvenor, Violet Keppel, Orazio Pucci and Harold Nicolson. Each of them was in love with Vita; increasingly each was aware of his or her conflicting claims on her affection. It was not the restful interlude doctors had prescribed, but Vita enjoyed the distance between herself and the debutante world of 'the little dancing things'; enjoyed too the tributes of those varied lovers whose suits she juggled with a degree of adroitness. She was instinctively proprietorial. The knowledge that one day she would lose Knole had long ago stimulated a strong possessive streak in Vita, and she does not appear to have questioned her right to the simultaneous admiration of Rosamund, Violet, Pucci and Harold.

In January, Violet wrote in need of reassurance: 'Do you know that you have ceased to be a reality for me? You are a mirage that recedes to the degree that one approaches it.'[86] Her letters were alternately loving and caustic, as she struggled to provoke a reaction in Vita. Violet was among Vita's last visitors in France and presented her with a ruby she had bought in Ceylon. Pucci took the opportunity to propose again. Again Vita turned him down. By contrast, in January 1911, Harold's departure from château Malet startled Vita on account of his apparent lack of regret. His behaviour provoked her in a way that neither Violet's nor Pucci's had. It was a revelatory response, her feelings strikingly at odds with Harold's. Vita was approaching a point where she could no longer disguise from herself the necessity of reaching a decision about her future; she was approaching a point where that decision would make itself. It frightened her nevertheless. At intervals over the next eighteen months she would appear to long for and to fear marriage to Harold, to take control of the situation and to relinquish it. 'I'm going to let everything be for a bit. Perhaps something will happen!!' she wrote at a moment of particular hesitancy.[87] To Harold himself, she pleaded: 'I am only twenty.'[88] Youth would be her excuse. It was only part of the story.

As in most aspects of Vita's emotional life, nothing was clear cut. With hindsight, knowing what we do of the mature Vita's sexual tastes, it is easy to assume that she must have known her true course. Such an assumption would be mistaken. Vita's self-knowledge was patchy. She understood herself as Cranfield Sackville. Already, convinced of her writer's vocation, she understood herself as Chatterton: 'A poet's work is art, and art is beauty,/ And beauty goodness.'[89] Behind these masks and this oversimplified moral scheme lay uncertainty. Rosamund wrote to her in 1912 of their relationship, 'I like to think that

"Men may come and men may go, but I go on for ever", which is what it amounts to, isn't it?'[90] Short-term intimacy notwithstanding, Rosamund too was mistaken. To Vita, her dilemma was less simple, its solution less restrictive: Rosamund's love was not enough. At moments she appeared overwhelmed by the scale of her confusion. She turned to Victoria for advice: she had no idea what it was she wanted. As throughout her life, Vita's moods oscillated regularly – prone, as she would describe them in an early poem, to 'vary with each variable day'.[91]

It was a situation outside Victoria's ken. Victoria was snobbish, materialistic and egotistical: twenty years earlier, her choice had been confined to selecting between rich, titled, adoring male suitors. By the end of 1911 Vita acknowledged her hope that Harold would propose to her. Nevertheless, the prospect inspired diffidence and scepticism, a surprising response given the extent of her romantic conquests.

To Victoria, Vita confided her desire to exist alone in a tower with her books, safe within an imaginary haven: 'In her immature philosophy, the first tenet was to shut yourself away in a stony fortress and then to consider what system of bluff would best defend you against the importunities of the world,' as she later wrote of one of her fictional heroines.[92] Far from choosing between loving men and loving women – Harold on the one hand, Rosamund and Violet on the other – Vita seemed to suggest rejecting both. In her uncertainty, wrestling with what she came to describe as 'this intricate I',[93] she preferred solitude, reading, writing, a 'system of bluff'. She had not wondered, as she would, whether books encouraged her to 'read life at second hand . . . content and withdrawn for a little hour from the dangers and fears'.[94] Like St Teresa in *The Eagle and the Dove*, she found in books security and fulfilment. 'So completely was I overmastered by this passion, that I thought I could never be happy without a book,' Vita quotes Teresa as saying.[95] In the case of both women, it was a statement of escape. At Sissinghurst in middle age, in her book-lined writing room in its red-brick Tudor tower, Vita would make good this aspiration; she leavened her solitude then with multiple affairs.

There were towers at Knole, too. In Bouchier's Tower, in Victoria's bedroom, Vita struggled to make sense of the tangle she had inadvertently woven round herself. Nervously her fingers moved among her mother's jewels as she talked, trying things on, setting things down. Most of all, Vita wanted to retreat to the safety of this great house, which she regarded both as friend and lover. In 'Night', the poem she dedicated to Harold, she celebrated her love for the country roundabout Knole: 'My Saxon weald! . . . the very heart of me . . ./ Always returns and finds its inward peace,/ Its swing of truth, its measure of restraint,/ Here among meadows, orchards, lanes, and shaws.'[96] Harold's very landlessness added to his attractions. Unlike Lord Granby, Lord Lascelles or Pucci, Harold had no reason for taking Vita from Knole and the Weald of Kent either physically or emotionally. Knole's pull was still stronger than Harold's, for Knole was a known quantity: its secrets were Vita's secrets. Harold was sensible enough not to fight it. Indeed he cultivated an admiration for Knole that he may not consistently have felt. 'My family are in a perfect glow of enthusiasm about Knole,' he told Vita tactfully in 1913.[97]

On the morning of 18 January 1912, Vita received a letter from her mother in London with news of Seery's death. Vita's first reaction was one of panic. That evening, at a ball at Hatfield House in Hertfordshire, she was certain that Harold would propose to her. In six days' time, he was due to depart for Constantinople. Despite her irresolution, Vita knew that she wanted the assurance of Harold's proposal: it was imperative that mourning not prevent her attendance. Victoria understood. Vita wore a new dress and Harold asked her to marry him.

They had spent the evening mostly apart. Alone on the second floor of the great Elizabethan treasure house, sitting on travelling trunks on a landing, Vita and Harold faced one another at midnight. Suddenly Vita's 'only idea was to prevent him from speaking'.[98] She failed. Instead she asked Harold to wait a year, a compromise indicative of her state of mind. Harold did not kiss her and Vita avoided his eye. His uncertainty matched her own. One by one, Harold tore the buttons from his white gloves. In her fictional account of the scene in *Marian Strangways*, which differs from her diary account, Vita wrote: 'He said, "I love you, I love you!" And all she could think was "Now I'm in for it", and all she could say was, "Don't, oh don't"; and she gave him her hand, and he almost crushed it.'[99] The spirit of that description is true to Vita's feelings. She told Harold that she did not love him. In her diary she told herself all sorts of things. She tried to comfort herself: 'at the bottom of my heart I know I'll marry him'. Later her behaviour puzzled her, her refusal to commit herself one way or the other. 'I don't want to lose him, at least not yet. I am selfish and despise myself for it.'[100] In Vita's diary and in the fictionalised version of *Marian Strangways*, this stilted scene reminds us of the relative naivety of both partners. Uncertainty and guilty secrets placed each of them on the edge of an abyss. That knowledge robbed the moment of romance, of laughter or rejoicing.

Harold departed for the Ottoman Empire and, in the spring, Vita went to Italy – 'that beautiful land, the home of all loveliness'[101] – with Rosamund. 'People say, after their fashion, "And did you have a good time in Italy?"' she wrote afterwards to a friend, 'and I say "Oh yes", but they don't know all that it conveys to me: the olives, and the sun, and the view, and the cross of light over Piazza del Duomo, and the little dirty [illegible] streets, and the fun of Perugia and Urbino and paddling in the sea.'[102] Not to mention, presumably, Rosamund. Vita's memories of Italy that year sparkled with the joy that was so notably lacking from her descriptions of Harold's proposal. When Harold first left for Constantinople, Vita had taken to her bed. 'I don't remember ever having been so unhappy. Only today I have begun to understand that I do not love him . . . I was in bed all day and have had time to think.'[103] It was an inauspicious beginning.

Victoria, currently enjoying Vita's confidence, ruled out an engagement proper for eighteen months. She forbad the 'lovers' to correspond on any but the most formal terms. In the event, albeit unwittingly, Victoria's proscriptions proved just what they needed and jolted their thoughts into focus. Implicit in the letters they exchanged in the interval before Harold's return in the autumn was an understanding that, at some point, they must decide whether or not to be married, and an acknow-ledgement that the decision lay chiefly with Vita. Vita advocated delay but took some care not to put off Harold entirely. 'Some day there will be no more away,' she wrote on 23 July. Prophetically she added, 'You mustn't make fusses about the people I speak to more than once because I will always tell you about it, and we can laugh at them together.'[104] As a picture of future dealings, it contained significant inaccuracies.

On her return from Italy, with Harold still abroad, Vita began redecorating her bedroom at Knole. She described its new appearance as 'so decadent' in a letter she wrote him on 29 May; it had previously been 'mock-Italian' in blue and gold and, before that, 'lovely with buff walls, with a frieze of big cornucopias with red and purple fruit (pomegranates and grapes) and the rest of the room red and purple . . . with a purple drugget, and a sofa with red and purple velvet cush-ions'.[105] 'From stern trecento it has become pure *Pelléas et*

Mélissande . . . I ought to have pale mauve volumes of Verlaine by my bed.'[106] It smelled of Madonna lilies and the incense she had brought back with her. The previous month, her bedroom at Hill Street had also been redecorated. 'My room is being papered black and gold with black furniture and gold stuff on the chairs. It will be very early Victorian, and rather macabre, and very eccentric, and people won't like it but I shall. Do you think it sounds hideous?'[107] Vita explained that such rearrangements happened every six weeks. They were for her own benefit and, like her literary self-projections, were a form of role play; their very theatricality was part of their point. She transformed her private spaces into stage sets. Harold responded by describing her as 'the distant princess of my exile'.[108]

In an article written for *Vogue* in 1924, 'Fashions in Decoration', Vita explained that the desire to make one's surroundings pleasing and colourful partly arose in response to the weather: 'if under our grey skies we feel the need of a brighter relief it is for no one to refuse it to us'.[109] In fact, in the years before her marriage, Vita's was an inclination of its time. The First World War had yet to challenge the serene existence of Britain's upper classes. A leisurely cavalcade of stately Saturday-to-Mondays remained the stuff of aristocratic life, balanced by London parties, as Vita remembered, of 'long dinner-tables covered with splendid fruit and orchids and gold plate, and people whose names I can find in the *Daily Mail* sitting all around'.[110] In that sumptuous world of privilege, houses played a key part. They provided the safe and cosseting backdrop for the life that Vita would expose in *The Edwardians* as shallow and amoral. They embodied wealth and prestige and a hostess's particular talents and style. In Vita's case, her relationship with Knole made her feelings about houses particularly acute. Visiting Ragley Hall in Warwickshire as a fifteen-year-old, the child of Knole observed, 'There are some fine things in the house but dreadfully arranged; it seems very comfortable and homely, but far from smart!'[111] Houses reflected their owners. In *The Edwardians*, Vita described in the banqueting hall at Chevron, 'two Bacchanalian little vines, dwarfed but bearing bunches of grapes of natural size, [that] stood in gold wine-coolers on either side of the door', just as, in Victoria's day, they did at Knole, Vita's model for Chevron.[112] The extravagance of gold plate drummed into service as planters symbolised Knole's grandeur, symbolised too Victoria's talent for excess and by extension, something of the joyous exuberance of her whole manner of life. The *grand luxe* of the Edwardian era was hedonistic: it was also a species of escapism. That Vita so often redecorated her rooms at Knole and in London says much about her fragile sense of identity and her desire to escape. Repeatedly in her arrangements she attempted to capture a memory or a mood: those memories were most often of visits to Italy, her favourite escape. Glimpsed against the backdrop of her decoration and redecoration, her uncertainty about her engagement to Harold makes sense. She is experimenting with different 'Vitas'. It is unclear how Harold will be assimilated within these varied rooms, just as it is unclear which Vita will suit him best.

Addressing the 'Italian' Vita of the blue-and-gold bedroom, Harold had sent her his first present soon after his departure. It was a sixteenth-century wooden figure of St Barbara, which he had bought the previous year in Spain. Vita's response was one of delight, though she assumed the figure was 'really only a little boy, unless he is John the Baptist'.[113] She commended its 'gloriously flat nose'. St Barbara would turn out to be an apt presiding deity for Vita; the figure accompanied the couple from home to home for the remainder of their lives. A well-born early Christian martyr distinguished by her beauty, Barbara had preferred to remain isolated and immolated in the tower in which her father confined her rather than marry the husband of his choice and risk compromising her beliefs (in Barbara's case, her Christian faith). A refusal to compromise and, over time, a growing desire for solitude within a tower that was at first metaphorical and at Sissinghurst a reality, became cornerstones of Vita's life.

Victoria's insistence that Harold and Vita's correspondence contain neither endearments nor intimations of affection resulted in a kind of phoney war. Neither knew exactly where they stood. Their letters suggest, not for the first or the last time in Vita's life, that they were frequently at cross purposes. 'I like things stripped down to truth,/ Un-prettied, unroman-ticised,' Vita would write in one of many unpublished poems.[114] It is not an assertion that rings true of her letters to Harold during their protracted engagement. Vita hedged her bets; Harold's letters indicate that he considered their marriage an inevitability. 'I will wait and wait and wait for you – and be patient unendingly – and unendingly will I resolve not to bother you.... or to be morbid,' Harold pleaded.[115] So easily did Vita take control. She gave with one hand and took with the other; in many ways shy and insecure, she was capable only of mastery. 'As we have always known, we are quite ludicrously suitable,' she wrote in July 1912, her words like the balm of summer breezes to Harold.[116] Reassured and confident, he gave himself up to a brief but all-consuming infatuation with Pierre de Lacretelle, a 'slender, dark, vivacious and highly intelligent' Frenchman based in nearby Therapia.[117] Invigorated by Lacretelle, Harold wrote begging her to marry him in the autumn. She read his letter within hours of receiving her first proposal from Lord Lascelles. To both men she responded evasively. Her behaviour remained consistent with that selfish-ness which, seated on a trunk in the moonlight at Hatfield, had encouraged her to accept Harold while doubtful of her own feelings: Vita's need to retain as many options as possible for as long as possible had deep roots. It arose from the certainty of dispossession that in turn arose from her inability to inherit Knole.

At Knole in late September, Harold kissed Vita in the garden. He kissed her again in the Venetian Ambassador's Room, with its enormous bed and faded tapestries of green and gold and pink. Confronted by what she interpreted as physical evidence of Harold's feelings, and undoubtedly swayed by his choice of setting, Vita responded instinctively. 'I love him,' she repeated over and over in her diary; it was a kind of empiricism. But love could not be wholly straightforward. 'I so much want to see R[osamund] again,' she added.[118] In December, with Harold back in Constantinople, Vita again returned to Italy, taking Rosamund with her. There she wrote what became her first published poem. She dedicated 'The Dancing Elf' to Rosamund, 'sweet Spirit of the night . . . for ever young, for ever fair'. It appeared, labelled 'To R.G.', in *The English Review* weeks before Vita and Harold's wedding.

Five months after Harold's autumn visit, Vita doused his confidence with ice. 'You know if I leave my beautiful Knole which I adore, and my B.M. [Victoria] whom I adore, and my Ghirlandaio room which I adore, and my books and my garden and my freedom which I adore – it is all for you, whom I don't care two straws about. Now I dare you to deny a word of all that.'[119] Such epistolary swaggering was partly a tease, Vita in the guise of Sackville cavalier appropriating what she took to be the language of male discourse. Almost two thousand miles away, Harold could not be certain. His uncertainty increased in May. After visiting Spain and Italy, Vita wrote proposing they call off their engagement. Her words, Harold replied, '[knocked] the sun out of my days and [made] even the clock tick differently'.[120] Hastily Vita retracted. While she was abroad,

Rosamund had become engaged to a thirty-eight-year-old naval officer, whom she met at Dartmouth. Suddenly alone, Vita panicked. 'I cannot let him out of my life. I shall marry him,' she wrote on 11 June.[121] She told Harold she wanted him back 'frightfully'. She apologised 'in sack-cloth and ashes'. She insisted he would be better off with a Rosamund: 'very gentle and dependent and clinging'. And having talked herself round and round in circles, she asked winsomely: '*Tu me pardonnes?*'[122] Harold's answer was a foregone conclusion. He understood fully, he explained, that Vita's feelings did not correspond to 'that absolute abandonment of self which I feel'.[123] For both of them, it was evidently enough. In March, walking in Hyde Park, Violet Keppel had again told Vita she loved her. Then in May, while she and Mrs Keppel were staying at Knole, Violet had appeared in Vita's bedroom in the middle of the night, 'grop[ing] my way down miles of passages, past the staterooms, through the long gallery, with its perennial smell of mothball'.[124] She had successfully extracted from Vita a promise that the latter was not in love with Harold.

That summer, Victoria faced the Scotts' lawsuit. Along with Rosamund, Harold was among those who accompanied Vita and her parents to the trial. 'The many who prophesied an engagement to take place between the Hon. Victoria Sackville-West and Mr Harold Nicolson as an outcome of the latter's assiduous attention during the lately settled Sackville–Scott lawsuit have the satisfaction of having prophesied correctly,' asserted one newspaper in the aftermath of Victoria's victory. The engagement was announced on 4 August and widely reported: with two salacious court cases behind them, the Sackvilles were decidedly newsworthy. The *Daily Sketch* linked Vita's engagement to Victoria's huge windfall: 'Eight days' wonder to end in wedding bells!' ran its headline. Victoria's courtroom victory enabled her to take care of the financial side of Vita's marriage to Harold.

It was what Seery himself would have wished: two days before his death, he had agreed to provide Vita with enough money to overcome Harold's 'supreme ineligibility'.

Their wedding was set for two o'clock in the afternoon of Wednesday 1 October in the Chapel at Knole. Before then Lord Lascelles, Rosamund and Violet wrote to congratulate Vita. Lascelles' letter was dignified, gentlemanly, friendly; Rosamund's despondent; Violet's withering in its scornfulness. Distraught, lonely and pathetic, Rosamund cried 'all night and every night', her tears fully audible to Vita in the next-door bedroom; 'cold as ice', Vita offered neither sympathy nor comfort.[125] Nor did she share the news with Violet. In her autobiography written forty years on, Violet wrote: 'Six months later she married without letting me know.' Her mistake had been to trust in Vita's confession, wrested from her on that moonlight night in May. She had failed to take into account Vita's invariable need in her relationships to appear to play the part required of her, to say what her listener wanted to hear regardless of the state of her emotions or the likely complications. 'As long as she did not tell me herself, I attached small importance to [rumours of her engagement]. I was stunned by what I took to be a piece of perfidy I did not deserve.'[126] Violet's revenge, when she exacted it, would be devastating in its impact on Vita and Harold's marriage. Predictably she did not attend the wedding. Instead Mrs Keppel gave Vita an amethyst and diamond ring in Violet's name. Other presents came from Rosamund, who steeled herself to act as Vita's principal brides-maid, Lord Lascelles and Orazio Pucci in Florence. Victoria began compiling a scrapbook. She included photographs of the newly engaged couple at Knole. In one image, they sit in deck-chairs outside the Colonnade Room. Harold gazes at his hands and Vita looks wistful. In the gulf between them stands an empty chair. It may be a coincidence.

Throughout the eight-week-long official engagement, news-papers continued to mine the slender pickings offered them. 'Kidlet is a poetess,' noted one; another described Vita as 'a young girl of versatile tastes [who] lately has had some verses published in the "English Review"'.[127] Overwhelmingly reporters fell back on the romance of the union. 'A Love Match' was one headline; more explosively another proclaimed, 'She Sacrifices a Fortune to Marry the Man She Loves'. Their reports scarcely varied. Had they uncovered the identity of the 'R.G.' of 'The Dancing Elf' – 'Thou crosst the room on tiptoe to my bed,/ One finger on thy lip' – they would have found a less common-place story. Instead descriptions of the bride's 'matchless English home' eventually gave way to well-intentioned gloating over the sumptuous wedding presents. These included historic jewels, a small bronze sculpture from Rodin, whom Vita had met in Paris earlier in the year and again within weeks of the wedding, a signed photograph of Ellen Terry and copies of the seventeenth-century candle sconces in the Colonnade Room which, at Victoria's suggestion, were the Knole estate staff's offering. At Chaumet in Paris, Victoria bought her daughter 'a string of emeralds and diamonds'. She added it to the necklace costing £2,000 that she had already bought on impulse from a jeweller in Bond Street. (She also took Harold shopping for an engage-ment ring for Vita: together, she reported in her diary, they looked at 'over 100 emerald and d[iamond] rings' before choosing 'a lovely one' for £185.[128]) In the first flush of her hard-won riches, Victoria was extravagant in her generosity.

Victoria commissioned Vita's wedding dress from William Wallace Terry, of Court dressmakers Reville & Rossiter. It was a striking and, at fifty guineas, costly ensemble. Described in the illustrated press as 'The Golden Wedding Dress', it featured a skirt of gold silk brocade of what was fancifully termed 'Persian' inspiration; *The Lady's Pictorial* likened the colour to 'the tassel of Indian corn, the silk shimmering bright like the silk on the cocoon'.[129] With it, Vita wore the Irish lace veil which had formed part of Victoria's Court dress for the coronation of Nicholas II in 1896. 'In lace and old gold,' one reporter commented predictably, Vita presented a 'spectacle for a painter'. Surviving photographs show an unsmiling Vita overwhelmed by clouds of veil. Her lengthy train was managed by Rosamund Grosvenor and Vita's other grown-up bridesmaid, Harold's sister Gwen; at Victoria's request the former was removed from the photograph of Vita afterwards released to the press.[130] Vita also had three junior attendants, including Viscount Moore, son of the Earl and Countess of Drogheda; all were dressed in costumes copied from Hoppner's late-eighteenth-century portrait of the children of the 3rd Duke of Dorset, which hung outside Knole's Music Room.

On a day of bright autumn sunshine, the effect of this consciously picturesque ensemble in the tiny fifteenth-century chapel was ethereal and lovely, 'a radiant vision of white and gold', hothouse lilies in pots along the altar, dust motes mobile against the Gothic tapestries, the congregation of only twenty-six shoe-horned around the choir under the gaze of the Bishop of Rochester. Outside, the bulk of the guests, including four duchesses, awaited the reception. Vita had decorated the Chapel herself. She noted that it was 'decked out like a theatre by me'.[131] Her wedding day provided a fitting climax to her youthful role play. Afterwards, inevitably, all reports granted the starring role to Vita, whom they invariably labelled 'Kidlet'. Like the Sackvilles, the newspapermen discounted Harold and his family. It was as it would remain. On the previous evening, Victoria had taken to her bed. She remained there throughout the service and the celebrations. It was probably a relief. In her absence, most prominent among the other women in the Chapel was Olive Rubens, who sang an anthem from Gounod's

Redemption: 'From Thy love as a Father,/ O Lord, teach us to gather/ That life will conquer Death.' She wore chestnut-red velvet trimmed with skunk, an appropriately extravagant costume for Lionel's mistress.

For months Vita had hardly written at all. Her energies were consumed in carefully constructing a house of cards in her letters to Harold, and by emotions which were volatile and unsettled. On and off during the course of 1912, she had worked at her latest historical drama, *Jarl Haddan*, a four-act play set incongruously in ninth-century Norway. Then in August, happy at last alone at Knole with Harold and an emollient Victoria, she began to write poetry again. The title of one of those poems is 1913 – 'MCMXIII'. It captures her mood of the moment; it suggests what Harold represented to her then: '"Oh, why so grave?" he cried to me,/ "Laugh, stern lips, laugh at last!/ Let wisdom come when wisdom may./ The sand is running fast."'

The night before her wedding, Vita wrote a poem in a different vein. It gives us as clear an indication of her feelings as the moment the following day when she set off for her honeymoon, wrapped in the leopard furs that were Victoria's parting gift and accompanied by her dog but having temporarily forgotten her husband. Vita called her poem 'To Knole' and subsequently included it in her first published collection. Written after an hour of crying, from which only Rosamund could shake her, it was a love letter to the house which had dominated her life. For all its self-indulgence 'To Knole' is among the most powerful of Vita's verse, evocative and percep- tive too. Vita admits her anthropomorphism of Knole, which had begun unconsciously in her childhood, and the extent to which she had permitted the house to usurp or replace more conventional relationships. Forcibly she demonstrates that she had never felt, and never would feel, that realisation which

Virginia Woolf attributes to her fictional Vita in *Orlando*: 'Chairs and tables, however richly gilt and carved, sofas, resting on lions' paws with swans' necks curving under them, beds even of the softest swansdown are not by themselves enough.'[132] At Knole they were enough for Vita in a way that newer chattels, newer homes, new lives and lovers, would not be. Unburdening herself of all that Knole had meant to her, she braced herself for departure: 'Friend of years,/ I rose a stranger to thee on the morrow.' That sense of enforced estrangement from Knole would permeate the remainder of Vita's life. She herself was mostly powerless to conquer the feeling; nothing Harold said or did significantly lessened it. Vita might claim, 'Our true and deep farewell/ Was spoken in the long preceding night.' As both she and Harold would discover, her farewell to Knole took longer than a single night.

If Vita's departure from Knole was a bittersweet affair, that mood was quickly dispelled in the short term. Vita said that she had cried away all her regrets on the eve of her wedding and left none for the day itself. This did not prevent her from ending the day's diary entry with the decidedly ambivalent: 'So it has come to this conclusion!'[133] She and Harold had driven to Somerset. Dorothy Heneage, described by Violet Keppel as resembling 'a furry little animal out of one of La Fontaine's fables',[134] had loaned the newlyweds Coker Court, near Yeovil. It was a house like Knole of fifteenth-century origins with Tudor additions. In the three days Vita and Harold spent there before their departure for Florence, 'rapidly, overwhelmingly, everything changed'.

In loosely fictionalised form, and in the third person, Vita described her wedding night in *Marian Strangways*. 'She knew nothing save that she lay crushed in his arms in the fierce night . . . She knew that at last an irresistible cosmic force of nature, no longer to be denied, had flung their two lives together and shattered them into one . . . She now knew the truth of all voids in her life, and they were plenteously filled as with the rush of many springing rivers.'[135] It was Vita's version of Victoria's diary accounts of 'Baby's' antics twenty years ago. That the child of such highly sexed parents should have reacted so wholeheartedly to her sexual initiation is unsurprising.

For four-and-a-half years Harold would fill all voids for Vita: she accepted what she regarded as irresistible and acquiesced in that cosmic force of nature which was in fact Harold's love for her and her own craving for contact and companionship. In her autobiography, Vita described Harold in those first years of their marriage as 'like a sunny harbour'. For the most part, 'tamed', her own response was equally sunny.[136] Only later did she repent of her description of her fictionalised Harold as 'her man and her master': 'in her awakening womanhood she desired nothing but that she might yield to him the most abased subjection'.[137] Neither abasement nor subjection came naturally to Vita. In her novel, she adopted the idiom of contemporary women's fiction: in practice it conjured up an unlikely guise for a young woman accustomed to independence and, latterly, the corrosive flattery of multiple admirers. Vita's rebellion was slow at first. In time, like Calladine married to Clare Warrener in Vita's novel *Grey Wethers*, Harold would find that 'he had married an elf and not a woman', a spirit impossible to confine.[138] But that was all to come.

Vita and Harold arrived in Constantinople after a month. Their journey had taken them first to Florence and afterwards via Cairo, where their host was an uncongenial Lord Kitchener. They travelled with Vita's maid Emily, who four years previously had made her Chatterton costume, and Harold's valet, Wilfred Booth, called Wuffy. Vita wrote frequent letters to

Rosamund, caught sunstroke, lost her voice; she suspected Emily and Wuffy of an unseemly intimacy. Egyptian sightseeing fell flat (in one of her novels Vita described the Sphinx as 'a most overrated object'[139]). The length of their journey bored Harold as well as Vita. Rosamund failed to respond to Vita's letters and Vita wrote a crabby, one-sided poem called 'Disillusion' about replies that never come: 'I waited, and the counted day/ Fruitlessly came and went.' Vita struggled with misgivings concerning both the diplomatic life and Constantinople itself ('beastly' was her pre-judgement of the latter): only the former proved well founded. For all her reservations, the lure of the exotic East inspired her. Her Uncle Bertie lived in Constantinople, employed by the Ottoman Public Debt Office. Anticipation went some way to salving her homesickness for Knole and her irritation at Rosamund's unexpected coolness. 'It is home which drags the heart; it is the spirit which is beckoned by the unknown,' she wrote. 'The heart wants to stay in the familiar safety; the spirit, pricking, wants to explore.'[140] Her heart for the moment content with Harold, Vita followed the pricking of her spirit.

From her first 'rose-shaded' daybreak, Vita adored Constantinople. 'She has an early morning of her own,/ A blending of the mist and sea and sun/ Into an indistinguishable one,' she wrote delightedly.[141] She and Harold found a house to rent in Cospoli and servants to staff it (including 'a beautiful Montenegrin' as a footman). It provided separate sitting rooms, a drawing room and, in keeping with upper-class practice of the time, separate but adjacent bedrooms. To Rosamund, Vita described the neglected building with its long views as 'the most attractive house you have ever seen. It is a wooden Turkish house, with a little garden and a pergola of grapes and a pomegranate tree covered with scarlet fruit, and such a view over the Golden Horn and the sea and Santa Sophia! And on the side of a hill, a perfect suntrap!'[142] She was apparently unaware that her description of the garden at 22 Dhji-han-Ghir corresponded closely to one of her 'Italian' decorative schemes for her room at Knole. 'Never in our existence/ Had life seemed brighter before!' Vita exclaimed with unaffected joy in the poem about the house she dedicated to Harold.[143] Again and again in the poems she wrote then she returned to the theme: 'Love hung about the rooms like smoke.'[144]

From Knole arrived furniture, paintings, and objects to fill the unfamiliar rooms; there were wedding presents too and in the bazaars Vita and Harold bought Persian pottery, coloured glass and white jade, revelling in their home-making as later they would revel in their joint creation of a garden. Vita's income of £2,400 a year from her marriage settlement enabled them to live up to 'an alarming reputation for originality and "art treasures"', which they found had preceded them.[145] Among Victoria's shipment from England were watercolour views of Vita's room at Knole. Like time spent in the company of her Uncle Bertie, these souvenirs of the recent past were occasionally counterproductive. Vita's mood oscillated; she missed Rosamund, Knole; the life that had suited her so well. In a poem of that period, 'Convalescence', she wrote: 'The thought of England, fresh beneath the rain,/ Will rise unbidden as a gentle pain.' Those were the days when Vita ignored Harold on his return from his work, when 'you used to go on writing with your pretty little head over your table refusing to turn round', as Harold reminded her later; when she withdrew from sunny domesticity into her other fiercer world of writing, building her tower around her even at this early stage.[146] Those were the days when she set aside her rapturous feelings about Constantinople, Dhji-han-Ghir, even Harold: it was in such a mood that she wrote 'Resolution', about her writer's vocation and her struggle to bring to fruition her 'struggling art': 'I see the work of others, and my heart/ Sinks as my own achievement I compare.' For the most part, and for the only time in her married life, Vita accepted diplomatic life with a semblance of good grace, successfully presenting herself, as she remembered with scorn, as 'the correct and adoring young wife of the brilliant young diplomat'.[147]

Her performance of those empty social duties which meant so little to her thrilled her admiring husband. In her own eyes – and to her subsequent surprise – Vita was 'gentle, self-sacrificing, chaste';[148] Harold called her 'little spirit of gentleness and love'.[149] On the flyleaf of her diary for 1914 she even inscribed the name 'Vita Nicolson'. Given her attachment to her maiden name and her disdain for Harold's family, it was a symbolic gesture. Harold's liveliness and good humour overwhelmed her taciturnity. His example taught Vita how to set aside her priggishness and enjoy simply being young. She described the first years of her marriage as unsurpassed 'for sheer joy of companionship'.[150]

Vita's poem about the house in Constantinople in which she would live for less than a year focuses on its abandoned garden: 'For none had cared for its beauty/ Till we came, the strangers.' She details the fruit trees growing there – pomegranate, quince and fig; the vines; roses, including the scrambling yellow Chinese *Rosa banksiae*; and the springtime carpet of daffodils and cyclamen naturalised in the grass, like the verdure in a medieval tapestry. Unlike the interiors they created in a spirit of companionable novelty, Vita and Harold did little gardening in Constantinople. Instead they stored up the memory of sun-drenched colour and successful natural pairings: the roses that twined through lilac bushes, the thick mat of cyclamen beneath the fig tree. Fecund, sunny and relaxed, their Turkish garden captured their own fleeting moods. For both of them, gardens would continue to possess this personal note.

Vita discovered that she was pregnant the week before Christmas. Harold's pleasure outstripped her own and she asserted her considerable force of will to compel him to silence on the subject outside the family. 'I belong to the old-fashioned school that thinks a baby should not be mentioned until it is in its cradle,' she once wrote.[151] Together they made plans for their return to England the following summer. The first of Vita's children, a son, was born at Knole on 6 August 1914. After fierce arguments with Victoria, he was christened 'Lionel Benedict'. (Vita and Harold had wanted simply Benedict: Lionel was a sot to Victoria. They referred to him as 'Detto', an abbreviation of Benedetto, and afterwards as Ben.) Vita was twenty-two and had been married less than a year. Two days previously, Britain had declared war on Germany. Unlike the majority of Vita's erstwhile suitors, Harold was exempted from fighting, transferred from the Diplomatic Service to the new War Department of the Foreign Office on 1 October. His battles would take a different form.

PART III

Invitation to Cast Out Care

'Her face was not beautiful – a red, sulky mouth, rather wide; a short straight nose; dark eyes, and a pale complexion – but with her smooth, rounded grace . . . and her composure, she would surely draw the eyes of men away from the untidy prettiness of English women.'

V. Sackville-West, *The Death of Noble Godavary*, 1932

ONLY A CATACLYSM could have made Vita forfeit her reputation. When it came, that cataclysm appeared in the familiar guise of Violet Keppel.

For Vita, though she seldom referred to it, the Scott lawsuit cast a long shadow. Its public parade of family secrets offended not only Edwardian double standards but her own innate Sackville reserve. Under the caption 'Society folk at the big will case', one newspaper printed a photograph of a woman arriving at court fashionably dressed and carrying a large cushion. The following week, on 16 July 1913, a painting of Vita in her Portia costume by Frank M. Bennett appeared on the cover of *The Bystander*. Neither Vita nor her parents enjoyed the experience of providing entertainment for their peers or the newspaper-reading public at large, much less being recipients of their sympathy or objects of speculation: afterwards Vita satirised 'women all jewelled and scented/ Smiling false smiles with the little sharp word in between'.[1] She described gossip as like thorns, 'as tangled as a blackberry bush, and just about as spiteful'.[2] 'How passionately one minds the meanness of people, how it hurts to find there is no generosity, only suspicion and mistrust,' she wrote later.[3]

It was no ordinary provocation that brought about the change of heart that, in the summer of 1919, led Vita to write to Harold: 'if you knew how it would amuse me to scandalise the whole of London! It's so secure, so fatuous, so conventional, so hypocritical, . . . so cynical, so humbugging, so mean, so ungenerous, so self-defensive, . . . so well-dressed, so up-to-date, so hierarchical, so virtuously vicious, so viciously virtuous. I'd like to tweak away the chair just as it's going to sit down.'[4] She wrote a poem on the same theme and called it 'Scorn'. Her rebellion was prompted by 'madness' – a combination of over-wrought emotions and sexual exhilaration. The cause of both was her childhood friend, Violet Keppel.

Since their bedside meeting in 1905, Vita had failed to keep faith with Violet. There had been visits to Knole, meetings in London, in Paris and in Florence, play-acting, presents from Violet to Vita. Once, memorably, Vita stayed with Violet at Duntreath Castle near Loch Lomond – home of the Edmonstones, Mrs Keppel's family. They sat up all night, intoxicated by the thrill of their closeness, as owls hooted from the pepperpot towers and velvet blackness obliterated the nearby hills of Dumfoyne and Dumgoyne. At dawn, peacocks shrieked; from across the castle courtyard a bell tolled. Violet knew then that she was in love with Vita. This impressionable and lonely girl fell victim to her own highly coloured dreams of romance. Her head was turned by Duntreath, which she regarded as worthy of the novels of Walter Scott: its ancient walls exuded historical fantasy; its distinctive scents of gunpowder, cedarwood and tuberoses made her dizzy. For her part, Vita was aware of a sensation in the darkness that troubled her. Violet worried that Vita would suspect her secret: in two years' time, in October 1910, she told her herself. Written between the lines of that letter was a further confession: that Violet had seen through Vita, understood her posturing, her search for an identity, the emptiness behind the bravado. Vita accepted her tribute as flattery without recognising hidden meanings. So it would remain.

Violet was infatuated, emotionally precocious, attuned to Vita's secrets and her fears; Vita was heroic, though less so than she pretended, unaware at first that Violet had glimpsed the Sackville detachment, 'part morgue, part melancholy', and determined always to exert control. 'I love you because you have never yielded in anything; I love you because you never capitulate. I love you for your wonderful intelligence, for your literary aspirations, for your unconscious coquetry. I love you because you have the air of doubting nothing! . . . I love you, Vita, because I've seen your soul,' Violet wrote.[5] It was as Vita would have wished to see herself.

In the short term, neither Violet's candour nor her percipience was rewarded. Vita was preoccupied with Rosamund Grosvenor, six years Violet's senior. They saw one another daily and slept in adjoining rooms. In July 1914, a heavily pregnant Vita wrote to Harold outlining the dispersal of her possessions (mostly jewels, including two tiaras) in the event of her death in childbirth. There were bequests for Harold's sister Gwen, Dorothy Heneage, Olive Rubens, Lady Connie, her maid Emily and a clutch of Vita's aunts. The largest gift was for Rosamund: a diamond watch, the diamond hatpin that had been Lord Lascelles' wedding present, and two of Vita's rings. As an afterthought, following instructions about her manuscripts and her dog, Vita asked Harold to give Violet 'my small sapphire and diamond ring'.[6] She omitted the Doge's ring entirely.

On 13 January 1913, Vita had written to Irene Lawley in Florence, 'Think of me (and pray for me) on Thursday night. In an attitude of apparent somnolence and unspeakable well-being, but a state of mind of agitation not easily expressed, I shall be lying on a divan surrounded by lovely Houris who all make up to me while I vacillate lazily among their charms.'[7] The occasion was a performance in Knole's Great Hall of 'a Persian play', to which Victoria had invited 'thousands of people'. 'Here I am living in a litter of addressed envelopes and endless telegrams,' Vita reported with some exasperation.

Her own role was that of the Caliph, with blackened face. At the end of the play she died 'in a realistic wriggle, which usually has something of genuine agony in it, as I have inadvertently fallen on my pipe or a pair of (very sharp, – I answer for that) cymbals'. Lightly she referred to her 'incense-laden Harem', which included Rosamund as a dancer called Zuleika, and Violet as a slave girl. Also taking part was the sister of a friend of Harold's, Muriel Clark-Kerr: she too was in love with Vita. Vita came closer to the truth than she realised in reporting her lazy vacillation between her lovely houris: all three women in their different ways clamoured for her affection.

From the first awakening of sexual maturity, Vita associated love and sex with choice. 'Round her revolved several enamoured young men,' remembered Violet of Vita during the years of Harold's courtship.[8] In *Family History*, Evelyn Jarrold asks, 'Doesn't everyone like to be loved? . . . One never gets enough love.'[9] Vita had seen it in her parents' lives. She was seven years old when Victoria first discovered a love letter from

Lionel to Joan Camden; the same year, Victoria met Seery. A sense of sexual opportunity – and, in time, opportunism – would characterise Vita's life. At intervals that metaphor of the 'incense-laden Harem' proved prophetic but also unhelpful. From Lionel and Victoria, Vita had inherited a vigorous appetite for sex: the harem, like the bordello, is a region of consumption free of emotional entanglements. It offers no training in fidelity; it insists on neither compassion nor consideration.

Unlike Rosamund, Violet had not followed Vita to Constantinople. She had remained with her formidable mother, entered into and broken off a 'suitable' engagement to Gerald Wellesley, future Duke of Wellington, and accompanied Mrs Keppel in the lavish entertaining, and equally lavish travel, which were the latter's preferred means of denying the passing of her Edwardian glory days. There would be other sham flirtations for Violet, including with the homosexual writer Osbert Sitwell. Misleadingly she described her motives in these pretences as 'compassion, curiosity, boredom, physical attraction'.[10] Behind the empty manoeuvres of Violet's public romantic life lay fear of Mrs Keppel.

In the summer of 1914, Vita and Harold returned to Britain for Vita's confinement. They swiftly rowed with Victoria. Taking baby Ben and his nursemaid with them, they moved to a rented house in London, at 182 Ebury Street; among their neighbours was the Irish novelist and poet George Moore. The following spring they bought a house in the country. Long Barn was an amalgam of fourteenth-, fifteenth- and sixteenth-century elements, reputedly the birthplace of William Caxton and lately restored by the wife of a local vicar: it cost Vita £3,000. Thereafter they spent winters in London, summer in the country. Meanwhile, Vita wrote. Long Barn was two miles from Knole, in the village of Sevenoaks Weald, which contained a number of estate cottages. Vita walked regularly between the two houses; among the recommendations of 'untidy and tinkly' Long Barn was Vita's sense of it as home from home.

Victoria suffered a nervous breakdown in September 1914. The suicide of her brother Henry in Paris, Lionel's call-up with the West Kent Yeomanry following the outbreak of war, and Harold's choice of the latter's mistress Olive Rubens as godmother to baby Benedict all contributed to her unhappiness. In her diary, Victoria admitted to 'feeling depressed enough to take my own life';[11] there were no further diary entries for ten months. Following her recovery in July 1915, her relations with Vita regained a semblance of normality. That equilibrium proved precarious, and Vita's eventual fictional portrait of her mother revealed the depth of her ambivalence: 'This old woman, beautiful and wicked and good, with a power of charm beyond reason, holds more danger and wickedness, beauty and goodness and wisdom in her than anyone I have ever met.'[12] In November, Vita gave birth to a stillborn son. 'It clouds everything,' she wrote, 'and I can't be happy.'[13] The agony of her grief made her dread being alone and she virtually stopped writing. In time, angrily, she would place that sorrow within a larger context of women's lives: it rooted her, she saw, in 'that anonymous crowd . . . of the women with the wasted lives, . . . women who had lost children or lovers, . . . women who had borne the long, mute burden of uncertainty'.[14]

In February 1916, Victoria loaned Vita the purchase price of the Ebury Street house. Vita's diary records the progress of her home-making with Harold: a 'jolly dessert service' bought on 6 January; a full-scale rearrangement of the entire house undertaken by the two of them on 7 February: 'Get dirty, tired, and rather cross; but quite successful on the whole.'[15] The birth of their second son, Nigel, on 19 January 1917, went some way to easing memories of Vita's stillborn child.

For her birthday in 1916, Harold presented Vita with a field at Long Barn; in the summer, at a cost of £700, Victoria purchased neighbouring Brook Farm. It increased the space around the house and guaranteed the Nicolsons a degree of privacy. It also went some way towards satisfying Vita's need, which she considered a birthright, for land ownership. With little prior knowledge, Vita began gardening. Later she commented that she 'took to gardening quite late in life: I must have been at least twenty-two'.[16] Previously she had grown handfuls of vegetables for her grandfather at Knole. She ordered pink and white thorn bushes for hedging, emulating a mix she had admired in Constantinople, and her first climbing roses, 'American Pillar' and 'La Guirlande'; both reminded her of the flower-laden tresses of *Rosa banksiae* in the garden at Dhji-han-Ghir.[17] Armed with catalogues from nurserymen and seed merchants, her first essays in gardening were predictable, straightforward: 'We planted rose and daffodil,/ . . . We planted yellow hollyhocks/ And humble sweetly-smelling stocks/ . . . We planted wallflowers in a row.'[18] She employed two gardeners; Victoria paid for one of them and also introduced Vita to Gertrude Jekyll. Miss Jekyll's example spurred Vita on to further rose plantings: to climbers 'American Pillar' and 'La Guirlande' were added 'Albéric Barbier', 'W. A. Richardson' and 'Gloire de Dijon', a handsome livery of creamy yellow and buff for Long Barn's crooked walls.[19] The old noisette climber 'Madame Alfred Carrière' would eventually entirely embower Vita's bedroom windows. In addition, Victoria gave Vita and Harold a Rolls-Royce.

Harold referred to Long Barn as 'our little mud pie'; he and Vita called it 'the cottage'. On Vita's instructions, Bentleys builders, of Tubs Hill, Sevenoaks, moved a sixteenth-century barn from Brook Farm and reassembled it at right angles to Long Barn to provide a fifty-foot-long drawing room, with bedrooms above. The Nicolsons called it the Big Room. Their extended cottage included seven bedrooms and four bathrooms, with separate sitting rooms for Vita and Harold, as well as Harold's small study. Vita's sitting room also served as her writing room. Placed centrally was the Italian desk that had been a twenty-first birthday present from Victoria. Windows on two sides of the room provided light and a view. Three indoor servants were employed. Virginia Woolf, visiting in 1927, noted an impression she characterised as predictably opulent: 'butler, silver, dogs, biscuits, wine, hot water, log fires, Italian cabinets, Persian rugs, books . . . all the inherited tradition of furnishing, so that [the] house is gracious, glowing, stately, but without novelty or adventure'.[20] Woolf overlooked the idiosyncratic element. Throughout Long Barn, floors sloped, oak beams extended at irregular angles, walls perceptibly tilted. It was recognisably the same house Vita described in her novel, *Heritage*, which she completed in first draft in November 1917: 'The eaves were wide, and in them the martins nested year after year; the steep-tiled roofs, red-brown with age, and gold-spattered stonecrops, rose sharply up to the chimneystacks . . . the furniture was propped up by blocks of wood on the south side, and I learnt not to drop round objects on to my floor, knowing that if I did so they would speedily roll out of reach.'[21] Vita explained current trends in interiors to readers of *Vogue*: 'Everything that is fusty or fussy we eliminate; we like hard surfaces and absence of ornament; we prefer hard stones to sculptured wood, marble to plush, Empire to Rococo, severity to comfort.'[22] In her own rooms she ignored changing fashions: she recreated as if unconsciously her memories of Knole. Typically it was a vision of Knole that excluded 'the rooms that our parents thought beautiful . . . those crowded rooms full of footstools and knick-knacks'.

In October 1917, Vita's first collection of poetry was published. *Poems of West and East* contains twenty-one poems, eight of which had previously been privately printed at Vita's expense in 1915. For the only time in her career, Vita appeared on the title page as 'V. Sackville-West (The Hon. Mrs. Harold Nicolson)'. The *Morning Post* and the *Observer* printed favourable reviews. After her passionate apprenticeship, Vita was excited at first publication. She wrote a poem, 'On seeing my first proof sheets'.

Despite intermittent tensions in her relationship with Victoria, and the trauma of her stillborn child, the first four-and-a-half years of Vita's marriage represented a period of contentment. For Vita, raised on stories of cavalier romance and the novelettish affair of Lord Sackville and Pepita, it came as a surprise. 'How undull love can be, even though it is married and has a little boy, two little boys, of its own,' she assured Harold.[23] Replete with happiness, she anticipated it lasting for ever: 'Let us to the road/ Which hides enchantment round each hidden bend,/ Our course uncompassed and our whim its end,' she wrote in *Poems of West and East.*[24] To her diary, on 31 May 1915, she exclaimed: 'I thank God that I have known absolute happiness.' Afterwards she concluded, 'I should think it was hardly possible for two people to be more completely and unquestioningly happy' than she and Harold during this prolonged honeymoon period.[25] She was sincere. She told Harold that he was 'the only thing that counts in the world. You are the vessel which contains the wine of life.'[26]

The war alone clouded the horizon. Harold's working hours lengthened; in the autumn of 1915 Lionel departed for Gallipoli, Palestine and France. Deprived of footmen, gardeners and carpenters, Knole was partly shut up; the newspapers carried their roll call of lost friends ('it required superhuman courage to open a newspaper,' Violet remembered[27]). Vita wrote a war poem, 'A Fallen Youth', which was printed in the *Observer*. In keeping with other poetry of the first years of the war, it emphasised heroism and the cheerfulness of noble sacrifice:

'laughing went he, till on that last day/ The hands stretched out to life were clasped by death'.[28] In fact, the war scarcely impacted on Vita. 'Noise of the Flanders guns quite distinct,' she reported on 1 July 1916 from Long Barn; on the day John Lane published *Poems of West and East*, Vita's diary noted without comment: 'Ebury Street nearly bombed, two bombs fifty yards off. Raid expected in the morning but they are turned back.'[29] Early in 1916, Vita had spent mornings working in an 'office for [the] wounded and missing'. She did not stick at it; instead she preferred to write.

In London she took part in a number of wartime charitable entertainments of the *Masque of Shakespeare* variety. In June 1916, she appeared alongside Olive Rubens in one of the *Omar Khayyam* tableaux organised by Viscountess Massereene at a private house in Arlington Street. Sumptuously dressed in a turban and patterned silks, she carried a shield and an unconvincing bow and looked studiedly unmoved. The following year she appeared in a charity matinée at the Lyric Theatre in aid of the Concerts at the Front Fund. The programme included a ballet inspired by Swinburne, the decadent Victorian poet whose biography Harold would write in 1926. Vita appeared statuesque and anything but decadent. In fact Swinburne's luscious romanticism suited her mood: 'All I can give you I give./ Heart of my heart, were it more,/ More would be laid at your feet –'[30] Two summers later, Violet quoted Swinburne to Vita in an attempt to bind the two women more closely together.

At home Vita recorded Ben's progress: height, vocabulary, his fondness for stories and picture books over toys. She decided that he was 'independent, undemonstrative, obstinate'.[31] Surprisingly, given her preoccupation with heredity, she made no comment on the origin of those traits. On the last day of 1916, she reported with wry humour: 'Ben says practically

In October 1908, the Hungarian-born society portraitist Philip de László told the sixteen-year-old Vita of his desire to paint her 'in a Velázquez style'. Two years later he did so. His image of extravagant languorousness initially delighted Vita. Later she dismissed it as 'too smart' and refused to hang it.

Vita with her parents
as a child at Knole.
She wrote that what
her difficult mother
Victoria (*above*) meant
to her was 'a mixture
of tragedy and – no,
not comedy, but sheer
fun'. Her bond with her
father Lionel (*left*) was
largely unspoken.

Knole, the love of Vita's life. She claimed it possessed 'all the quality of peace and permanence; of mellow age; of stateliness and tradition. It is gentle and venerable.' It was also imbued with intense romance for Vita, who was a lonely and imaginative child.

In a hidden drawer in an ebony cabinet in the King's Room (*below*), six-year-old Vita left a note: 'Dada, Mama and Vita looked at this secret drawer on 29th April 1898.'

In 1913, Lionel and Vita were accompanied to court during the Scott case by Harold Nicolson and Rosamund Grosvenor (*left*). Both were in love with Vita.

'Never before or since, have I felt so much like royalty,' wrote Vita following Lionel and Victoria's success in the Sackville succession case of February 1910 (*below*).

For a fundraising Shakespearean masque in the summer of 1910, Vita, as Portia, borrowed the velvet robes worn by Ellen Terry in a production of *The Merchant of Venice* in 1875. Clare Atwood's portrait depicts her as a romantic Italian youth.

Vita and her father's mistress Olive Rubens in one of the *Omar Khayyam* tableaux staged by Viscountess Massereene in aid of war charities in June 1916.

'When you see a person, a body, marvellous casket and mask of secrets, what do you think?' Vita asked in her first novel, *Heritage*.

A young Harold Nicolson –
in his own words 'supremely
ineligible', in Vita's not 'the
lover-type of man', 'a playmate,
clever and gay'.

Among Harold's contenders
for Vita's hand was Henry
Lascelles (centre), heir to the
Earl of Harewood and an
income of '£31,000 a year
from his land alone, plus
plenty of cash'.

Violet Keppel in 1919, in a portrait by John Lavery. Vita described her as 'this brilliant, this extraordinary, this almost unearthly creature'. Their affair changed the course of Vita's life.

anything he wants to now, though not very distinctly; he also recites "Little Bo-peep", "Pat a cake" etc., not at all distinctly and leaving out all the smaller words.'[32] For all her fondness, Vita brought a degree of detachment to motherhood. She described children as 'quarrelsome, competitive, envious, cruel, herd-primitive and generally uncivilised';[33] 'domesticity destroyed you in the end', she wrote in an unpublished poem about a friend whose enthusiasm for motherhood she considered excessive.[34] Following an operation on 12 April 1916, the twenty-month-old Ben was sent to Eastbourne to recuperate. He and Vita were not reunited until 17 July. In the intervening fourteen weeks, Vita visited her son three times. It was Harold who spoiled the boys. On 5 February 1917, he bought Ben 'a gramophone which he adores'.[35] In a discussion about women's careers in the context of marriage, Vita subsequently denied 'most emphatically' that the loss of a woman's career could be balanced by 'the joys of motherhood'.

'Love was all that ever grew,' Vita had written in her short poem, 'The Garden', in the summer of 1915. In her own way she embraced domesticity; she gardened and she wrote. Together she and Harold decided that, in decorating, 'flowers, chintz and Jacobean furniture were the happiest companions'.[36] Harold's interest was greater than Vita's. Vita paid more attention to what lay outside the house, setting the pattern for the future. For Christmas 1916, Vita and Harold gave one another a fishpond; Vita reported Ben's delight. She began, but did not always finish, a number of plays, including *On the Road, an episode*, set two days after the destruction of Pompeii and, on and off throughout 1916 and 1917, worked at her monumental history of the Italian States from 1300 to 1500. It was, she remembered, 'full of murderous and probably inaccurate detail'. It was an undertaking born of love rather than inspiration or particular insight: an escapist venture. Of the relationship between Umbria and Rome, for example, Vita noted: 'The nearness of Rome affects the politics of the province much as her nearness as the centre of Christianity would seem to cast the rays of religion into the narrow streets of Umbrian towns.'[37] Later she attributed her enjoyment of the abandoned project 'to the amount of research it involved, for I had not yet shed the priggishness and pedantry of my schooldays'.[38] Having set aside her thousand-page-long uncompleted manuscript, Vita transferred her priggish, pedantic instinct to her commonplace book: she collected extracts from the works of authors including Chaucer, Dr Johnson, Balzac and Keats. Also included was Lionel Johnson, the Victorian poet who died of a stroke at the age of thirty-five: Johnson's battle against his homosexuality had turned him into an alcoholic.

Vita embarked on a new novel. 'I was then twenty-five and old enough to know better, but prose was still only a contemptible stopgap for the days on which I couldn't write poetry.'[39] After a lengthy rewrite on the advice of George Moore, that novel, *Heritage*, became Vita's first published work of fiction. It is notable among her novels for its use of a female rather than a male alter ego as the principal means of resolving aspects of her own character, in this case her perceived divide between Pepita's unruly legacy and that of the Sackvilles: 'the separate, antagonistic strains in her blood, the southern and the northern legacy'.[40] By the time the novel was published, in May 1919, not only Vita but Harold and indeed Violet thought they knew the answer to this divide.

Motherhood, the war and Harold's work did not interfere unduly with the couple's social life, which retained the exclusive quality of pre-war socialising. In July 1916, Vita won £12 playing poker in Lord Ribblesdale's rooms at The Ritz; lunch guests at Ebury Street in February 1917 included Winston Churchill, a long-term favourite acquaintance, and Osbert

Sitwell. Contemptuously Vita described herself and Harold at that point as 'a nice young couple to ask out to dinner'; Harold was reliably good-humoured and an accomplished raconteur.[41] Contentment made Vita relaxed and unaffected, and tempered her priggishness: afterwards she reflected that this was 'the only period of my life that I achieved anything like popularity'.[42] She labelled it a halcyon interlude. In January 1918, she wrote a poem describing a typical Long Barn day. 'One Day' is a study in contentment: a morning walk across the Weald, followed by gardening; a meal of eggs, bread, meat, an apple; poetry to read. 'Joy have I had of life this vigorous day/ . . . Freedom I drank for my delirious wine,/ . . . What more could heart desire?'[43] Looking back with new eyes in the aftermath of her affair with Violet, she seemed to see herself as a person sleepwalking, half awake, half fulfilled; she regretted the predictably 'Edwardian' aspect of their social lives. For one of Vita's hungry and assertive appetites, such somnambulism could not satisfy indefinitely.

'At her own sarcastic request', Violet stood as godmother to Ben. Among fellow godparents was Vita's own godfather Kenneth Campbell, who had first tried to rape her and then suggested marriage. Little wonder the experience of Ben's christening, orchestrated by Victoria, was one of such acrimony that Harold told Vita they had no choice but to take measures against her mother's 'destructive personality', 'her vain empty insincere nature'.[44] Victoria's was not the sort of character measures could be taken against and neither Harold nor Vita successfully resolved her role in their lives; eventually Harold dismissed her as 'not mad . . . just evil'.[45]

Violet did not interest herself unduly in Ben's infancy. She described Long Barn as 'a Tudor cottage in Kent, very pretty in its way, but too self-consciously picturesque for my taste. Life in a Tudor cottage is like living *under* the furniture instead of above it.'[46] That tone of acerbic superiority was her defence against Vita's domestic bliss; behind it lay bitterness and furious jealousy. As the war continued, Violet accompanied Vita to an occasional exhibition or to a matinée but did not renew her assertions of love. In late September 1917, she made a week-long visit to Long Barn before Harold and Vita's return to London for the autumn; she visited again the following April. Her contempt for Vita's married life grew with the degree of her exposure. She lampooned the narrowness of their interests, the predictability of their conversation: 'At dinner, you will have the eternal furniture-decoration conversation, interlarded with scraps of Roman reminiscences, and conjugal badinage,' she snapped in a letter to Vita.[47]

Vita had not forsworn what Violet described as 'the rackety element' of herself. Happiness simply imposed a check on her 'duality', subduing a part of her nature. In time she came to see her life with Harold – 'two little boys; a cottage; money; flowers; a farm; three cows'[48] – as 'only one side of the medal'.[49]

Intimations of the Vita who had played at being Sir Redvers Buller, Cranfield Sackville, the Man in the Iron Mask and Chatterton, persisted, albeit confined to her imagination and, very occasionally, her writing. Her only visible outlet was the play-acting of the charitable tableaux, and that was of an exceedingly tame variety. Nevertheless, in a poem called 'Nomads', included in *Poems of West and East*, Vita had written: 'with narrow bonds and limits never could we be content,/ For we have abolished boundaries, straitened borders have we rent,/ A house no more confines us than the roving nomad's tent.' This was the voice of that Vita with whom Violet had fallen in love when she was ten years old, but who, in Vita's explanation, 'had always repulsed her (when things seemed to be going too far), out of a sort of fear':[50] here was the refusal to yield, the failure to capitulate, 'the air of doubting nothing'. Harold might dismiss this tendency, part gypsy and part aggressor, as 'your bloody Sackville looniness':[51] he must have known that Vita would discard no part of herself that was recognisably 'Sackville'. Even as she cherished the rich tranquillity of her emotional life with Harold, she was exploring in her writing something quite different. In *Heritage*, Vita described the relationship of Rawdon Westmacott and Ruth Pennistan as 'not merely an idle, rural or cousinly flirtation. The man's blood was crazy for her.'[52]

Tartly, Violet wrote to Vita within weeks of publication of *Poems of West and East*, 'I simply can't get on without a periodical glimpse of radiant domesticity.' With greater sincerity she added: 'We are absolutely essential to one another, at least in *my* eyes!'[53] It was a statement of that obsessive single-mindedness which had characterised Violet's thinking about Vita for the better part of a decade. As it happened, and quite by chance, Violet's timing was fateful.

Vita's diary notes the Nicolsons' departure for Knebworth in Hertfordshire, home of Lord Lytton, parliamentary secretary to the Admiralty, on 28 October 1917. It records too a post-dinner session of planchette, the wooden board on castors used for automatic writing and in séances. Vita made no note of the 'messages' received during that planchette session: they would, anyway, have paled beside Harold's revelations in the aftermath of the weekend's party.

On 6 November, Harold told Vita that, during their stay at Knebworth, he had contracted a venereal infection. That admission inevitably involved further disclosures. It was, potentially, a watershed moment. Harold was upset and afraid. He struggled to convince Vita of the unimportance to their marriage of his homosexuality. The next day Vita set off for Oxford and the home of a married friend, Irene Pirie. In the space of twenty-four hours, three letters from Harold pursued her: 'Let's face it together and bravely,' he begged her.[54] Vita was the braver of the two. She responded to Harold's pleading with a reassuring telegram. Relieved, Harold acclaimed her as his 'saint', his 'true angel'.[55] Vita confined her real response to her novel. In *Heritage*, Mrs Pennistan offers: 'It's hard, isn't it, to see into people's hearts, even when you live in the same house with them?'[56] For the moment that thought applied in equal measure to Vita and to Harold.

Vita herself had not been infected by the disease, which Harold had caught from a fellow guest or a Knebworth servant. Nor, in the short term, did the disease or Harold's revelations significantly estrange husband and wife. Within less than a fortnight Vita's diary includes a vignette of companionable domesticity incompatible with marital breakdown: 'Read "Heritage" right through with Hadji [Harold]; so happy.'[57] Harold's doctor ordered a six-month hiatus in their sex lives, to which Vita appears to have agreed without remonstrating; Harold was the more regretful of the two. Yet the cessation of that six-month term would not be marked by a return to conjugal felicity. Instead, two days before the date earmarked by Harold's doctor for the all-clear, Vita embarked on the most passionate sexual encounter of her life.

It would last, on and off, for three years. At the height of his disillusionment and unhappiness, Harold described it as a 'scarlet adventure'; at other moments, he attributed it more flaccidly to liver. Vita was at first clear about her motives, if disingenuous. 'You are wrong. I don't want that sort of adventure, having *you*,' she wrote; 'It is real Wanderlust I have – the longing for new places, for movement, for places where no one will want me to order lunch, or pay housebooks.'[58] Four years into her marriage, the girl who had struggled so hard to demonstrate her boyish qualities had rebelled against the minutiae of a woman's life. It was not, of course, the whole story.

Vita's affair with Violet Keppel has been recounted before.

As Vita's mother noted, it contains all the elements of a sensational novel. It contains, as well, the temporary realisation of aspects of Vita's character and her particular brand of boldly coloured storytelling, which had been present since childhood: cross-dressing, a swaggering male alter ego, foreign travel and exotic escapism, emotional heroics (not to mention histrionics), jewels pawned, reputations tarnished – and all for love.

The truth, though every bit as melodramatic, is also darker. Prevented at this stage from satisfying powerful homosexual urges within any visible relationship – a conflict she later resolved by conducting discreet lesbian affairs behind the shield of her marriage to Harold – Vita indulged in emotional role play. It resembled a form of short-term schizophrenia and was sometimes conscious, at others not. She ceased to be the 'gentle' Vita of the early-married days in Constantinople and became instead someone more brutal, whom she and Violet christened 'Mitya' or 'Julian'. Her sense of herself as possessing a 'dual' nature – the English half continent, married and decorous; the Spanish half passionate, homosexual and reckless – enabled her to justify indulging contraband desires while exonerating herself from blame. 'It is so neat, the division in me, more neat than you'll ever know,' she insisted.[59] She would find that she was wrong and that it was impossible to live a life of divided selves with any degree of happiness or equanimity. Her internal struggle, when it came, ought not to be dismissed as self-indulgence: it imposed a severe strain on Vita as well as those around her. Vita emerged bruised from her affair with Violet: a part of her retreated further within herself. 'To me, who knows her pretty well, she is a "beautiful mask",' Victoria wrote in 1922. 'She has put on a thicker mask since the distressing V[iolet] affair.'[60]

For three years Harold kept faith with his errant wife. He did so by blaming everything on Violet Keppel, 'that little tortuous, erotic, irresponsible, irremediable and unlimited person'.

Memorably he likened her to a 'fierce orchid, glimmering and stinking in the recesses of life and throwing cadaverous sweetness on the morning breeze', and he wished her dead.[61] Violet's culpability has since become an established element of the story. This is partly because the story has been told most often from Vita's point of view; it is partly because Vita chose ultimately to return to the trappings of her 'English' self — Harold, her children, material possessions, upper-class society. Her own rejection of Violet in favour of other, more pressing, claims seems to imply a value judgement. It could just as easily have been a failure of nerve. Vita and Violet were both dominated by their mothers: both Victoria Sackville and Alice Keppel played their part in the unravelling of this fantastical story. The irony is that Violet celebrated her mother's relationship with Edward VII as the acme of romance: 'I adore the unparalleled romance of her life . . . I wonder if I shall ever squeeze as much romance into my life as she has had in hers; anyhow I mean to have a jolly good try!'[62] She ignored Mrs Keppel's hard-headedness and her significant material gains as a result of her glittering liaison. For Violet it was Vita who became her 'King', but in Violet's case, unlike that of her mother, the relationship was based solely on love. Vita by contrast came close to castigating her own mother as selfish and acquisitive (despite the income of the Sackville estates falling far short of Mrs Keppel's ill-gotten £20,000 a year): she failed to appreciate the depth of Victoria's love for Lionel. Condemning her mother's emotional caprice, she herself behaved in a manner that was equally capricious. With Violet she lived out a fantasy life whose roots stretched deep into her childhood. Then she discarded Violet. She had damned the whole of London society, played out her rebellion and survived to the extent of later being invited by the BBC to give a radio broadcast with Harold on the ingredients of a successful marriage. Like Miles Vane-Merrick in *Family History*, she chose to return to '[her] own life, parallel with the life of love, separate, independent'. Her separation was from Violet. 'The life of love' remained central to Vita: never again did it overwhelm her to the same extent.

Having made her choice, Vita believed she could retrospectively contain the affair. It became a youthful transgression and youth could not be protracted indefinitely. She saw this even as, with Violet's help, she worked on *Challenge*, the novel that would become their own fictionalisation of their affair, begun while that affair was full of promise. 'Were the years of youth the intuitive years of perception? Were the most radiant moments the moments in which one stepped farthest from the ordered acceptance of the world? Moments of danger, moments of inspiration, moments of self-sacrifice, moments of perceiving beauty, moments of love, all the drunken moments!'[63] Afterwards she referred to Violet darkly as an 'unexploded bomb' whose destructive power terrified her. Vita would continue to pursue 'moments of perceiving beauty' and 'moments of love': never again would she come so close to danger or self-sacrifice.

Without her mother's level-headedness, Violet became a tragic victim, destined never to achieve a fulfilling relationship. She had invested everything and lost. Truthfully she had told Vita, 'I can never be happy without you.'[64] Half a century later, she played out her final days as a parody of her mother. Queenly in jewels and Balenciaga, at the end of her life she ran her Florentine household like a miniature court with herself as exacting sovereign. 'Across my life only one word will be written: "Waste" – Waste of love, waste of talent, waste of enterprise.'[65] Vita, on the other hand, emerged from 'Julian's' escapades to reclaim the spoils of war that had come to her on her marriage. She had tasted a new and different kind of love: with a string of partners that love remained a part of her life. It existed alongside Harold's tolerant devotion, conventional family relationships with Ben and Nigel, houses in London and the country, a Rolls-Royce, a chauffeur, a cook, gardeners, jewels and Jacobean furniture from the attics at Knole.

Although their worst 'misdemeanours' were committed abroad, both women came close to social ostracism. Yet while Violet retained an aura of transgression, Vita rehabilitated herself, knowledge of her peccadilloes afterwards confined to a small, mostly discreet inside circle. It was as Violet foresaw in the summer of 1918: 'what is so killing is that you will probably . . . become a celebrated poet/novelist and I shall [achieve] nothing but disreputability!'[66] Violet described them both as 'absolutely indifferent to the world's opinions': Vita's response has not survived. Vita did indeed become a respected, prize-winning and commercially successful literary figure and, in time, a horticultural authority; later still, she was appointed Companion of Honour by George VI. Few members of the reading public recognised her portrait in *Little Victims,* a novel written in 1933 by a former lover of Harold's, Richard Rumbold: 'She speaks like a man in a deep bass voice . . . She is horribly ugly . . . and gives lurid, detailed accounts of her affairs. She started at sixteen and has kept going pretty well ever since.'[67] Although she repented the unhappiness she had caused Harold, Vita did not regret the adventure of her wanderlust. It was her riposte to the hypocrisy of Edwardian double standards. In her short biography of the playwright Aphra Behn, written in 1927, Vita offered a triumphalist endorsement of her subject's mores: 'in her private life she followed the dictates of inclination rather than of conventional morality'.[68] It was, ever after, as Vita would live her own life. Such was the prize she had coveted and won.

The story of Vita Sackville-West's affair with Violet Keppel is one in which everyone is a victim: Harold, Vita, the Nicolson children, Violet and, as we will see, Violet's husband Denys

Trefusis. But there are degrees of victimhood. While Harold and Vita recovered from the cataclysm, Violet, Ben, Nigel and Denys Trefusis all remained scarred by a sense of abandonment, misuse or both that none fully understood. All, in their different ways, were hostages to fortune.

It was Violet who fired the opening salvo. On 25 January 1918 she wrote a letter to Vita that was more than usually calculating. Formerly she had appealed to the would-be indomitable strain in Vita – the Vita who liked to think she never yielded, never capitulated. Now, in the aftermath of *Poems of West and East*, Violet appealed to Vita's sense of herself as an artist. She described an artist as 'the supreme luxury that the gods toss to the world' and, pointedly, as one who 'must necessarily belong to both sexes, his judgement is bisexual, . . . he must be able to put himself with impunity in the place of either sex'. She couched her appeal in the form of a parable: 'Once upon a time, there lived an artist and a woman, and the artist and the woman were one.' Inevitably, the artist-woman – Vita – surrendered a side of herself to become a wife and mother: 'The artist was temporarily forgotten: wrapped in comfortable torpor, the artist slept, and the woman gloried in her womanhood and in the happiness she could give . . .'[69] No matter that it was not true. Vita had not forgotten the artist nor was her artistry asleep; she had written poetry and a novel; she had received happiness as well as giving it. Violet laid her cards upon the table. Since 1913, she had watched and waited, excluded from Vita's life, angry and hurt. Now she intended her letter as a wake-up call to Vita. In combination with Harold's revelations and the temporary halt to Vita's sex life, it served its purpose.

On 18 April 1918, Violet had already been at Long Barn for five days. She was bored, playing her waiting game. Vita, too, anxious to be writing, chafed at the restraints of her company, a sign of the gulf between them. The previous month, at

Thornton Manor on the Wirral, Vita had stayed with another of Victoria's wealthy admirers, Sunlight Soap magnate Lord Leverhulme. 'Go over the soap works at Port Sunlight, great fun,' she recorded in her diary.[70] A seed was sown. It would grow into the novel that, in 1921, became *The Dragon in Shallow Waters*, a violent, darkly melodramatic story that begins with a description of a soap factory and culminates in a gruesome death by immolation in a vat of boiling soap; throughout its inception Harold and Vita referred to the novel simply as 'Soap'. Vita was writing poetry too. Her second collection of verse, *Orchard and Vineyard*, would also be published in 1921 (by then it included a number of poems about Violet and about Vita's fleeting moods at moments in their affair). In this orderly routine there was no room for Violet's wiles.

And then there was the garden. Vita had previously worked outdoors in the long skirts and smock-like blouses that were accepted gardening apparel for women of her class. A photograph of 1917 shows her stripping lavender on the terrace at Long Barn with Harold and Ben. She is dressed in white, she wears a straw hat with a petersham ribbon and a white shirt with billowing sleeves. At the time of Violet's visit she had just taken delivery of 'clothes like the women-on-the-land were wearing'.[71] Twenty years after Victoria vetoed trousers as part of Vita's khaki suit for Boer War games with the Battiscombes, Vita had at last obtained practical, mannish clothes for her work outside, inspired by the costumes of the Women's Land Army, formed the previous year. With Violet's disconcerting presence preventing her from writing, Vita swapped her clothes, 'and in the unaccustomed freedom of breeches and gaiters I went into wild spirits; I ran, I shouted, I jumped, I climbed, I vaulted over gates, I felt like a schoolboy let out on a holiday; and Violet followed me across woods and fields'.[72]

In Vita's account, the effect is instantaneous. Like a magic cloak in a fairy tale, the new clothes transformed her into the person she was always destined to become. Unexpectedly, unaffectedly, Vita's Land Girl guise liberated something deep within her. It should not surprise us that this defining moment in her life occurred when she put on a 'costume' and embraced in real life a further instance of masquerade. Throughout her formative years she had found fulfilment and self-expression imaginatively, through just these means. On an April day in the last year of the war, 'in the rich warm-blooded rush/ Of growth, and mating beasts, and rising sap',[73] the catalyst for Vita's sexual epiphany was a uniform of breeches and leather gaiters. She would wear it for the rest of her life.

As she ran across the Weald, bounding from garden to field, Vita described Violet 'never taking her eyes off me, and in the midst of my exuberance I knew that all the old under-current had come back stronger than ever, and that my old domination over her had never been diminished'.[74] Shedding the clothes of Harold's 'gentle' wife, Vita was reborn in a new identity. Violet chased behind her, and to the exhilaration of freedom was added a frisson of sexual conquest. That night, Vita and Violet remained talking after the servants had gone to bed. They talked until two o'clock in the morning. Then they kissed. They then went to bed. For Violet it was the natural corollary to that night of owl song at Duntreath Castle. In this instance only Vita had spoken. 'Violet had struck the secret of my duality,' Vita wrote; she rationalised it as an alternate preponderance of 'the feminine and the masculine elements' in herself.[75] In unravelling her duality aloud, Vita found that she had talked herself into becoming Violet's lover. It was a moment of overwhelming excitement – as Virginia Woolf imagined Orlando–Vita's dawning love for Sasha– Violet in *Orlando*, 'the thickness of his blood melted; the ice turned to wine in his veins; he heard the waters flowing and the birds singing; spring broke over the hard wintry landscape'.[76] In her diary, Vita wrote simply but feelingly: 'How eventful a day!'[77] Ten days later she and Violet ran away to Cornwall.

There was no resumption of sexual relations for Harold on 20 April, nor would there be now. Now Vita had a different lover. After two nights in a 'very primitive' fisherman's cottage, on 30 April she and Violet moved into a house belonging to novelist Hugh Walpole: it was Harold who, in an emollient gesture, had arranged for their use of it. Perched on a cliff above Polperro, it was remote, romantic, full of books and the tireless cry of gulls; noisily the sea crashed beneath its walls. They read, they walked the cliff path to Fowey and back, Violet filled the rooms with flowers. Vita was dominant and masterful as she had always longed to be. Violet compared her to 'a dazzling Gypsy . . . a Gypsy potentate, a sovereign': it was the illusion both craved.[78] Together they began writing the novel that became *Challenge*. It tells the story of a wealthy Englishman called Julian (Vita), living on the Greek coast and torn between love for his mercurial cousin Eve (Violet) and the offshore island of Aphros (Harold). Julian inspires an uprising on Aphros: he himself becomes the island's president. *Challenge*'s working titles included 'Rebellion', 'Rebels' and 'Vanity'; Harold called it 'Smuts'.

Harold wrote to Vita in Cornwall of the loneliness of London Sundays and his hatred of being a bachelor; he suggested drowning himself in the Thames.[79] Vita wrote to Victoria, her letters light, voluble, misleading. 'We live on boiled eggs . . . but we are very happy, and the sophisticated Violet is getting quite refreshingly simple. Today we went to Hugh Walpole's cottage, he is not there, but he said we were to use his sitting room and borrow his books.'[80] Meanwhile 'sometimes', wrote the sophisticated Violet, 'we loved each other so much we became inarticulate, content only to probe each other's eyes for the secret that was secret no longer'.[81] Their relationship was rapturous in its physicality. In a poem written in French,

Vita celebrated Violet's twin roles as companion and lover: 'In the heavy fragrance of intoxicating night/ I search on your lip for a madder caress/ I tear secrets from your yielding flesh/ Giving thanks to the fate which made you my mistress.'[82]

A precedent had been set for a pattern that would repeat itself over the next three years: Vita and Violet escaping to an inaccessible lovers' hideaway with Harold's assistance, Harold at the same time critical but endlessly forgiving; Vita physically, emotionally and mentally absent from Harold, reassuring him of her love as she indulged another love, and exacting from him his own similar reassurances; Violet, like a novelist or playwright, creating and enforcing roles for herself and Vita, slaking Vita's thirst for drama, manipulating her (even if subconsciously) in order to perpetuate their escape into romance.

If visual sources can be trusted, Vita's sexual awakening in the spring of 1918 constituted a form of self-discovery. On 12 June, Vita gave the first of six sittings to Dumbarton-born painter William Strang. Strang's portrait, for which Victoria refused to pay, claiming she had commissioned a much smaller image, is justly celebrated. *Lady with a Red Hat* contrasts with de László's portrait of eight years earlier. Both are theatrical images, which owe something of their drama to bold contrasts of light and shade; in both Vita adopts a role. But while the sfumato extravagance of de László's painting lacks conviction, Strang's picture of modernist hauteur depicts a sitter who has taken possession of her own iconography. Loosely, Vita holds a book. Its red cover matches the red hat which was Victoria's inspiration for the commission, after Vita wore it with a matching red dress. The hooded Sackville eyes, dark and glassy pinpoints, ignore the viewer. Gone is the beseeching of the earlier painting. Strang's Vita is aloof in her confidence, comfortable in the self she presents unblinkingly. It was an image Vita herself liked enough to send as postcards after its purchase from the Grosvenor Gallery by a museum in Glasgow. Harold shared her enthusiasm, describing it as 'so absolutely my little Mar [the Sackville word for 'little' or child, which became Harold's name for Vita]: she's all there – her little straight body, her Boyhood of Raleigh manner, and above all, those sweet gentle eyes which are so familiar to me'.[83] On first glance it is an image of swagger, the 'splendid . . . dauntless' Vita of Violet's puppetry. Throughout Vita's affair with Violet, Harold would continue to insist on her gentleness. It was his way of reminding her of the other side of her duality, her place in *his* life.

Like Raleigh himself, Vita had other journeys to make before her ship returned to shore. In July, she and Violet travelled to Cornwall again. Vita read *Sex and Character* by the Austrian philosopher Otto Weininger. Weininger's book, published in English in 1906, makes a clear division between male and female, characterising women as passive and illogical in contrast to active, productive, creative, logical, rational men. It was a thesis guaranteed simultaneously to infuriate Vita and to confirm her in her attachment to her theory of her own duality and, in particular, to the masculine side of her nature; passages in her copy are heavily annotated. She underlined Weininger's statement: 'All that [men] care about is that their work should glitter and sparkle like a well cut stone.'[84] Vita would never *only* care about her work, and she wrote in the margin beside Weininger's claim that 'when [women] marry they give up their own name and assume that of their husband without any sense of loss', 'I disagree'.[85]

Already, according to Vita, something had changed by that second trip to Polperro. She herself now suspected their affair was 'an adventure, an escapade' and unlikely to last (an opinion she would change).[86] Outside forces clamoured. Letters followed Violet to Cornwall from Denys Trefusis in France. Vita believed Violet hardly knew him; at first she was not jealous. But Violet was playing a double game.

Throughout the summer, Violet had written to Major Denys Robert Trefusis of the Royal Horse Guards, veteran of Ypres and the Somme. Mrs Keppel lay behind it; the Trefusises were well connected, if lacking in cash. Violet's mother had made it clear that Violet must marry: she was not a woman to brook resistance. Inspired by her mother's example, Violet envisaged an arrangement in which she and Vita, both provided with understanding husbands, would continue their affair from the safety of their positions as respectably married women. She even told Vita so. Via letter she flirted with her battle-scarred but honourable victim. To make good her fantasy she reinvented Denys in her imagination as a male Vita. She described him as 'an Elizabethan. He had a pale arrogant face . . . It was impossible to look better bred, more audacious. Slim and elegant, he could not help dramatizing his appearance . . . he made the most ordinary clothes appear picturesque.'[87] Aligning Denys with the new Vita of Strang's portrait, Violet claimed that he was 'intrepid, rebellious . . . adventurous, exciting'. She told Vita they would be friends. The reality, as Violet knew by the time she wrote that description, was somewhat different.

Vita and Violet discovered swiftly that accommodating their relationship within the routines of ordinary life would be more difficult than they had foreseen. Vita had a whole life separate from Violet, the world of Long Barn and Ebury Street, the nursery, the Foreign Office, her poetry; Violet remained firmly beneath her mother's watchful gaze. Just as Harold and her sons made demands on Vita, ditto Mrs Keppel and Violet. Denied time together, both became irritable and unhappy. Vita resented the well-upholstered social round she and Harold pursued in leisurely Edwardian fashion. They argued: Vita disparaged Harold to Victoria, accusing him of physical coldness; in public Harold was uncharacteristically snappish. Violet's letters oscillated between hope and despair, building fantastic castles in the air, or operatic in their tearfulness. She was less resilient than Vita, whose tone of 'profound indifference and nonchalance' chilled her.[88] She found that the more heated the argument, the greater Vita's apparent withdrawal: like Victoria berating Lionel, Violet mishandled Vita's horror of confrontation. A new note entered their correspondence: Violet's repeated protest against the dishonesty of dissimulation. Vita's reply no longer exists. In her adolescent writings, the possibilities of dissimulation had thrilled and sustained her.

Diplomatic, assuasive and mindful of his own part in triggering this crisis in his marriage, Harold offered Vita a compromise: 'a little cottage in Cornwall or elsewhere' for hidden liaisons. He assured Vita that it would 'be hers absolutely, and she can go there when she likes and be quite alone and have whom she wants. Then the Padlock [promise] is that Hadji never goes there and can't . . . even know when she is there or who she has got with her.'[89] Vita ignored his offer. She knew that it represented the very outcome Violet dreaded most – a severance inadequately leavened by snatched illicit nights together – and perhaps, at that point, one she also disdained. Over and again Violet insisted to Vita the inevitability of their union, willing her to give in. She could not conceive of sharing Vita, limiting their love to hidden assignations. She wrote that she wanted, 'not only the physical you, but your fellowship, your sympathy, the innumerable points of view we share. I can't exist without you, you are my affinity . . . my twin spirit. I can't help it! no more can you! . . . *Nous nous completons* [We complete each other].'[90] She railed at the furtiveness of their liaison. Their dashes to Cornwall had already given rise to ill-natured gossip. Such speculation increased their troubles. They must quash it – or run away from it. They responded with recklessness.

*

On 11 October, after a matinée performance with Violet of Rimsky-Korsakov's *Scheherazade* – appropriately a story of the seductive and redemptive power of storytelling – Vita returned to Ebury Street and changed into men's clothes. She took a taxi to Hyde Park Corner. There she met Violet and, like lovers (which of course they were), the two women strolled the streets of Mayfair in the autumn darkness. Vita smoked a cigarette, her confidence in her disguise gaining by the minute. She had become Violet's 'Julian'. At Charing Cross, they took a train to Orpington in Kent and stayed the night in a boarding house as husband and wife. In the interests of verisimilitude, Vita deepened her voice to talk to their landlady. 'Oh, the wet dark evening at Hyde Park Corner!' she exclaimed in her diary. 'Then down here . . . This is the *best* adventure.'[91]

'Nothing is an adventure until it becomes an adventure in the mind,' Vita wrote later.[92] So it was with this dazzling, dangerous other life as Julian. It was the culmination of all Vita's years of play-acting; she was back in the attics of Knole performing *Chatterton* in Emily's improvised breeches and shirt, only now the drama ended happily. Vita felt heroic, liberated: what struck her most forcibly was how natural it felt. The next morning, 'Julian' and his 'wife' went to Knole, where Vita changed into conventional clothes in the stables. 'There are other ways [than love] of resolving the confusion of life into some kind of synthesis,' Vita wrote in *Gottfried Künstler* in 1932. 'Gottfried resolved it simply by becoming another person.'[93] In Vita's case that other person was a facet of herself that she had always recognised.

Orpington proved to be a dress rehearsal for events ahead. That month, Violet faced the challenge of Denys's leave. He had told her he loved her in a letter written on 1 September; he was waiting for an answer. Before his return to his regiment on 26 October, he proposed to Violet in person. He knew by then something of the complexity, if not the full unorthodoxy, of the situation in which, unwittingly, he found himself. Like Vita before her, Violet responded evasively. As often as she could she struggled to escape Denys for Vita; Mrs Keppel easily outwitted her. Denys left London for Paris. Before the Armistice was declared, he 'was cheered and acclaimed . . . by two regiments for his magnificent daring and skill'; the following summer he received the Military Cross.[94] Ironically it was Denys's presence in the French capital which persuaded Mrs Keppel to agree to the next step of what Violet termed 'the Great Adventure'. On 26 November, Vita and Violet set off for France.

By then, an affair which had begun so happily was sullied by acrimony, mistrust and bad behaviour. Both Harold and Violet had attempted to enlist the sympathies and support of Vita's mother. Harold had told his mother-in-law that Violet intended to destroy his marriage; Violet told Victoria that Harold stifled Vita's creativity and that Vita cared more for her literary ambitions than for Harold. Victoria listened to Harold and discussed with Vita his performance as lover. Later she confided to her diary the extent of her bafflement: 'If [Violet] was a man, I could understand, but for a woman, such a love beats me.'[95] In a spirit of calculated mischief she enlightened Violet about a husband's sexual needs. Persuaded of Victoria's support, Harold continued to treat Vita with tolerance and agreed to help obtain for Violet as well as Vita passports and the necessary papers for travel. Victoria's disclosures reduced Violet to something like hysteria; her previous knowledge of sex had evidently been scant. Now there must be a new condition to her marriage to the war hero Trefusis, an understanding that their relationship could not be consummated. Vita for her part had stopped wearing her wedding ring. On the eve of their departure for the Continent the women argued, as they would continue to.

In a poem called 'Dissonance', Vita attributed the strains in the relationship to other people: 'Clamour has riven us, clamour and din.' She did not shy from the extent of those strains: 'the closer we clasp one another, the further apart [we] remain'.[96] But four months passed between Vita's departure with Violet and her return, four months in which they were frequently very close indeed.

Their time was spent in Paris, in Avignon, St Raphael and Monte Carlo. From the outset their progress was fanciful, imaginative. They were Vita and Violet, Julian and Eve, Mitya and Lushka, reality and unreality in constant elision. They dressed up, they wore disguises, they effected a lovers' patois based on Romany – a sot to the dream they shared of Vita as a gypsy king. Around themselves they wove fictions: in addition to *Challenge*, Vita's poems about Violet, 'Eve' and 'Eve in Tears'. Eve is 'fickle as the flame/ And sweet as music irresponsible'; she possesses superhuman power: 'You wept, and all the music of the air/ . . . Was stilled.'[97] It was a delicious, shared delusion, which Vita would ultimately reject. It was also a delusion facilitated by less romantic realities. Vita and Violet's bohemian idyll was made possible by Vita's income from the Sackville estates and Violet's allowance, paid for by investments made for Mrs Keppel on the instructions of Edward VII. They made good their shortfall by pawning jewels, taking £130 from Harold and a loan from Gerald Wellesley, heir to a dukedom. At Monte Carlo, they were forced to change their hotel in a hurry after a fracas when Julian danced in public with Eve; Harold described such antics as 'vulgar and dangerous' in a letter unusual for its sternness. Correctly Harold accused Vita of muddle-headedness: Vita appeared confused even about her feelings. Her diary recorded the unequivocal 'hate life . . . wish I was dead'; in the confession that became *Portrait of a Marriage*, she painted an alternative picture: perfect happiness, perfect love, perfect Violet. Whatever the truth, Vita and Violet's French leave suggests elements of calculated perform-ance and a degree of uncontrived narcissism on Vita's part: this was the moment when, on a day-to-day basis, she lived out her theories of her duality. Months later, on her final trip to France with Violet, she wrote to Harold: 'You are good and sweet and lovable, and you are the person I loved in the best and simplest way; but there is lots that is neither good or simple in me, and it is that part which is so tempted.'[98] So long as she was playing a part, Vita was happy. She was tempted by a vision of herself as much as by Violet.

They remained away for Christmas, gambling in the Casino at Monte Carlo, while Harold spent the day alone at Knole with the Sackvilles, Ben, Nigel and eccentric composer Gerald Berners, a curious Father Christmas substitute for two small boys.[99] In January, Vita failed to join Harold in Paris for the beginning of his work at the Peace Conference. At home, baby Nigel was described as having forgotten who his mother was. Harold had read Marie Stopes's *Married Love*, in an attempt to convince Vita of the value he attached to her happiness; when she ignored his letters, he embarked on an affair of his own with Victor Cunard and ensured that Vita knew about it. By the time of her return in March, Vita had exhausted the patience of both her parents. Although she admitted that she was to blame, she was appalled by the coldness of her mother's fury. She described Victoria as looking at her 'with eyes of stone'; Harold encouraged her to 'recover your confidence in yourself, and your serenity in life'.[100] In the short term, there was to be no escape from the consequences of her actions. In the summer of 1919, Vita sacked Ben and Nigel's nanny after the latter walked about Sevenoaks Weald dressed in a suit belonging to Harold.[101] The inference was clear, and Vita was not prepared to be made ridiculous.

On 21 March 1919, Violet told Vita that she and Denys Trefusis were no longer 'even on friendly terms'.[102] It was an unfortunate development in the light of the formal announcement of their engagement, which happened five days later. Vita read it in a newspaper in Brighton, where, with the assistance of architect Edwin Lutyens, whom she called 'McNed', Victoria was converting three enormous townhouses into one even larger house as a retreat from Knole and Lionel's antipathy. Vita almost fainted when she saw in black and white confirmation of what she already knew. It was proof of the continuing strength of her feelings. Vita escaped to Paris, where Harold would remain until June assisting with the peace talks; inevitably Violet's letters pursued her. After travelling to London in May for publication of *Heritage* (the novel was widely and favourably reviewed; Collins issued a reprint in July), she returned to Paris. It was two days before Violet's wedding and Vita, who had promised to elope with Violet the following day, symbolically snatching her from the altar, did not trust herself. 'I shall do something quite irretrievable and mad if I stay in England,' she told Harold by way of explanation as she set off to rejoin him.[103]

Vita reneged on her promise to Violet. As it happened, the 'something quite irretrievable and mad' took place not in England but France. For on Denys and Violet's arrival at the Paris Ritz, Vita abducted Violet. She took her to the Hotel Roosevelt, a less opulent setting, and roughly, unthinkingly, madly, had sex with her. 'I treated her savagely, I made love to her, I had her, I didn't care, I only wanted to hurt Denys.'[104] The real hurt to Denys occurred the following day, when jointly the two women confronted him and, at last, told him most of the truth. Violet informed him of their plan to elope.

Once, Violet had flirted with the handsome Major Trefusis. She had procrastinated, bandied evasions, issued conditions.

She had scorned his repressed, well-behaved, musical family and ignored the extent of his emotional vulnerability in the aftermath of what he called a 'disastrous war'. She had postponed their wedding, rebuffed his patient affection. She had allowed him to be the plaything of her mother's scheming in the desperate hope that the prospect of marriage to Denys would force from Vita the tangible commitment she repeatedly avoided. Throughout it all, Denys had kept faith with an idea of something lovable in Violet; when she drew his portrait during their engagement, he interpreted it as a speaking gesture. Only now, with his eyes finally opened to the true nature of her love for Vita, did Violet allow him to dislike her as she deserved. Confronted by these women who had used too many words, shared too many charades, exploited too many romantic fictions to imbue their passion with legitimacy and grandeur, his most powerful response was wordless. He turned so white that Vita thought he was going to pass out. Yet she was not moved to pity. That night, in a gesture of deliberate provocation, she dined alone at The Ritz. Violet watched her from her suite. Behind Violet stood Denys. He was crying. He would take his revenge by destroying all of Vita's letters to Violet.

If Denys was in a position to think clearly, he could not have anticipated that it would be Harold who would next help Vita and Violet in their plans. Vita returned from Paris to Long Barn. She was like Clare Warrener in *Grey Wethers*, unable to settle down to her 'suitable' marriage, but tortured by the thought of making good her bolt for freedom: 'She returned, of course; every time she duly returned.'[105] She immersed herself in *Challenge* and the garden; at an auction in July she bought an additional thirty-three acres next to Long Barn, with two cottages and standing timber.[106] Her occupations were symbols of the two halves of her life, both of them more easily managed

in the absence of her co-players. Of the experience of writing
Challenge she wrote to the absent Harold that she was 'playing
gooseberry to the oddest couple';[107] of the garden she sent
tempting, lyrical descriptions which belied the tumult into
which she had plunged both Harold's life and her own, and
reassured him of the solidity of her long-term commitment to
him. 'I wonder what else in the garden you will want to hear
about,' she wrote in June. 'I went out and walked round it to
see – and have come back determined that another year we
must have masses and masses of flowers.'[108] It was letters of
this sort, with their promise of 'another year', which persuaded
Harold to agree to Vita's suggestion late that summer that she
again go away with Violet. The excuse this time was a trip to
Greece as research for *Challenge*. Later, one of Vita's fictional
alter egos regretted gardening as a taming of 'uncultivated'
nature.[109]

Vita and Violet did not reach Greece. Instead they lingered
in Paris, Vita again dressed as Julian, and afterwards travelled
south to Monte Carlo. Vita had suspected her passion was on
the wane but quickly learned she was mistaken. 'There was no
abatement, rather the reverse, in our caring for one another;
there was no abatement either in my passion for the freedom
of that life.'[110] Again Violet implored Vita to commit herself
to her irretrievably; again, presumably, Vita agreed. In Monte
Carlo in December, she and Violet again decided on an elope-
ment. This time Vita's nerve held. Bluntly, she told Harold of
her plans. He was predictably distressed and, reunited for
Christmas, they temporarily resumed their life together, going
through the motions of family celebrations and failing to discuss
either their present or their future. It was characteristic of the
whole muddled interlude. Vita had partly surrendered to
Violet's demands; simultaneously she refused entirely to
relinquish Harold who, for his part, ignored their predicament

when they were together and, in his letters when they were apart, chided Vita in one sentence while, in the next, assuring her of his limitless forgiveness and Violet's poisonous reprehensibility. At times Vita pleaded with Harold to demolish all of Violet's arguments and win her back by sheer force of love and daring: 'I long for weapons to fortify myself with,' she told him.[111] Grand gestures were more in her line than his: she concluded that he mistook the seriousness of the ongoing crisis. The well-intentioned intervention of Harold's mother served only to prove to Vita how much better suited she was to Violet's company. Vita dispatched the now completed manuscript of *Challenge* to William Collins and, on 3 February, she and Violet left London for Lincoln. Their purpose was again research for Vita's writing, in this case the fenland setting of *The Dragon in Shallow Waters*. In that angry and brutal novel, only the landscape itself emerges unscathed from the quarrels of men.

'Like a great bowl opened to the gold-moted emptiness of heaven the country lay, recipient of the benediction,' Vita wrote of the Lincolnshire wolds irradiated by spring sunshine.[112] In February 1920, at Lincoln's Saracen's Hotel, Vita felt no corresponding benediction. She blanked Violet's attempt to explain to her that she and Denys had each broken their vows – Denys to Violet, Violet to Vita; it was unclear how far their attempts at sex had gone and Vita was not listening anyway. Instead Vita 'urged [Violet] *so* much' to go back to Denys.[113] Violet refused. Within a week the women were again in France. From Dover they travelled separately, as they had arranged, Violet crossing first. Vita made the journey with an unexpected travelling companion in the form of Denys Trefusis. Also with her in spirit was Harold, to whom Vita wrote constantly, updating him of her movements and her plans. Denys had followed Violet to Dover but instead found Vita; he refused to leave her without first seeing Violet. All this Vita reported to Harold. Even with her resolve apparently at its strongest – 'You think that you will win,/ But that's just where you are wrong, wrong, wrong,' she wrote of an unnamed opponent, presumably Denys, in a hastily scribbled poem en route to meet Violet[114] – Vita maintained the lifeline to her other life of husband and home.

What happened next has become a byword for unhappy farce. Amid the to-ings and fro-ings, the angry mothers and grieving husbands, the hotel bedrooms and station buffets, the boats and trains and a plane, which play their part in this staccato narrative, the underlying emotional struggle can fade from view: we should not lose sight of it. Vita and Violet's plan was to meet in Amiens. In the aftermath of the First World War it was a suitably battle-scarred setting. Denys decided that Amiens was as good a place as any for his own final showdown with Violet: he intended to offer her a last chance to return with him and resume their tattered marriage. But Violet, whose life, like Vita's, had been sheltered by wealth and position, had never previously travelled without a companion – at the very least her maid or chauffeur. The experience frightened her. She deposited her luggage at Amiens' Hôtel du Rhin and returned to Calais to await Vita there. She found her, with Denys, in the station buffet. Surprised but undeterred, all three comforted themselves with chicken and Champagne. It was, Vita admitted, a 'ludicrous situation'.[115] Denys suggested 'that we should all three live together in Jamaica growing sugar!'.[116] Extreme nervous tension contributed a brittle sort of humour. They spent the night in three adjoining rooms and, the next day, continued to Amiens.

No sooner had Denys arrived in Amiens than he left. He knew, he said, that Violet had rejected him and, in tears, he returned to London. In London, Mrs Keppel had other ideas. Rejecting Denys was not an option she would countenance for Violet. She found a two-seater aeroplane. On the morning of

St Valentine's Day – though the date lost its significance in that welter of conflicting emotions – she arranged that Denys fly to Amiens and reclaim his wife from her lover. Thanks to Victoria's intervention, Harold accompanied him. Two husbands and two wives confronted one another in the Hôtel du Rhin. Their strongest emotions were hatred, shock and anger. The first belonged to Violet, directed at Denys. The second and third were Vita's. Swiftly she passed from one to another. Violet's treatment of Denys shocked her: what she learned of Denys's treatment of Violet angered her to the extent that she could no longer bear to look at either of them: 'I *had* to go, I should have killed her if I had stayed an instant longer.'[117] It was extreme sexual possessiveness which goaded Vita to fury: she learned at last that the man she had cuckolded had attempted to return the favour. Frantic with rage she departed for Paris with Harold, with whom she had also argued; at a distance Violet and Denys followed them. That evening, Denys told Vita that her suspicions were unfounded: he had not slept with Violet. 'Broken with misery', Vita allowed herself to be partly mollified; although she did not admit it, it was her vanity that had been hit hardest. The next morning Violet and Denys embarked on their journey to the south and continuing unhappiness for Violet.

Five nights later, at the Casino de Paris, Vita was briefly distracted from her angry misery. She saw 'the most lovely woman, almost entirely naked, but so lovely that one forgets to think of anything but her sheer perfection'.[118] In fact Vita had no desire to forget anything bar the horror of that hotel showdown in Amiens. She reread *Anna Karenina* and wallowed in the proofs of *Challenge*. The publishers requested a change of title; Vita chose *Endeavour*, fully aware now of the sheer hard work of such crises of the heart. The novel was not published in Britain until 1974. Victoria had decided 'the book will give rise to gossip'; she wanted Vita to cancel its publication. To persuade her, she enlisted the help of popular novelist Marie Belloc Lowndes. On 15 March 1920, after a long discussion, Mrs Belloc Lowndes did as Victoria wished and arranged a meeting with Vita. 'She [Mrs Belloc Lowndes] wants me to cancel it,' Vita recorded in her diary, 'says, if L [Lushka] were dead, would I publish it, etc. This hits me – gossip I don't care a damn about. Mrs Lowndes is kindness itself. So I give it up.'[119] It was Victoria who paid William Collins £150 to cover the expenses of the printed book and recover Vita's rights.

Within days of her interview with Mrs Belloc Lowndes, Vita set off for Avignon. There she was reunited with Violet. They had been apart for six weeks and immediately quarrelled. They travelled to Cap d'Antibes, Bordighera and San Remo, where Vita described Violet as 'horrible to me all day, and makes me very miserable and exasperated'.[120] They travelled to Milan, then by Orient Express to Venice. In Venice, Violet's spirits revived, with a corresponding effect on Vita; after a day, reality bit. 'It is horrible,' Vita wrote. Their next stop, after a lengthy delay, was Verona. From Verona they returned to Paris. Harold met them for the return crossing to Dover. For much of their journey they had been accompanied by Pat Dansey, a friend of Violet's, authorised by Mrs Keppel as a chaperone: birdlike in appearance, stuttering, obsessive, ultimately duplicitous. Despite the volatile atmosphere, in which no one appeared to advantage, Pat was falling in love with Vita. It was an added complication, typical of the climate of confusion and unreality which seemed to surround Vita; later she and Pat would become lovers. Moments of intimacy for Vita and Violet were few. 'Sanctuary should exist on earth;/ Some private place, where life may be./ . . . For boisterous love and puppy mirth,' Vita wrote afterwards in an anti-hunting poem, 'To Any M.F.H.'; she may have been thinking as much of hunted lovers as foxes.[121] In the spring of

1920, Vita and Violet struggled to find any 'private place': much of the boisterousness and 'puppy mirth' of their love had vanished. They had shunned, and eventually forfeited, secrecy.

On 17 April, one week after her return to Kent, Vita entertained Mrs Belloc Lowndes at Long Barn. They spent 'most of the day talking' and Vita found the older woman 'almost unbelievably nice and kind'.[122] At the latter's suggestion, Vita returned to her writing. She described the effort poignantly as disconsolate, but the weather was 'windy, showery, cold' and there were limited opportunities for gardening. By the end of the month she had persuaded herself her gift had vanished: 'O my good Lord! I can't write nowadays. It drives me wild to remember my fluency of once upon a time – ten or twelve sheets a day! And as for poetry, it's gone, gone, gone from me.'[123] It came back early the following month when Vita spent a whole day in bed and wrote two poems. 'Distinctly more cheerful in consequence,' she noted.[124] The return to any semblance of normality was fitful; there were setbacks along the way. A cruise with her father on *Sumurun*, the yacht Victoria had bought for Lionel after her victory in the Scott lawsuit, and the present of an elkhound puppy from Harold, went some way towards restoring her equanimity. She was rebuilding her life.

In September, Vita finished *The Dragon in Shallow Waters*. Violet read it the following month and dismissed it as 'coarse'.[125] Neither woman appears to have questioned Vita's choice of subject matter, but this shilling shocker tale of brothers Silas and Gregory Dene had a curious aptness. 'They lived in a double-cottage; Gregory with his wife in one half; Silas and his wife . . . in the other . . . Of the two brothers Gregory had been deaf and dumb from birth, and Silas blind.'[126] Their physical impairments mean that each brother is incomplete: only when they are together do they function fully. That idea is emphasised by their occupation of twin halves of the same house. Silas and

Gregory also embody opposing character traits, the former violent and destructive, the latter patient, thoughtful, creative. That neither is wholly believable as a character is due to Vita having attempted to depict the dualities of a single nature in two different people. Remote as the fictive Denes' lives are from Knole and the Sackvilles, *The Dragon in Shallow Waters* is another of Vita's attempts to work out in fiction uncomfortable aspects of what she imagined to be her own character. She wrote the novel at a moment of crisis, when that schism seemed more than usually real and powerful to her. Vita's towering fury in the hotel at Amiens, when she learned, as she thought, that Violet had deceived her by sleeping with Denys, became Silas's loathing for his brother: 'Silas appeared to be possessed by a senseless, impersonal fury of destruction. She thought she might as well argue with the unleashed elements as with Silas.'[127] The act of writing helped resolve parts of the crisis: the novel's very existence is proof that, for all the savagery of her feelings, brutal Silas–Vita had not destroyed creative Gregory–Vita. Despite Violet's reservations, it was to Violet that Vita dedicated the novel. She offered no explanation of its contents. The madness had passed. Vita retreated behind what Victoria called her 'beautiful mask'. Like Lady Anne Clifford, whose diary she would shortly reread, she 'strived to sit as merry a face as [she] could upon a discontented heart'.[128]

Vita would travel abroad with Violet once more, for two months at the beginning of 1921: she departed within days of assuring Harold that she had refused Violet's invitation. There was a valedictory quality to parts of this final sojourn. It could not be otherwise. In July 1920, Vita had begun writing the 'confession', which subsequently formed the basis of *Portrait of a Marriage*. The very act of ordering her thoughts sufficiently to form a coherent narrative imposed distance, however artificial. In her account of those events which had left her, as she acknowledged, unfairly 'safe, secure and undamaged save in my heart',[129] Vita attempted complete candour: she discounted the distortions both of Violet's letters and Harold's.

Evidently Harold did not share Vita's certainty of an end of the affair. The letter he wrote to her on 8 February was determined and emphatic, and he threatened to leave her if she failed to return to Long Barn within a fortnight of the letter's receipt (she didn't and he didn't). At the same time, resorting to memorable imagery, Harold continued to attribute all blame to Violet: 'I know that when you fall into V's hands your will becomes like a jelly-fish addicted to cocaine.'[130] Vita returned to Harold on her birthday in March.

In the past Vita and Violet had had recourse to flame imagery in their descriptions of their shared passion: 'The eager muscles of your throat were bare,/ The candid passion lit you like a flame,' Vita wrote in 1919.[131] By 1921 the flames burned less dangerously. For Christmas 1920, Vita gave Violet a fur coat: Violet was struck more forcibly by the coldness of Vita's manner on the telephone.[132] (Later, Vita exonerated herself from such accusations on the grounds that she hated the telephone.[133]) The flame had not died, Vita simply grew more adept at ignoring it. The other side of her nature reasserted itself. She bought Ben a pony for his birthday; she revelled in the seven puppies produced by her elkhound Freya. She pictured herself 'bewildered and uncertain between . . . my two lives': she chose 'my house, my garden, my fields, and Harold'.[134] This was the Vita who had once written to Violet about rabbits. If Violet had had access to Vita's diary, with its focus on puppies and whelping, she would have known the extent of her defeat. But she was never completely vanquished. In 1940, the women met again after an interval of eighteen years. 'We must not play with fire again,' Vita wrote to Violet on that occasion, holding her lover firmly at arm's length.[135] She reverted to former imagery. Her letter betrays fear and the power of a fugitive infatuation.

After their last trip to France that spring of 1921, the tsunami of Violet's letters to Vita dwindled and dried; all the triumphalism, the grandiloquence, the daring were past, meaningless now in the light of Vita's rejection. At intervals in the future Vita would resume the rhetoric of heroism that was so essential to her self-esteem. 'Better to fall with such reverberation/ That nation looks aghast across to nation,' she proclaimed in typically vaunting mode in her poem 'Reddín' in 1926; other lovers would admire in her the venturesome qualities that Violet had thought she glimpsed. Vita mostly deceived herself. By the autumn of 1921, worn out with misery, her only wish was for respite. How much she allowed herself to dwell on Violet's misery is questionable.

Her thoughts drew solace from what she described possessively as 'my Saxon weald! my cool and candid weald!'.[136] She had received a jolt from Lionel's attempt, in April, to find tenants for Knole. An advertisement in *Country Life* highlighted 'a family suite of sixteen bedrooms, eleven bathrooms, nine reception rooms and a billiard room, tennis lawns and a covered squash court . . . everything to make . . . a convenient country house of our own day', but failed to attract serious interest. The threat of dispossession, albeit temporary, returned Vita to her senses.[137] 'I have been absent,' she wrote in a poem dedicated to Harold. 'I have found unchanged/ The oaks, the slope and order of the fields.'[138] It was by way of being an apology, also a reassurance to herself.

On 4 September, she conceived the idea that would become *The Land*: a single long poem celebrating the cycle of the agricultural year and the traditions of the English countryside. She did not begin her first draft until 6 June 1923. In the meantime, from 'the things I know, the things I knew/ Before

I knew them'[139] and daily observation of husbandry close at hand, Vita gathered material for a poem which is a compendium of disappearing practices and, equally obviously, disappearing language; later she would work from the four-volume *Encyclopaedia of Agriculture* that Harold sent her in November 1925. In its first draft, *The Land* included a quotation from Hesiod's *Works and Days*: 'Work is no disgrace; the disgrace is in not working.'[140] It was as Violet had foreseen. While she herself remained under a cloud, living in exile in Paris with Denys, Vita addressed the business of turning herself into a successful writer. Work was a way out of her 'scarlet adventure'; it was also her atonement. With its portrait of dependable permanencies, *The Land* was a long way from a love affair so scandalous that Mrs Keppel worried it would jeopardise the engagement of Violet's younger sister Sonia to Roland Cubitt, son of the immensely rich Lord Ashcombe. And Vita's focus was more than agriculture: 'All . . . dies in its season; all perplexities,/ Even human grief with human body dies,/ Such griefs that press so wildly on the heart/ As to crush in its shell.'[141] At the sturdy Italian table in her sitting room at Long Barn, with its views over her garden and the landscape she had known all her life, Vita had reason to understand her own words.

At the end of June 1929, Vita cut from *The Listener* the two-page abridged version of the discussion on marriage she and Harold had broadcast on the radio, and pasted it into her cuttings book. She underlined a single sentence: 'I think that the secret of a successful marriage is the capacity to treat disasters as if they were incidents, and not to magnify incidents into disasters.'[142]

PART IV

Orlando

'Love in fantastic triumph sate,
Whilst bleeding hearts around him flowed,
For whom fresh pains he did create
And strange tyrannic power he showed.'

Aphra Behn, quoted by V. Sackville-West in
Aphra Behn: The Incomparable Astrea, 1927

VITA WAS EMOTIONALLY promiscuous. In a poem called 'Sometimes When Night . . .', she imagined a couple content to 'read, speak a little, read again', an evening scene in a house in the country. Its tranquillity is shattered by the sound of a shot. 'But we read on,/ Since the shot was not at our hearts, since the mark was not/ Your heart or mine, not this time, my companion.'[1] The key words are 'not this time': next time may be different. About the soundness of her heart, Vita makes her companion no lasting promises.

Like her parents', Vita's was an intensely passionate nature. Sex, intrinsic to Julian's mastery over Eve, played an important

part in her relationship with Violet, as it would in future relationships. Her depiction of thwarted sexual desire in a late
novel, *The Easter Party*, bears the hallmark of truth to experience. Vita pictures her heroine 'pacing up and down her room
at night, twisting her hands, throwing her head back, heaving
her shoulders, breathing quickly and heavily, in an anguish . . .
trying to regain control'.[2]

Vita's choice of Harold over Violet did not mean that she
had conquered or forsworn such urges, despite her earlier decision, in the face of Harold's desire for another child, that sex
would play no further part in their marriage. She forswore
those urges only in relation to Harold: even in Harold's case
she occasionally relapsed in the early days. Instead Vita had
determined to resist for a second time the complete physical
and emotional surrender of her relationship with Violet: her
motives were self-protection and belated loyalty to her marriage.
'You know what infatuation is, and I was mad,' was Vita's final
verdict on the affair to Harold, in December 1922.[3] Other lovers
would follow in Violet's footsteps, all but one of them female.
Although several sacrificed their own stable, long-term relationships in order to reciprocate feelings they misattributed to
Vita, none again threatened the safety of her marriage. Harold
referred to them glancingly as Vita's 'muddles'.

The ability to remain unharmed by emotional and sexual
entanglements points to a capricious quality in Vita's make-up.
Novelty aroused her, so too pursuit, seduction, dominance.
Narcissism sharpened her pleasure: the realisation of that image
of herself in the male role of conqueror that Violet had recognised,
'the abandonment of mastery and surrender in the hours of night',
as she described it in *Challenge*. Most of her believed, as she wrote
in her diary, that 'love makes everyone a bore, but that the excitement of life lies in the *béguins* [infatuations], and the "little moves"
nearer to people'.[4] Those feelings were necessarily fleeting; Vita

told her mother that her *béguins* lasted a matter of days and left no imprint. 'Few delights bear the strain of investigation,' she wrote in a different context in 1926; 'they bruise, as tender fruits after handling. It is safer not to know too much.'[5] She enjoyed and needed sex, enjoyed the anticipation of fulfilment: she learnt to separate this need from all but temporary emotional involvement. Vita never accepted any lover's argument that sex implied commitment. That refusal became her means of preserving herself and her marriage. Its consequence was that Vita hurt anyone who felt more strongly than she did.

In her biography of Aphra Behn, begun on 7 June 1927, Vita itemised Behn's images of love. Her focus is illuminating: 'there are in the quiver of the god a great many different darts; some that wound for a day, and others for a year; they are all fine, painted, glittering darts . . . but the wounds they make reach the desire only, and are cured by possessing'.[6] Vita recognised her own desire as a chimera but necessary, and accorded it a corresponding place in her priorities. For much of the time, she accepted Behn's assertion that there are higher aims than physical fulfilment: ''tis that refined and illustrious passion of the soul, whose aim is virtue and whose end is honour, that has the power of changing nature . . .'.[7] Couched in terms to satisfy a latter-day Sackville cavalier, this was the 'passion' that Vita ultimately realised in her platonic marriage to Harold. More than her relationship with Violet, her decision that her marriage should succeed irrespective of her own physical desires set the course of Vita's life. Inevitably, at intervals, she fell short of her own lofty resolutions, 'swept by a sensation I cannot logically explain to others;/ . . . an irrational passion'.[8]

In the decade following the collapse of her relationship with Violet, Vita's affairs resulted in three broken marriages, at least one career ruined, threats of legal action and the publication of a vicious satirical poem intended to expose to public outrage the unconventional (and in Harold's case, illegal) nature of the Nicolsons' proclivities. At the same time, Vita's own marriage regained much of the serenity of the early years in Constantinople and at Long Barn. That the latter should have been possible is a tribute to Vita's ability to compartmentalise her life and satisfy sexual desire without committing herself beyond the heady moment; a tribute too to Harold's patient lack of jealousy. Vita reminded herself of the separation between her love for Harold, which she described as 'real' and 'pure', and what she later dismissed as 'the cheap unworthy tricks that lure the flesh'.[9] She quoted Khalil Gibran: 'Fill each other's cup, but drink not from one cup', and pursued her quarry with a degree of discretion, a degree of detachment, while keeping faith with Harold in spirit. 'The liaisons which you and I contract are something perfectly apart from the more natural and normal attitude we have towards each other, and therefore don't interfere,' Vita wrote to Harold in May 1926; she was wholly sincere.[10] As she must have known, that statement was more true of Harold's affairs, which avoided tempestuousness, than her own.

Vita first met Dorothy Wellesley, then Dorothy Ashton, called Dottie, in March 1914 in Constantinople. Dottie was engaged to Harold's friend, Lord Gerald Wellesley, like Harold a secretary in the Diplomatic Service. Gerry Wellesley had recently been engaged to Violet; his sister, Lady Eileen Wellesley, was Harold's former fiancée. On that occasion, Vita's diary records only Dottie's wealth (she had inherited an estate in Cheshire). She does not mention Dottie's aspirations to be a poet or her striking appearance: 'blazing blue eyes, fair hair, transparently white skin'.[11] She also failed to notice the demons that lurked so close below the surface and, unsurprisingly, what another observer described on Dottie's skull as 'the three bumps of temper, pride and combativeness more developed than [in] anyone I have ever known'.[12] Within a decade this triple endowment would combine to destroy Dottie's marriage to Gerry, which took place the month after she and Vita met. Vita also played her part in the collapse of this marriage of friends.

In July 1920, dented in spirit and harried by their families, Vita and Violet told their story to novelist Clemence Dane, whom Vita had met with Mrs Belloc Lowndes. Among Clemence Dane's novels was a girls' school story, *Regiment of Women*, which Vita had read; ambiguously she likened Dane to the novel's villain Clare Hartill. *Regiment of Women* has strong lesbian components, but ultimately endorses the desirability of marriage in preference to the hothouse emotional effusions it attributes to single-sex schooling. Dane's response to Vita and Violet that last summer was consistent with the message of her novel: she suggested they give each other up. Confronted by the bleakness of this advice and Violet's increasingly histrionic demands, Vita turned to Dottie for distraction. Dottie came to Long Barn; Vita discovered their shared interest in poetry, a bond. The same year, to lukewarm critical reception, Dottie published a collection of verse, entitled simply, *Poems*, which Vita read and advised on prior to publication. The last weekend in August, Vita went to Sherfield Court, the house Dottie had bought on the edge of her father-in-law's Stratfield Saye estate. 'I like Dottie but can't stick smug Gerry,' she recorded tersely in her diary.[13] The women saw more of one another, their intimacy endorsed by Harold's longstanding friendship with Gerry. Dottie accompanied Vita as her guest to a PEN Club dinner where they met the distinguished novelist John Galsworthy; the veteran author was full of praise for Vita.

The following autumn, on 14 September 1921, Vita, Dottie and Gerry set off for Italy; Harold joined them in Rome on 6 October. It was to be a holiday marred by the Wellesleys' bickering and squabbling. At intervals Gerry left Vita and Dottie; the women pursued interests of their own. They were alone in Ravenna, Split, Ragusa, Cattaro. In Ravenna, Vita wrote, they 'left the motor and went into the wood, and lay under the pines, and read snatches of the more obscure poets to one another. We said, "Here Dante, Boccaccio, Shelley and Byron walked," and again, "Oh my God how the canal does stink."'[14] Vita wrestled with a new novel, but failed to make headway; later she abandoned it and rewrote it over a two-year period as her poem 'Reddín'. Instead she wrote a short poem about Dottie at Long Barn. It is among her sunniest, and depicts an unnamed Dottie, exotically dressed, skipping in a moonlit Kentish lane.

The lightness of tone of 'Full Moon' reveals the scale of Vita's unawareness of the situation into which she had blundered. She recognised Dottie as 'a born romantic', 'a fiery spirit with a passionate love of beauty in all its forms, whether in flowers, landscapes or works of art'.[15] In verse she acclaimed her whimsically as a 'small impertinent charlatan' and imagined her as a fey child; in person she called her 'Aprile'. She did not see that, like Violet before her and, to some extent, Vita herself, Dottie was damaged and unhappy, the victim of a childhood that combined immense material privileges with emotional deprivation. Jointly and separately, Dottie's commanding mother, Lady Scarbrough, and her elderly nanny, Wa-Wa, had treated her with cruelty and contempt. Remembering Wa-Wa, Dottie wrote in a tone of mounting hysteria in her poem 'The Deserted House': 'There, there, was the bed,/ Where she beat me and shook me,/ When I cried with terror at night.'

Vita and Dottie became lovers. Afterwards one of Vita's servants claimed to have seen them together 'in a very amorous position, D with no clothes on'.[16] But Dottie needed reliance and reassurance more than sex; she craved the care and attention that had formerly been withheld from her. Not for the last time, Vita found herself in the double role of lover and mother.

The price she exacted, as always, was unquestioning devotion. For her part, she described her relationship with Dottie limply as 'our casual journey'.[17]

By the time Harold expressed serious concern about the nature of Vita and Dottie's involvement, the Wellesleys' separation was only weeks away. Harold warned Vita that Gerry would be likely to look for a scapegoat: it was too late. At Christmas 1922, Gerry moved out of Sherfield. Seven weeks later, on 9 February, he inscribed beneath a photograph of Dottie three lines from an ode by Horace, translated by Dryden: 'The joys I have possessed, in spite of fate, are mine./ Not Heaven itself over the past has power;/ And what has been has been, and I have had my hour.'[18] For the next forty-six years, until its theft from a hotel bedroom, he placed beneath his pillow when he slept the watch that Dottie gave him in 1914.[19]

Harold blamed Dottie for the breakdown of the marriage. 'I do think Dottie makes a mistake in trying to be at one and the same time the little bit of thistledown *and* the thistle,' he wrote in his diary before the final split.[20] As in Vita's relationship with Violet, it was his way of avoiding blaming Vita. Vita herself implicitly acknowledged the part she had played: her reaction emphasises self-preservation over sympathy. To Harold she wrote: 'I do *not* want people to say I have anything to do with her marriage having gone wrong, which probably they would be only too pleased to say . . . I do *not* want to be dragged into this, either for your sake or my own. We have had quite enough of that sort of thing, haven't we?'[21] But it was Vita whom Dottie repeatedly summoned to her aid, threatening tears in the face of Vita's reluctance, Vita whom she chose to support her in her wretchedness. Vita responded to Dottie's summons, though she would find an increasing number of draws on her time as the year progressed.

*

At thirty, Vita was beautiful. Even one of her less fanciful observers described her as being 'in the prime of life, an animal at the height of its powers, a beautiful flower in full bloom. She was very handsome, dashing, aristocratic, lordly . . .'[22] Her hooded eyes were dark and clear under attractively heavy brows, her nose long and straight, her profile strongly modelled. She was tall and often strikingly colourfully dressed, a 'remarkable person in black and scarlet' as she described herself in an unpublished short story she wrote about herself called 'The Poetry Reading'.[23] She still, at this point, made regular trips to the hairdresser, she wore dangling earrings, ropes of coloured beads or the pearl necklace Seery had left her; large rings crowded her fingers. Victoria took credit for her dazzling complexion, attributing it to the mercilessness with which she had prevented Vita from eating 'chocolates and bonbons' in childhood. 'She must be grateful to me now that she is thirty, that her cheeks are like two ripe peaches, with a sun-kissed look and a bloom that is the envy and the admiration of everyone.'[24] Victoria drew attention to Vita's 'dignity and repose': there is a quality of stillness in the photographs of Vita taken by émigré German portraitist E. O. Hoppé at sittings in February 1923 and again in February 1924, as well as that easy confidence Strang had captured five years previously. Only Sir William Rothenstein, drawing Vita in 1925, missed her iconic allure. Rothenstein's portrait, today in the collection of the National Portrait Gallery, reimagines Vita as a pre-Raphaelite sleepwalker: heavy-featured, expressionless, apparently with a cast in one eye, stolid rather than statuesque. 'Vita was a beautiful woman and this is an ugly one,' Harold commented, when presented with the drawing years later.

None of these images suggests that the 'virile' quality in Vita, identified mischievously in 1923 by novelist Ronald Firbank, was yet visible in her appearance. In his novella *The*

Flower Beneath the Foot, Firbank satirised Vita as Victoria Gellibore Frinton, the Honourable Mrs Chilleywater, 'the sole heir of Lord Seafairer of Sevenelms, Kent', writer of 'lurid studies of low life (of which she knew nothing at all)'.[25] 'Virility' *was* a part of Vita's make-up – after her epiphany with Violet, Vita understood it as one half of her dual nature. To the casual observer it revealed itself only in a certain boldness of gesture and mannerism, the habit of striding that so struck Leonard Woolf, and outside her immediate circle Vita had no intention of advertising her duality further than in her choice of deliberately masculine hats. 'Charlotte was . . . surveying Sackville-West,' Vita wrote in 'The Poetry Reading'; 'she saw the dark felt hat, the heavy cream lambskin coat, black dress, scarlet earrings, scarf, and shoes, yet apart from these externals the quality that held the audience and Charlotte in particular was not the beauty of the rather tired face, but its exceptional sincerity.'[26] In describing her own appearance, Vita chooses sincerity over virility, depth of feeling over physical forcefulness. As much as the swashbuckling characteristics of earlier self-fictions, it possesses a heroic dimension: Vita's 'sincerity' in the story persuades the frustrated Charlotte to break free from the smothering influence of her elder sister, Amelia. As in fiction, so in Vita's life. Without any idea of doing so, unaware even of her own power, the fictional Vita destroys the Pringle sisters' bond. With equal sincerity would the real Vita destroy relationships in her path. It was never her intention. Nor did she take responsibility for fallout from her *'béguins'*.

Vita had met Geoffrey Scott before she saw him in Rome with Gerry and Dottie in the autumn of 1921 – in Florence, in 1909, while travelling with Rosamund Grosvenor. Geoffrey Scott was married, the author of a highly praised architectural monograph, *The Architecture of Humanism*, published in 1914; tall, humorous, darkly attractive behind round spectacles, melancholic for all his easy wit. Financially he was supported by his wealthy wife, Lady Sybil, younger daughter of the Earl of Desart; they lived in Fiesole, in Michelozzi's fifteenth-century Villa Medici, amid manicured formal gardens. Three years into their marriage, in 1921, the Scotts had embarked on a trial separation: Geoffrey had fallen in love with another woman. His was a chequered romantic career, with numerous affairs before his marriage to Sybil Cutting and a reputation for philandering. Contemporary slang denounced him as a 'bounder'; Vita would call him Tinker. As much as Vita, he was driven by desire and a kind of recklessness over consequences. Like Vita, he understood the perils of love.

At the end of July 1923, Geoffrey left Italy for London, his third appearance in Vita's life; his purpose was Vita herself. He was working on a biography of eighteenth-century novelist Madame de Charrière, *The Portrait of Zélide*, while Sybil completed translations of four of Madame de Charrière's novels, also for publication; in 1926 the former won the James Tait Black Memorial Prize. In addition Geoffrey Scott was a poet. *A Box of Paints: Poems* was published in November 1923 to enthusiastic reviews. It included the lines: 'I locked the gold Sun with a key/ That lasting joy might dwell with me;/ The sun did scorch my hands and feet/ But to my heart refused his heat;/ So the swift flame with captive rage/ Consumed me in his glowing cage.' In London that summer and subsequently with Vita in Italy, Scott failed to heed his own warning; Vita herself fell fleetingly in love with him. From the ruins of Dottie's marriage to Gerry, Vita stepped open-eyed into another passionate liaison. Inevitably she withdrew once the love she had demanded in turn exacted its own demands; again the *béguin* was temporary. It was Geoffrey who eventually found himself consumed by the 'captive rage' of love's flame. Sybil divorced him. He lost wife, wealth, reputation and failed to win Vita.

Before that, Vita and Geoffrey spent a week together in the Lake District (Ben and Nigel were safely out of the way in Brittany with their French governess, Mademoiselle Nadré, known as 'Goggy'). In the autumn they met again in Florence, where Vita arrived ahead of Harold. In Florence, the Nicolsons stayed with the Scotts at the Villa Medici. By the time of Harold's arrival, thanks to a combination of Florentine moonlight and overwrought emotionalism, Vita had fallen in love with Geoffrey and he with her, much to Sybil's distress. Vita confided in her mother. Victoria's anxiety was balanced by healthy enjoyment: she was certain that sex with Geoffrey would successfully banish memories of Violet. Vita and Geoffrey discussed *The Portrait of Zélide* and the long poem that would become *The Land*; Geoffrey referred to them as 'our book' and 'our poem'. Shared literary aspirations nourished the lovers. After parting, they wrote to one another daily; Geoffrey fretted over Sybil's reaction. On her return to Long Barn, Vita wrote emolliently to Sybil, a gesture in which worldliness and unworldliness combined in equal measure. Like a lover in a story, sincere in her role play, Vita offered to renounce Geoffrey. Sybil was temporarily placated. Her equanimity did not survive Geoffrey's return visit to London in the New Year.

'At 3.30 Geoffrey rang me up to say he had arrived,' Vita wrote on 10 January 1924. 'At 7 he came for me, we dined at the Berkeley; and came back here afterwards; a bewildering and not very real evening. Rainy London; taxis; champagne; confusion.'[27] The following day she took Geoffrey to Knole. Geoffrey and Dottie were among guests at a lunch party on 15 January, which Vita described as 'uncomfortable . . . by reason of the tension between Aprile [Dottie] and Geoffrey'.[28] On Sunday 20 January, Vita took Geoffrey to Knole again, in company with Harold and Ben: in her diary she listed her companions in order 'Geoffrey, Harold, Ben'. The following night she stayed on at

Knole, alone with Geoffrey; they dined and lunched together in the week ahead and, on 31 January, following a furious argument with Victoria over a plate warmer, Vita noted Geoffrey's 'consolation' in her diary. On 1 February, at a lunch party, Vita 'talked to Sybil [Colefax] and tried to enlist her help in diminishing talk about me and G'.[29] Three days later she took Geoffrey in Harold's place to a PEN Club dinner after Harold had to 'chuck at the last moment as he has to do a draft on the relations of France and England for Ramsay McDonald'.[30] On 7 February, after an afternoon alone together at Ebury Street, Geoffrey bought Vita a ring. And so it continued for another week.

Vita understood the symbolism of the ring, understood the direction of Geoffrey's thoughts – and maintained the pattern of frequent meetings. It was surprising behaviour given her stated 'confusion' and typical of what Harold regarded as Vita's 'muddled' approach to her love affairs. As he wrote to her later, 'I have every confidence in your wisdom except where this sort of thing is concerned, when you wrap your wisdom in a hood of optimism and only take it off when things have gone too far for mending.'[31] Vita could have stopped seeing Geoffrey, just as she could have resisted parading him in front of literary London at a PEN Club dinner only days after asking for help to quash gossip. In the latter aim she failed anyway. In her letters written from Florence she had confided too much to Victoria; now she introduced Geoffrey to her mother in person. And Victoria, even when her relationship with Vita was not riven by arguments of the plate-warmer variety, was dependably indiscreet. Once Geoffrey returned to Sybil in the middle of February, his cause was lost. As Violet had discovered, Vita's loyalty seldom survived physical separation: she excelled at epistolary equivocation.

Geoffrey came back to England and Vita in the summer. His visit to Long Barn, cut short by Vita and Harold's imminent departure for the Dolomites, was unsatisfactory: his furious reaction to Ben and Nigel bursting into his bedroom to find him naked, changing for dinner, is indicative of his unsettlement. Harold was similarly unhappy about developments. He told Vita: 'I dislike Geoffrey because: a) he talks better than I do; b) he worries you; c) he has a yellow face & sits up late & is flabby; d) because he is more emotional than I am, and because you are impressed by emotion.'[32] Geoffrey would continue to worry Vita in his letters for the remainder of the year. As in Vita's relationship with Violet, their correspondence took on a one-sided quality: all the urgency, ardour and – increasingly – suffering, belonged to Geoffrey. Vita responded either inadequately or with careful promises that she must have known she would not keep. Only Victoria took pity on Geoffrey. She found him 'so unhappy' before his return to Italy that she treated him to lunch: 'I think I cheered him up with lobsters stuffed with caviar.'[33] But she signalled her approval of Vita's growing detachment by cancelling her loan on Ebury Street and offering Vita and Harold £500 a year towards its running costs; she also offered to clear Harold's tax debt. It was a symbolic gesture.

Like Violet, Geoffrey found it impossible to accept the obvious explanation for what he interpreted as Vita's contradictory behaviour: her initial insistence on his wholehearted surrender followed by an unexplained withdrawal once that surrender had been granted. 'To ask for a possessive lover, and do everything to show him he "possesses" nothing, is not only damnable, it's idiotic,' he wrote to her.[34] It was an inconsistency Vita would never resolve, this need for abject submission that contained within itself the seeds of her disillusionment. 'It made love richer to have something saved up for a later day. One did not give everything out at once. An essential of love was to keep something in reserve always,' she wrote in *Grand Canyon* in 1942.[35] But Vita did not encourage reserve in her lovers, and she consistently attracted those whose need was to give everything out at once, prostrating themselves completely, help-lessly, childishly. Geoffrey had decided that Vita did not share the sexual excitement that for him was as fundamental to their relationship as their literary communing. He told her she responded to the *appearance* of emotion. It could not be other-wise given the element of play-acting that shaped her recep-tivity to the idea of love.

Throughout the spring of 1925, Vita's diary records her meet-ings with Geoffrey; in April, in Venice with Harold and Ben, she spent her mornings with the man she knew now she would never marry. Despite Sybil's decision in May to file for divorce, and Geoffrey and Vita's shared fear of Vita being cited in proceed-ings, they continued to meet in London that autumn, not only in the privacy of the Nicolsons' Ebury Street house but publicly, in restaurants like the Criterion. Vita's progress on *The Land* was well advanced: current muddles did not prevent her from describing life as 'too exciting altogether'. One particularly good day she wrote seventy-one lines of her poem – 'a record I think?'.[36]

At the end of the year her mood changed again: Geoffrey was threatening to kill himself; Vita explained his visit to Long Barn in October as 'very much against my will'.[37] On 29 December he telephoned Vita in the evening 'in a state of hysteria (or so it sounded)'. Her response was one of baffle-ment, compounded by disappointment that, having allowed him fruitlessly to destroy his marriage, they could not 'have remained good friends'.[38] The following day she described him starkly as 'very sinister'. If he threatened physical violence on that occasion, it would not have been the first time: afterwards Vita claimed that Geoffrey had once nearly strangled her.

Again it was Harold who saved Vita from her predicament. On 24 September 1925, he told Vita he had been posted for two years to Tehran, beginning in November. Excited by the idea of Persia, though still hostile in general to Harold's diplomatic career, Vita decided to join him in the New Year. The day before she left, on 19 January 1926, she had a farewell lunch with Geoffrey. They were not alone. Also present was Dorothy Warren, a niece by marriage of Lady Ottoline Morrell. Dorothy was in love with Geoffrey. She was also in love with Vita. There were suggestions of history repeating itself: Violet and Pat Dansey all over again, one lover replaced by their substitute. This time Vita reacted differently. She had learnt at least one lesson. Dorothy's importuning, her shyly insinuating letters, irked her.

Later that year Sybil divorced Geoffrey and married in his place the writer Percy Lubbock. 'A memory, a bird flown,/ A wild bird's claw prick in the moon,/ . . . love is so,' Geoffrey had written in *A Box of Paints*. So it proved. In October 1927, he travelled to the States as first editor of the James Boswell Papers, which had recently been bought by American businessman Colonel Ralph Isham. He did not marry Dorothy Warren. Vita discouraged further contact, writing to Harold on 28 June 1926: 'Geoffrey writes but I have refused to see him, and he has accepted that. He now writes me sentimental letters about "Remember what I was once . . ."'[39] Despite her dislike of sentiment and her relief at having extricated herself, she may have taken his injunction more to heart than she realised. Long after his death, Vita claimed that Geoffrey was one of the two people she missed most (the other was Virginia Woolf). In the meantime she avoided Dorothy, whose reappearance in Vita's life four years later proved equally unwelcome.

Vita had remained close to Dottie during her affair with Geoffrey. She did not confide in her: their own relationship was too recent for that and she recognised Dottie's jealousy, which she discussed with Geoffrey. Vita's principal confidante remained her mother, notwithstanding upheavals brought about by frequent arguments. Given the complexity of her emotional life, Vita needed a confidante. A third liaison, conducted in tandem, ended so badly that, at the beginning of 1924, Vita reported herself 'hav[ing] moments of wishing most people at the bottom of the sea'.[40] It ought not to have happened.

On the table beside her bed in her flat in Cumberland Mansions in Bryanston Square, Pat Dansey had a copy of Vita's second volume of poems, *Orchard and Vineyard*. It was signed 'with love from DM'.[41] 'DM' was Vita, the book her gift to Pat, Pat's name for Vita 'Dark Man'.

'"That brilliant creature Vita Sackville-West" is a darling, I think, to have sent me her book of poems. I am dreadfully proud to have been given them. Vita, thank you a thousand times,' Pat wrote on 12 November 1921. 'I spent the whole of last night dreaming about you. I expect it was because I had taken your poems to read in bed. Queer dream it was too . . .'[42] Two months later Vita and Pat became lovers. In both cases, their motives contained traces of cynicism.

Pat was the confidante and chaperone Mrs Keppel had sanctioned for Violet and, until Violet's letters to Vita ceased in November 1921, the women's go-between. A niece of the last Lord Fitzhardinge, she spent formative years in medieval splendour at Berkeley Castle in Gloucestershire, living with her childless, elderly, 'crochety ogre' of an uncle. Physically diminutive, she was self-willed, with an active fantasy life; she may have been, as Lord Northumberland described her, 'not quite right in the head'.[43] She found a degree of emotional fulfilment early on with Joan Campbell, a granddaughter of the Duke of Argyll, who would remain nominally her partner for life. Her emotional volatility matched Vita's own but she was less adept than Vita at regulating her feelings. Her friendship with Violet included an overt sexual dimension – she described inventing 'the most erotic pastimes to appeal to [Violet's] taste'.[44] She was determined that sex would also play its part in her relationship with Vita.

Vita's relationships invariably encompassed an element of manipulation, Vita herself alternately villain and victim. She first met Pat in 1918 with Violet; afterwards, we know, in the spring of 1920, Pat travelled with Vita and Violet from Verona to Paris. Pat's loyalties were initially clear. Once the lovers had parted, she kept open a channel of communication between them; she sent Violet money, cigarettes, press cuttings of Vita's poems. Then something changed. Pat's covering notes to Vita, included alongside Violet's letters, which she forwarded, set out to drive a wedge between the women: she described Violet as deceitful, given to trickery and lies; spitefully she suggested that Violet could only 'ever be happy in *being* unhappy'.[45] Slowly, insidiously, Pat attempted to usurp Violet's position in Vita's thoughts. It is a measure of Vita's own unhappiness that she apparently failed to spot, or chose to overlook, Pat's feline duplicity.

Pat was well equipped to claim Vita's attention. Not only was she her last link with Violet, with whom she remained in love, since 1917 she had been privy to all of Violet's confidences about Vita. Pat had listened well. She wooed Vita exactly as Violet had unwittingly instructed her, and seduced her, as Violet had, with a fantasy of herself, the image of the Dark Man: she was strong, handsome, masterful. 'I do wish, Vita, that when you come to see me you could manage to look ugly,' she wrote. 'You make me forget all the important disagreeable things I want to say.'[46] Just to be certain, she wrote to Vita pointing out, in a safely round-about way, that she was in love with her; afterwards she whispered that Vita attracted her 'in a way which I cannot describe'.[47] Beside her copy of *Orchard and Vineyard* stood a framed reproduction of Vita's portrait by William Strang, the picture painted while Violet had sketched in the background of Strang's studio. For Vita the transition from Julian/Mitya to Dark Man was easy.

Like Violet and Geoffrey, Pat gave Vita a ring. She went one better and gave her two rings, one of diamonds, the other emeralds. With lover-like abandon she showered Vita with presents: Champagne and Sauternes from the cellars at Berkeley Castle; oranges from South Africa and flowers from the South of France; a fountain pen; a Burberry mackintosh; she described a Daimler coupé she meant to buy her. She absorbed herself wholeheartedly in Vita's life, 'your dogs, cats, garden, books, children, husband and mother!'.[48] She gave Vita a copy of the *Arabian Nights*, perhaps hoping to kindle Vita's memories of *Scheherazade* and that rainy October evening in 1918 when, following a matinée of Rimsky-Korsakov's ballet, Vita first transformed herself into Julian. Then, in December 1922, Pat declared herself terminally ill and promised to leave everything she owned to Vita; Vita described her as 'the queerest fish I ever came across'.[49] That Christmas, Pat joined the family party of Vita, Ben, Nigel and Victoria at Victoria's huge house in Brighton (Harold was in Lausanne, at an international conference debating the future of Turkey). It was the same month Gerry Wellesley moved out of Sherfield Court.

There was a desperate quality to the scale of Pat's generosity. Like Victoria she exploited the magpie lure of her gifts to bind Vita closer to her. She offered Vita the very concession Violet had failed to make good: a sham marriage as a screen for their continuing liaison. Pat was in the grip of a sexual infatuation every bit as strong as Vita's for Violet or Violet's for Vita. Even the thought of their lovemaking unsettled her: 'hot waves rush all over me. Little electric needles of sensation prick all through me.'[50] Vita's own feelings, muddied from the outset by her unresolved love for Violet and the less assertive dependency of Dottie, were characteristically slippery. The poem she wrote for Pat, 'Black Tarn', lacked the urgency and earthy directness of her poems to Violet, a lengthy description of a hill walk, terminating in 'a pool in a crater'. It is a poem about a landscape, which never fully makes the leap to examining

Vita's own interior landscape. Even its central metaphor of climbing beyond the familiar and 'leaving a discontent/ With the lake in the valley, and the road beside the lake,/ And the dwellings of men, the safety, and the ease' makes no reference to Pat herself, much less to happiness, love, exaltation, desire.[51] The pool in the crater is suggestive: it too falls short of becoming the sexual symbol it first appears. Nor is it, the poet insists, the only pool in those 'rough, negative hills'. Inevitably Vita would soon make good that threat.

By the summer of 1923, Geoffrey Scott vied with Dottie and Pat for Vita's attention. From Florence in November, Vita wrote to Pat explaining that she had fallen so hopelessly in love with Geoffrey that she could no longer go on seeing her. Her letter inspired desolation swiftly followed by fury. Unlike others among Vita's lovers, Pat would not be content to slake her rage in silence. She demanded the immediate return of all her presents and refused Vita's easy reassurances. 'I centralised on you for three solid years *as my life*, and you just shut me off bang! stranded,' she wrote.[52] In the New Year, Vita's diary reported alarming developments: 'Quarrel with Pat in full swing; letters exchanged, she threatening lawsuits, and I being rather pompous.'[53] Vita discussed her latest 'muddle' with Harold, 'and finally wrote her a conciliatory letter'. Harold resisted blaming Vita and Vita avoided blaming herself. Instead she described her mood as one of boredom.[54] She followed up her letter with a short meeting two days later, which she described as 'perfectly amicable', and pursued her tottering relationship with Geoffrey.

Pat had no intention of quickly fading away, however. She was deeply in love, humiliated and vengeful. She had flattered Vita in her careful fantasy of the Dark Man, knowing from Violet Vita's susceptibility to appeals made to her conviction of her own duality. And now she had been defeated by the flipside of Vita's posturing, 'your obsession that you are a romantic young man who treats women badly'.[55] Like Violet, Pat threatened suicide; unlike Violet she consulted a lawyer and told Vita she would take her story to the newspapers: 'I shall tell the despicable way in which you treated me throughout . . . How you dropped me when it suited you.'[56] She accused Vita of playing her off against Dorothy Wellesley. Violet had accepted Vita's abandonment, continuing to love her even after Vita chose Harold, Ben, Nigel and Long Barn in her stead: Pat's love was not so selfless. 'You have *always* only considered *your* feelings, *your* wishes, *your* wants,' she spat.[57]

On 8 March, Vita described Pat inadequately as 'very cross'. It was a dramatic encounter. Pat produced a pistol; with a fight Vita wrenched it from her. 'If it had been loaded it was *bound* to have gone off,' Pat wrote afterwards of their rough, clumsy fight.[58] In the face of melodrama worthy of one of her own novels, Vita maintained commendable sangfroid in her diary: 'Pat came in the morning . . . suggested blowing her brains out and leaving a letter to be read at the inquest saying it was all my fault for having been so unkind to her – but melted finally – and we parted friends, me wiping the sweat of surprise off my brow.'[59] Pat may have regarded their 'friendship' in a different light. She herself had manipulated Vita through storytelling, bolstering the legend of the Dark Man; she is unlikely to have been swayed by more words. Notwithstanding the gun, it was typical of the way Vita shirked resolving romantic conflicts which she had entered voluntarily. With hindsight her grounds for surprise seem slender. In her assessment of Vita's focus on what she described as '*your* feelings, *your* wishes, *your* wants', Pat hit upon a truth of all Vita's short-term relationships. Vita admitted other considerations only in her relationships with Harold, Victoria and the boys – and in her long and loving friendship with Bloomsbury writer Virginia Woolf.

*

Virginia Woolf admired Vita Sackville-West's legs and her ancestry; she considered her a second-rate writer. Vita for her part admired Virginia Woolf unreservedly, while remaining ambivalent about Bloomsbury, which she labelled 'Gloomsbury': 'She had the warmest and deepest and most human of affection for those she loved. They were few, perhaps, and she applied alarmingly high standards, but her love and humanity were real, once they were given.'[60]

Vita conceded Virginia's superior artistry: she attributed to her a 'mysterious power . . . to make certain words, – perhaps quite ordinary words – start up out of the page like partridges out of a turnip field, getting a new value, a new surprise', a power she knew that she herself did not possess.[61] Virginia was exhilarated by Vita's forcefulness as a presence, her 'full-breastedness; her being so much in full sail on the high tides'.[62] Insisting on her intellectual superiority – she labelled Vita and Harold 'both incurably stupid' within weeks of meeting them[63] – Virginia admitted inferiority in other areas. In that way her relationship with Vita adopted the model of mastery and submission that characterised Vita's affairs with Violet, Dottie and Pat. Unlike her predecessors in Vita's affection, Virginia did not relinquish control completely.

Vita and Virginia's nineteen-year correspondence is notable for a degree of self-dramatisation on both sides. Their epistolary flirtation was energetic and imaginative, their physical intimacy gentler and of shorter duration. Vita told Harold that she and Virginia slept together only twice. Given Virginia's nervous fragility, it is unlikely that Vita exaggerated their abstemiousness. Both women recognised the danger to Virginia's mental stability of any full-scale physical awakening. Virginia's inspiration for Vita was cerebral rather than sexual, 'a mental thing; a spiritual thing . . . an intellectual thing', as Vita explained to Harold:[64] her influence is clearest in *Seducers in Ecuador* and, to a lesser extent, *Gottfried Künstler*, allusive novellas that are indebted to Virginia's writing thematically and stylistically.

On her side, Vita inspired Virginia romantically, imaginatively, historically; on and off their letters tingle with the idea of sex. 'She is a pronounced Sapphist, and may . . . have an eye on me, old though I am,' wrote the forty-year-old Virginia, at the outset of their acquaintance.[65] 'I lie making lovely plans, all firelit and radiant,' Vita wrote to her on Christmas Day 1926. 'My bed's at least nine feet wide, and I feel like the Princess and the Pea, – only there is no Pea. It is a four-poster, all of which I like. Come and see for yourself.'[66] Vita's 'radiance', a byword for her easy sensuousness and commanding vigour, became a given between the two women; Vita labelled herself an 'honest sensualist'[67] and encouraged Virginia to project her fantasies on to her. In Virginia's last novel, *Between the Acts*, she itemised Vita's physical impact in her descriptions of Mrs Manresa: 'goddess-like, buoyant, abundant, her cornucopia running over'.[68]

Virginia's earlier novel *Orlando* is a celebration of what Vita meant to her. Vita's son Nigel Nicolson called it an extended love letter: undertaken once the flush of first intimacy had passed, it is also the literary equivalent of a shackle. It was Virginia's means of skewering Vita in print in order to possess at least a part of her in person and prolong indefinitely aspects of their closeness; she explained its inception as arising from an 'overmastering impulse'.[69] It is also a valediction, Virginia's permission to Vita to stray sexually. 'It was certain indeed that many ladies were ready to show [Orlando] their favours'; 'he was excessively generous both to women and to poets, and both adored him', Virginia writes: a nod from one woman to the other in this hybrid fantasy.[70]

Predictably Vita adored both *Orlando* and Orlando. She fell in love with a vision of herself that replicated in essentials personal fables stretching back to her childhood. As Virginia had read *Challenge*, which Vita loaned her in the summer of 1927, *Orlando* is partly inspired by Violet's vision of Vita as Julian: lover, Byronic hero, gypsy leader. It is a refinement of the Julian/Mitya/Dark Man myths of Vita's sexual history, coloured by the lascivious snobbery that Vita always stimulated in Virginia ('it's the breeding of Vita's that I took away with me as an impression', Virginia recorded of her first visit to Knole[71]). *Orlando* was the nearest Vita came to inheriting her father's house. The novel imagines Vita–Orlando as the sum of all her ancestors, every Sackville rolled into one through three centuries, and returns Knole to Vita as hers by right of temperament as well as birth. For all these reasons – romantic, narcissistic, possessive, proprietorial – Vita loved not only the book but its creator.

They met for the first time on 14 December 1922, at dinner with art critic Clive Bell, while Harold was in Lausanne. Virginia's diary betrays her curiosity about Vita; Vita's diary is blank. Three weeks earlier, Vita had published *Knole and the Sackvilles*, her second book of the year, following *The Heir*. Of the two of them, as Virginia was aware, Vita was the better-known, bigger-selling, commercially more successful author and would remain so throughout their friendship. But it was Virginia, proprietor with her husband Leonard of the Hogarth Press, publishers of T. S. Eliot, who had the reputation for cleverness.

Virginia's first impressions of Vita established from the outset the terms of their engagement: Virginia regarded her as a physical specimen and, under the influence of *Knole and the Sackvilles*, an embodiment of a social type; she dismissed her intellectually. Vita was 'florid, moustached, parakeet coloured, with all the supple ease of the aristocracy, but not the wit of the artist . . . The aristocratic manner is something like the actresses [sic] – no false shyness or modesty . . . She is a grenadier; hard; handsome; manly; inclined to double chin.'[72]

Virginia was intrigued. Vita, she noted, made her 'feel virgin, shy & schoolgirlish'; she observed that Vita knew 'everyone – But could I ever know her?' and accepted an invitation for the following week. She marvelled at Vita writing '15 pages a day' and clung doggedly to her conviction of her own superiority, however 'schoolgirlish', in the face of Vita's creative facility, her 'supple ease' and 'grenadier' manner. On 15 January, she referred to 'the new apparition Vita, who gives me a book every day'.[73] Something of that sneering tone would persist, though she would find that Vita did not warrant so spiky a dismissal. Virginia did not reveal in her diary that it was she who had requested from Vita copies of *Knole and the Sackvilles* and *Orchard and Vineyard*, did not mention, as Vita reported to Harold with dismay, the orange woollen tights and pumps that she had worn to Clive's dinner.

As ever, Vita made up her mind quickly. 'I simply adore Virginia Woolf, and so would you. You would fall quite flat before her charm and personality,' she wrote to Harold five days after their first meeting. She described her as simple, 'utterly unaffected', 'both detached and human' and told Harold candidly: 'I've rarely taken such a fancy to anyone . . . I have quite lost my heart.'[74] Correctly she surmised that Virginia reciprocated her *béguin*; she was unaware of the extent of Virginia's equivocation in private (even three years on, Virginia still characterised her feelings about Vita in her diary as 'very mixed'[75]). 'I like you a fabulous lot,' Vita wrote to Virginia frankly and straightforwardly in August 1924.[76] On both sides, albeit translated in time into a safely sexless *tendresse*, this fancy would endure.

Vita never doubted the importance of Virginia Woolf in her life. She swiftly came to occupy a place similar only to Harold's – that of an enriching, devoted friendship. 'I don't think I have ever loved anybody so much, in the way of friendship; in fact, of course, I know I haven't,' Vita told Harold four years after

she and Virginia met.[77] Only Enid Bagnold, novelist and playwright, came close to offering Vita friendship that resembled
her relationship with Virginia, and that on an altogether
different, lesser scale: a mutually supportive understanding
between women of shared literary aspirations, touched by love.
In Enid's case, she lacked Virginia's literary genius; the love
and admiration Vita felt for her were less pure, less selfless.
For all Vita claimed, 'I never loved you, Enid, save as a friend',
she may not have been wholly truthful.[78] In 1933, she wrote
to Enid of her 'qualms . . . a sudden horror and dismay' about
including in her *Collected Poems* 'that doggerel I once wrote to
you, which seemed to me not so bad as I reread it, and not too
terribly indiscreet either'.[79] Vita's friendship with Enid probably
included unresolved sexual tension on Vita's part; their closeness suffered after Enid's marriage to Sir Roderick Jones of
Reuters. By contrast, Virginia's marriage to Leonard served to
illuminate Vita's understanding of their relationship; Vita was
Leonard's friend too. The sexual aspect of their friendship
would be briefly but satisfactorily resolved without lasting
damage to Vita, Virginia, Harold or Leonard; innuendo added
liveliness to their correspondence, a shared joke, concord.

Vita had continued to work at her long poem *The Land*
throughout the upheavals of her affairs with Geoffrey and Pat;
along with *The Portrait of Zélide*, it formed part of the 'glue' of
her affair with Geoffrey. Now she discussed it with Virginia.
She divided the poem into four sections, named after the seasons
of the year; within each season were stand-alone elements. In
October 1923, the *London Mercury* printed 'Bee-master' from
Spring and 'Making Cider' from Autumn; Dottie wrote to
congratulate Vita on the former. It was prose, however, that
Vita chose when Virginia invited her to contribute to the
Hogarth Press. 'I hope that no one has ever yet, or ever will,
throw down a glove I was not ready to pick up,' Vita wrote by

way of reply on 16 July 1924. It was a characteristically gran-
diloquent response to what was in fact a commonplace request
that a professional writer write; it echoed the masterful rhetoric
of *The Tale of a Cavalier* and *The King's Secret*. From such statements would Virginia build up her picture of Orlando's swank.
Vita was with Harold in the Dolomites, the walking holiday
that had cut short Geoffrey's visit to Long Barn; on her return
she reshaped the holiday into an article for the *Evening Standard*.
'You asked me to write a story for you,' Vita wrote to Virginia.
'On the peaks of mountains, and beside green lakes, I am writing
it for you. I shut my eyes to the blue of gentians, to the coral
of androsace; I shut my ears to the brawling of rivers; I shut
my nose to the scent of pines; I concentrate on my story.'[80] The
result was *Seducers in Ecuador*, dedicated to Virginia, its contract
negotiated – to his annoyance – without the intervention of
Vita's new agent Alec Watt of A. P. Watt and Son, and published
to warm reviews on 30 October 1924 by the Hogarth Press.

To Alec Watt on 9 October, Vita called her novella 'a very
slight thing'.[81] Virginia's response was altogether more positive.
She recognised her own influence in the fantastical tale of a
man who retreats from reality behind coloured sunglasses, and
preened herself that Vita had 'shed some of the old verbiage,
and come to terms with some sort of glimmer of art . . . and
indeed, I rather marvel at her skill and sensitivity; for is she
not mother, wife, great lady, hostess, as well as scribbling?'.[82]
(Over time Virginia would continue to marvel at Vita's ability
to keep 'her hands loosely upon so many reins: sons; Harold;
garden; farm'.[83]) Vita delivered her manuscript in person.
Against the shabbiness of Monk's House – the Woolfs' white-
painted, weatherboarded house in the Sussex village of Rodmell
– Vita, with her smart car, expensive dressing case and night-
dresses wrapped by her lady's maid in sheets of tissue paper,
appeared particularly splendid to Virginia.

Her splendour aside, and discounting the flatteringly imita-
tive quality of *Seducers in Ecuador*, Virginia allowed herself to
venture no further than a tentative 'this might be a friendship
of a sort' in her diary.[84] Virginia's attitude to Vita continued to
waver. Vita decided Virginia was 'curiously feminist': 'She
dislikes possessiveness and love of domination in men. In fact
she dislikes the quality of masculinity. She says that women
stimulate her imagination, by their grace and their art of life.'[85]
For all her womanly plenitude, Vita provided ample evidence
of 'the quality of masculinity' in her possessiveness and love of
domination; as *Orlando* proves, her stimulation of Virginia had
little to do with grace. In Vita's company Virginia was moved
to 'childlike dazzled affection',[86] roused by what she described
in March 1926 as 'the glow and the flattery';[87] in her absence
a note of detachment, even reserve, asserted itself. Early in their
friendship, Virginia was hurt when Vita accused her of 'lik[ing]
people through the brain rather than through the heart';[88] it
was her means of maintaining her balance, but she worried that
Vita would hold it over her. In that she misjudged Vita.

As with Geoffrey Scott, Vita's decision to join Harold in
Tehran acted as a catalyst on Virginia. In Geoffrey's case, Vita's
departure provided final severance; in Virginia's case, fear of
that parting and its consequent loss of intimacy encouraged
her to decisive action. Virginia had been ill for much of the
summer and the women's meetings had been few and brief. In
December 1925, at Leonard's suggestion, Virginia proposed
herself for a visit to Long Barn. She stayed three days. Without
any conscious effort Vita dazzled her guest physically – 'she
shines in the grocer's shop in Sevenoaks with a candle-lit
radiance, stalking on legs like beech trees, pink glowing,
grape clustered, pearl hung'.[89] Vita felt confirmed in the
pleasure of Virginia's company, but wrote to Harold that, while
loving Virginia, she knew she would not fall in love with her.

The next day she added that her affection contained no 'back-stairs' (homosexual) element; the day after that she repeated her assurance that she was not in danger of falling in love with Virginia. So many emphatic denials might have worried Harold: he reassured Vita that he 'was not really bothered about Virginia and think you are probably very good for each other'.[90] On the second day of Virginia's visit, Vita's 'goodness' took the form of listening to her talk until three o'clock in the morning. 'Not a peaceful evening,' was Vita's comment in her diary. Their conversation roved widely, flirtatiously, amorously. Subsequently Vita referred to 'the explosion which happened on the sofa in my room here when you behaved so disgracefully and acquired me for ever'; Virginia described it as 'the night you were snared, that winter, at Long Barn'.[91] Without meaning to, Vita had snared Virginia too.

Vita spent her last afternoon before her departure for Persia with Virginia, crossing London to be with her after her farewell lunch with Geoffrey. In the evening, at Ebury Street, she read over Harold's latest letters. With her was writer Raymond Mortimer, himself a friend of the Woolfs and Harold's lover since 1924. He and Vita read the letters together.

Harold did not have to go to Tehran. He chose it over the alternative of Peking for Vita's sake. 'Of all foreign posts it will be the one Vita will dislike least,' he wrote in his diary.[92] He was right. But Vita's preferences were flimsy foundations on which to base important decisions about his career: her dislike of diplomacy was too marked, too unreasoned, her refusal to accompany Harold full time unorthodox in a diplomat's wife and potentially damaging. The truth was that Vita wanted Harold to have no career but her own one of writing – she described it as his 'legitimate' pursuit[93] – and her own pastime of gardening: 'You love foreign politics. And I love literature, and peace, and a secluded life. Oh my dear, my infinitely dear Hadji, you ought never to have married me.'[94] On the eve of another departure, Harold pleaded with her in vain that 'being parted is only like standing back from the picture to see it better'.[95] More successfully, in December 1925, he wrote requesting tulip and hyacinth bulbs, cuttings of rosemary and lavender for his new Persian garden. Vita dispatched a box of rosemary the week before Christmas.

Despite her 'muddles', Vita had done her best to make good her return to 'my house, my garden, my fields, and Harold' following her 'scarlet adventure'. She had published *Orchard and Vineyard*, with its poems about her relationship with Violet, including 'Bitterness', in which a lover is reluctantly 'rescued' from his mistress: 'Let your heart heal. Forget!/ She was your danger and your evil spirit';[96] she had published *The Dragon in Shallow Waters*, with its investigation of her own double nature and its dedication to Violet. Then she appeared to turn her back on rebellion. She wrote the history of Knole, the house she longed to call 'mine', and followed it with an edition of Lady Anne Clifford's diary; she wrote a love story, *The Heir*, about the joy of inheritance, and elevated the ecstasy of possession above sexual ecstasy: 'He suddenly stretched out his hands and passionately laid them, palms flattened, against the bricks.'[97]

In both subject and style, Vita's books proclaimed her return to the fold. Seven poems from *Orchard and Vineyard* were included in the fifth and final volume of *Georgian Poetry*, published in November 1922. They confirmed Vita's aesthetic credentials as those of a traditionalist and a conservative. When, the following year, her novel *Grey Wethers* appeared, with its rebellious heroine Clare Warrener who, 'like a hobbled colt . . . wanted to kick herself free' of conventional expectations,[98] no one but Harold would have understood Clare's struggle between acceptable love, represented by Calladine, and unacceptable love, in the person of Lovel, as an image of Vita's own life so recently at a crossroads. Only Harold knew that Vita was simultaneously Clare *and* Lovel and that each was characterised by incompleteness. He told Vita that ex-Viceroy Lord Curzon had described *Grey Wethers* as 'a magnificent book. The descriptions of the downs are as fine as any in the language. Such power! Such power! Not a pleasant book of course! But what English!'[99] Husband and wife avoided talking about the novel's ending, when Clare abandons her husband for her lover. For it is Clare, not Lovel, who suggests escape: '"We had better go," she said, inviting him.'[100]

'It's no use writing novels which are only the observations of life,' Harold had told Vita at the height of her unhappiness in September 1921, 'the point is to write books which are the explanation of life.'[101] Like *The Dragon in Shallow Waters,* and so much of her writing, *Grey Wethers* endeavoured to explain Vita to herself. It was not necessarily what Harold had intended, and confirmed his anxiety about Vita's weakness for striking heroic attitudes: 'No poet is a hero to himself (except my Vita who is a heroine to everyone including her own darling self).'[102] Uniquely Harold recognised the nature of Vita's inner struggle. With his dislike of confrontation, he mostly veered away from addressing the issue, save occasionally in his letters. Instead, between 1921 and 1924, he concentrated on his own writing. He wrote a novel, *Sweet Waters,* about diplomatic life in pre-war Constantinople; in the character of Eirene, it included a loose fictional sketch of Vita. He also wrote a clutch of literary biographies (of the poets Verlaine, Tennyson and Byron). He did so without as yet any intention of resigning from the Foreign Office.

In Harold's absences, and missing Violet, Vita spent time with her mother. The final unravelling of Lionel and Victoria's marriage was protracted and painful. For all his surface courtesy, Lionel did little to mitigate Victoria's unhappiness at his lost love. In November 1917, Victoria had discovered that Lionel had removed from his room her two portraits, which had hung there since 1889. She interpreted their removal correctly as symbolic and began to look about for an alternative house of her own.

She found the answer in a large townhouse in Sussex Square in Brighton. 'It was a huge house,' Vita remembered, 'a great echoing mausoleum of a house, with vast naked staircases and still vaster drawing rooms, large enough to accommodate four generations of descendants.'[103] Victoria was enchanted. Greedily she acquired the two neighbouring houses, both of equal size, and set about remodelling the charmless pile. The process was a costly one – airily Victoria estimated she had spent something in excess of £50,000 – but the result was a house of twenty-four bedrooms which, she explained to Vita, would make an ideal holiday house for Ben and Nigel. Vita was forced to acknowledge that there was something 'ripping' about the sheer scale of her mother's folly. Her own room, decorated in 1918, was papered in metallic emerald green, with sapphire blue doors and curtains, furniture painted the same bright blue and an apricot ceiling, a vigorous scheme inspired by the Ballets Russes settings of Léon Bakst, designer of *Scheherazade*. It was a far cry from the 'flowers, chintz and Jacobean furniture' of Long Barn, a dramatic and theatrical space closer to Violet's sultry eroticism than Vita's life of elkhounds and climbing roses; a last exercise in the decorative artifice of Vita's rooms at Knole and Hill Street in the years before her marriage and a window on to something unresolved in Vita.

Despite her expenditure and its size, Victoria meant at first to use the Brighton house only as a bolt hole. She took no more furniture from Knole than the bare minimum, transported in seven lorries. Events in April 1919, however, forced her hand. Victoria returned to Knole in the early evening. She went into the garden looking for Lionel, and discovered him with his mistress Olive Rubens. They were 'under one of the tulip trees,

O and L in each other's arms and kissing!! Just like any soldier and his girl in the park. I got away as quick as I could and tore to the sycamore seat.' The sight haunted her; she described it as an 'evil day' when Lionel fell in love with Olive; she returned to the memory again and again, unable to banish it: 'Oh, shade of that tulip tree, where they were kissing and hugging and God knows what, as I did not stop long enough to look.'[104] The final humiliation was Victoria's certainty that Lionel had seen her. Her 'Book of Happy Reminiscences' demonstrates the extent, and the longevity, of her anger at Lionel's betrayal. She exacted the only revenge left to her by mulishly refusing his repeated requests for a divorce.

From the moment of Victoria's final departure from Knole, on 19 May 1919, Vita's challenging relationship with her mother would be further complicated by this angry disaffection, which never went away, and a coruscating loneliness for which Vita felt in part responsible. In 1923, Victoria sold the house in Sussex Square at a loss of more than £45,000; she dispersed many of its contents in an equally unsuccessful two-day auction. She moved to the smaller White Lodge, on a cliff at Roedean perched above the English Channel, where Vita visited her assiduously. Bar a brief flirtation with an ugly red-brick villa standing in five acres close to Streatham Common, Victoria remained at White Lodge until her death.

Dottie was Vita's companion on 20 January 1926. Together they travelled from London via Egypt, Port Said and Aden as far as Agra and New Delhi, before Dottie turned back and Vita continued alone up the Persian Gulf to Baghdad and thence to Tehran and Harold. Vita left behind her Ben and Nigel, at preparatory school at Summer Fields in Oxford, and Virginia, to whom she gave a copy of her latest manuscript of *The Land*. In her diary the latter noted: 'I feel a lack of stimulus, of marked days, now Vita is gone; and some pathos, common to all these partings.'[105] Vita travelled with her jewel case and her emeralds, a fur coat and fur hat against the cold, Harold's statue of St Barbara, a flask of Dottie's best brandy and another copy of *The Land*, which she had almost completed. She carried messages from Victoria to Lutyens, with whom she had tea in Bombay on 12 February; within her she carried the idea of Virginia. 'I miss you horribly,' she insisted on 29 January. From now on Geoffrey would vanish from her consciousness. Pat's disappearance too was already becoming a memory; at intervals she wrote to Vita. Over time the list of former lovers who continued to write became a long one, proof of the strength of Vita's hold on their affections for all that her *béguins* were transitory.

On the SS *Varela*, from Bombay through the Persian Gulf to Baghdad, Vita fell ill with fever. It did nothing to diminish her sense of her journey as an adventure and, on 20 February, goaded into writing by envy at Virginia's descriptions of progress on *To the Lighthouse*, she recorded her start on 'my new book'. It became *Passenger to Teheran*, a chronicle of Vita's four-month odyssey, published by the Hogarth Press in November. An instance of her need to separate distinct aspects of experience, Vita discusses landscape, impressions of Egypt, India and Persia, Persian culture, the diplomatic life of the British legation and the coronation of Reza Shah, but makes no mention of Dottie. On the printed page Vita travels alone, hers as solitary a progress as Orlando's. Dottie was understandably infuriated.

Passenger to Teheran is an account of a love affair. Out of sight of Virginia and Dottie, disentangled from Geoffrey and Pat, as sanguine now as she would ever be where Violet was concerned, Vita fell in love with Persia. She thrilled to its visible reminders of a past that, compared with English history, seemed infinitely distant; she noted the features of Persian gardens, with their flowering Judas trees and peach blossom, and water rills lined with rich blue tiles; and she rejoiced, outside the legation compound, in the open spaces, the expansiveness of a landscape that extended infinite possibilities of solitary escape. 'One is allowed to be lonely . . . in more civilised communities no one is allowed to be lonely; the refinement of loneliness is not understood.'[106] The same impression stirred Vita to poetry: 'Are there not hearts that find their high fulfilment/ Alone?' she asked, anticipating her own future reclusiveness; in the poems she wrote about Persia, Vita celebrated isolation as 'pure'.[107] When she came home, she wrote verses about a migrating English swallow glimpsed against the red rocks of the Persian desert; so long as she remained away, she found it impossible to acknowledge the reality of England.[108]

Like all Vita's affairs, first love for Persia was intense but brief. She returned early in 1927, before Harold's final departure; together they journeyed into the Bakhtiari mountains to visit the tomb of Cyrus the Great. Their expedition formed the substance of *Twelve Days*, Vita's second Persian travel book. While both books include passages that are among Vita's best – lyrical, insightful and colourful – the later account also records the disillusionment that seized her when she saw the Abadan oilfields and confronted face to face the unromantic reality of Persia's future: an end of sorts to the affair.

In February 1926, Vita stayed in Baghdad with Arabist and archaeologist Gertrude Bell. Bell took her to tea with the King of Iraq, whom Vita reimagined in her own image as her classic fictional hero: 'a tall, dark, slim, handsome man, looking as though he were the prey to a romantic, an almost Byronic, melancholy'.[109] She acquired a Saluki puppy, 'a marvel of elegance, – long tapering paws, and a neck no thicker than your wrist',[110] and met Harold in Kermanshah; at the very end of Vita's life, Harold singled out 'the great moment at Kermanshah' as a shining nugget of happiness. Husband and wife travelled the last 300 miles of the journey together, the yellow Saluki curled on Vita's knee. On arrival, Vita dismissed Tehran as squalid; she reacted predictably to the prescriptive formalities of European life in the compound and what she described to Virginia as the 'eventless weeks',[111] but she was happy in her reunion with Harold and fascinated and delighted by Persia as a whole. With an appearance of good grace, if limited anticipation of enjoyment, she accompanied Harold to entertainments connected with the forthcoming coronation of the new shah; she shared the Persians' excitement at celebratory fireworks. There were moments of freedom too. Every morning at seven, Vita and Harold went riding, dazzled by 'the freshness and beauty of the morning', and to Virginia, Vita described 'days of going into the mountains, and eating sandwiches beside a stream, and picking wild almonds, and of coming home by incredible sunsets across the plain'.[112]

There was a makeshift quality to diplomatic life in Tehran, and indeed to Reza Shah's monarchy, that surprised Vita: ahead of the coronation, she found herself mixing paints in the great hall of the Gulestan Palace and advising on the peach-coloured distemper of the throne room walls. She was invited to see the crown jewels. 'Knowing too well by now the shabby condition of everything in this ramshackle country, I was not very much excited at the prospect of seeing the treasury of imperial Iran.'[113] The experience astonished her. Green and gold, it glittered in her memory. It would remain vivid in its otherworldliness, a direct appeal to that side of Vita that had revelled in *Scheherazade* and decorated her room in Brighton in jewel-like, Bakst-inspired colours. She likened the treasury to Aladdin's Cave: in Persia, fact and fable merged. 'I am blind. Blinded by diamonds,' she wrote. 'Sacks of emeralds were emptied out before our eyes. Sacks of pearls. Literally. We came away shaking the pearls out of our shoes. Ropes of uncut emeralds. Scabbards encrusted with precious stones. Great hieratic crowns. All this in a squalid room, with grubby Persians drinking little cups of tea . . . It was simply the Arabian Nights, with décor by the Sitwells.'[114]

Vita discovered a different story in Persia, too, though sharing an element of transformation: that of nineteenth-century French archaeologist's wife and cross-dresser, Jane Dieulafoy. She recounted her history in *Vogue*: '"What," said the Shah, "is that boy a woman?" On being assured that it was so . . . Why, he enquired, was she not dressed in the long skirts and garments of European ladies? Jane replied that she found man's dress more convenient.'[115] At the beginning of April, Vita wrote teasingly about Madame Dieulafoy to Virginia: an arrow shot in their extended, long-distance flirtation. She labelled her simply 'a ravishing character'.[116]

Vita began her fortnight-long journey home on 4 May. With her she carried iris and tulip bulbs plundered from the Persian plains. She potted them up in Dottie's greenhouse at Sherfield and wrote to Harold on 12 October to report on their progress. The previous month she had sent Harold his own consignment of spring bulbs: tulips, scilla and *Iris reticulata*, which she instructed him to plant in a shallow bowl to flower in February. In return she asked for cuttings of wild broom, sage and pink-flowered lavender, packed in damp moss and sealed in a biscuit tin. She sent him *Passenger to Teheran* in proof form and a copy of *The Land*, which Heinemann published on 30 September; she had written the last ten lines in Isfahan in April.

Harold praised both books generously, though he was hurt by *The Land*'s dedication to Dottie, who is also the subject of the poem's best-known section, 'The Island', about the gardener of the manmade island in the lake at Sherfield, 'laughing at her flowery escapade'.[117] 'It is such a lovely thing, darling, so beautiful a thing,' Harold wrote on 7 November. That opinion was echoed by *The Land*'s reviewers. Fellow poet John Drinkwater

claimed in the *Observer* that 'it contain[ed] some of the loveliest
verse written in this century';[118] on the strength of a similar
review, Vita announced in her diary that she had 'started writing
a poem about gardens' (the partner poem to *The Land*, which
would eventually be published in 1946 as *The Garden*).[119] But
it was Virginia's view that resonated loudest. She had read *The
Land* while Vita was in Tehran and written that it lacked 'a
little central transparency: Some sudden intensity.'[120] In
November, she suggested that the absence was in Vita as much
as in her writing, a void, 'something reserved, muted'.[121] This
verdict haunted Vita. At the end of the year, despite Heinemann
ordering a reprint of the poem and indications (which would
be proved right) that it would win her the Hawthornden Prize,
Vita sat down to write a poem that reveals the extent of her
uncertainty about her abilities. 'What have I gathered?' she
asked in 'Year's End', weighing up not only the passing year
but her working life in its entirety. The only answer she could
give herself was 'one unprofitable naught'. Despondently the
poem ends with a question: 'Shall I not clear my goods and
quit the ring?'[122] It was a markedly different Vita from the
woman who had told Virginia she would always be ready to
pick up any glove thrown down. She did not quit the ring,
though she set aside *The Garden*. Throughout the following
summer her letters to Virginia increased their provocative,
teasing note. If she could not triumph as a writer, she would
insist on her superiority as a woman.

A string of blue Persian beads bought for sixpence coiled on
Vita's writing table at Long Barn. 'Now, in a bowl, in exile,
they/ Speak Persia to an English day,' she wrote in 'A Bowl of
Blue Beads'. She added that the beads proved 'that Persia is no
lovely lie/ For me, but sharp reality'.[123] Except in her relationships with Harold and Virginia, it was physical proof that for
Vita kept love alive. The idea of Persia remained a powerful one,

even if her excursion to the Bakhtiari mountains shattered some illusions. At the time of her death, among the debris on Vita's desk was a packet of seeds: Sutton's wallflowers, Persian Carpet.[124]

In the winter of 1927, a young woman with raven hair and pale skin was painting a picture of Long Barn. It is a truncated image which simplifies the outline of Vita and Harold's garden and reduces in length the barn that had become the Big Room.

Her name was Mary Campbell. Physically she resembled Ruth Pennistan in *Heritage*, an untamed Romany beauty invariably dressed in coloured breeches and a velvet cloak; hers was a restless, rebellious, unconventional nature. The eldest of nine children of a wealthy Midlands doctor, she had studied art at Heatherleys and, six years previously, in a long black dress and golden veil, married penniless South African poet Roy Campbell. Vita met her in the post office in Sevenoaks Weald on 22 May. Roy was there too: tall, thin, blue-eyed. He was also hard-drinking and intemperate, but Vita could not have known that on first meeting. Vita invited them to dinner the following day.

Vita and Roy Campbell shared a weakness for bravado. 'We never kiss but vaster shapes possess/ Our bodies: towering up into the skies,/ We wear the night and thunder for our dress,' Roy wrote in his poem, 'We are Like Worlds'. Vita would discover that they also shared a weakness for sexual jealousy. Roy had fallen in love with Mary Garman at first sight, describing the experience as an 'electric thrill'; his was a possessive, aggressive, angry love and his ideas of marriage, he explained later, were 'old-fashioned about wifely obedience'.[125] Vita had read and partly admired the collection of poems Roy Campbell published in 1924, *The Flaming Terrapin*, which she discussed in letters to Virginia. The book failed to sell. With an income of £20 a month following the death of Roy's father, a baby, Anna, and a three-year-old daughter Tess, the Campbells

struggled financially. Vita turned their heads, Virginia repri-
manded her afterwards, 'with her silver, and her coronets, and
her footmen'.[126] Cynically Mary referred to Vita as 'our latest
acquisition . . . the daughter of Lord Sackville'.[127]

As May gave way to June, Vita continued to work on *Twelve
Days*. She began her short biography of Aphra Behn, which she
completed in nine weeks despite the inevitable disturbances of
Ben and Nigel's summer holidays, visits to and from Dottie at
Sherfield and Virginia at Rodmell, a daily tally of lunch and
dinner invitations. At the end of August she and Harold heard
to their horror that the Foreign Office intended sending Harold
to Budapest (he refused the posting and was ordered to Berlin
instead); both worked out their uncertainty about the future
through gardening. Vita decided to spend the £100 she received
for the Hawthornden Prize on 16 June on new plantings of hazel
and poplar in the woods at Long Barn. Observing her daughter's
appearance of happiness at a similar moment of quietus, Victoria
imagined she had glimpsed emotional tranquillity after recent
tempests. Darkly she noted then: 'She seems contented now, but
the Volcano is there, ready to burst into flame, I am sure.'[128] In
the summer of 1927 Victoria was proved right.

The previous August, Vita had reassured Harold that her
friendship with Virginia was not about to develop into one of
her 'muddles'. 'I *have* gone to bed with her (twice), but that's
all,' she wrote, referring to a visit to Rodmell earlier in the
summer. In stark terms she explained, 'I am scared to death
of arousing physical feelings, because of the madness.'[129] Harold
praised her restraint: 'it's not merely playing with fire; it's
playing with gelignite'.[130] If Vita wanted physical stimulation
– and she invariably did – she needed to look elsewhere.

What Victoria mistook for settledness was lingering discon-
tent. In Tehran at the end of February, Vita had reflected on
an unhappy month: 'Very depressed all this month owing to

1) inability to write, 2) fear of Hadji continuing in diplomacy. The Foreign Office says he will have to come back in September for another year. God help us! I had hoped to find him disgusted with exile and social duties, but it is quite the contrary.'[131] Vita's assessment fell wide of the mark. Harold's diary records a morning during Vita's second visit to Tehran when he woke up 'with a conviction that I shall chuck the diplomatic service. I have been fussing and worrying about this problem for months.'[132] Nothing came of his first attempt at change. An interview with Sir John Cadman, chairman of Anglo-Persian Oil, failed to produce the hoped-for offer of a job in the company's London offices. It was Vita's hopes, as much as Harold's, that were dashed.[133] With plenty to occupy her, Vita did not immediately focus her attention on the Campbells following their meeting in the post office. Mary went to Long Barn for tea a fortnight after the first dinner invitation; three weeks later, she and Roy returned to dinner, this time in company with Vita's cousin Eddy and Bloomsbury writer David Garnett. Roy dined alone at Long Barn in July and, on 22 August, Vita went for tea with Mary. That invitation was reciprocated within less than a week; three days later, Mary appeared at Long Barn in the evening and she and Vita went for a walk. In Vita's diary she remained 'Mrs Campbell'.

And so it might have continued, if Mary had not declared her hand as Vita drove her to the station on the morning of Friday, 2 September. Unsettled and evidently surprised, Vita frittered the following day in idleness, 'unable to read or write, upset about MC'.[134] Ten days later, the women had become lovers: the volcano burst into flame and Vita, as she imagined herself later, was straying again in 'whispering galleries . . ./ That like a sea-cave or a fluted shell/ Reverberate with love's whole ocean swell'.[135]

Vita was heroic, reckless. 'Love's the lion that with golden eyes/ Shames the unruly pack and makes them cower,' she trumpeted with the braggadocio that came naturally to her in the grip of one of her *béguins*.[136] Then Nigel came down with influenza and a temperature of 102. For a single night Vita parted from Mary. At considerable risk of detection, they spent the following night together at Long Barn – in the small room next door to the room into which Vita had moved Nigel. The next night she and Mary again had sex in the room beside Nigel's. It became a repeating pattern: Mary spending nights with Vita whenever Roy went to London – and neither woman told their husband. 'I have just acquired a new friend who takes up all my time while Roy is working,' Mary wrote obliquely.[137] Vita was excited and persuaded herself that her excitement was love: Mary's feelings ran deeper. Like all Vita's lovers until Evelyn Irons, there was a neediness in Mary Campbell. She told Vita that she was 'sometimes like a mother to [her]. No one can imagine the tenderness of a lover suddenly descending to being maternal. It is a lovely moment when the mother's voice and hands turn into the lover's.'[138]

Their idyll lasted two months. On 1 October, after the beginning of the school term, the Campbells moved into Ben and Nigel's cottage, to live there rent-free. Five weeks later, Roy told Vita he knew about their affair. It was a tit-for-tat announcement: in the same breath he revealed his own affair with Geoffrey Scott's old flame, Dorothy Warren. Later his mood changed and a frightened Mary briefly returned from the cottage to Vita. That night, Roy's threats alternated between suicide and murder. It was the beginning of what he later called a 'comically sordid and silly period'; he denounced 'vice' as 'a sort of obligation for board and lodging'.[139]

Without revealing her own part in the affair, Vita wrote to Harold in Berlin, updating him on the progress of the Campbells' rapidly unravelling marriage. 'I think he is absolutely crazy. I feel most frightfully sorry for Mary. He went for her last night with a knife.'[140] Three days later, Vita reported, his anger was more focused. He had offered Mary two alternatives: a suicide pact on the one hand, both of them slashing their wrists with Roy's razor; on the other, Roy's own suicide or his return to South Africa. Mary allowed herself to waver. Uncontrite, she was anxious only to be reunited with Vita and 'naked except for a covering of your rose leaf kisses';[141] Vita congratulated herself on the calming effect on Roy of her own presence and her arguments in favour of moderation. Meanwhile Harold, contemplating his marriage long distance and distracted by lunch in Berlin with Noël Coward, stuck to his conviction 'that our love and confidence is absolute'.[142] On the evening Mary fled from Roy's anger, Dottie was at Long Barn. She kept watch through the night with a shotgun across her knee. 'Gin-soaked, a shot-gun in her clutches/ The Fury was a future duchess,' Roy commented later in verse.[143]

Vita confided the truth of the 'muddle' to Virginia, whose response was sharply critical. 'I felt suddenly that the whole of my life was a failure,' Vita wrote of her chastisement.[144] She had failed to reckon with the importance attached by Bloomsbury to relationships: in Vita's tangled amorousness, Virginia saw only bungling and an inability to commit herself wholeheartedly to any single individual (herself included). Privately Virginia admitted that she was jealous; she told Vita she hated being bored, but gave herself away in her letters: 'heart you have none, who go gallivanting down the lanes with Campbell'.[145] Virginia knew of the night Vita had recently spent with Mary Hutchinson, Clive Bell's former lover; she suspected the young actress Valerie Taylor, who had fallen in love with Vita and kept her talking late into the summer nights, or dressed up as Byron for Vita's titillation. Confronted by Virginia's disappointment, Vita cried, admitted her incapacity for 'creating one single perfect relationship', and swiftly reassured herself: 'Well, at least I won't create any further mistakes!' It was a vain hope.

Roy dropped his plans to divorce Mary and wrote soberly but resignedly to Vita that he was tired of trying to hate her. 'I realise that there is no way in which I could harm you (as I would have liked to) without equally harming us all. I do not dislike any of your personal characteristics and I liked you very much before I knew anything. All this acrimony on my part is due rather to our respective positions in the tangle.'[146] He and Vita agreed to a halt in Vita's affair with Mary and a semblance of normality was restored. Vita frenziedly wrote sonnets about Mary ('a sort of catharsis,' she explained to Harold[147]), Mary began her painting of Long Barn and Roy internalised his anger. He would mine its rich seam to devastating effect in what he called 'a satirical fantasy in verse', *The Georgiad*, published in 1931. Although the satire of *The Georgiad* roves widely through the Bloomsbury Group, Harold and Vita feature prominently. Roy's depiction of the 'frowsy poetess' Vita – 'too gaunt and bony to attract a man' – indicates the damage Vita had inflicted on his sexual vanity.[148] With some justification, the poem deprecated Harold and Vita broadcasting on the radio 'about married life,/ As if their life were one protracted kiss,/ And they the models of connubial bliss'.[149] As late as 1952, Vita declined an invitation to a Foyle's lunch for Stephen Spender 'because I didn't fancy the idea of meeting Roy Campbell'.[150]

With a degree of understatement, Harold had recently warned Vita that she lacked a happy touch where married couples were concerned. He resisted reminding her of this warning and instead did his best to restore her equilibrium. He countered Virginia's criticism by pointing to their marriage as proof of her 'genius for *durable* relationships', indicated as well her relationships with Dottie, the children, her parents.

In the middle of December, Vita spent five days with Harold in Berlin, letters of protest from Mary following in her wake; on her return she persuaded Roy to go on living in the cottage. To her diary Vita confided that she was 'very depressed at leaving [Harold] alone in that beastly place [Berlin]'; her dislike of the German capital would grow.[151] Neither Harold nor Vita had any idea that one of Vita's 'durable' relationships was about to end, with long-lasting consequences for Vita. At the relatively young age of sixty-one, Lionel was weeks away from death.

Lionel Sackville-West, 3rd Baron Sackville, died on 28 January 1928 of pericarditis (inflammation round the heart). Knole passed by ancient right to Vita's Uncle Charlie and his American wife, Anne, whom Vita loathed. Bar a handful of occasions, she would never return and so her mythologising of Knole became complete: it was the house of her memories, the house in her dreams, a region of fantasy and her own perfect panacea. 'I dream quite often about Knole. I dream about the deer galloping down the stable passage, their hooves rattling on the wood boards,' she wrote in her Dream Book. 'I like this dream. I like any dream that takes me back to Knole. I wish I dreamt oftener about Knole . . . I wish I did. It used to be a sort of substitute for not going there.'[152]

Lionel had been attended by Sir Thomas Horder, a 'short, friendly specialist in cancer and heart disease' with a roster of royal clients, and nursed at Knole by Olive Rubens and Vita, who described him as suffering 'agonies of pain'.[153] Victoria's wretchedness at his death focused at first on these nursing arrangements: it was Vita, henceforth labelled 'the Vipa' in her mother's diary, who bore the brunt of her anger. Vita made arrangements for Lionel's funeral and his burial in the family chapel at Withyam church: cart horses drew his coffin. She also answered more than three hundred letters of condolence and conceived a novella, *The Death of Noble Godavary*, about heredity, inheritance and the destruction of an ancient family home by an outsider of mixed blood (like Victoria, and indeed Vita herself). 'It is a dismal affair for her,' Virginia wrote to Eddy Sackville-West, son of the new Lord Sackville and now heir to Knole; 'and your aunt's [Victoria's] behaviour could only be tolerated in an Elizabethan play. That she might take a dagger to her own throat or drink broken glass is rather my hope.'[154]

Virginia's thoughts were running on Elizabethan history. At the time of Lionel's death she reported herself 'hacking rather listlessly at the last chapter' of *Orlando*.[155] Its publication in October would offer Vita consolation of sorts in this year of dispossession when Knole slipped irretrievably from her grasp. 'When she left the house behind the old carthorses, she went for ever,' Virginia reported Vita telling her in the aftermath of Lionel's funeral. Virginia was sympathetic if detached: 'Can one really be in love with a house?'[156] But *Orlando* made good Vita's symbolic return.[157]

Accurately Harold told Vita that it was a book 'in which you and Knole are identified for ever, a book which will perpetuate that identity into years when you and I are dead'.[158] Vita described it as containing 'romance, wit, seriousness, lightness, beauty, imagination, style'.[159] Since all those qualities belong not only to the novel but to Orlando himself, she could not help but be flattered. Virginia's diary records *Orlando*'s critical reception and its commercial success: she does not dwell on Vita's reaction. Perhaps she knew she could take her excitement for granted, so accurate is her realisation of Vita's mythomania. Photographs of Vita were included among *Orlando*'s illustrations – Vita as a portrait by Lely, as a Victorian and in modern times, beside a five-bar gate at Long Barn; she was its dedicatee and identified in reviews. Lesbian novelist Radclyffe Hall, who did not know her, wrote to Vita on 16 December 1928 after seeing her, 'it must have been you because it was someone who looked so exactly like Orlando'.[160]

To Virginia, Vita signed her ecstatic, admiring, respectful letter of thanks for a special leather-bound copy of the novel, which arrived a day ahead of publication, 'Orlando'. In September the women had spent six days together in France, as a result of which Vita considered that both she and her friendship with Virginia had been regenerated (Virginia, by contrast, spent much of the time missing Leonard, but concluded that Vita was not as unintelligent as she had assumed). During the summer, Vita had signed her notes to Mary Campbell with the same alias. *Orlando* helped Vita face the altered reality of life without Knole after her father's death; in providing another mask in her romantic armoury, it helped her to escape again into unreality.

Of the two readers who complained about *Orlando* to Vita, Victoria railed against what she interpreted as Virginia's lesbian agenda and her desire to separate Vita and Harold, and Mary lamented the passionlessness of Virginia's portrait. 'Orlando is too safe too sexless and too easy-going to be really like you, but then I am thinking of him as he appears to *me* . . . Ah an entire book about Orlando with no mention of her deep fiery sensuality – that strange mixture of fire and gloom and heat and cold – seems to *me* slightly pale.'[161]

Vita's relations with both women were in a state of flux. In the third week of February, while Roy remained incapacitated following an operation for appendicitis, Vita had resumed her affair with Mary. There were passionate nights and more poems on Vita's part, but the giddiness of first infatuation had passed. In April, Roy left the cottage for Martigues in the South of France; like Geoffrey's initial parting from Sybil, it was understood as a trial separation. Roy wrote to Mary constantly, imploring her to join him. On 11 May, Mary did so. She was still in love with Vita but recognised now, like other lovers before and after, the gulf between her own feelings and Vita's. As ever, Vita channelled her feelings into the safe containment of the written word. *King's Daughter*, published in 1929 and the last of Vita's collections of verse, captured the lights and shades of this vanished *béguin*: 'Time was our banker once . . ./ Now he's turned sour, and our account does edit.'[162] Harold disliked the poems' overt lesbianism and advised against publication; Virginia overruled his reservations. Vita also wrote a short story based on the affair for a women's magazine. The Roy of the story, treated sympathetically by the narrator, shoots himself.

There would be no similar disappearance on Victoria's part: instead, a hiatus in relations between mother and daughter. This came about on 18 April 1928, the short-term cause a 'terrible scene' in the office of the Sackville family solicitors.

For too long Victoria had exploited the money that came to her from Seery as an unwieldy instrument of power. Houses, jewels, Rolls-Royce motor cars, furniture, tapestries, gardeners, school fees and tax bills all fell within the remit of her munificence when she wished it. But her character was mercurial: the fairy godmother was also a witch. On this occasion Victoria's fury focused on twelve extra pearls she had added to the pearl necklace that was Vita's posthumous twenty-first birthday present from Seery. She surprised Vita at Pemberton's, signing documents. Amid floods of 'the vilest abuse . . . like a mad woman, screaming Thief and Liar, and shaking her fist at me till I thought she was going to hit me', Victoria demanded the return of her dozen pearls.[163]

'She was made to take the pearl necklace from her neck, cut it in two with a pocket knife, deliver over the 12 central pearls [and] put the relics, all running loose, in an envelope the

solicitor gave her,' an incredulous Virginia noted in her diary.[164]
Victoria had retreated to the comfort of her Rolls-Royce. Vita
followed her. Outside, amid the clangour of the London street,
she broke apart the necklace and handed over the pearls.
Victoria screamed that she hated her, hoped she would die then
and there, that very minute, standing in the street, run over
by a bus. Then she sent her secretary after Vita into Pemberton's
office to demand the return of all the other jewels she had ever
given her: they were to be brought to her room at The Savoy
the following morning and Vita would wait outside in the
corridor while Victoria made her inventory. Vita agreed to
their return, but refused to be treated 'like a servant' in a hotel
corridor. When the breathless Victoria began to abuse Harold,
Vita took refuge in a taxi. The episode lasted from 12.30 to
2.15, almost two hours of unremitting invective, and created
a rift that lasted until February 1930, when, symbolically,
Victoria returned to Vita the twelve contested pearls. Of greater
significance to the Nicolsons than the shortening of Vita's pearl
necklace was Vita's decision to give up the allowance Victoria
paid her. At a single blow, Harold and Vita found not only
Vita's pearl necklace but their income drastically reduced.

In a letter to Harold that evening, Vita described the morning's events with as much calmness as she could muster; her
diary is laconic. At lunch with Raymond Mortimer afterwards,
she drank half a bottle of Champagne. She spent the afternoon
at London Zoo with a supportive Virginia. In the evening, for
the first time, Vita broadcast live for the BBC. It was an unset-
tling preliminary to this important new development in her
career.

Vita fell in love at the BBC. As with other *béguins*, her fancy
was generously rewarded. The relationship she embarked on
with Director of Talks Hilda Matheson took a familiar course:

obsession, physical rhapsody, letters, concealment, a holiday
abroad, friendship after the damping of the flames. Hilda's self-
effacement prevented it from becoming a 'muddle'. 'I want you
to love me – to have me – to possess me utterly – I want to
give myself to you,' Hilda wrote to Vita on 15 January 1929;
she offered Vita adulation, devotion, submission. Her love was
physical as well as emotional: 'My body is yours as my heart
is yours . . . sometimes I want you so terribly physically that
I can hardly bear it.'[165] Hilda fell in love with a private Vita,
'the most beautiful person that's ever swept across my horizon';
she loved the public Vita too, the acclaimed novelist and poet,
the Vita who, in April 1930, after the death of Robert Bridges,
was considered for the position of Poet Laureate.[166] Vita called
Hilda 'Stoker' (Virginia claimed the name was Harold's). It
suggested the hard-working stoker men of steam engines, an
appropriate moniker for Hilda, who shunned the limelight,
happiest in reflected rays. And Vita returned Hilda's love. Then
the moment passed and Hilda the lover became Hilda the friend.

They met on 18 April and again on 4 June, when Vita read
passages from *The Land*. Hilda wrote to congratulate Vita on
that broadcast; Vita returned the compliment three weeks later
after listening 'with the tears pouring down my face' to Robert
Harris read Shelley's 'Ode to the West Wind' and 'Ode to a
Nightingale'.[167] Hilda invited Vita to discuss broadcasting
poetry; Vita invited Virginia to accompany her to the BBC.
Hilda spent a weekend in July at Long Barn: in Vita's diary
she was still 'Miss Matheson'.

On 2 October, Vita broadcast the first of six talks on 'Modern
English Poetry'. By the following May she had begun the
fortnightly radio reviews of new fiction that would continue
until December 1931 (after which, for the next year, Vita shared
with former literary editor of the *New Statesman*, Desmond
MacCarthy, a half-hour-long slot, 'Literary Criticism'). Vita

received ten guineas a broadcast, with an additional payment for subsequent publication in the *Radio Times* or *The Listener*. Hilda was Vita's producer; the women met regularly and often. Elaborating her invitation to Vita to 'contemplate a fortnightly review of new novels' in January 1929, Hilda wrote: 'It would be so perfect from my point of view – excuse for your coming to my office, benefit untold to my listeners, prestige of the most exalted kind for the BBC.'[168] By then, for both of them, the first reason carried the day.

They became lovers in December 1928. Vita broadcast a discussion on 'The Position of Women Today' with novelist Hugh Walpole who, a decade earlier, had loaned Vita and Violet his cottage in Polperro. Hilda and Hugh spent the preceding weekend at Long Barn; broadcast over, Vita spent the night in Hilda's flat in South Kensington. The morning after, Hilda stayed with Vita, too faint to go to work. The same day she sent Vita her first love letter. 'I love you more than ever I can tell you . . . it's the most completely comprehensive sweep I ever dreamed of, all of me, in every sort of different way. I bless you and Heaven and creatures generally for having made it possible for this to happen; and you in particular . . . for being so perfect and so good to me, and most of all for loving me.'[169] Wholeheartedly, Vita returned Hilda's love. It was obvious even in her letters to Harold. It was also obvious, and a source of disgruntlement, to Dottie, whom Vita continued to see regularly. Hilda wrote to Vita and Vita, with her customary zeal, wrote back, fifty letters in a matter of weeks.[170] Following Vita's departure on 19 December for Berlin and Christmas and the New Year with Harold and the boys, Hilda wrote up to three times a day. Their intimacy then was a novelty. 'Here we are writing to each other every day, without any apparent barriers or obstacles or reserve . . . I have this incredible feeling of naturalness and absence of shyness or reserve or *anything* towards you,' Hilda marvelled.[171] As Vita had predicted, in the short term they came to know one another better on paper than in person.

Hilda's letters punctuated a five-day visit to Berlin in the middle of January by Virginia and Leonard. They were joined by Duncan Grant, Virginia's sister Vanessa Bell and her nephew Quentin. It was an unsatisfactory visit, pressed on Virginia by Vita. The day after Virginia's departure, Vita began writing *Gottfried Künstler*, 'a story about skating' influenced by Virginia's descriptions of the Great Frost in *Orlando*. Vita dedicated it to Hilda. It was all grist to the mill of Virginia's jealousy.

Virginia Woolf deplored Hilda Matheson as an 'earnest middle-class intellectual . . . drab and dreary'.[172] To Vita she wrote: 'She affects me as a strong purge, as a hair shirt, as a foggy day, as a cold in the head.'[173] She parried Hilda's invitations that she too should broadcast for the BBC, gave in with all ill grace, delivered a talk on Beau Brummell in November 1929, claimed that Hilda had made her 'castrate Brummell' and, broadcast over, 'poured . . . rage hot as lava over Vita'; she was determined not to be considered alongside Hilda and Dottie as part of Vita's 'second-rate' schoolgirl clique.[174] Vita admitted the validity of the criticism but remained loyal to the loyal Hilda.

Hilda stayed at Long Barn in the spring, when Vita started writing *Andrew Marvell*, the first of a new series launched by Faber & Faber called 'The Poets on The Poets'. Vita had begun collecting budgerigars: her diary records a gift of two birds from Deirdre Hart-Davis. For three days in the middle of April, Vita and Hilda made an aviary; after Hilda's departure, Vita finished it with Ben. The next week Virginia was with Vita when she bought a pair of blue budgerigars. On a rainy night in May, Vita stayed with Hilda in London after broadcasting: she excused herself on grounds of the weather. A fortnight later it was Hilda, not Ben and Nigel, who inaugurated the new swimming pool built at Long Barn by Harold. In June, Vita's first budgerigar chicks were born; her excitement was in line with her fondness for rabbits and dogs, derided by Violet. The radio discussion on marriage Vita broadcast in the middle of the month with Harold, who was briefly at home on leave, would also have provoked Violet to derision. Ditto a follow-up discussion on happiness, broadcast in April 1930.

Vita travelled with Hilda to Savoie and Val d'Isère in July; clumsily she attempted to lessen Virginia's jealousy by presenting the holiday as a last-minute decision. In France she wrote a pair of poems for Hilda. 'Storm in the Mountains (Savoy)' and 'Peace in the Mountains (Savoy)' are landscape descriptions like the poem she had once written for Pat, but lacking the earlier poem's ambiguity: colourful, pictorial, post-cards in verse. Vita was reading Ethel Colburn Mayne's newly published *The Life of Lady Byron*, which thrilled her. It drew on previously unpublished sources, among them letters from Byron to different, jealous lovers; Vita's diary does not record any train of reflection set in motion as a result. The high point of the trip had nothing to do with Hilda. 'Came down in the morning and found a very exciting letter from Hadji saying he had been offered a job by Lord Beaverbrook,' Vita reported.[175] Four days later, Harold sent more details. On 1 August, having parted from Hilda, Vita met Harold in Karlsruhe for 'endless discussions about Beaverbrook!'.[176] She described the news to Virginia as 'a happy bombshell'.[177]

Lord Beaverbrook was the proprietor of the *Evening Standard* and the *Daily Express*. He offered Harold £3,000 a year to join the staff of the *Standard*. Harold requested a higher figure and his political independence and was granted the latter.[178] Vita was delighted. In her diary the previous summer, she had written herself a memorandum: 'Many discussions with H as to our future. He seems determined to remain in diplomacy, and quite cheerfully contemplates years spent in foreign capitals. Don't think he realises in the least what this means to me – and I don't want him to.'[179] Virginia shared Vita's pleasure. For his part, Harold suspected he was trading the certainty of an embassy for moonshine. It was a suspicion that would never leave him. He lamented 'the tug always at my heart of diplomacy in all its forms', but contemplated with pleasure a life in which there would be no more lengthy separations from Vita and the boys.[180] His contract with Beaverbrook began on 1 January 1930. Harold would endure it for twenty months.

At Long Barn, Vita stumbled walking upstairs. Lumbago set in, acutely painful and debilitating; the condition would return at intervals until her death. She described herself to Virginia as 'only able to hobble from room to room on two sticks, or else drag myself along the floor'; she was too incapacitated to broadcast.[181] Hilda helped to nurse the thirty-seven-year-old invalid. With Harold set to return to Britain full time in December, she recognised now the curfew on their intimacy; she had always acknowledged Vita's 'other claims': 'You know I am the sort of person to whom you can always say without any kind of compunction – please keep away from Long Barn, or please after all don't come tomorrow, or next weekend, or whatever it is.'[182] For all her devotion, such selflessness occasionally cost her dear.

Her back recovered, Vita spent three days looking for a London flat for Harold (she had sold the Ebury Street house in 1926). She found it at King's Bench Walk in the Inner Temple, on 7 October. The next day advance copies arrived of *King's Daughter*, proof to Vita as well as to Hilda of the changeability of the former's affections. Vita organised 'plumbers, painters, electricians' for King's Bench Walk; she chose chair covers and, in the second week of December, unpacked Harold's cases from Berlin, hung pictures and arranged furniture. She even bought a painting by Duncan Grant, perhaps a sot to Virginia given Vita's previous hostility to Bloomsbury painting. She hung it too in the new flat, which was within walking distance of the *Standard* offices; King's Bench Walk would become Harold's Monday-to-Friday home in his new existence. Before Harold left Berlin he was commissioned by the BBC to broadcast a series of talks called 'People and Things'. Hilda Matheson would remain part of Vita's life. Though there would be flashes of disillusionment and considerable pain in her loss of Vita's love, Hilda mostly adjusted to her altered status with characteristic lack of recrimination. When internal politics at the BBC forced her resignation in 1931, she briefly licked her wounds with Vita and Harold, working as the equivalent of their personal assistant. 'I respond unlimitedly to kindness,' she had once told Vita.[183]

In the novella Vita dedicated to Hilda Matheson, Gottfried Künstler 'fall[s] on the back of [his] head on the ice' and becomes a different person. He calls himself Klaus and finds a companion called Anna. Like Hilda, Anna is patient and ripe to fall in love. In his new life in the icy wilderness, Gottfried revels in the patterns that his ice skates slice into the surface of the frozen lake, 'a scratch . . . that next day would turn to water'. His skating, the patterns in the ice, his progress across the lake with Anna are no more than 'a gesture . . . that might break a limb, or a heart; and all for nothing . . . "As our life together," [Anna] said, looking at him very sadly, and expecting perhaps some human reassurance, some warm contradiction; but he only said, with a philosophy that amounted to indifference, "Just so – as our life together."'[184]

PART V

The Land and the Garden

'The deepest roots of all are those one finds in one's own home, among one's own belongings.'

Vita to Ben Nicolson, 25 March 1932

'IT WAS THE Sleeping Beauty's castle with a vengeance, if you liked to see it with a romantic eye; but if you also looked at it with a realistic eye you saw that Nature run wild was not quite so romantic as you thought,' Vita wrote in the autumn of 1950.[1] Her subject was her home of two decades, Sissinghurst Castle.

Vita first saw Sissinghurst on 4 April 1930, with Dorothy Wellesley, whose land agent Donald Beale had alerted her to its sale, and a thirteen-year-old Nigel. It goes without saying that she saw it with a romantic eye. April habitually inspired Vita to eulogy. It was the month when the Kentish country, 'my own county', looked 'absurdly like itself': 'Cherry, plum, pear and thorn whiten the orchards and the hedgerows; lambs frolic; the banks are full of violets and primroses; the whole landscape displays itself as an epitome of everything fresh and innocent.'[2] Vita had recently bought four new fields at Long Barn; she had also learnt in March of a threat to Long Barn's privacy in the form of a proposed chicken farm on land immediately adjacent.

There was nothing fresh at Sissinghurst in the meagre sunshine of that April afternoon: it was cold and muddy and wet. It had been for sale for two years: the rot had set in long before. In an instant, Vita fell 'flat in love'. 'Contact with beauty, for me, is direct and immediate,' she wrote.[3] Transfixed by a tower of pinkish Tudor brick, 'like a bewitched and rosy fountain [pointing] towards the sky', she told a sceptical Nigel that here was somewhere they would be happy.[4] She telephoned Harold 'to say she [had] seen the ideal house – a place in Kent near Cranbrook', some twenty miles from Long Barn and Knole.[5] For the simple reason that she did not see it like that, she did not describe to him with any accuracy the two tired cottages, the tower shorn of the adjoining buildings it had once adorned, the entrance arch with its shabby flanking ranges, the rusty bicycles and iron bedsteads that choked the moat, the woodland dark and overgrown. Her affections would never waver.

Vita was in a mood to fall in love with Tudor ruins. The emotional tumults of the last decade were fleetingly quelled; in her romantic life she had achieved stasis, a moment of calm. In all her relationships – with Violet, Dottie, Virginia, Mary and Hilda – intoxication lay behind her; Geoffrey Scott had died of pneumonia the previous August, alone in New York. Her attachment to Virginia ran deepest. Now, as she had written to Mary in a different context, Vita had begun to crave privacy above all: she described it as constantly under attack from 'myriads of noisy urgencies'.[6] 'I shun all voices, shrink from every task,' Vita had written in a sonnet to Mary included in *King's Daughter*. She wanted to be alone. Where better than in a tower, surrounded by 450 acres of Kentish greensward?

Four weeks earlier, Vita had finished *The Edwardians*. Two years had passed since her father's death and her final departure from Knole. Her novel was a symbolic undertaking, though she did not reflect on it as such and we should resist assuming that its completion provided her with closure or resolution; there would be no resolution to Vita's misery at Knole's loss. *The Edwardians* was a paean of sorts to an idealised version of her own upbringing. It celebrated not only the setting of her childhood in its fictionalised Knole, complete with heraldic leopards, faded tapestries and broad expanses of roof, but its ideological landscape too: that 'good system' of 'a good understanding between class and class', a feudal order of inherited overlordship described by Sebastian in reactionary mode as currently being destroyed by 'too many people . . . too much industrialism'.[7] Sebastian surely spoke for Vita.

Like much of her fiction, *The Edwardians* was an exercise in make-believe. She had spent busy days researching in the London Library; diligently she had applied herself to recreating the below-stairs hierarchies she remembered so vividly; she had plundered her memories of corsets, jewels and table settings, of Christmas presents for the estate children and even of George V's coronation, which she had attended with her father − all in the interests of verisimilitude in this novel inspired by *Orlando*. But in the end, while *Orlando* offered its admiring audience a celebration of Vita, *The Edwardians* attempted instead no more than a picturesque divertissement and, again, an explanation of Vita for Vita's benefit. The novel began as a whim − 'Such a joke it will be,' Vita told Virginia in February 1929:[8] she proved incapable of taking either Knole or herself less than seriously. Writing was not an act of exorcism: Vita was as much in thrall to Knole as she had ever been. As Eddy Sackville-West wrote in his novel, *The Ruin*, published the following year, the house exercised a peculiar power over its children: 'The pictures – the countless pictures – the china, the carving, the silver, the gold, the furniture – all possessed a composite soul with which to rule their masters.'⁹ Later *The Edwardians* embarrassed Vita. Even with the solace of *Orlando*, it did nothing to lessen the pangs she felt about expulsion from her personal Eden.

On publication, however, *The Edwardians* did increase Vita's spiritual ownership of the great house she had lost for ever on Lionel's death. In the minds of the reading public, it reaffirmed her 'possession' of Knole, which she had established with *Knole and the Sackvilles* and Virginia had consolidated with *Orlando*. The novel also offered a partial verdict on her relationship with Violet. Vita was thinking of Mrs Keppel and Victoria when she described the older generation as 'envious, spiteful and mercenary; arrogant and cold. As for us, their children, they leave us in complete ignorance of life, passing on to us only the ideas they think we should hold, and treat us with the utmost ruthlessness if we fail to conform.'¹⁰

Up to a point, Vita recognised her careful illusion for what it was. She also came to see that the Knole she had lost was in the process of being lost in another sense; that knowledge was anything but a comfort. On 30 May 1929, she recorded in her diary a trip to London with Eddy. He told her about the imminent sale of Hoppner's portrait of the three children of the 3rd Duke of Dorset to Thomas Lamont of New York for £65,000. There would be other sales and other losses, including the Flemish tapestries depicting scenes of the Passion of Christ from Knole's Chapel. Hoppner's portrait had inspired page and bridesmaid costumes for Vita's wedding: it was among her favourite of the Knole paintings. The tapestries had served as the backcloth to her marriage to Harold on a bright October afternoon two decades earlier. It was as if Vita's memories were being dismantled, the stage-set of her life plundered and dispersed. For all its criticism of turn-of-the-century moral vacuity, *The Edwardians* celebrates an unpillaged Knole, an idyllic vision unsullied by rich New Yorkers or the outstretched arms of American museums (on 3 October 1929 the tapestries entered the collection of the Museum of Fine Arts in Boston).

In the mud of Sissinghurst, in a tract of Wealden Kent unspoiled by 'too many people . . . too much industrialism', Vita found a new focus for her romanticism. For her, Sissinghurst was indeed 'the Sleeping Beauty's castle with a vengeance': she hoped it would never awaken to the full horror of the present, and its attraction lay in its ability to transport her into its timeless dream world. It became the tower she had told Victoria she longed for, somewhere to be alone with her books; like St Barbara's tower, it became her sanctuary. Sissinghurst was a refuge from a world in which even Knole was vulnerable, a world of chicken farms and invasive new developments, a surrogate but not a replacement for the home of which she claimed as late as 1943 to be 'too greatly moved by the merest thought of it to write or think of it with . . . objectivity'.[11] It was an appropriate setting for an existence Vita repeatedly rationalised through her own private myth-making and fables. As Vita would later describe gardening in wartime, her engagement with Sissinghurst was an exercise in 'daring to find a world in a lost world,/ A little world, a little perfect world'.[12] Vita's tower acquired the status of metaphor made reality. In a review of her *Collected Poems*, published by Leonard and Virginia in 1933, the *New Statesman* described Vita's poetry as 'a frontier tower on the border of a land that we are leaving behind. That land is the England which is vanishing; the England of a ripe and comely rural civilisation.' Vita's agreement was unqualified; in her tower she would hold on to her own (part-fictionalised) version of vanishing England.

Vita acted quickly. The next day, 5 April, she took Harold and Ben to inspect; two days later, she and Harold returned alone. Externally there was no garden, nothing but an old quince tree with 'flat, pink-white blossoms' and a 'shrubby, woody old rose'.[13] They discovered a nutwalk and Harold's enthusiasm grew. The buildings which became the Nicolsons' house were ruins. Euphemistically the sales particulars described them as 'picturesque': at first sight Harold labelled them 'big, broken down and sodden'. The only liveable space on offer was mid-Victorian: Castle Farmhouse, with ten bedrooms, 'well-matured grounds with lawn and rhododendrons', walls 'well-clothed with choice creepers' and views of 'the Towers of Sissinghurst Castle in the background'.[14] It never crossed Vita's mind to live there. Castle Farmhouse was 'that horrid farmhouse' in which she refused to sleep even during Sissinghurst's restoration.[15] For Vita the background became the foreground.

Primitive and derelict, the castle itself – last remnants of a large Tudor house built around a courtyard – had most recently offered patchy shelter to families of farm labourers. Vita's assessment did not spare their feelings. 'The slum-like effect produced by both man and Nature, was squalid to a degree. There was nothing but a dreadful mess of old chicken houses and wire chicken runs; broken down . . . fences; rubbish dumps where cottagers had piled their tins, their bottles, their rusty ironmongery and their broken crockery for perhaps half a century; old cabbage stalks; and a tangle of weeds everywhere.'[16] The central gateway and the tower which today symbolise Sissinghurst were described by the agents as in passable repair;[17] photographs show broken windows on the first floor of the tower but little other evidence of decay. Referring to this assortment of mismatched, apparently purposeless, structures, the surveyor instructed by Meynell & Pemberton, the Sackville solicitors, stated: 'I understand that Mrs Nicolson proposes to occupy [these].'[18] The dominant note was one of astonishment. Unlike Vita, the

surveyor did not see the resemblance to Knole, with its courtyards, arches and towers, its leisurely unfolding of views, its
promise of enclosure, of gates barred against the world; did not
see, as Virginia and Leonard used to say to Vita, that she was
'only really comfortable in a castle'.[19]

Vita and Harold spent most of April debating their purchase.
Although Vita's decision was instinctive, Harold vacillated. The
shocked reaction of his mother, visiting in a downpour, proved
a setback. Subsequently other early visitors would echo Lady
Carnock's reservations. Harold's lover Raymond Mortimer
remembered thinking Sissinghurst 'a gloomy place in hideous
flat country, with commonplace cottages and no view, [we]
couldn't think why they wanted it'; Virginia Woolf described
'Vita's tower; lovely pink brick; but like Knole, not much view,
save of stables'.[20] For Vita, by contrast, acquisition was reflexive.
It was Harold who rationalised the arguments for and against.
Amid the rusting bedsteads and broken tools, the chicken wire,
barbed wire and discarded fencing, the brambles, bindweed,
bulrushes, couch grass and ground elder, Vita had glimpsed at
once the vision of benign collapse in which creeping ivy bound
together a tottering structure of chipped brick and crumbling
casements, which she celebrated in her poem 'Sissinghurst',
written that year: 'Invading nature crawls/ With ivied fingers
over rosy walls,/ Searching the crevices,/ Clasping the mullion,
riveting the crack . . .'[21]

Vita felt something else besides: the tug of atavistic possessiveness. It was a pull like that she attributed to Peregrine
Chase in *The Heir*, the novella she had written almost a decade
ago. After spending his whole life in Wolverhampton, Chase
finds that he rapidly becomes enmeshed in the house in the
country which he has inherited from his last surviving aunt.
In Vita's romantic narrative, contrary to expectation, including
his own expectation, Chase resists every (sensible) pressure to

sell: he is motivated not by greed, acquisitiveness or snobbery, but drawn by 'laws [that] were unalterable' into 'a rhythm that no flurry could disturb',[22] the unchanging rhythm of inheritance and single-family ownership. Chase has no choice but to remain at Blackboys: it is an act of fidelity and family piety occasioned by visceral promptings. Vita disguised her own greedy longing for all that she had decided Sissinghurst represented as similarly beyond her control. She was delighted when, on 6 May, her offer of £12,375 was accepted by telephone. At Victoria's request the trustees were persuaded to advance £13,000 for the purchase. Victoria's compliance was a sign of mother and daughter's temporary amity.

For in Vita's eyes Sissinghurst was a Sackville house. She and Harold discovered that the entrance arch was the work of Sir John Baker, purchaser of the site in 1533; the tower was a later addition by his more extravagant son, Sir Richard Baker. In 1554, John Baker's daughter Cecily married Thomas Sackville, 1st Earl of Dorset: their marriage forged a link between Sissinghurst and Knole. The Bakers went on to entertain both Mary I and her sister Elizabeth I at Sissinghurst. Knole too boasted Tudor royal connections. Lord Dorset was among Vita's most distinguished ancestors, appointed by Elizabeth I High Steward and Lord High Treasurer of England; Vita described him as a 'grave and solemn personage'.[23] He was also the author, with Thomas Norton, of *Gorboduc*, a play of 1561 regarded as the first English drama written in blank verse. A political piece, it is concerned, like much of Vita's writing, with questions of inheritance and female vigour: 'Gorboduc, King of Britain, divided his realm in his lifetime to his sons, Ferrex and Porrex. The sons fell to division and dissension. The younger killed the elder. The Mother that more dearly loved the elder, for revenge killed the younger.'

Sissinghurst's connection to Dorset and the Sackvilles through

Cecily Baker enabled Harold to legitimise Vita's decision to buy the house that, he recognised from the outset, would prove a costly and impractical drain on their resources; he estimated restoration costs at £15,000 on top of the purchase price. 'It is most wise of us to buy Sissinghurst,' he wrote to Vita on 24 April, after presenting all the arguments against its purchase (mostly financial or relating to the absence of amenities like hot water: in fact Sissinghurst in 1930 lacked mains drainage). 'Through its veins pulses the blood of the Sackville dynasty. True it is that it comes through the female line – but then we are both feminist, and after all Knole came in the same way. It is, for you, an ancestral mansion.'[24] In April 1930, Vita's concurrence was wholehearted. Sissinghurst, she remembered, 'caught instantly at my heart and my imagination';[25] it acquired a magic quality too, 'the ivory tower/ Like a tall lily in the moonlight risen'.[26] Her fervour for the house included a measure of need: here at last was her distraction from her severance from Knole. That she could trace a line of descent from the house to herself and therefore claim it as a Sackville legacy, hers 'by birthright far from present fashion', made good the illusion.[27]

For Vita as well as for Harold, Sissinghurst would become the joint venture of their lives. Its garden gave both immeasurable pleasure at the same time as providing an ideal arena for their distinct but complementary talents: Vita as plantsman, Harold as designer. Vita's earliest motives, even if she did not pause to analyse them, were personal expediency. As in all things, her craving for 'an ancestral mansion' took no account of the Nicolson side of her marriage. Flanking the restored entrance arch she would display two coats of arms, those of the Sackville-Wests and the Bakers; Nigel Nicolson later described wheelbarrows, tools and farm equipment as 'indelibly' stamped with her own initials 'V.S-W'. In all aspects of her life, Vita enjoyed possession, an affirmation of herself in the inarguability of ownership or the unquestioning loyalty of friends and lovers. To have enfranchised Harold's family, however symbolically, and shared her possession, would have destroyed the version of Sissinghurst Vita first created for herself.

Harold is similarly absent from Vita's poem about the house, in which she imagines it as a secret place lost in time, 'where stirs no wind and penetrates no sound'; she dedicated the poem to Virginia. At times that comprehensive exclusion would extend to Harold in reality as well as in verse. If Vita's writing was autobiographical, it was also frequently egotistical. As in her writing, so in her outlook. It was part of the cruel side of her nature inherited from Victoria, the side that loved dominance. Later, similar feelings found an echo in her portrait of Louis XIV's cousin, Anne Marie Louise d'Orléans, 'La Grande Mademoiselle', the subject of Vita's last biography. 'There was a touch of the bully in her, perhaps especially provoked when her feudal feeling for her provincial properties was involved.'[28] In Vita's case it was unwitting, but nevertheless thoughtless.

At Long Barn, Vita and Harold had perfected first essays in fragmented family living: separate bedrooms, separate sitting rooms, separate studies or working rooms, a large, family drawing room and the shared space of the garden, with its tennis court and the swimming pool that Harold made out of a pond. The house was shaped by the same ideas that governed Vita and Harold's marriage, as described in Vita's last novel, *No Signposts in the Sea*: 'Mutual respect. Independence . . . both as regards friends and movement. Separate bedrooms – no bedroom squalor . . . Separate sitting rooms if the house is large enough. Separate finances.'[29] Ben and Nigel had slept in a separate cottage a hundred yards from the main house, the cottage later borrowed by the Campbells: as young children, they joined their parents at six o'clock each evening in the company of their nanny or governess.

Sissinghurst would enforce a further degree of separation. Having discarded Castle Farmhouse, Vita and Harold found that they had bought nothing resembling a conventional house – as Nigel had said to Vita on 4 April 1930: 'There's nowhere to live.'[30] Instead there were two small cottages: the Priest's House, once the Elizabethan garden banqueting house, and the South Cottage; the entrance range, in which, within the Tudor stables, they eventually recreated Long Barn's Big Room in the form of the Library; and the tower, which became for Vita a domain-within-a-domain, her own private sanctuary, mostly, but not exclusively, barred to other people.

That Vita and Harold ever considered this curious agglomeration of unrelated living spaces as a home indicates a sea change in their approach to their own lives. As an adult Nigel Nicolson remembered Vita quoting from Khalil Gibran's *The Prophet*: 'Let there be spaces in your togetherness. Love one another, but make not a bond of love . . .'[31] That philosophy would be fully realised at Sissinghurst. The arrangement Vita and Harold devised mirrored that of Long Barn in its 'separations', the 'spaces in its togetherness'. So, too, in its staffing levels of two gardeners (three from 1937), a chauffeur, a cook, Vita's lady's maid Louise Genoux, under-servants and secretaries for both Vita and Harold; the longest-serving of Vita's secretaries, Miss Macmillan, known as Mac, stayed for twenty years, including a period in 1938 as Vita's lover.[32] Only one important detail differed: there was no guest room at Sissinghurst. Vita's desire to escape 'noisy urgencies' prevailed. In her diary Virginia reported Vita telling her, on 26 March 1931: 'We want to turn those stables into guest bedrooms: & build a library across the courtyard'.[33] In the event only the library was built, in 1935. The South Cottage would provide space for Vita and Harold's bedrooms and Harold's study; in the Priest's House were separate sitting rooms for Ben and

Nigel and a shared bedroom, a kitchen and the family dining room; Vita's sitting room was in the tower, and the entrance range, in addition to the Library, accommodated Mrs Staples the cook and her family, and the family of Jack Copper, the chauffeur-handyman. And that was that. None of the buildings was connected: progress to and from meals, to and from bedroom, sitting room and dining room, was entirely at the mercy of the weather.

Vita and Harold had entertained extensively at Long Barn. After the weekend parties, the lunch and dinner parties, the stream of houseguests and Vita's perpetuation in miniature of the Edwardian entertaining of Victoria's Knole, Sissinghurst would embrace a different Knole. It was here, over the next thirty years, that Vita realised that fantasy of her father's house she had described to Harold as long ago as 1912. 'I am all alone here for the moment, and all this big house is mine to shut up if I choose, and shut out all the rest of the world by swinging the iron bars across all the gates. But instead of doing that I have locked all the doors of my own tower, and nobody will come near me till tomorrow morning, or even know whether I am still alive . . . And I think I have gone back five hundred years.'[34] There would be lunch guests at Sissinghurst, guests who came for tea and garden visitors, including, after its first official opening through the National Gardens Scheme on 1 May 1938, paying members of the public, Vita's 'shillinges' − 'the people I most gladly welcome and salute'.[35] Invitations to stay, which required Ben and Nigel's absence, were altogether rarer. Sissinghurst became the symbol of Vita's gradual withdrawal from the world.

It became the house in which Vita was able at last to 'lose myself within a slumber/ Submerged': dream made reality.[36] It was a feature of the place she recognised from her first visits. Once, she had retreated into the past in her novels and plays.

Within the coloured covers of Murray's exercise books, she had imagined herself among vanished heroes, including members of her own family. On 20 June 1911, she had posed for the photographic company Speaight Ltd, dressed in a hybrid version of cavalier costume: gauntlets, an extravagant sash, puff sleeves slashed and laced. There had been tableaux, masques, the Persian play in Knole's Great Hall, Shakespeare in the rain; Orlando gave Vita the possibility of vicarious time travel at will. At Sissinghurst, Vita confined conscious historical role play to her biographies of Joan of Arc, St Teresa, Saint Thérèse, 'La Grande Mademoiselle'. Given the objectivity required of nonfiction writing, her submersion was necessarily lesser. Instead, she contrived an illusion of past and present merging that she interpreted as intrinsic to the atmosphere of Sissinghurst. It resembled the feeling she had experienced at Knole as a child, alone by candlelight amid the long shadows and dusty glitter of galleries and state rooms. Vita considered Sissinghurst's Tudor buildings timeless – as emblematic as Knole itself or the Avebury stones which dominate the physical and mental landscape of her novel, *Grey Wethers*. 'The heavy golden sunshine enriched the old brick with a kind of patina, and made the tower cast a long shadow across the grass, like the finger of a gigantic sundial veering slowly with the sun,' she wrote in the first novel she completed in her tower room.[37] Like Knole, Sissinghurst existed for Vita as a physical presence, a force and powerful too.

In the decoration of the Library, as in Long Barn's Big Room, Vita returned to the dark wood and Jacobean dash of the home of her childhood. With its Sackville portraits, candle sconces and seventeenth-century chairs of blackened cane and needle-point, with its farm, its tenants, its ancient brewhouse and woodland Wealden setting, Sissinghurst became Vita's new inheritance. It belonged to her alone: Harold never legally shared its ownership. On the cusp of her fortieth birthday, established in her tower like a spider at the centre of a web, Vita would exchange some of Orlando's amorous skittishness for a role closer to that of Lady Anne Clifford, landowner and matriarch. As Virginia Woolf had noted, Vita was an astute and competent businesswoman; there were limits to her romantic spirit.

As ever Vita signalled the direction of her thinking in her writing. With *The Edwardians* finished she quickly embarked on a novel which, like its predecessor, examines the nature of personal choice. *The Edwardians* had highlighted the inescapability of Sebastian's destiny as Chevron's heir: Vita's focus in *All Passion Spent* is on Deborah Slane's role as Victorian wife. 'Even had she been in love with [Henry], she could see therein no reason for foregoing the whole of her separate existence. Henry was in love with her, but no one proposed that he should forego his.'[38] Among the novel's themes are renunciation of worldly riches and love for a house. Vita herself would never manage the former – in her writing, her diary, her letters and her speech she was continually possessive – 'I', 'my' and 'mine' pepper statements on everything from jewellery to England – but she could and did empathise wholeheartedly with the latter.

Octogenarian widow Lady Slane is externally modelled on Harold's mother: her character is closer to Vita's. Following the death of her distinguished husband, a former viceroy of India, Lady Slane withdraws from her attentive but worldly family to the relative seclusion of a house in Hampstead with which she had fallen in love thirty years earlier (the house itself is inspired by Keats's house, which Vita had visited with Virginia). Without regret she divests herself of jewellery and possessions, shedding the uniform of the wife of a great man; trophies and trinkets fail to move her. Her intensest emotion is reserved for her new house, which displaces not only former glories but her family too. Lady Slane's challenge is to justify her choice of the Hampstead house over nearer 'claims'. This passionate engagement with a building, added to a tendency to imbue it with human characteristics, is Vita's own trait. Assessing her ecstatic response to the landscape of Persia four years earlier, Vita had admitted the extent to which places, not people, affected her: 'These brief but frequent fallings-in-love gave me cause for serious anxiety; such vibrations of response ought, I felt, to be reserved for one's contact with human beings, nor should nature have a greater power than human nature to excite and to stir the soul . . . The external world had too much importance for me; my appreciation was altogether too painfully vivid.'[39] In consigning this response to the past, Vita misleads her reader: it remained indelibly part of her psyche. Disingenuously she refers to 'cause for serious anxiety'; nothing in her subsequent behaviour suggests she repented of this tendency in herself. 'The external world' of landscape, building and place remained critically important to Vita. She allows the heroine of her novel to be overwhelmed by the small house in Hampstead just as she herself was overwhelmed by Knole and had since succumbed to Sissinghurst; the novel invites the reader's judgement of those who criticise Lady Slane: 'Duty, charity, children, social obligations, public appearances – with these had [Lady Slane's] days been filled.'[40] It was the very formula Vita herself had resisted in her marriage to Harold the diplomat, the formula Harold's mother had more successfully embraced. Within the context of the novel, it is as much a plea for individual freedom as a feminist manifesto. In the emotions to which it gives rise and its symbolic place in her affections, Lady Slane's house in Hampstead is another Knole, another Sissinghurst.

Work at Sissinghurst began on Vita's tower, a clear statement of priorities. Against its walls Vita planted a climbing

rose called 'Richmond' and clumps of rosemary. Even before
contracts were signed, she had made sorties from Long Barn;
invariably this proprietorial woman planted something during
her visit, staking out her territory in lavender bushes. But it
was inside the tower rather than its surrounds where work
started in earnest; in the short term, garden plans were confined
to 'large paper sheets ruled into squares'.[41] On 12 July, Vita
recorded her decision to use the room on the first floor of the
tower as her writing room. Once the dividing wall between
the two spaces had been knocked through, she saw that she
could accommodate a small library in the octagonal turret
adjoining it (initially referred to by Vita as 'the oratory'[42]).

Bookshelves were built along the two window walls of Vita's
writing room and a working fireplace across a corner; there
was a single radiator. The majority of her books were housed
in floor-to-ceiling shelves in the turret. Here, once the dust had
settled, she kept her notes and manuscripts, including those
exercise books filled with neat, hand-written drafts of the
unpublished novels and plays of her childhood. There were
books of Elizabethan history, literary criticism and literary
biography, Vita's growing collection of gardening books and
books about sexuality and gender, including, by 1937, seven
volumes of Havelock Ellis's *Studies in the Psychology of Sex*,
which Harold also read.[43] Most were inscribed 'V.N.' or 'Vita
Nicolson'. At the time of Vita's purchase, walls of the tower
room were papered. Vita's first act of beautification at
Sissinghurst was to strip away the layers of 'hideous' Victorian
wallpaper and replace it with distemper. The distemper was
never applied. 'I found the old brick so pretty that I left it all
rough as it was, the colour of pot-pourri,' Vita explained, 'a
sort of half-pink, half-grey, and mottled.'[44] Aesthete Stephen
Tennant, visiting in December 1945, described it as the colour
of 'squashed ripe pomegranates'.[45] And so it remained, unchanged

until her death. When builders mistakenly plastered the walls of her bedroom in the South Cottage, Vita insisted they strip off the plaster to reveal the ancient brick beneath.

Vita's first night at Sissinghurst was spent not in her bedroom, where the builders also uncovered 'the most lovely, huge, stone Tudor fireplace', but in the turret room. By mid-October it was wired for electricity; cardboard sheets shielded the windows from wind and rain. Vita took her dogs with her from Long Barn. The following night Hilda joined her and gardened all day, the next night Harold. Weeks later Vita and Harold spent their first night in the South Cottage.

That night Harold's lack of enjoyment, coloured by the all-pervasive anxiety he felt as a result of unhappiness with his change of career (Harold quickly decided he loathed working for the *Evening Standard*), contrasted with Vita's bluffness in the face of overwhelming discomforts. Harold made light of the night's experiences in a humorous radio broadcast made soon afterwards; his diary tells a different story. Vita's character dominates the broadcast. Harold calls her 'Edith': she is commanding, capable and dismissive of his difficulties. Without apparent regret, he presents himself to listeners as a man 'not born to be a settler's husband': damp logs, fragile crockery, a well reluctant to yield water and his least favourite picnic food successively defeat him. Edith–Vita, by contrast, revels in 'the mellow light of candles' and provides soda water with which to clean their teeth; Harold mislays the syphons. Edith–Vita is forthright, decisive, controlling. Harold fails in every task he attempts, including preparing their simple breakfast of coffee and boiled eggs. Edith–Vita is sanguine: neither Harold nor Vita flourished in the absence of domestic help (Vita once protested at 'being asked to produce various domestic utensils which I do not even know by name'[46]) and, as Vita had written earlier, she required few creature comforts to feel at home: 'my own house, dogs, and servants; my luggage . . . unpacked. The icebox . . . in the kitchen, the gramophone on the table, and my books . . . on the shelves.'[47] Affection between the couple is at best implicit. Beneath the humour are suggestions of role reversal and an easy assumption of mastery on Vita's part. It was not the whole truth. Later Harold dismissed himself as 'the most incompetent man since Noah'.[48]

Vita did not immediately sell Long Barn, despite its drain on the couple's diminished resources once she had renounced her allowance from Victoria. To Virginia she wrote of the cost of Long Barn's upkeep, but Virginia was puzzled by the Nicolsons' inability to retrench. For two years, Vita, Harold, Ben and Nigel lived between the two houses: they moved into Sissinghurst on 9 April 1932. Two years later Vita sold Long Barn to Victoria for £8,000 (Victoria would return it to Vita in her will). The house was let. On a visit in October 1934, Vita noted with sadness the first tenant 'making every room as hideous as possible'.[49] Nine years and several tenants later, in the winter of 1943, Vita sold the house, along with many of its contents, including three thousand books. Harold regretted its loss. In his diary he associated it with 'all the happy days of youth'.[50] He was fifty-seven years old. Given his marked unhappiness during much of Vita's affair with Violet, his memory played him false. Although she did not know it at the time, during the sale Vita lost her key to the garden gate at Knole.

By the spring of 1932, restoration work on Sissinghurst, though unfinished, had progressed apace, and Vita and Harold were able to start laying out the garden they had been planning throughout what Vita called the 'impatient' intervening period. Much of their first two years had been devoted to clearance work. The moat wall was revealed hidden under rubbish. They laid rudimentary paths, sited a handful of borders and planted trees. In 1932, they increased their tree planting. 'We had to get on with the hedges. We planted hornbeam where we couldn't afford yew; and we also planted an avenue of young limes in a rough place and left them to look after themselves.'[51]

The substitution of hornbeam for yew on grounds of cost was important. That year the continuing loss of Vita's income from the Sackville estates, added to the shortfall caused by Harold's decision in 1931 to leave the *Standard* ('that urinal of futility', as he dismissed it) in order to edit *Action,* the newspaper of Sir Oswald Mosley's New Party, combined to create an unaccustomed and, to Harold, deeply troubling hole in their finances. The New Party journal folded after the party's disastrous electoral defeat in October 1931, leaving Harold unemployed. In her role as secretary-cum-manager Hilda Matheson pointed out the acuteness of the problem. At £6,000 a year, the couple's outgoings were double their income. Harold himself also owed £3,000 in income tax, with further debts of another £800.[52] At the beginning of 1932, Vita and Harold had £300 in the bank between them to support two houses in the country, the flat in King's Bench Walk and two boys now at Eton. Happily the discovery of Sissinghurst had coincided with a burst of creative energy on Vita's part, which showed no sign of abating. Although her literary earnings could not rival Victoria's giving power, the period proved both fertile and lucrative. For diversion there would be gardening. Vita took comfort from her conviction that gardening was 'the daughter of painting'; that association raised it 'from the rank of a fiddle-de-dee hobby to the royal dignity of a serious pursuit'.[53]

As Vita had intended, *The Edwardians,* published on 29 May 1930, became a bestseller. On 27 June, in its roundup of 'the books most in demand from the *Times* Book Club', the *Spectator* placed *The Edwardians* at the head of its list. It sold 30,000 copies in its first six months and netted for Leonard and Virginia, its publishers, a profit of £2,000 in the first year. For the Woolfs, this boon came on top of a doubling of Virginia's literary earnings since publication of *Orlando* two years previously.[54] On 13 August 1931, Vanessa's husband Clive Bell described to a friend the improvements made to Monks House with revenues from *Orlando* and *The Edwardians*: 'Monks is now a place fit for socialists to live in – electric light, central heating, a Frigidaire and two WCs. And all paid for by Virginia and Vita which makes it more romantic.'[55]

For their part, in December 1930, Vita and Harold had allocated £125 of recent income to make a lake: the money was spent on damming the nearby stream and flooding two meadows to the south of the house. 'It was a creation romantic beyond my hopes,' Vita wrote. 'Extravagantly I ordered a boat from the Army and Navy Stores.'[56] They found they were able to cut corners. The wisterias they planted that year were sent over from Victoria's house in Streatham, which she would shortly leave; foxgloves came from the nearby woods, tracked down by Harold and transplanted in an old pram. For Harold, Sissinghurst's garden, and its all-consuming demands on his time and energy, provided a necessary distraction. On 20 March 1932, of a morning devoted to the usually uncongenial task of weeding the delphinium bed, he wrote: 'I cannot get a job and am deeply in debt. I foresee no exit from our financial worries. Yet Vita and I are as happy as larks alone together. It is a spring day. Very odd.'[57] It was as Vita would claim at the beginning of her second long poem, *The Garden*, written during the Second World War: 'Small pleasures must correct great tragedies.' Thinking of her own gardens at Long Barn and Sissinghurst, she described a garden as 'a miniature endeavour/ To hold the graces and the courtesies/ Against a horrid wilderness'. In the summer, the Nicolsons plundered Vita's royalty

cheques to pay for a family holiday in Italy. In five days in
Portofino, Harold returned to his continuing preoccupation
with diplomacy. He wrote a comic play about diplomatic life,
The Archduke, which was never performed. Later, the joint
proceeds of *The Edwardians* and *All Passion Spent* contributed
substantially to Ben and Nigel's school fees.[58]

'We must not forget the unparalleled prestige the aristocracy
enjoy among the middle and working classes in England, even
today,' Violet Trefusis wrote in her novel *Broderie Anglaise*; 'nor
the eagerness with which those classes seize upon everything
the privileged class does, applauding and admiring all their
exploits, like a child at a circus.'[59] So it proved not only with
The Edwardians but its successors *All Passion Spent* and *Family
History*, published in successive years. Though the later novels
did not match *The Edwardians'* undilutedly aristocratic flavour
– nor the scale of its commercial success – both offered Vita's
readers snapshots of a world that was uniquely her own, in
the case of *Family History* a portrait of Vita's elder son Ben in
the guise of the seventeen-year-old Dan and a fictional castle
that resembles Sissinghurst in every essential: 'They passed
through an archway beneath the tower and came out on a
cleared space with an old orchard beyond. The dark shape of
a cottage rose up, and other walls, all of the same Tudor brick.
Miles' castle seemed to consist of isolated buildings, connecting
walls and the dark background of the country lands. It was
very lonely.'[60] In 1931, *All Passion Spent* sold 15,000 copies in
its first year and earned the Hogarth Press £1,200. Leonard
described it as the best novel Vita ever wrote. On 12 October
1932, Virginia wrote to Vita with the news that 6,000 copies
of *Family History* had been sold pre-publication. 'My God! And
my fingers are red and wheeled with doing up parcels inces-
santly . . . Orders pouring in – we all working till 7.30 – thought
we were just finished – then a last batch of orders discovered

hidden in a drawer another hours work – clerks panting – telephones ringing carriers arriving – parcels just finished in time to catch the vans – Oh Lord what it is to publish a best-seller . . .'[61] From now on the bulk of Vita's income from writing would be diverted towards Sissinghurst.

Vita was working at a considerable rate. Her three biggest-selling novels were produced at yearly intervals; Harold too wrote a book a year between 1931 and 1937. It was against this background of shared hard work that the garden at Sissinghurst was created. At the same time, although her position was increasingly precarious since Hilda's departure from the BBC, Vita continued until October 1932 to review fiction and nonfiction for her radio broadcasts and to contribute articles to a range of publications. In addition to *The Listener*, these included the *Spectator*, *Week-end Review*, *Life and Letters* and the *Graphic*. 'My own production has become simply terrific (in quantity I mean, not quality),' she wrote. 'I never stop writing stories and articles . . . I must make the most of it while the fit is on me – but they are cheap stuff.'[62] Once he had agreed to take over its editorship in June 1931, Harold invited Vita to contribute 'a weekly article containing hints to the amateur gardener' to the New Party's *Action*.[63] Although her efforts were to be unpaid, it was the beginning of Vita's horticultural journalism and led to a series of Friday evening gardening broadcasts for the BBC and, in the summer of 1938, a short radio series about the gardens of the West of England. Reflecting her own inclinations, Vita's *Action* contributions included 'Flowers that are like Dutch paintings', 'Irises possess every virtue but one' and 'Flowers you must sniff very closely'.

She also continued to write poetry and featured in numerous anthologies, among them *Poets of Our Time* and *Younger Poets of Today*, both published in 1932. The previous year Vita's translations of German poet Rainer Maria Rilke's *Duineser*

Elegien were published as *Elegies from the Castle of Duino* and widely reviewed. Vita had conceived the idea during her visit to Harold in Berlin in the spring of 1928. She was encouraged in the project by the American wife of a Berlin-based British journalist, Margaret Voigt, who rapidly became Vita's lover. Following Vita's return, Margaret visited her at Long Barn: in this instance familiarity bred detachment on Vita's part and Margaret's fantasy that Vita was her aristocratic lover 'David' was of brief duration. Vita did not allow sexual disillusionment to interfere with her work. Instead she completed her translations in collaboration with her cousin Eddy. The book was published under both Vita and Eddy's names, though Vita was the more highly regarded, commercially successful of the pair.

Previously, discussing Aphra Behn, Vita had suggested 'the fact that she wrote is much more important than the quality of what she wrote. The importance of Aphra Behn is that she was the first woman in England to earn her living by her pen.'[64] Had she revisited those words in the early 1930s, Vita must have found in them a prophetic ring.

Her output was prodigious: in the short term, quality kept pace with quantity. Struggling with the ending of *Challenge* during the turbulence of her relationship with Violet, Vita had confessed to Harold her conviction of her own limitations: 'I shall never write a good book; at least, I might write dozens of *quite* good books, but I shall never write a great one. And to be great is the only thing that really counts, whether for books or people.'[65] There is poignancy in the accuracy of this self-assessment, also in the vehemence of Vita's characteristic longing for greatness.

Vita won a large popular following both for her novels and her poetry. *Orlando* and her radio broadcasts conferred a degree of fame; her striking looks added to her distinctive appeal. Her appearance in the early 1930s as guest of honour at speech day at Tonbridge County School for Girls inspired cheering and autograph-hunting on the part of the assembled girls; a horrified headmistress lamented that 'such unwarranted and vulgar scenes had never been witnessed at Speech Day'.[66] Yet despite *The Land*'s award of the Hawthornden Prize, the Heinemann Prize in 1946 for *The Garden*, respectful and often enthusiastic reviews and impressive sales figures for a number of her books, Vita would stake no lasting claim to unequivocal greatness through writing. In 1922, the *Spectator*'s reviewer of *Orchard and Vineyard* claimed, 'Miss Sackville-West has interesting thoughts, but she does not make very good poems out of them.'[67] A decade later the same magazine reached a different conclusion: 'Her poetry does not merely describe nature; it does not merely express her feeling: she describes, and in what she writes Nature and her feeling are one.' Subsequent readers have tended to agree with the first assessment and much, though not all, of Vita's poetry has failed to achieve longevity. Posthumously, as in the second half of her career, her reputation as a poet suffered as a result of her allegiance to the forms and focuses of so-called Georgian poetry: orderliness of rhyme and rhythm and an anti-modernist agenda of pastoralism, romance and detachment from the quotidian. She once described herself as 'so out of touch with poetry as it is being written today'[68] and, partly regretfully, as 'a damned out-moded poet'.[69]

Vita's reputation as a novelist reflects in the same way her avoidance of formal experimentalism, her sensationalism and her particular brand of non-realism, alongside her perceived fixation with the ramifications of class. Posterity has mostly disdained Vita's prose fictions. Her son Ben described her as 'a remarkable writer manqué', her 'true quality' concealed beneath her 'snobbery, the assumptions of superiority'; but Ben, whose relationship with Vita was latterly vexed to the point of collapse, is a highly subjective commentator.[70] Vita was only concerned for her poetry. In her own mind she was quite clear about the different spheres occupied by poetry and fiction. 'A poet's dream costs nothing; yet is real,' she wrote in *The Garden.*[71] In response to a letter from a member of the public protesting about the secondary role accorded to poetry in her radio broadcasts, Vita wrote gratefully on 9 May 1930: 'I would gladly exchange novels for poetry, but what about the great British Public which enjoys the former more than the latter? . . . I get plenty of letters, but few people ask for more poetry. That's *their* loss.'[72]

At her best, in prose as well as poetry, Vita wrote with insight, verve and colour. Her lingering descriptions of landscape and nature, described by a contemporary reviewer in the *Daily Telegraph* as a 'generous glow of enthusiasm for beauty',[73] retain an intensely visual, sensuous and moving quality; in her 'Country Notes' for the *New Statesman,* she categorised herself as someone in whom 'the love of nature and the natural seasonal life [had attained] the proportions of a vice'.[74] 'I looked out of my porthole and saw . . . the dawn scarlet behind a range of hills,' Vita wrote of her first sighting of India. 'Small craft were dotted about; kites swept over the placid surface; yellow lights ringed the water's edge; rigging pencilled the flaming sky. Here was all the business of land again, albeit a land unawakened as yet.'[75] Vita's description separates colours into the blocks of an artist's palette; unravels the different threads; builds up its picture simply but lingeringly.

In her examination of character and motive she is sometimes intrepid and often unpredictable; necessarily discreet, given the climate of the time, her lesbian explorations contribute an element of tension, even subversion. Vita had a storyteller's instinct and, as Leonard Woolf saw, enough honesty, romance and sentimentality to capture the popular imagination.[76] These qualities came to fruition in all three of her best-known novels, within narrative formats which in each case offered opportunities for the self-exploration that consistently shaped Vita's fiction. What's more, she wove her tales, with their often startling effects – sado-masochism in *The Dark Island* and life after death in *Grand Canyon* – with a minimum of writerly fuss and consistent ease; as Virginia described her: 'Vita . . . writing another novel; but as careless about it all as ever.'[77] On the debit side is an inclination to purple prose and a taste for improbably heightened emotionalism. 'How marvellously well she writes . . . She carries into her writings the quiet tranquillity of manner which is so characteristic of her,' her mother wrote in 1927. Modern readers may reach the opposite conclusion. Vita's style is invariably in keeping with that of popular fiction of its time: as she wrote in 1929, in her short biography of seventeenth-century poet Andrew Marvell, 'so strong, so instinctive, is the habit of mind of one's own age'.[78]

It is not necessary to second Virginia Woolf's dismissal of Vita's 'pen of brass', a critique of her commercial instinct and ready facility, those ten, twelve or fifteen pages Vita wrote sometimes in a day, her assessment of *The Edwardians* as 'not a very good book',[79] or her generalised disdain for what she termed Vita's 'sleepwalking servantgirl novels'.[80] Vita herself made no claims for her early fiction, 'the vile indiscretions of youth', as she labelled them in 1927.[81] Even Virginia agreed that 'never was there a more modest writer'.[82] It would not have occurred to Vita to suggest parity with Virginia's writing. As we have seen, her acknowledgement of Virginia's pre-eminent talent was a cornerstone of their relationship: Virginia enforced the gap by labelling Vita 'Donkey West'. Vita enjoyed the act of writing: her novels were bread-and-butter undertakings, her purpose material gain. Reflecting Virginia's influence, Vita told an interviewer in October 1930 that she wished she could 'make a bonfire of all my novels . . . I particularly dislike my novels. The only one I can tolerate at all is *Seducers in Ecuador*.'[83] The following year she summed up her literary achievements in a flippant doggerel obituary as 'a few cheap novels as bad as sin/ And some honest lines of verse'.[84] Her self-criticism was unnecessarily bleak. Virginia herself claimed that 'all creation is the result of conflict'.[85] There was no shortage of conflict either in Vita's writing or her life. The ultimate weakness of Vita's writing is that its autobiographical dimension too often stopped short of self-revelation; her instincts for concealment and privacy were too great. 'Those things which are felt, and those things which are seen . . . are not the business of words,' she once wrote, a curious, if revealing, statement for any writer.[86]

On 31 December 1932, Virginia recorded in her diary: 'Vita is on the high seas, sailing to America.'[87] Two days previously, Vita and Harold had left Sissinghurst for a four-month lecture tour of the States. With Harold still without a job, their motives were financial.

Both had published well-received novels during the course of the year – Vita's *Family History* and Harold's *Public Faces*; in May, American publishers Doubleday, Doran & Co. had also issued a collection of Vita's stories, *Thirty Clocks Strike the Hour*. The title story was her fictional recreation of Seery's apartment in the rue Laffitte; 'Elizabeth Higginbottom' concerned 'a severe and serious person' who 'attained the age of forty before romance entered her life'; 'The Poet' offered an up-to-date variation on the death of Chatterton, which had so absorbed the teenage Vita, and revisited the themes of plagiarism and artistic fraudulence that underpinned the earlier drama. All engaged with characteristic foibles and preoccupations. In the title story, Vita reimagined Seery's apartment as belonging to her great-grandmother, a means retrospectively of asserting her possession of it and claiming it as an 'ancestral mansion'. In 'Elizabeth Higginbottom', Vita's unlikely heroine yearns for marriage in order to escape from her maiden name, the reverse of Vita's own outlook. She blames her parents for her dissonant surname and is eventually made ridiculous in her one misguided attempt at passion, as if her unfortunate name had fixed her destiny, much as Vita's own destiny was shaped by heredity. Nicholas Lambarde's claims to greatness in 'The Poet' are exposed as a sham when the narrator recognises that his best poems are unwitting copies of other men's work; only his picturesque death moves the reader. Several of the stories in the collection had previously appeared singly in magazines. The publishers described them as 'eight stories, brilliant, fantastic, exquisite, by the author of "All Passion Spent"' and paid Vita $500.

A well-oiled publicity machine, orchestrated on Vita and Harold's behalf by a public-speaking agency called the Colston Leigh Bureau, ensured that, even at the height of the Great Depression, as many as possible of the book-buying American public were aware of the couple and their work. From the moment of their arrival in New York on 5 January, they found themselves objects of fascination. Reporters described Harold as 'one of the cleverest men in England'; Vita's connection with Knole and the long roll call of her Sackville ancestors inspired a degree of New World dizziness.[88] Testily Harold dismissed the 'slushy adulation' that pursued them.[89] Vita's attitude, by contrast, was consistently one of wry amusement. 'There were several descriptions of my personal appearance,' she told Harold in February, referring to newspaper reports in Minneapolis. 'My eyes, you will be pleased to hear, are (1) blue, (2) deep blue, (3) brown, (4) hazel. So you can take your choice. They got very puzzled as to what my name was, and there is a touching reference to my modesty in preferring to be called

Miss S-W instead of Lady "which is her rightful title". I think they thought I was being tactful in a democratic country.'[90]

Vita had first been published in the States in August 1919, when George H. Doran brought out an American edition of *Heritage*. Doran's publicity material had claimed then that 'in its passion, its pervading sense of beauty and detached pity, [*Heritage*] is reminiscent of Conrad and – strange to say – of *Wuthering Heights*', an assessment of suitably exaggerated hyperbole that nevertheless attributes to Vita's first novel characteristics more fully realised in her life: emotionalism, a pervading sense of beauty and, in terms of the lovers she abandoned so easily, detached pity. In the intervening period, all Vita's books except *Poems of West and East, Orchard and Vineyard* and *Andrew Marvell* had been published in the States. Vita's American following was considerable; both she and Harold found that they were better known there than in Britain, despite their radio broadcasts for the BBC, large sales and Vita's early notoriety as Kidlet.

Harold would calculate that by the end of their tour the couple had travelled 33,527 miles; in seventy-two different journeys they had crossed the length and breadth of America and visited fifty-three different cities. As Vita wrote to Virginia in March: 'I never realised the size of this darn country till I came here.'[91] It was a frequently gruelling experience, with repeated nights on sleeper trains; at Des Moines in February, Vita was so tired she fell asleep at the station, 'on a wooden bench among my luggage, looking like an immigrant'.[92] Occasionally they shared the stage for joint lectures, more often they were apart. Vita's repertoire was larger than Harold's. She discussed 'Changes in English Social Life', with references to *The Edwardians*; 'Novels and Novelists' and 'The Modern Spirit in Literature', amply supplied with material for both from her broadcasts for Hilda and her friendship with Virginia;

less often she spoke about her Persian travels. Press attention followed her wherever she went – 'Mummy is lionised like nohow. She is given orchids and met by groups of people at stations,' Harold wrote to Ben at the end of their first week;[93] she worked hard to ensure that her talks were well received. 'Americans are easily and unexpectedly amused,' Vita reported in her diary on 27 February. There were inadvertently entertaining incidents: 'In the middle of my lecture a screen falls down on the heads of the audience but they do not appear to mind,' she noted in Chicago.[94] There were also a great many parties, invariably hosted by the local branch of the Women's Club of America. 'I don't think I can stand many more women,' Vita wrote to Harold at the midway point, 'America is rapidly curing me of any weakness I may ever have entertained for my own sex.'[95] At times Vita found both Americans in general and specific individuals trying. 'It is awful how these people talk in trains,' she noted;[96] the following week, having been prevented from going to bed by an over-attentive host, she added 'with all their kindness, these people have very little imagination'.[97]

Vita retained her ability to inspire powerful responses of physical attraction in those she encountered, despite recent weight gain and the increasingly ruddy complexion which caused one photographer to request that she remove her rouge. Typically the press referred to her as 'Juno-esque', 'Portia-like' and 'Orlando';[98] others reacted more idiosyncratically. At Cincinnati, Vita recorded in her diary: 'A lady comes up afterwards and tells me she has had a vision during my lecture, and that I was Balkis, Queen of Sheba in a previous incarnation. Try to look suitably grateful.'[99] She too was not wholly immune to her new acquaintances. In Columbus, Ohio, on 20 February, she was particularly struck by a Mrs Edmunds, 'who is really lovely without a hat – lovely wide brows and a serene look;

dark hair; a Madonna-like type'.[100] At Northampton, Massachusetts, she found respite in the company of the wealthy Mina Curtiss. The latter's farm in the Berkshire Hills reminded Vita for the first time on American soil of the way of life at Long Barn and Sissinghurst: pigeons colonised the roofs of the wooden buildings, in the meadows Jersey cows grazed.[101] Vita felt a pang of homesickness and dedicated a poem to Mina, her thanks for a fleeting escape from 'voices, cities, trains,/ . . . the clamour of a city street/ And vapid endless talk of books, books, books'.[102]

Predictably Vita's reaction to America itself was similarly varied. While dazzled by the South California desert, which reminded her of Persia, and the Grand Canyon, which would later form the centrepiece of her wartime novel of the same name (she described it to Virginia as 'the most astonishing thing in the world'[103]), she was less impressed by American cities. 'A large, elderly, Edwardian-looking lady called Mrs Thompson then drives me off to "see Pittsburgh – such a beautiful city",' she reported on 27 February. 'It reminds me of Sheffield.'[104] From the west coast she wrote simply: 'Los Angeles is hell.'[105] Publicly she was circumspect in her pronouncements to the American press. Her fury on 28 January at 'a newspaper article saying we had been rude about America' was justified: she defended herself on the grounds that she would not be so ill-mannered or so unintelligent.[106] In return she inspired uniformly positive coverage in the American press. As Harold told her: 'They adore your shy dignity, your regal modesty.'[107]

On her return to Sissinghurst, Vita described herself as 'enriched' in more than the financial sense. Harold, whose attitude to their host country was less benign, told Raymond Mortimer that, despite appalling living expenses, 'we shall bring back a pretty pile', a profit in the region of £2,000.[108] Vita brought home, in addition, books, bogus native American trinkets of a sort she would later deride in *Grand Canyon* but which currently delighted her, and several large cowboy hats.

During their absence, areas of woodland at Sissinghurst had been thinned and tidied. Vita and Harold would continue improvements to the garden that year with the addition of a covered terrace attached to the Priest's House, in what is now the White Garden but was then the Rose Garden; they used it for outdoor dining. The Erechtheum is a pergola constructed of salvaged fragments of columns supporting a wooden trellis. Vita and Harold planted a vine to cover it and, prompted by Harold's philhellenism, named it after the temple of Athena on the Acropolis that had once been plundered by Lord Elgin. The idea was not theirs exclusively, but had been suggested by architect Albert Powys (known as A. R. P.), secretary of the Society for the Protection of Ancient Buildings, whose help at Sissinghurst Vita and Harold had enlisted.

Vita's diary for her American tour is engaging and funny. She seldom employed her diary for self-scrutiny and the entries for this period are no exception, but the woman who emerges from its pages during the first quarter of 1933 appears at ease with herself. She was 'lapped in happiness and security . . . so ordered, rational', as she described herself elsewhere;[109] she was confident in her likes and dislikes, impatient perhaps but polite, hard working, mostly without cynicism, prepared to be amused, entertained and interested; at this point she was more open-minded than her ex-diplomat husband. The smooth surface of Vita's American diary reveals no trace of the woman who, only months earlier, had written for the first and only time in her life: 'Pass from my heart towards the heart of others;/ But in your passing, half-remember me.'[110] In the spring of 1931, Vita had fallen in love again. The following summer, she learned that the object of her affections had fallen in love with another woman. It had never happened to her before and would never happen again. Vita would discover at first hand what it was to face rejection by a lover.

She fell in love at a moment of unhappiness. Vita could not explain the cause of what Virginia called her 'vague mood of depression', and yet it hung, heavy, refusing to budge, darkening her final weeks' work on *All Passion Spent*. 'If I, who am the most fortunate of women, can ask What is life for?, how can other people live at all?' she asked Virginia on 22 January.[111] Neither woman could pinpoint an answer. Although Vita did not identify her as such, Virginia herself was part of the problem: their relationship had stalled through Vita's fault, that cooling of ardour that sought distraction first with Mary, afterwards with Margaret Voigt then Hilda. Virginia revenged herself by making Vita jealous of her own new friendship with septuagenarian composer-turned-writer, Dame Ethyl Smyth.

As long ago as 1909, Vita had identified 'the gnawing doubt of self' as 'worse than any outward suffering':[112] Virginia retained enough of a hold over Vita to challenge the careful balance of her self-confidence. At the same time, Harold and Ben were also unhappy. Harold jibbed against what he saw as his mistaken change of career – 'I simply loathe writing for a newspaper, and have got an anti-vulgarisation complex';[113] as late as 1935 he was still dreaming he had been asked to return to the Foreign Office and waking to disappointment on discovering that his hopes were only dreams. As with Vita's relationship with Violet, he refused to allow himself to blame her for his unsettlement. Ben was miserable at Eton. In the autumn of 1931 he suffered a nervous breakdown. Harold was too busy to visit him and Vita bore the brunt alone. On the plus side, Victoria underlined her ongoing (if temporary) truce with Vita by dispatching to Sissinghurst weekly grocery hampers from Selfridges and a drip feed of treasures from Knole. Among highlights of the latter was a copy of one of the two portraits by Kneller of Charles Sackville, 6th Earl of Dorset, poetaster and hero of Vita's early historical novel *The King's Secret.*

A consignment of 'moth-eaten but superb' carpets from Victoria's house in Streatham inspired Harold to reflect on the inconsistencies in their lives. 'It is typical of our existence that with no settled income and no certain prospects, we should live in a muddle of museum carpets, ruined castles, and penury.'[114] Most lasting among Victoria's gifts would be two lead vases with covers and eight bronze urns from the gardens of Bagatelle, two of which were sold after the war; Victoria also sent the statue of a bacchante that stands today at the head of Sissinghurst's Lime Walk. Less pleasing to reflect on was Roy Campbell's overtly hostile and dangerously transparent verse satire, *The Georgiad.* Its publication in 1931 added to Vita and Harold's dissatisfaction. Wisely, the Nicolsons responded to its very public drubbing with silence.

The woman who startled Vita out of her 'ordered, rational' state was a journalist eight years her junior. Simply dressed, eschewing make-up, with her short hair and strong face, she was boyish in appearance; she possessed none of Mary's gypsy wildness or Hilda's earnest diffidence. Her name was Evelyn Irons. They met in a drawing room in Belgrave Square. Vita had accepted a request to read to an invited audience from *The Land.* Briefly, afterwards, Evelyn, who was the editor of the Women's Page of the *Daily Mail,* attempted to interview Vita: she found herself reduced to a daze by what she regarded as 'headily emotional stuff' and the questions she wanted to ask Vita eluded her. When she set off to return to the office, Vita followed her. Vita suggested lunch at Harold's flat in King's Bench Walk. Evelyn's response was contained within a letter full of the questions she had failed to ask in Belgrave Square. Vita replied: 'I really do hate newspaper stunts and try to keep away from them as much as possible,' ignored Evelyn's questions and again suggested lunch – 'to show me you forgive me'. Evelyn accepted.

Two days later, on 6 March, Evelyn went to Sissinghurst and stayed the night. By evening it was cold, the moon glinted on frozen turf, made reflections in the lake, silvering the willows, the outlines of wild ducks; Evelyn admitted to herself that she had fallen in love. She invited Vita to a party in the flat in Royal Hospital Road, Chelsea, which she shared with her lover, Olive Rinder. Vita took olives. Evelyn offered drinks, issued a challenge: 'I suppose you know that I'm desperately in love with you.'

Not since Lord Lascelles and Ivan Hay had Vita resisted the aphrodisiac of being loved. Evelyn's visits to Long Barn and Sissinghurst became a routine, a weekly occurrence, usually on Fridays. She left on Saturday mornings, ahead of Harold's return. Vita insisted on secrecy: like Violet before her, Evelyn balked at its constraints. For her part, Olive Rinder encouraged Evelyn's romantic truancy; she too was halfway to falling in love with Vita. Once, Vita cooked the first Sissinghurst asparagus for Evelyn: she steamed it in a syrup tin over a primus stove. The two women worked together in the garden: Evelyn's photographs show Vita in a spotted shirt, belted at the waist, over breeches, or a shapeless dress of indeterminate colour like an overall, with gardening gauntlets and a spaniel in attendance. In her new novel, Vita called her heroine Evelyn. It was a lover's joke. For all her desirability and attractiveness as a character, Evelyn Jarrold in *Family History* is decorative, feminine, trivial: her dressmaker, Mr Rivers, is 'in the habit of saying that few of his clients could afford to look both picturesque and chic, but that Mrs Tommy Jarrold was one of the exceptions'.[115] Evelyn Irons was bored by clothes and would shortly leave the paper's Women's Page; her interests were serious, hard-hitting. Neither picturesqueness nor chicness interested her any more than they interested Vita. She would never, like the fictional Evelyn, make herself foolish in love.

Reversing the roles she had shared with Pat Dansey, Vita bought Evelyn extravagant presents – a monogrammed leather writing case for her own daily letters; a suitcase filled with silk pyjamas; a diamond watch. She loved Evelyn extravagantly too and deluged her with poems. But her instinct erred. In a poem written in May called 'Warning', Vita suggested that the springtime of love contained within it seeds of its autumn decay: 'love's revenges their fruits for us shall bear/ The darkened fruits of passion so fresh in spring begun'.[116] Possibly she anticipated the cooling of her own passion and was preparing the way for her disentanglement.

When it happened, it would be Evelyn who disentangled herself from Vita, not vice versa, Evelyn's the passion that cooled. In *Family History*, which she had finished by the beginning of July, Vita attributes to the fictional Evelyn characteristics she must have recognised as her own. Of Ruth, who is secretly in love with Evelyn, we read: 'She had no illusions as to the depths of woman's cruelty where love or vanity were concerned. Evelyn, she knew, had a cruel and ugly side to her nature. She stated it in those terms, crudely, going no further, and not realising that in Evelyn she had to deal with an exceedingly complex and passionate temperament.'[117] In the novel, those Vita-like characteristics contribute to Evelyn's superiority over Ruth; in Vita's relationship with the real Evelyn, cruelty on the latter's part was inadvertent and Vita lost the upper hand. She was defeated by a greater love.

Before that, at the end of September, Vita and Evelyn went to Provence. They visited Tarascon, Arles, Nîmes, Les Baux. In Nîmes, both were revolted by the spectacle of a bullfight: the Spanish instincts of Pepita's granddaughter were tempered by that English side of her duality which revelled in rabbits, budgerigars, her dogs and their puppies. In the ruined hilltop village of Les Baux, the combination of Evelyn, love, autumn sun and the beauty of the setting inspired Vita to further poetry. Vita concealed from Harold that she was not alone – 'Their absolute seclusion . . . invested their secret love with idyllic colours,' she wrote in *Family History*.[118] When he found out, Harold dubbed it 'Lez Boss'. After the Violet debacle, he could be excused his displeasure at the idea of Vita and a girlfriend in France.

The holiday was a success: Vita wrote, Evelyn took photographs; they made bonfires from dried lavender and the aromatic cones of cypress trees. Vita was expansive, unguarded. 'Oh northern mists of doubt and fear,/ You are not here, you are not here,' she wrote.[119] She made jokes about her adventure with Violet, and Harold and Denys's dash by plane to Amiens; she talked about Mary, also about Hilda and Dottie who had found common ground in their shared loss of Vita and forged a surprisingly warm friendship from that unpromising beginning. Vita referred to them jointly as 'The Sicilian Expedition' after a holiday the two had shared on the island. Later, they returned the favour. Given the difficulties certain to arise from Evelyn already having a partner, Hilda and Dottie referred to her as Vita's scrape. The label stuck and Vita adopted 'Scrape' as her name for Evelyn. Once Vita also became Olive Rinder's lover, early in 1932, she rapidly found herself in a triangle of conflicting jealousies, a scrape indeed. That this was entirely of her own making, she was honest enough to admit, both to herself and to Evelyn, apologetically, when the latter found out; less apologetically she told Evelyn that she was 'more than ever convinced that it is possible to love two people'.[120] Again she did not tell Harold (the third person she loved). Instead she wrote cryptically to Virginia (a fourth love object): 'Life is too complicated, – I sometimes feel that I can't manage it at all.'[121] Virginia replied with concern, but Vita declined to explain herself. Nor did she hasten to resolve the increasingly acrimonious tangle in which she had embroiled Evelyn and Olive. That would be left to Evelyn's defection.

In the meantime, Vita used her poems to impose conditions on Evelyn: 'Love thou but me . . ./ . . . with my own cipher [I] would imprint thee,/ That thou should'st answer to my single voice.'[122] It was her habitual refrain, insisting on unswerving devotion, regardless of the mobile and omnivorous character of her own emotions. In a poem written at Les Baux, she promised to love Evelyn until death: in practice she interpreted to suit herself Gibran's injunction about making bonds of love. She acknowledged to Evelyn that her poetic promises sounded like 'threadbare vows' and denied that they were such. They were, and the intensity of her feelings proved typically evanescent. So too did Evelyn's. In Evelyn's case, her feelings for Vita were knocked sideways by a *coup de foudre* at a party on 14 July 1932.

Evelyn fell in love with an older woman with 'features cut like a Greek intaglio', Joy McSweeney: Joy would remain Evelyn's partner until her death in 1979. With a degree of trepidation, Evelyn told Vita of her change of heart in the first week of August. Coming on top of a disastrous Cornish holiday in Lamorna, where Vita, Evelyn and Olive had argued bitterly, Evelyn's revelations cannot have surprised Vita. Vita was regretful nevertheless. On 11 August, she sent Evelyn a poem, which she published in her *Collected Poems* the following year. 'Do not forget, my dear, that once we loved,' she wrote in 'Valediction'. 'Remember only, free of stain or smutch,/ That passion once went naked and ungloved,/ And that your skin was startled by my touch.'[123] Those memories, with their unapologetic emphasis on the physicality of their love, were alive and real for Vita.

Vita did not comment on Evelyn's transferral of her affections. Although she described herself as 'very revengeful when I love',[124] a tendency she had proved before in hotel rooms in Paris and Amiens, she was sensible enough to accept defeat and write out her unhappiness in verse. She clung to the memory of Les Baux and would invoke it in her occasional letters to Evelyn, which continued for the rest of her life. Her American lecture tour provided welcome distraction. On her return Vita took a deliberate step away from the dangerous, talkative, disloyal world of newspapers and bohemian London parties into the safety of her tower at Sissinghurst; she planted water lilies in the lake and *Iris kaempferi* by the moat.[125] In the future, other helpers than Evelyn would work alongside her in the garden.

But Vita remained stung, unexpectedly on the defensive. Although her retreat appeared to be endorsed by advice Harold received from Lord Eustace Percy on the couple's return from America that 'serious people ought to withdraw from life nowadays', she wondered if in fact she had any choice.[126] In an unpublished diary poem written in May 1933, she described herself as 'a broken mirror that once gave a whole reflection' and asked 'What have I to give my friends in the last resort?/ An awkwardness, a shyness and a scrap,/ No thing that's truly me.'[127] Eventually she took cover in her writing, explaining her feelings in what would become her next novel: 'In her immature philosophy, the first tenet was to shut yourself away in a stony fortress and then to consider what system of bluff would best defend you against the importunities of the world.'[128] It was St Barbara's philosophy, passive, discreet: far removed from the cavalier swagger that remained a part of Vita's self-identity.

Vita compartmentalised her life. It was a form of pragmatism, her means of juggling conflicting loyalties. It also, at times, represented a genuine failure of imagination. 'It is almost as hard, in Persia, to believe in the existence of England, as it is, in England, to believe in the existence of Persia,' she wrote in Tehran in 1926.[129] At times that 'blindness' extended beyond England and Persia to Vita's dealings with people. Her emotional life was seldom simple. In 1931, she had fallen in love with Evelyn, encouraged Olive Rinder to fall in love with her, remained hurt at what she saw as Virginia's abandonment, worked alongside Hilda and written and gardened at a furious rate. Her support for Harold and her sons was boundless in theory but circumscribed in practice by these multiple claims on her time and energy.

Harold had joined the staff of the *Evening Standard* on 1 January 1930. Before the month was out, he knew that he had made a mistake, disliked journalism, slithered into depression. That depression lingered. His aversion to Grub Street dented his self-esteem. His early dreams with Vita taunted him. In January 1913, apprehensive about her dislike of diplomacy as a profession and a way of life, Vita had begged Harold to re-assure her that 'the truth is a rose-coloured story culminating in you and me making a State entry into Delhi on an elephant with a golden howdah, and you receiving deputations of Indian princes'; in May 1926, the Nicolsons' butler George Horne, known as Moody, confided to Vita that he shared the same dream for Harold.[130] Harold soon discovered that Lord Beaverbrook's gossip columns were a far cry from following in the footsteps of his Uncle Dufferin as Viceroy. Distaste for journalism lay behind his decision to join Sir Oswald Mosley's New Party in January 1931 and stand as a parliamentary candidate in October; Virginia described his political oppor-tunism to Vita as 'rash, foolish, perverse, incalculable', as indeed it proved.[131] Predictably the collapse of New Party hopes in the 1931 elections had also dealt a body blow to the party's

Vita as mother – with Ben (left) and Nigel (right) in 1924.

Vita's lover Mary Campbell painted this view of Long Barn in the winter of 1927.
Vita had bought the part-medieval, extended cottage for £3,000 in 1915.

Vita broadcast for the BBC for the first time on 18 April 1928. After embarking on an affair with Director of Talks Hilda Matheson, she became a regular and highly regarded broadcaster for the Corporation.

Nigel, Vita and Ben at Long Barn. Vita's decorating included distinctive features of the rooms of her childhood: tapestries, seventeenth-century looking glasses and Jacobean oak furniture.

Vita 'in the prime of life, an animal at the height of its powers, a beautiful flower in full bloom. She was very handsome, dashing, aristocratic, lordly...'

'You do like to have your cake and eat it, – and *so* many cakes, so many, a surfeit of sweet things', one lover teased Vita in 1932 of her habit of juggling multiple lovers. Among Vita's lovers were (*clockwise from top*): Dorothy Wellesley, Hilda Matheson and Virginia Woolf.

At Sissinghurst, Vita realised her long-held fantasy of retreating into a tower with her books. Her writing room was on the first floor of the tower, with a small library in the adjoining octagonal tower.

Vita conceived the idea that would become the White Garden, beside the Priest's House, in December 1939. It has since become one of the most famous planting schemes in the world.

In a photograph taken in 1948 by John Gay (*right*), Vita, on the steps of the tower at Sissinghurst, wears the uniform of breeches and gaiters she had first adopted thirty years earlier. The cigarette, in its holder, is also a feature of an equally theatrical image taken by John Hedgecoe four years before Vita's death (*below*).

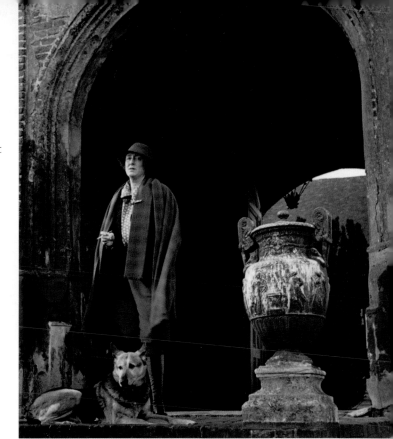

Vita's desk on the day she died, 2 June 1962, with her preferred collection of small-scale flower arrangements, a photograph of Harold and sheets of stamps.

paper, *Action*, and Harold was forced to use his own money to settle some of the journal's outstanding debts. With a degree of accuracy, he noted in his diary at the end of the year, 'Everything has gone wrong. I have lost not only my fortune but much of my reputation.'[132] In the short term, he would remain equally preoccupied with both.

With his financial prospects 'so black that I groan to gaze into the abyss', Vita visited Harold's bank on 23 December 1931 and successfully 'extract[ed] an unwilling loan from them'.[133] Harold acknowledged Vita's role in his life as one of calmness, comfort and consideration; he omitted to mention the lack of interest in either politics or journalism which had caused her to fall asleep the night they sat beside the fire discussing his future: 'When I reach the point where I picture myself riding on an elephant at Delhi, I find that for the last half-hour she has been asleep.'[134]

Airily Vita reassured her husband that he could make £2,000 by writing a novel; it was still less than the income she had forsworn from Victoria. Vita's admiration for Harold's writing was sincere and wholehearted. In her diary in January 1924 she had described herself as 'so impressed with [the] vividness' of his *Byron: The Last Journey*, which she read as proofs. 'I like his lucid mind, and his ease of expression. He is like a person who knows how to use a scythe,' she wrote to Virginia.[135] Her dislike of the bulk of the careers open to Harold was equally sincere. In addition, Vita struggled to take seriously any mention of the precariousness of their finances. In March 1932, Harold described her reaction to just such a conversation: 'Our discussion is interrupted by a sudden desire on her part to take the Blue Train to Biarritz, or why not Syracuse, or why, if one has got as far as that, not to Greece or the Lebanon? I point out that we CANNOT AFFORD IT – THAT WE ARE POOR PEOPLE THESE DAYS.'[136]

But Vita was not listening. She parried Harold's misgivings with her proposed new plantings for the front of Sissinghurst, 'a wall of limes, framing the two gables and the arch, and following on to a poplar avenue across the fields'.[137] For the considerable sum of £5, she bought four large yew trees for the courtyard. 'We found them in a nurseryman's garden, to which they had just been transplanted from Penshurst church-yard. The parishioners of Penshurst apparently thought them too gloomy and threw them out. They were old trees but they were just what the courtyard at Sissinghurst demanded and we chanced it.'[138] At further expense the trees' roots were thoroughly doused with bull's blood during planting. From the same nurseryman Vita acquired a neglected climbing hybrid perpetual rose that was afterwards identified as Souvenir du Docteur Jamain. It remained one of her favourites. In August 1957 she described it with customary lushness as 'nostalgically scented, meaning everything that burying one's nose into the heart of a rose meant in one's childhood, or in one's adolescence when one first discovered poetry, or the first time one fell in love'.[139] Harold's warnings affected Vita glancingly: she was never constrained by the ordinary or the small scale. 'It is always possible to paint any picture in dark colours, but that means that one has left out the essential part,' she wrote later. 'Life depends largely on how you take it.'[140] Her boldness was a tonic to Harold. When Vita was away, his confidence faltered.

During Vita's absence in Provence with Evelyn, Harold identified in his diary 'what it is that makes us so indispensable to each other'. He focused on four points: their respect for one another; their ability to relax completely in one another's company; their stimulation of one another and the harmony of their togetherness.[141] He highlighted Vita's understanding; he did not refer to love, either given or received. And he never forgot Vita's underlying dislike of marriage as an institution, of which she had given him ample proof. 'I know you loathe marriage and that it is not a natural state for you,' he wrote on their twenty-first wedding anniversary in 1934.[142]

Vita's financial phlegmatism appeared to be rewarded by the success of the couple's American lecture tour at the beginning of 1933. This benison was followed by another in the autumn, when Vita received a letter from her French bank announcing a balance of £2,600. It was not enough to assuage Harold's fears completely. 'Unless we begin to make more money by books, we are in for a very difficult time. This is for me a constant anxiety,' he wrote on 31 December. Both Harold and Vita knew that they were playing a waiting game: Vita would become a wealthy woman on Victoria's death.

Naturally less anxious about such things than Harold, Vita was wrestling with different anxieties. Once Evelyn had set up home with Joy McSweeney, Olive Rinder was homeless: suffering from tuberculosis, she was too weak to support herself by working. Vita's financial support exceeded her emotional benefactions. She recognised that Olive, like Violet before her, had seen through her: the picture Olive painted of Vita was less heroic than Violet's. 'You do like to have your cake and eat it, – and *so* many cakes, so many, a surfeit of sweet things,' Olive had written to Vita on 11 January 1932.[143] It was a repetition of Pat Dansey's criticism about Vita's deluded play-acting as 'a romantic young man who treats women badly'. Again the accusation of selfishness, however deserved, was unwelcome. Vita asked Evelyn to go on visiting Olive, but Evelyn had broken free. In the years to come, neither Olive nor Vita would see her often. Vita found a bungalow for Olive. Olive's letters to her were pathetic entreaties. For Vita the spell was broken. The depression that had assailed her early in 1931 returned.

*

'It goes without saying that a book by the author of "The Edwardians" is ably written, that every part of it, taken singly, is good, and that it holds the interest,' wrote Basil Davenport in his review of *The Dark Island* in the *Saturday Review* on 24 November 1934. 'But it holds the interest only to disappoint it; the new "Wuthering Heights" is still unwritten, and the self-tormenting sadist still awaits his genius.'

On 10 October 1934, the Hogarth Press printed a first edition of 10,590 copies of what would prove to be Vita's last novel for almost a decade. By the end of the year only half had sold, 4,000 of them ahead of publication and a raft of mostly ambivalent reviews.[144]

The Dark Island is the most disturbing of Vita's novels. It tells the story of a marriage between Shirin, a woman who, like Vita, prefers 'harshness to sentimentality', and Davenport's 'self-tormenting sadist', her husband Venn. Venn too resembles Vita: he has been shaped by his childhood, 'too well trained by his own temperament, and by Storn [his ancestral home], always to choose the more cruel, more dangerous path'.[145] At some length Vita examines the angry and self-destructive emotional make-up of her handsome protagonists. She summarised her melodramatic plot as 'the trouble which ended in two persons losing their lives and in one criminal receiving an expression of sympathy from the coroner instead of a sentence of death from the judge'. It is brooding, intense stuff played out against a backdrop of equal intensity.

The dark island of the title is Storn, crowned by a Norman castle, the home of the le Breton family. Both husband and wife are more in love with Storn than one another; like Vita's feelings for Knole, their passion for the island exceeds simple love and overrides other loyalties. Like Vita's Sissinghurst, Storn is a retreat from the world: Shirin relishes 'the bliss, the release of living for ever on Storn away from people'.[146] For husband

and wife, Storn is their journey's end: physically and metaphorically it lies 'at the end of that path of sunlight, symbol
of all romance and of all escape from the humdrum weariness
of life, from its meannesses, its falsity, and its pain'.[147] Their
tragedy is to take into that path of sunlight their own meannesses and falsity. Despite its vigorous emotions, *The Dark
Island* is a novel by an older, wearier, less sanguine Vita.

On delivery of Vita's manuscript, Leonard Woolf described
the novel to Virginia as 'perilous fantastic stuff, a woman fla-
gellated in a cave'.[148] Astutely he questioned how much of Vita's
lurid Grand Guignol the public would stand. Harold, Nigel and
Ben, who designed the dust jacket, combined in disliking *The
Dark Island*; Harold protested that it was 'morbid and distressing'.
Sexual violence and calculated cruelty were curious subjects for
a popular writer of bestsellers in 1934. Where recently Vita
had wooed a large, middle-class readership with a story of
Edwardian aristocratic amorality, in *The Dark Island* she exposed
to their bewildered gaze unlovely subtexts drawn from her own
atypical experience of upper-class life, conflicts centred on inheritance, territorialism and the inequalities of men and women.
The tragic story of Shirin le Breton offered Vita's readers no
picturesque distractions from an uncertain decade. The violence
that in *The Dragon in Shallow Waters* had appeared simply stir-
ring here acquires a darker, more lingering impact, which made
for uncomfortable reading. The *Times Literary Supplement*
acclaimed the novel as a work of 'fervid' imagination: it was
that very fervour which alienated other readers. Virginia
suggested Vita was too close to her material. Afterwards she
acknowledged that the emotional revelations contained within
the novel made her jealous and lessened her enjoyment.

The key, as always, lay within Vita herself. Soon after her
return from America, she had fallen in love with her sister-in-
law. Gwen St Aubyn was one of two grown-up bridesmaids at

Vita and Harold's wedding. *The Dark Island* is dedicated to Gwen and Gwen is the inspiration for its heroine, Shirin; Storn is St Michael's Mount in Cornwall, which Gwen's husband Sam would inherit on his father's death. Even Shirin's name, Persian for 'sweet', was Vita's pet name for Gwen; it was more appropriate in Gwen's case than that of the fictional Shirin. As Vita's son Ben recognised, the novel is a double portrait of Gwen and, in the guise of old Lady le Breton, Victoria. It also, of course, encompasses images of Vita herself, a fragmented reflection divided between several characters. The Venn who whips the chained and naked Shirin in Andromeda's Cave is an adult version of the nettle-thrashing Vita of those Boer War games with the Battiscombes; like Vita, Venn is torn between his hatred of democracy and mistrust of privilege. Shirin shares Vita's obsessive belief in the redemptive power of place; like Vita, she is casual in her approach to romantic conquest, studiedly without regrets and secretive. Vita's description of Shirin's friend Cristina suggests self-portraiture, 'with her tawny appearance and her big limbs; her large gestures, her large generosity, her love of bright colours, her coltish way of striding about, her impatient way of pushing her hair back, her strong square hands, her direct speech – all rather Wagnerian'.[149] Cristina's affection for Shirin clearly transcends the ordinary bounds of friendship. She admits that she wants 'the whole of Shirin greedily',[150] a statement in itself to account for Harold's dislike of the novel. In her ponderous ratiocination, Cristina repeatedly resorts to horticultural imagery. In *The Dark Island*, Vita wears many masks.

On 18 August 1933, Vita had written to Virginia, 'I've got my sister-in-law staying here, and she's been ill, and I am supposed to provide the cure. Country rustication and all that.'[151] Gwen was Harold's only sister, ten years his junior, four years younger than Vita. Despite a strong sibling bond, she had played little part in the Nicolsons' lives since 1913, although she and her husband rented Vita and Harold's Ebury Street house early in their marriage. It was a motor accident involving serious head injuries that brought her to Sissinghurst to convalesce. Her arrival provoked a mixed response in Vita. The women were not close. Gwen and her husband led safe, predictable lives in county society, accepting its values and shibboleths; Gwen mostly appeared preoccupied with bringing up her large family of five children. At the time of her accident, she was working on a book, *The Family Book*, subtitled: 'A comprehensive guide to family life from before marriage to the adolescence of children: primarily for parents'. Both title and subject seemed to confirm Gwen's conventionalism.

Vita's letter to Virginia suggests the way the wind was blowing. She described her pleasure in looking after Gwen as increased by Gwen's work on *The Family Book*: 'We sit on the steps of the tower discussing why some women get their physical satisfaction interiorly or exteriorly, and what connection there may or may not be between the inner part of the nerve and the outer – and what connection there may be between perversion and normality – and so on. A very interesting question.'[152]

Gwen had reached a crossroads in her life. More important to her than *The Family Book* was her long, thoughtful spiritual journey towards Catholicism. That change represented a move away from the solid certainties of St Aubyn county life; in the aftermath of her accident Gwen embraced a larger-scale questioning of the building blocks of her existence. Vita, who had warned Harold during their engagement that she was incapable of submission, interpreted this development as a rejection of Gwen's former docility in marriage and encouraged her rebellion. The women's friendship grew. Gwen's doctor insisted she needed at least a year's full convalescence: with her husband's acquiescence, and in the absence of guest rooms, she moved in to a room at the top of Vita's tower at Sissinghurst that was specially prepared for her. With intervals she would continue to live with Vita and Harold until 1942.

Following an operation in January 1934, Gwen was taken by Vita to Portofino to recover. Harold expressed concern at his 'poor cracked sister' travelling so soon, but no other uneasiness.[153] The women stayed in Castello Brown, the small sixteenth-century hilltop castle perched above the harbour, which had inspired Elizabeth von Arnim's novel of the previous decade, *The Enchanted April*. In ironic vein, Harold wrote to Vita: 'Well, I am all for that sort of thing, as you know. I liked being turned out of my dear little suburban home [Long Barn] and made to sleep in a ruined tower on a camp-bed [Sissinghurst]. And I see no reason why, in the present state of our finances, you did not buy the Castello outright . . . It all comes from Gwen reading . . . the works of Elizabeth Russell [von Arnim].'[154]

Von Arnim had described the Castello as ideal for 'those who Appreciate Wisteria and Sunshine', a prescription calculated to appeal to Vita.[155] She had also drawn a picture of women frustrated in marriage, temporarily abandoning their husbands. 'A picture had flashed across her brain, and there were two figures in it sitting together under a great trailing wisteria that stretched across the branches of a tree she didn't know, and it was herself and Mrs Arbuthnot – she saw them – she saw them.'[156] Like Vita in 1918, von Arnim's women reject the constraints of unrelenting domesticity. 'There ought to be a break, there ought to be intervals,' one exclaims, referring to the married woman's monotony of 'see[ing] about the dinner and the fish'. As in von Arnim's novel, in which, within a fairytale scheme, wives are fondly reunited with their husbands against a backdrop of glittering Mediterranean,

Harold joined Vita and Gwen in their harbourside eyrie. In this case, there had been no crisis. Vita had made her protest long ago and Gwen had no need to shirk domestic responsibilities, having already, as she said, entrusted all responsibilities to Vita.

In 1940, Gwen published an account of her conversion to Catholicism, *Towards a Pattern*. It consists of letters written to an unnamed recipient, who is almost certainly Vita. In describing a mystical vision that appears to her while she is writing, Gwen tells her correspondent, 'I heard your pen scratching as you wrote . . . The room, and you, were there, and so was I, but I was conscious of an enormous change in me.'[157] That change in Gwen had begun before 1940. It began when Vita reimagined her as a flawed and tragic romantic heroine in *The Dark Island* and, in the way of Vita's fiction, merged their two personalities in her picture of Shirin. In turn Gwen would influence Vita. At first those changes happened in small ways: Virginia noted with disapproval that Vita had begun to wear nail polish and lipstick, inexpertly applied. Afterwards Gwen's preoccupations shaped both the subject matter of Vita's writing and her handling of those subjects.

The mysticism that characterises the biography of St Joan of Arc which Vita wrote during the period of her intimacy with Gwen St Aubyn arose out of the latter's religious odyssey: it is already discernible in *The Dark Island*. Shirin succumbs to the 'beauty and magic of Storn': 'like a faith, like an ecstasy, it transformed her, filling her with strength and purity and ardour, with a passion that transcended all material love'.[158] Gwen's journey towards spiritual renewal inspired similar questioning on Vita's part: Vita described her as 'you, who opened first my shuttered eyes/ To the first difficult and deep surmise'.[159] The Hogarth Press promoted Vita's long poem *Solitude*, written under Gwen's influence and published in 1938, as 'the poet's intimate reflections induced by the solitude of night, reflections upon love, God and the universe, beauty and truth, life and death', territory Vita would visit again, in different guise, in *The Garden*. In fact she was no newcomer to such questions. On and off throughout the last decade she had struggled to unravel a workable philosophy of living, most notably in 'Reddín', the long poem she finished in 1928, having previously attempted to write it as a novel, including during the trip to Italy with Dottie and Gerry in 1921.

The poem is named after an architect who builds a temple that 'compelled each man to find his way anew/ Round corners and by paths that no guide knew'.[160] Reddín's philosophy is explicitly non-Christian – 'No vision of the martyr or the saint/ Shone down from domed mosaic'. It is a creed which, rather vaguely, embraces everyone: 'all were welcome there,/ Since the great doors stood open'.[161] In its vagueness lies both its strength and its weakness: after a decade the Vita who had once described herself as 'disgracefully happy-go-lucky' was still searching for answers.[162] *Solitude* included her attempt at a fuller, more personal answer; she also offered images of transformation in *Saint Joan of Arc* and *The Eagle and the Dove*. After the cool critical reception of *The Dark Island*, Gwen's example provided Vita with fresh inspiration and, in her biography of Joan of Arc, published by Cobden-Sanderson in June 1936, a popular commercial success. Vita's mother, who read the book in manuscript form, lamented the absence of any love interest in her heroine's life; her friends were caustic, and baffled by a development they regarded as out of character. No one who had read 'Reddín' or Vita's assessment of Joan of Arc's first dilemma – 'the practical inconvenience of belonging to the wrong sex must be faced and overcome'[163] – could fail to find the connection.

Vita celebrated completing her new book by planting quantities of old-fashioned roses. In the same year, a large greenhouse and an orchid house were erected at Sissinghurst and Vita bought thirty new budgerigars for her aviary. The Lime Walk was planted and paved. It would become Harold's particular suzerainty, referred to as 'My Life's Work' or 'MLW'; he employed his own gardener, Sidney Neve, for its upkeep and kept detailed notebooks on its progress.[164] Gwen continued to help Vita in the garden. Together they rowed on the lake, gathered apples in the orchard, filled cushions with the 'delicious silky floss' contained in bulrush stems. Whenever they were at home, Ben and Nigel also helped their parents in the garden, part of Sissinghurst's 'monastic' routine in which gardening formed the only alternative to writing. But it was not *Saint Joan of Arc* which so richly endowed Vita and Harold's garden. On 30 January 1936, following a minor stroke or heart attack, Victoria died peacefully in her sleep at her house, White Lodge, near Brighton. She was seventy-three. In his diary Harold described Vita as 'much harassed and shattered, but inwardly, I think, relieved'. Vita, who had rushed to her mother's bedside, described herself as 'stunned'. She felt fragile; the onset of the menopause exacerbated the uncontrollability of her responses. Eight days later, Harold returned to Brighton to bury Victoria, as she had requested in 'a pathetic typewritten note', by scattering her ashes out at sea, in sight of White Lodge. Vita did not accompany him.

It was a vignette, like others in this story, which balanced sobriety with slapstick. More than twenty years after Victoria's triumph in the Scott lawsuit, the Sackvilles remained noteworthy. Members of the press seized upon news of Victoria's death. Vita and Harold took precautions. Victoria's ashes were removed from the undertakers' premises after cremation and entrusted to a local oyster seller, Mr English. English turned out to be a drunkard: only with difficulty was he dissuaded from keeping Harold company in his hired fishing boat. Assisted by the two sailors who owned the boat, Harold travelled two miles out to sea; also with him was Victoria's last secretary, Cecil Rhind. Kneeling at the gunwale, the sailors and Rhind standing behind him, their hats in their hands, Harold tipped into 'an angry brown sea' the handful of Victoria's last remains. In place of prayers was a simple valediction, hurled by Harold into the wind: 'B.M. – all who love you are happy that you should now be at peace. We shall remember always your beauty, your courage and your charm.'[165] Inevitably the wind changed direction. It threw the ashes back into Harold's face. They settled in the seams and creases of his greatcoat.[166]

Harold reported proceedings selectively to Vita. After death duties, the estate she inherited from Victoria provided her with an annual income of £5,000. There was also £1,000 a year each for Ben, now twenty-two and embarked on the first steps of his career as an art historian, and nineteen-year-old Nigel, at Balliol College, Oxford, where he had followed in Ben and Harold's footsteps. Among Victoria's possessions were garden benches designed by Lutyens which made their way to Sissinghurst. In the short term, Vita and Harold's financial worries were over. Seery's gift to his 'chère petite amie' extended its lifeline to a third generation.

For Vita, Victoria's death demanded resolution. She achieved it, as always, through her writing. The following October she offered the public a careful, affectionate and misleading account of her relationship with her mother: what Victoria meant to her, she asserted, was 'a mixture of tragedy and – no, not comedy, but sheer fun'.[167] In a double biography of Victoria and Pepita, entitled simply *Pepita*, Vita imposed order on disorder and replaced questions with answers. She did so by presenting the lives of her mother and her grandmother as case studies in the Latin temperament. *Pepita* became Vita's fullest exposition of her personal theory of her own duality.

She rooted the 'Spanish' side of her nature in an inescapable maternal continuum and exploited national stereotypes to explain away troubling behaviour. Of Pepita's mother (her own great-grandmother), Vita wrote: 'Catalina lavished on her own daughter the fierce and possessive love which Latin women do often display towards their children, injudicious to a degree and mischievous in its consequences, but certainly not malevolent in its intention.'[168] At a stroke, Vita appeared to solve the riddle of Victoria's own approach to motherhood; the pattern she outlined came close to describing her own behaviour in her sexual relationships with other women. This pat quality to *Pepita* reassured Vita; it also trivialised more extreme aspects of Victoria's bad behaviour. Its writing proved an act of exorcism. In none of her fiction written after *Pepita* did Vita explore with the same urgency and intensity the emotional and sexual ebullience of earlier fictions. She had settled the record.

Separately Leonard and Virginia Woolf wrote to Vita about the manuscript to express their delight: Virginia claimed she 'read it like a shark swallowing a mackerel'.[169] In private they accused Vita of consciously downplaying Victoria's devilment: Virginia remembered too vividly the horror she had felt in 1929 when Victoria took it upon herself to enlighten Ben and Nigel about their parents' sexual proclivities. In this case, Vita's instinct for myth-making was stronger than the careful objectivity she had demonstrated in her biography of Joan of Arc. Again she plundered fairy tales for easy explanations: 'The bad fairy who attended the christening of Sleeping Beauty must have attended my mother's also. Gifts had been showered on her: beauty and charm and energy, abounding vitality, courage, determination . . . But the bad fairy ordained that she should fritter everything away.'[170] Like much of Vita's writing, it was an exercise in wish fulfilment. Her American publishers aligned it with her fiction. 'Witty, frank, completely devoid of reticences,' claimed Doubleday Doran, 'this unconventional memoir of the extraordinary Sackville-West family could only have been written by the brilliant author of *The Edwardians* and *All Passion Spent.*' The Hogarth Press published four editions in six months and, at the end of March 1938, paid Vita royalties on sales of 12,198 copies.

Meanwhile, Vita had embarked on her first gardening book: *Some Flowers* was published by Cobden-Sanderson in November 1937. Despite her growing reclusiveness, she had made a new friend of Maidstone-based rose expert, Edward Ashton Bunyard, author of *Old Garden Roses*; she included four roses in *Some Flowers*, alongside crown imperials and the pomegranate, *Punica granatum*, which she had first seen a decade before growing untended in Persian myrtle groves. From the outset Vita's horticultural writing betrayed an idiosyncratic quality. She offered commonsense advice and observations while celebrating favourite plants with the sensuousness typical of her writing. 'It is improbable that we shall ever lie on a bed of roses, unless we are very decadent and also very rich,' she wrote of *Rosa gallica*, 'but we can imagine ourselves doing so when we hold a single rose close to our eyes and absorb it in an intimate way into our private heart.'[171]

On 8 June 1937, Harold wrote to Vita: 'Never has Sissinghurst looked more lovely . . . we have got what we wanted to get – a perfect proportion between the classical and the romantic, between the element of expectation and the element of surprise.'[172] Up to a point those neat polarities represented Harold and Vita themselves; Vita's romanticism took the form of the lavishness which she claimed was 'an inherent part of my philosophy', her principle of 'cram, cram, cram' that, as much as anything, hallmarked a distinctive Sissinghurst style.[173] By the late 1930s, Vita and Harold's complementary outlooks had sculpted Sissinghurst's six acres into a richly satisfying aesthetic and horticultural mélange: in their garden they proved to one another that in their divergences lay much of their strength and each was touchingly eager to accord credit to the other. That Vita shared Harold's assessment of Sissinghurst's loveliness is indicated by her agreement the following summer to open the garden twice to paying visitors. The Nicolsons charged them a shilling a head. Over the course of two days they raised £25 14s 6d. The same year Vita made her first plantings in the Herb Garden and between them they completed the carpet of polyanthus in the Nuttery. Harold celebrated the success of their open days by giving Vita a plant token. In the unpublished poem she wrote to him in response, she linked plants' growth with the growth of love and, reflecting on their marriage, resorted to her planting philosophy: 'let us cram with flowers each threatened rift'.[174]

The Sackville flag was hoisted at Sissinghurst for the first time in the second week of March 1939. It was Harold's present to Vita. 'The flag streamed out five minutes after I had passed under the porch and made me feel awfully grand,' Vita wrote in her diary on 24 March.[175] Later she told an American friend that it was Harold who valued the symbolism of the flag: 'as Harold says of the flag I fly in the tower: "It grands the place up."'[176] It hardly matters. Bold above her tower, it was the pennant of her possession. In the fullest sense, Sissinghurst was Vita's. The last of the 'fragments of an age gone by' that she had described in her poem 'Sissinghurst' had been 'assembled'. From now on possession would be reversed: Vita would belong to Sissinghurst.

PART VI

All Passion Spent?

'When I came into the country, and being seated among silent trees and meads, and hills, had all my time in my own hands, I resolved to spend it all, whatever it cost me, in search of happiness, and to satiate that burning thirst which nature had enkindled in me from youth. In which I was so resolute, that I chose rather to live upon ten pounds a year, and to go in leather clothes, and feed upon bread and water, so that I might have all my time clearly to myself . . .'

Thomas Traherne, quoted in 'Buying a Farm',
by V. Sackville-West, *New Statesman*, 15 April 1939

VITA DESCRIBED SEX as 'the arch-deceiver'. In a diary poem she claimed 'sex deludes one into the belief that one has attained real contact with another person;/ And since the horrible loneliness of the soul makes one crave for some contact,/ One turns gratefully to sex as a short-cut to contact'.[1]

Vita knew at first hand the deceits of sex. She knew from her *béguins* the potential elusiveness of real contact with another person. At moments throughout her life she had known 'the horrible loneliness of the soul'. In *Solitude*, published in 1938, she dismissed the 'lure' of the flesh, suggesting its 'cheap unworthy tricks' failed to satisfy.[2] In vain Hilda wrote to Vita to protest, hurt to be likened retrospectively to a trick, even by implication.

In middle age, Vita did not forswear the romantic impulses that had directed so much of her life: those energies found a more certain outlet, a fuller satisfaction, in Sissinghurst. Previously, in novels and plays, she had transformed herself into the Sackville cavalier of her imagination; in the same guise she had wooed friends and lovers. In her last – and best – act of creation, she channelled that heroic bravado into her garden. 'Dare/ Th' unorthodox; be always bold; be prince;/ . . . Fail if you must . . ./ But gloriously fail: the dream, the brag,/ No prudent pose,' she wrote in *The Garden*.[3] It was, for Vita, characteristic rhetoric, with its insistence on unorthodoxy, glory, a vaunting dream and the combined suggestions of masculinity, power and status in the injunction: 'be prince'.

Sissinghurst had provided solace and distraction for Harold, battling rising debts, unhappiness at the *Evening Standard* and the sense of futility that followed his departure from the Foreign Office. It would provide the same solace – and significant excitement – for Vita. Leonard Woolf wrote that, 'in the creation of Sissinghurst and its garden [Vita] was, I think, one of the happiest people I have ever known, for she loved them and they gave her complete satisfaction in the long years between middle age and death'.[4] Vita's work on her garden was a retreat and recognised as such by those nearest to her. On 9 March 1938, Harold concluded a letter discussing the threat of Nazi Germany with: 'My dearest, do not worry about these things but cultivate your lovely garden.'[5] Like the purchase of Sissinghurst itself, Vita's immersion in gardening represented a running away in order to 'sink down through centuries to another clime,/ And buried find the castle and the rose'.[6] That immersion was imaginative as well as physical. Her garden became Vita's final act of defiance. She approached it, as ever, in vigorous spirit. 'Come, flame; come, tongue of courage; scorch me, sear,' she entreated in *The Garden*, 'Better, I swear, to be consumed entire/ Than smoulder, knowing neither zest nor fear.'[7] But her withdrawal into horticulture was also the symbol of something akin to defeat. In 1929, writing about Victorian essayist Leigh Hunt, Vita had claimed 'he could not stand back and estimate the taste of his own day in any detached perspective'.[8] As she must have known, any suggestion of ambivalence about one's own times applied equally to her. 'One ought to be able to adapt oneself – and not struggle to go back to, and live in, an obsolete tradition,' she lamented in December 1944.[9] Vita's efforts were half-hearted and predictably failed. Later, in her dream diary, she wrote a heading: 'Vita's Book of a Thousand Pities'; among her suggestions for pities were committees, clothes, politics, relations, socialists, society and voices. At Sissinghurst, Vita would live life at a remove.

On 22 August 1945, Vita replied to a letter from the daughter of a friend, asking if she had a new book out in time for Christmas. 'Alas the answer is no. I am trying to finish a long poem (a sort of sequel to *The Land*) but that won't come out till next year. The only thing I can recommend to you, as a convenient Christmas present, is a little anthology which Harold and I have rather carelessly thrown together, called "Another World Than This". The title may appeal to you, as I don't think you like *this* world any better than I do?'[10] In a letter to Ben, she had written: 'You know I loathe the modern world quite as much as you do, if not more'; angrily she castigated it as 'this horrible new world'.[11] Vita had described herself as 'worldly-sick' in the dedication of *Solitude* to Gwen St Aubyn.[12]

As long ago as 1924, Vita had recorded simple everyday occurrences guaranteed to make her happy: 'walking on crisp snow;

running a stick along railings; stamping on a nut; stripping the shell from a hard-boiled egg; writing with the really ideal nib; plunging into the sudden comfort of warm water on a cold night'.[13] Each inspired a sensation she labelled 'through leaves' on the analogy of the uncomplicated pleasure inherent in kicking one's way through dry leaves on an autumn walk. Though not intended as an inventory of personal fulfilment (Vita's list omitted Harold, poetry, gardening, her houses, Ben, Nigel, dogs and intimate friends), it indicates something of the nature of her engagement with her world. In *The Land*, Vita claimed for herself the role of 'scholar of simplicity': she found that simplicity in fallen leaves, in nature and the cycle of the seasons.[14] 'I find my God alone in his creation,/ Magnificent or detailed, in the skies/ Or in the leaf unfolding to the spring,' she concluded in *Solitude*.[15] It was nature that moved her to a sense of wonder, awe and comfort. The pleasure of life in the country, she explained, lay in 'the eternally renewed evidences of the determination to live'.[16] Those 'evidences' became the basis of the beliefs she articulated in *The Garden*, as near as she came to resolving her search for spiritual clarity. In country life lay both the simplicity and the reassurance Vita craved in middle age. It provided the background she needed for her life of the mind; she was always, and absorbedly, a creative artist.

'The country habit has me by the heart,' Vita asserts in *The Land*.[17] She defined herself as countrywoman as much as daughter of Knole. In 1938 she began her 'Country Notes' column for the *New Statesman*. She recorded the visit to Sissinghurst of 'metropolitan friends' in 'A Country Life', published the following February. 'They ask me if I have seen this or that play, these or those pictures, and I always find myself obliged to reply that I have not.' But her composure was not ruffled: 'They leave me feeling that I am getting more out of this short life than they, for all their agitations.'[18] As at Long Barn, she bought additional parcels of land over a period of years, thrilled atavistically by her delight in landowning. There were acquisitions along Sissinghurst's boundary with neighbouring Bettenham. Then, in November 1940, at a cost of £5,000, she added 110 acres at Brissenden, north of Sissinghurst. After the Bettenham purchase, she wrote a 'Country Notes' column entitled 'Buying a Farm': 'I love the fields and the orchards so much that I want to feel them safely mine';[19] in a diary poem she referred with greedy hauteur to 'my lands in Kent'.[20]

Vita's vision of country life was selective, possessive and idealised. In *The Women's Land Army*, a short wartime account published in 1944, she imagined a farmhouse kitchen at suppertime: 'The white tablecloth is spread under the lamp and the table is set with yellow plates, and there is a huge loaf and a bowl of tomatoes and jade-green lettuce in the centre. The fire glows behind the bars of the grate, the kettle bubbles gently.'[21] Vita imagines the farmer and his family: the father reading the newspaper with his sleeves rolled up, mother in the scullery, well-behaved children, inevitably a dog. Certainly she did not, as she had written in August 1945, always like *this* world: as in so much of her life, Vita preferred her own version.

Vita's romantic engagement with the country arose in part from her poet's vocation; the privileges of wealth also shaped her vision. Increasingly central to Vita's country life was her solitariness. At Sissinghurst, as she had always intended, she realised her dream of a lonely tower full of books; in time her tower became home to a flock of white pigeons, which she fed on the steps every morning, a scene reminiscent of the Knole of her childhood.

That she came to spend Monday to Friday consistently alone for the last three decades of her life began, on 14 November 1935, as a result of Harold's election to the House of Commons. Parliamentary duties kept Harold in London and his flat in

King's Bench Walk; he spent his weekends with Vita at Sissinghurst. Physical separation reflected profounder gulfs in Vita and Harold's marriage. 'I suppose Hadji and I have been about as unfaithful to one another as one well could be from the conventional point of view, even worse than unfaithful if you add in homosexuality,' Vita commented.[22] By 1935, they had learned to reconcile those differences. The conviction that they did so successfully, supportively and lovingly became key to the value each attached to their resilient marriage. As Vita wrote to Harold: 'I swear no two people could love one another more than we do after all these years . . . I do think we have managed things cleverly.'[23]

Harold became an MP with a majority of eighty-seven votes and a loan from Vita of £500 towards his campaign expenses. Vita offered no further support, resisting with considerable vehemence 'the "Candidate's Wife" stunt' and refusing to make a single visit to the West Leicester constituency he was fighting.[24] 'Don't run away with the idea that I "have never taken any interest," as you said, in the things which mattered to you,' Vita pleaded with him, following a disagreement on this score. 'You know as well as I do . . . that this is an absurd contention!'[25] It was not absurd to Harold, who came as close as he ever would to direct criticism of Vita over her lack of interest in this development in his career. Far from being flattered, he was irritated by her insistence that she had 'always cared very very deeply about your writing and even your broadcasting'. As ever, Vita's 'care' applied to those aspects of his career that matched her own. 'My idea of heaven on earth would be for you to live here and bury yourself all morning and evening in your room and write, with perhaps one very interesting job that took you to London once every six months,' Vita wrote in 1943.[26] In the afternoon, they would garden together.

In terms of party loyalty, Harold's political affiliations were fluid and opportunistic. It was necessarily so: his beliefs, like Vita's, were at odds with developments in contemporary politics. 'I have always been on the side of the underdog,' he wrote in 1940, 'but I have also believed in the principle of aristocracy.'[27] He claimed he had been brought up with a Victorian idea of 'privileged classes with nice clean Sunday-school discipline for the poor'.[28] He stood for the National Labour Party, formed to coordinate Labour support for Ramsay MacDonald's Conservative-dominated National Government. His candidacy was suggested by Vita's cousin, the suitably aristocratic Herbrand Sackville, 9th Earl De La Warr, known as 'Buck'. Harold represented West Leicester for the next decade. Vita was never interested in politics and did not pretend, for Harold's sake, to an interest she did not possess. Her outlook was that of the Edwardian grandee; in *The Edwardians* she sketched aspects of her preferred paternalism. Her feudalism was unapologetic and she shared Harold's belief in the principle of aristocracy. In February 1945, a proposed new bus route skirting Sissinghurst woods roused her to a political credo: 'I detest democracy. I hate *la populace*. I wish education had never been introduced. I don't like tyranny but I like an intelligent oligarchy. I wish *la populace* had never been encouraged to emerge from its rightful place. I should like to see them as well fed and well housed as T.T. [dairy] cows – but no more thinking than that.'[29] His political life would rebuild for Harold the sense of purpose and self-worth he had forfeited by abandoning diplomacy; Vita's experience of politics happened at second hand, in Harold's daily letters. At Sissinghurst, Vita settled into a routine she would maintain until her death of writing, gardening and her dogs, Martin and Martha, both Alsatians; with her secretary Miss Macmillan, she occasionally drank too much sherry, a habit that would grow. The majority of her time she spent alone or with Gwen, who remained at

Sissinghurst until 1942. After Gwen's departure, Vita relied more and more on the companionship of her dogs.

The more perceptive of Vita's friends saw the warning signs. As long ago as June 1926, Vita had recorded in her diary an ideal Long Barn day: 'Alone; gardened; wrote';[30] days later she spent an evening with Dottie 'discuss[ing] solitude and eccentricity'.[31] On 13 April 1934, Virginia wrote pointedly to Vita: 'The week after next we go to Ireland . . . And there I may be windswept into the sea. But what would Vita care. "No," she'd say, we had the *Petulaneum Ridentis* in that bed last year: we'll try *Scrofulotum Penneum* there this." So she'd bury me under, wouldn't she Vita?'[32]

Vita did, as Virginia feared, bury her friends under. Not completely and not all the time, but the contact became sporadic. At the outset of their marriage, Vita and Harold had spent half the year in London and the warmer months at Long Barn, visited by a large circle of friends and acquaintances. By the end of the Thirties, Vita compressed her London life into three days before Christmas. She stopped buying clothes (the single evening dress remaining in her wardrobe at the time of her death had been bought in 1927); she was careless about her hair. Until a severe attack of pleurisy in 1938 resulted in her losing two-and-a-half stones, Vita had grown significantly heavier, 'more matronly and voluptuous than ever', as Virginia described her in October 1937.[33] Virginia regretted the dark shadow of a moustache and puffy cheeks which hid her eyes. Vita lost her unselfconsciousness about her looks and, doing nothing to address the cause, became nervous about the impression her appearance created. Poet and biographer Peter Quennell remembered an encounter in 1936: 'From beneath the brim of a hard black Spanish hat sprang locks of wiry black hair. Her eyebrows were heavy; her eyes were very dark; her cheeks had a vivid carmine tinge; and she made no effort to disguise the perceptible moustache . . . She had all the impressiveness that surrounds an archaic cult statue.'[34] Memorably, if unkindly, the breeches- and gaiters-clad Vita was compared to Lady Chatterley and her lover rolled into one.

Much to Harold's annoyance, Vita refused to attend a banquet at Buckingham Palace in March 1937; she refused a similar invitation in November 1938, to a banquet in honour of the King of Romania. On both occasions she blamed her lack of a suitable dress. Explaining her second refusal, she told Harold: 'I am writing this letter with my jewels littered all around me – emeralds and diamonds, just taken out of the bank – and they make me feel sick. I simply *can't* buy a dress costing £30 or wear jewels worth £2,000 when people are starving.'[35] She had discovered that white evening gloves cost £2 a pair, that shoes and suitable underwear would add another £10. Behind the well-meant principle were self-consciousness and fear of exposure: she admitted to Harold: 'I hate the idea of being examined under electric lights.'[36] Vita had changed in the twenty-five years since she announced to Harold how much she preferred *'un bal un peu propre* . . . powdered footmen announcing duchesses' to 'scrimmages at the Ritz'.[37] The change was more than surface deep. As her desire for solitude grew, her confidence in herself socially declined steeply. She told Harold she felt decreased by people. And so she avoided them and so the fear grew. With the loss of Knole came a degree of severance from the world of powdered footmen and duchesses, a realignment of her identity.

Harold's concern lay in what Vita had once labelled 'the family failing of unsociability'.[38] He was afraid, given time, that Vita's inherited tendency to reclusiveness would extend even to himself and the boys. That Vita initially felt differently is clear in her portrait of their marriage outlined in *Grand Canyon*, the novel she completed in March 1942 and which Leonard Woolf turned down for the Hogarth Press on account of its wartime defeatism and variable quality. In this instance, Vita's marriage to Harold, with its degrees of separation and consenting independence, appears in the description of an ideal platonic friendship between heroine Helen Temple (another exercise in fictional self-portraiture: a woman who loves silence and solitude) and safe, sexually neutral Lester Dale. The picture Helen draws resembles in every particular that of Vita and Harold's marriage during the Sissinghurst years as preserved in their letters and their diaries. 'His company gave her a curious sense of completion, and when he was not there she felt that something was lacking, that something had gone cold and grey and would return to life only when he reappeared. They did not always talk much. Their conversation came in bursts which might last for hours, since there seemed to be so much they could talk about, and so many by-ways of communication down which they wanted to stray, so that their talk was always inconsistent, rich and variegated, as though they never finished one subject before they were darting off on another; but equally they could sit silent for hours, or meander together through the incredible kingdom they had been given to explore, roving without fatigue or effort in a contentment that neither of them had ever known.'[39] Helen's reflections constitute a love letter from Vita to her absent husband. They are also an explanation. Their 'incredible kingdom', the Grand Canyon itself, was, like Sissinghurst, another Eden. Loving Vita as he did, Harold understood Helen Temple's needs, above all those 'times when the human voice made her want to put her hands over her ears'.[40]

*

On 17 May 1940, Winston Churchill invited Harold to become parliamentary secretary to the Ministry of Information; in time Harold served as unofficial link between Churchill's government and de Gaulle's Free French. Vita's war work was of a more local character, concerned with the Women's Land Army. She wrote *The Women's Land Army* in 1944, at the invitation of the Ministry of Agriculture and Fisheries, and donated her royalties to the Women's Land Army Benevolent Fund; from early in the war she helped the Kent Committee with recruitment and administration, not always with a good grace. Her letters to Harold include details of 'bad land girls giving a good deal of trouble'; 'this afternoon I must go touring after land girls, blast them'; in *The Women's Land Army*, she permitted herself only cautious criticism: 'Of course it would be absurd to pretend that . . . the conduct of every girl had been model, heroic, and in every way beyond reproach.'[41] Despite the flamboyance of her driving, Vita was also enlisted as an air-raid ambulance driver. Ben joined an anti-aircraft battery outside Rochester as a private, afterwards serving as an officer in the Intelligence Corps in the Middle East; Vita overlooked the extent of his unwillingness to fight. Nigel became an officer cadet at Sandhurst, was commissioned into the Grenadier Guards and saw action in North Africa and Italy. Both survived. Six months after it was first hoisted, Vita and Harold lowered the Sackville flag on Vita's tower for the war's duration. Vita's flock of white pigeons, endowed with a sixth sense, flew away.

With all but one of Sissinghurst's gardeners called up, Vita was helped by the epileptic William Taylor and a single Land Girl. After his call-up to the RAF in 1941, she had agreed with new head gardener Jack Vass to do her best to keep the hedges in order. 'I hated those hedges when I looked at my blistered hands,' she remembered.[42] Much of the garden fell victim to the conflagration: its unkemptness, and her inability to reverse the trend, intermittently overwhelmed Vita. 'It reverted to the wildness in which we had found it in 1930,' she wrote in 1950.[43] At the time her depression prevented her from writing: *Grand Canyon* became 'my bloody book'.

The outbreak of war inspired powerful feelings in Vita: outrage, anger and deep wells of sadness. She described 'the alternations between the dreadful troughs and the tiny crests, the muted anguish with which one met bad news, the piteous optimism with which one greeted good, trying not to be lifted up, not daring to hope, still less daring to despair'.[44] She was frequently unsettled. In a 'Country Notes' column, she recorded one sleepless night when, in inky darkness, she walked down to the lake in search of peace. She took out the boat and rowed across the black expanse to cut water lilies. Overhead, she watched the fighter planes, listened to a fox bark at the disturbance, admired the eerie phosphorescence of the unwieldy white flowers. Afterwards she struggled, but failed, to transform this experience, which she likened to 'a fable curiously up to date', into any sort of written coherence.[45] She oscillated between certainty of defeat and a Churchillian belief in British greatness; from the former conviction arose the premise of *Grand Canyon*, which Vita explained in her Author's Note: 'Germany, by the use of an unspecified method of attack, is assumed to have defeated Great Britain.' For the most part her belligerence was marked, Boudicca in gardening gauntlets.

Harold instructed her to have the car always ready for escape by the back roads to his brother's house in Devon in the event of a German invasion of Kent. He suggested she pack her jewels, his diaries and the statue of St Barbara; Vita's own list of essentials included her sables, gardening clothes and cigarettes; her current manuscript, an annotated copy of her *Collected Poems*, *Roget's Thesaurus* and her spectacles; and the suicide tablet that Harold had obtained for each of them.

As at the beginning of the First World War, Vita's complicated feelings inspired her to poetry. In July 1941, the Hogarth Press published her *Selected Poems*. It was slighter than the

Collected Poems of 1933, with only excerpts from *The Land*, but included five new poems, among them 'September 1939'. On and off she continued to toy with *The Garden*. Although it would not be finished until after the war, the thought of it became Vita's answer to brutality and destruction: 'the gardener in little way/ Maintain[s] the bastion of his opposition/And by a symbol keep[s] civility'.[46] True to that philosophy, at Sissinghurst Vita continued to plant for the future: more than 10,000 bulbs in the first six months of the war alone and a Japanese cherry tree with greenish-white flowers which she imagined her grandchildren admiring. She wrote to Harold: 'Let us plant and be merry for next autumn we may all be ruined.'[47]

Vita continued to submit morale-boosting 'Country Notes' columns to the *New Statesman* until October 1941, her first, most potent contribution to the war effort. Like *The Land*, they enshrined her belief in the wholesomeness of country life; like Jan Struther's earlier Mrs Miniver columns for *The Times*, they offered readers a vision of Britishness worth defending. 'How much one regrets that local turns of speech should be passing away!' Vita lamented in January 1939, opening a window on to a different, older, less angry world. For the most part, the picture she drew for her readers was one in which renewal and rebirth retained the upper hand. In 1941, Vita wrote *English Country Houses* for the 'Britain at War' series of patriotic illustrated books, covering every aspect of British life from poetry to farm animals; the series was Hilda's brainchild and Dottie was briefly a member of its editorial committee. In *English Country Houses*, Vita emphasised the spirit of place, the rootedness of great houses within a landscape: she presented the country house as a quintessence of Englishness. Inevitably she drew attention to Knole: she had always regarded it as pre-eminently an 'English' house, 'no alien fabrication, no startling stranger seen between the beeches and the oaks. No other country but England could have produced it, and into no other country would it settle with such harmony and such quiet.'[48] Vita's was among the best selling of the 126 books in the series. She sounded similar notes in a trio of articles about Sissinghurst written for *Country Life* the following summer. She could not resist her own hobbyhorses: 'it may, I think, fairly be claimed that the spirit of the place is very strong at Sissinghurst . . . The more instinctive visitor exclaims that it is like the castle of Sleeping Beauty.'[49]

Despite *Grand Canyon* and her first misgivings about British military strength, Vita was determined not to give in to the war. From a secret radio station in Renby Grange near Tunbridge Wells, she recorded a number of broadcasts in French for Radio Paris between March and May 1940. The idea, like the 'Britain in Pictures' series, was Hilda's – in this instance in her role as director of the Joint Broadcasting Committee with responsibility for media propaganda. On mainstream radio, Vita broadcast on the Women's Land Army, 'The English Countryside', sixteenth- and seventeenth-century poetry, and the poems of Andrew Marvell. She gave two readings from Virginia's *To the Lighthouse* and a Home Service broadcast on Knole. Her airwaves contributions form a miniature compendium of her passions.

Vita's thoughts never strayed far from her garden. On 12 December 1939, she wrote to Harold: 'The Lion Pond is being drained. I have got what I hope will be a really lovely scheme for it: all white flowers, with some clumps of very pale pink. White clematis, white lavender, white Agapanthus, white double primroses, white anemones, white camellias, white lilies, including *giganteum* in one corner, and the pale peach-coloured *Primula pulverulenta*.'[50] The scheme was not carried out until after the war, and not on the site of the drained Lion Pond but beside the Priest's House, in the old rose garden; a decade later Harold added suggestions for silver and grey foliage. Conceived as a statement of faith in the first months of fighting, her poet-gardener's belief in the redemptive power of beauty, Vita's White Garden would become one of the most famous planting schemes in the world.

Hilda Matheson died suddenly on 30 October 1940, during an operation to remove part of her thyroid gland; Vita wrote an obituary for the *Spectator*. Virginia Woolf committed suicide on 28 March 1941; a shaken Vita wrote an obituary poem, 'In Memoriam: Virginia Woolf', published in the *Observer*. In 1942, Gwen St Aubyn, since her father-in-law's death Lady St Levan, left Sissinghurst for Cornwall; Vita described her as 'living at St Michael's Mount in grandeur, but so far as I can make out in a perpetual gale straight off the Atlantic, so that on most days they can neither open nor shut the front door'.[51] Dottie's alcoholism escalated beyond Vita's intervention. In 1943 she was prevented by drunkenness from taking part with Vita in a poetry reading in aid of the Free French in the presence of the Queen and Princesses Elizabeth and Margaret. In July 1944, Vita's first love, Rosamund Grosvenor, was killed when a bomb fell on the Savoy Chapel, London. 'It has saddened me rather,' wrote Vita, 'that somebody so innocent, so silly and so harmless should be killed in this idiotic and violent way.'[52]

The coterie of Vita's girl friends that had incited Virginia to rancour all but disappeared, Virginia among them. In their place Vita made weekly visits to Katherine Drummond, an elderly, wheelchair-bound neighbour who shared her interest in gardening and to whom, in 1946, she dedicated *The Garden*. For Christmas 1939, Mrs Drummond had given Vita a weeping pear tree, *Pyrus salicifolia* 'Pendula', which was eventually transplanted into the White Garden; Vita in turn created for her a series of miniature gardens in pans and shallow bowls. Katherine

Drummond became a temporary substitute mother: 'I felt your love as a benediction/ In tranquil branches above me spread,/ Over my sometimes troubled head.'[53] She also introduced Vita to her daughter-in-law, Bunny, the latest in a line of married women to fall under Vita's spell. Vita warned Bunny Drummond against playing with fire and maintained for the time being a careful, if kindly, distance.

A bomb exploded close to Knole in February 1944: windows along the Green Court, the Stone Court and in the Chapel were broken. Vita told Harold she minded 'frightfully fright-fully frightfully'. Long Barn had also been hit. In the *Observer*, Vita published a poem called 'Blast': 'This house lived; sparkled once; had eyes.'[54] With no wartime supply of birdseed, the budgerigars in the Sissinghurst aviary died of starvation. The moat wall collapsed and weeds overwhelmed the flowerbeds.

Knole and Long Barn were damaged, Sissinghurst over-grown, friends and lovers dead; Vita herself was suffering from arthritis of the spine, an advance on her former lumbago; in time it would affect her hands and her knees. She worried about 'the weakness it brings to my limbs' and her ability to go on gardening.[55] She resorted to Benzedrine as a pick-me-up and stimulant, describing it to Harold as 'rather like Champagne only less expensive. It makes your brain work like fun.'[56] On other days she drank sherry to staunch pain that was emotional as well as physical. Vita's post-war world would include signif-icant omissions.

As the toll of everyday unhappiness mounted, Vita struggled to find distraction in her writing. Although her work on *The Garden* stalled and *Grand Canyon* brought her limited satisfac-tion, not to mention a clutch of adverse reviews, in January 1943 she took up an idea she had conceived six years previously in Lisieux while holidaying with Gwen: a double biography of St Thérèse of Lisieux and St Teresa of Avila. She acknowledged

the esoteric nature of her subject and made her case forcefully
for a wartime examination of the advantages of the contemplative life. To some, Vita acknowledges, such contemplation
'appears . . . as a form of escape from reality; almost as a form
of self-indulgence, of selfishness, an evasion of responsibility,
a withdrawal from the unpleasantness of a world which nevertheless is everyone's charge to help within their own range to
run'; she sweeps aside such dismissals.[57] Escape, self-indulgence
and withdrawal from unpleasantness had always shaped Vita's
writing, with its inclination to fantasy and mythomania: in *The
Eagle and the Dove* she defended herself thoughtfully, making
her case for an alternative life of the senses. Vita told Harold
how much her new book excited her. She claimed it absorbed
her completely, and she wrote with the speed and relish she
had feared she had lost. Occasionally aspects of her own experience break through her sensitively handled narrative: 'No
amount of recurrent personal experience, nor the recorded and
similar experience of other people, can alleviate the soul in
such accesses of despair.'[58] Her new publishers Michael Joseph
released the book on 8 November 1943; in December 1944
they issued a fourth reprint.

Challenges to Vita's equanimity were manifold. Even as she
grieved for lost friends, Ben and Nigel remained overseas and
in danger. She worried about Knole and about Sissinghurst,
both in the flight path to London; to Harold she described a
night-time air raid when 'the whole of the South Cottage shook'
and the sky glowed red; the distant cry of doodlebugs was as
noisy as Piccadilly Circus.[59] Listlessly she watched nature's
sure-footed encroaching on her garden. Once soldiers with
tanks occupied Sissinghurst's woods and the lake at the end
of 1944, Vita announced that both were spoilt for ever; her
recurrent depression returned. 'I shall never love the lake or
the woods again in the same way as I used to . . . I mind more

about this than you would believe. It was a thing of beauty now tarnished forever,' she told Harold.[60] It was an extreme reaction and probably unwarranted, but there had always been an extreme side to Vita's nature. She herself only partly understood it. That lack of comprehension, and the fear it bred in her, accounts for the tenacity of her theory of her duality, Englishness versus Spanishness, with all that both terms came to signify for Vita. Previously she had channelled what Harold called the 'rather cruel and extravagant' side of her nature into her novels, satisfying vicariously what could not safely be satisfied any other way. Since *The Dark Island*, fiction had failed her. Harold had noted her increasing neurosis. He knew that Vita's refusal to accept invitations, for example, arose from more than stubbornness, symptomatic of a deep-seated anxiety in the presence of anyone outside her immediate circle. 'I cannot establish contact with anybody;/ They are all unreal to me, the charming intelligent people,/ And I daresay I seem as unreal to them,' Vita wrote in a diary poem at the beginning of the war.[61] Harold knew too about Vita's drinking. The combination added up to what he called her 'muzzy moods', which he struggled to penetrate.[62]

Against this backdrop, Violet re-entered Vita's life. Following Denys Trefusis's death in 1929, she had remained in France. Like Vita she lived in a tower – at St Loup de Naud, eighty kilometres from Paris on the road to Provins in the Ile de France. Violet's feelings for her tower mirrored Vita's for Sissinghurst: she considered St Loup 'both romantic and mysterious. It could even lay claim to a certain magic all its own.'[63] In the summer of 1940, the Fall of France drove Violet from her tower back to England. The magic of St Loup was not enough to safeguard it against occupation by German soldiers.

Violet telephoned Vita. Caught between hesitancy and muzziness, Vita proposed a visit to Sissinghurst. Violet accepted and Vita wrote to tell Harold. On 28 August, the day Vita expected her, Violet cancelled. Instead she suggested 31 August: 'I lost my head and said yes,' Vita explained to Harold.[64] On the 31st, Violet cancelled for a second time. Vita was relieved and disappointed and wrote Violet a letter in which she jumbled up persuasion and discouragement. 'We must not play with fire again,' she warned, and she described memories they shared, as if to underline former intimacy. 'The very sound of your voice on the telephone upsets me,' she wrote.[65] Her letter proved the extent of that upset. For weeks Vita and Violet held one another at bay. No arrangement was made, but their letters returned them to life for one another. They resumed the old names of Lushka and Mitya, referencing love, insisting without conviction that love was in the past. 'I was so worried about you when France collapsed,' Vita wrote a fortnight after their cancelled meeting. 'I couldn't bear to think of you in danger and distress.'[66] Violet suggested meeting anywhere but Sissinghurst: Vita demurred; it was their own version of the Phoney War. News that the Germans had overrun St Loup in mid-October brought another expression of sympathy from Vita. Violet's halfway meeting point won the day. Vita agreed to meet her on 15 December, almost four months after their letters began, at The Red Lion in Pulborough, Sussex.

Their meeting was a success. The same evening, Vita wrote to Violet: she admitted her fear of falling in love again. 'I don't want . . . to become involved with you in a way that would complicate my life as I have now arranged it,' she explained. 'You and I can't be together. I go down country lanes and I meet a notice saying "Beware unexploded bomb" so I have to go round another way. The unexploded bomb is you, Lushka.'[67] The letters continued. Vita declined to visit Violet in her rented house, the Manor House at East Coker, decorated by Dorothy Heneage with paintings by Titian and Van Dyck, Chippendale furniture and Chinese lacquer in the manner of Mrs Keppel's London houses; she resisted any resumption of regular contact. She repeated her fear of Violet as an unexploded bomb, her attachment to the orderliness of the life she and Harold had evolved. 'I don't want you to explode. I don't want you to disrupt my life.'[68] Violet remained in Somerset and Vita proved incapable of ignoring her.

By the summer of 1941, Vita felt able to pass the buck. Ben was stationed near Yeovil, Violet was his godmother: they would meet at Dorothy Heneage's house, Coker Court. Vita prepared her son for their meeting, describing Violet's charms and her snares, like an epicure remembering a favourite meal. To Harold, she worried that Ben would fall in love with Violet. The suggestion is revealing. Harold attributed it to Vita's muzziness and correctly trusted Ben's good sense. For all her protests, Vita allowed herself the indulgence of falling in love with Violet a second time – through Ben, who had already told both his parents he thought he was gay (a conclusion he would subsequently reconsider).

Two years later, the women arranged to meet at Sissinghurst. Again Violet cancelled. She arrived a week later, on 11 May 1943, and stayed a single night. After some deliberation, Violet slept in Vita's room, Vita in Harold's room. Both women admitted their embarrassment and the visit passed successfully. Afterwards Vita described the experience as 'shattering', an indication of the effort it cost her.[69] There were no repercussions nor any sense of resolution. Violet went on to London, where more than once she and Harold found themselves at the same dinner party. Harold surprised Vita by calling Violet 'a good old sort', but deprecating her laborious wit.[70] After the war, Vita wrote to Violet again: 'I think we have got something indestructible between us, haven't we? . . . It has been a very strange relationship, ours; unhappy at times, happy at others;

but unique in its way, and infinitely precious to me and (may I say?) to you . . . our love has lasted for forty years and more.'[71] In a roundabout fashion it constituted an apology.

Violet signalled her acceptance by contacting Vita whenever she returned to England. In January 1952, from her suite at The Ritz, she dispatched to Vita at Sissinghurst what the latter described as a 'shower of Madame de Vilmorin's books' and made an arrangement to meet for lunch two weeks later.[72] Louise de Vilmorin's latest novel, *Madame de*, told the story of a wife destroyed by her inability to keep from her husband the secret she is determined not to share. There would be other, safe, amicable meetings, including visits by Vita to St Loup and by Harold and Vita to l'Ombrellino, the large, part-fourteenth-century villa on the top of the Bellosguardo hill south-west of Florence that Violet had inherited from Mrs Keppel.

With the end of the war Vita's half-empty glass began to refill. Ben came home in March 1945, suffering from head injuries, and remained at Sissinghurst to recover. On 21 April Vita told a friend: 'I have to go and fetch my boy who has just emerged from the hospital at Tunbridge Wells – free and unplastered.'[73] Harold joined Vita and Ben later in the spring, before returning to Leicester for summer electioneering; in the meantime he and Vita continued work on their joint poetry anthology, *Another World Than This*, which was published in December and sold 10,000 copies within the month. To celebrate VE Day, Harold, Vita and Ben unfurled the Sackville flag and hoisted it on Vita's tower. On 17 June, Nigel also returned to Sissinghurst.

In January 1946, after a five-year absence, Jack Vass was back at work as head gardener. Vita described him as 'a gardener after my own heart . . . only I think it is a good thing to be behind him to check his love of over-neatness with my own more romantic and more untidy view of what the garden should be'.[74] Jack Copper reclaimed his job of handyman–chauffeur and Mac returned from overseas duties with the Queen Alexandra Nursing Service for another eight years as Vita's secretary; by mutual consent she would reduce her workload to three days a week.

Harold lost his West Leicester seat in the general election of July 1945 by 7,215 votes. Three days later he learned that he had also lost his rooms at King's Bench Walk: bomb damage to the Inner Temple meant they were needed for practising barristers; Vita shielded him from the news during the final days of campaigning. 'I feel as if chapter after chapter was being closed, finished, put away,' he confided to his diary; he minded badly about both losses.[75] Vita had warned Harold that Churchill's wartime performance could not be counted on to win the election, and with less sensitivity than she had shown over King's Bench Walk, swept aside his public life of the last decade. 'Why on earth you want to go and get mixed up in politics when you could stay here and write books passes my comprehension. Idiot!'[76] She overlooked the political aspect of any number of Harold's books.

Anticipating the worst, Harold had written to Nigel ahead of polling day, 'If I learn that my political career is over (perhaps for ever), I shall accept it with philosophic resignation and devote such years as may remain to me to serious literary work. I have a domestic retreat of the utmost felicity and a second string to my bow. My God! what right have I of all men to complain?'[77] His resignation proved less philosophical than he had imagined and he made no plans to return permanently to his felicitous domestic retreat. Harold found that he was not ready yet to retire from public life. He longed to return to Parliament, either through a by-election or, via a peerage, to the House of Lords. As a consolation prize he set his sights on chairmanship of the British Council. In all three ambitions he was thwarted. A suspicion that he made a fool of himself in his manoeuvring to obtain a peerage would add to the unhappiness of his post-war mood.

Harold made plans to live in London with Ben and Nigel. The former resumed his pre-war position as Deputy Surveyor of the King's Pictures, while Harold retained his governorship of the BBC and remained, after fourteen years, a committee member of the London Library; later Ben left the Royal Household to edit the *Burlington Magazine*. They found an ugly Victorian house in Neville Terrace, South Kensington, which Harold hated from the outset. He called it Devil Terrace, but remained there until the summer of 1952, when he moved into a shared set in Albany with Nigel, who had recently been elected Conservative MP for Bournemouth East. Harold wrote a weekly column for the *Spectator* and continued to contribute to French newspaper *Le Figaro* accounts of 'British events of interest to the French public', as he had since 1934. Having joined the Historic Buildings Committee of the National Trust in 1944, in 1947 Harold became vice chairman of the Executive Committee, a position he retained until 1961; Vita sat on the Trust's newly formed Gardens Committee. It was not enough. With a degree of misgiving Harold joined the Labour Party and stood as candidate in the North Croydon by-election on 11 March 1948. Though he increased the Labour vote, he lost to a large Conservative majority. Vita hoped electoral defeat would pave the way for Harold's long-awaited peerage. Like Harold, she hoped in vain.

Vita's own post-war mood became unpredictable. For all her fantasy that Sissinghurst was Sleeping Beauty's Castle, she could not herself take on the role of Sleeping Beauty: she needed the affirmation of specific contact with the outside world, an audience for her poetry, readers for her books. And so, as she had written in *All Passion Spent*, 'one was happy at one moment, unhappy two minutes later, and neither for any good reason'.[78] On 23 December 1944, the *Times Literary Supplement* published an extract about the Nativity from the 'Winter' section of *The Garden*. Three months later, Vita threw a birthday party at King's Bench Walk. James Lees-Milne, a former lover of Harold's and a friend since the early thirties, noted her 'regal' appearance and the absence of any 'frolicsome' qualities in Vita (in contrast to Harold).

Vita's token return to a social life of sorts may have laid ghosts and bolstered her fragile confidence. If so, these feelings would be of short duration. Vita resumed work on *The Garden*, and was assailed by doubts about its quality: 'Flatness has come with increasing competence,' she wrote.[79] They were the same anxieties she had voiced twenty-five years before in relation to her second collection of poetry, *Orchard and Vineyard*, and perhaps typical of many authors' responses to their work. As she wrote to Harold after completing *The Eagle and the Dove*, 'I think it has some merit, but of course, as one always does, I wish that it were better.'[80] The award of the Heinemann Prize by the Royal Society of Literature and a reprint six months after publication only partially allayed her anxieties. Vita spent the £100 prize money on azaleas for the Moat Walk (she determinedly ignored Harold's objections to azaleas, as she overlooked his equally vehement dislike for red-hot pokers); she noted that both *The Eagle and the Dove* and *The Women's Land Army* were more widely reviewed. With no new writing project, Sissinghurst was increasingly claiming her attention. In the spring of 1946, Vita would need all the healing balm of her garden.

*

The Poetry Committee of the Society of Authors met under the chairmanship of Society Secretary Denys Kilham Roberts.

A racing enthusiast and former contract law barrister, 'DKR', as he was known, had recently edited a five-volume anthology of British poetry, *The Centuries' Poetry*. Its fifth volume, 'From Bridges to the Present Day', excluded Vita. It was a sign of things to come. The committee, of which Vita was a member, met in March 1946 to discuss a poetry reading on 14 May in the Wigmore Hall in the presence of the Queen and Princesses Elizabeth and Margaret. Henry Reed, who was also present, described it as a 'rather fractious gathering convened to decide which verses in our language might not be too tedious or indecent for the young ears of the Royal Family'.[81] A programme was compiled and poets chosen. Vita was not among them. It proved a defining moment.

'The only inference to be drawn is that they didn't think me worth putting up on the platform – in other words, my poetry wasn't good enough,' Vita wrote later. 'It had the effect on me that I have never written a line of verse since then.'[82] As his assistant Elizabeth Barber remembered, Denys Kilham Roberts enjoyed claiming that 'he could use the "evil eye". Every time that anyone died or was taken inexplicably ill after quarrelling with him, he took credit for it. It was a sinister side of his character that could not be underrated.'[83] Vita's fellow committee members included Louis MacNeice, Walter de la Mare and Edith Sitwell, who had once dismissed *The Land* as the worst poem in the English language; in 1938, at the invitation of Victoria's troublesome sister Amalia, Edith Sitwell had embarked on (but not completed) a novel, *Spring Torrents*, intended to retell *Pepita* from Amalia's point of view.[84] The combined judgement of her peers had an effect on Vita very like the evil eye. 'They destroyed me for ever that day in Denys Kilham Roberts' rooms,' she noted simply. Her nature was not of the sort to draw comfort from the view of *The Times* correspondent that, 'if the second part of the programme, which was devoted to contemporary work, declined in splendour, it was more the fault of the poets than the poetry. Mr C. Day Lewis, Mr Louis MacNeice and Mr Thomas came off much better in reading their own work than Mr Walter de la Mare, Mr T. S. Eliot and Miss Edith Sitwell.'[85]

For as long as she could remember, Vita had aspired to renown for her poetry. She had grown up surrounded by poets, dining with her parents in the Poets' Parlour at Knole. She counted poets and a playwright among those ancestors who meant so much to her. She had discussed prosody with Poet Laureate Robert Bridges and, on the evidence of her diary, the business of writing with Virginia Woolf, Arnold Bennett, George Bernard Shaw, Lytton Strachey, André Maurois, Aldous Huxley, Beverley Nichols, Hugh Walpole, Rudyard Kipling, W. B. Yeats and John Galsworthy. Five of her lovers – Violet, Dottie, Geoffrey, Virginia and Margaret Voigt – were published authors; she was also married to a writer. Her exclusion, in a 'fractious gathering' in March 1946, inflicted a devastating blow not only on Vita's pride, for Vita the writer was essentially modest, but on her very sense of herself. So deep was that blow that she told no one for five years and never told Harold.

Harold had spent the day of the poetry reading at Chelsea Flower Show. His letter, written that evening, must have gone some way to raising Vita's bruised spirits. 'I believe that before we die we shall make Sissinghurst the loveliest garden in Kent . . . There are certain things [i.e. plants] which are adapted to Sissingbags and those things should be improved and improved and improved until they reach the perfect standard.'[86] With poetry closed to Vita, the pursuit of perfection at Sissinghurst would go some way to filling the void. By serendipity, she would shortly be given an opportunity to combine her love of her garden with her need to write.

Vita's gardening column for the *Observer* began on 29 September 1946; the following month Harold began a fortnightly book review for the same paper. It continued until February 1961, becoming a weekly fixture early in 1950. For more than twenty years, Vita had been a prolific and successful author. She enjoyed a high public profile as a result of her radio broadcasts, her glamorous association with Knole – which she had exploited – and her striking appearance. The columns she wrote for the *Observer* won her renewed and long-lasting popularity and acclaim of a different variety; she was photographed by Beaton, Hedgecoe, Snowdon. They also garnered an impressive mailbag – in excess of two thousand letters one bumper week. Vita replied to them all. This shy, remote, occasionally aloof woman recoiled from parties: 'There are times when I cannot endure the sight of people./ I know they are charming, intelligent, since everybody tells me so,/ But I wish that they would go away,' she wrote.[87] Yet she mustered endless patience with her 'shillingses', the paying garden visitors to Sissinghurst, and, for the most part, the same patience with her *Observer* readers. Her columns were friendly and confidential in tone. They offer a vision of that gift for intimacy which had beguiled a succession of lovers, and suggested in the minds of Vita's readers warmth and sympathy to which they in turn responded. In May 1954, at a loss for a subject, Vita mentioned being ill: a flurry of 'so many deeply concerned letters of sympathy and enquiry' appalled Vita with a sense of her own fraudulence.[88]

Vita's lovers typically responded to her as maternal, dominant, richly imaginative: she brought the same attributes to her gardening columns. She was encouraging and inspiring. She resorted to an element of heroic daring to persuade the doubtful: 'The only thing is to be bold; try the experiment; and find out.'[89] True to her Sackville roots, she had a weakness for historic associations: she recommended medlar trees, the common quince and sweet woodruff, which Elizabethans used for scenting linen. Her column simultaneously increased Sissinghurst's fame and benefited from it, though Vita resisted naming her own garden, careful not to forgo the inclusive quality of her advice. She never lost sight of those who gardened on a small scale. 'Even the smallest garden can be prodigal within its own limitations,' she trumpeted on 26 March 1950. It was a call to arms, a mission statement, an antidote to the privations and drabness of post-war Britain. She recycled earlier experience. Untended wartime gardens she had visited in her capacity as a Land Girl representative proved to her, she argued, the desirability of pruning roses only lightly. And she discussed her own gardening plans, beginning in January 1950 with 'my grey, green and white garden'.[90] 'I cannot help hoping that the great ghostly barn-owl will sweep silently across a pale garden, next summer, in the twilight – the pale garden that I am now planting, under the first flakes of snow,' she wrote in her cosiest novelist's manner.

As in all Vita's writing, she herself was among her beneficiaries: in her *Observer* columns she held at bay her fears that she would be prevented from gardening by physical incapacity. In the winter of 1946, Harold twice discovered Vita reduced to immobility in the garden. On one occasion, leaning against a lime tree to support her back, she wept with combined pain and frustration. 'May I assure the gentleman who writes to me (quite often) . . . that I am not the armchair, library fireside gardener he evidently suspects . . . and that for the last forty years of my life I have broken my back, my finger nails and sometimes my heart in the practical pursuit of my favourite occupation,' she wrote in April 1957.[91] There was a romantic quality to her self-sacrifice, grandeur in the wholeheartedness of her immersion.

Eventually Vita protested against the unrelenting tyranny of her gardening articles, which she disparaged as 'sticklebacks': in the short term, the orderliness and discipline of a weekly column replenished her appetite for her work. On 8 January 1947, she told Harold she was ready to begin work on her biography of 'La

Grande Mademoiselle', an idea of long gestation. 'She isn't *quite* my sort of thing, but there are some aspects of the story which I find interesting . . . Her own description of herself is fascinating as a psychological document. It is a study in self-delusion by a most sincere person. It is on these lines that I shall try to base my portrait of her.'[92] In the event, years would pass before Vita applied herself to her 'study in self-delusion by a most sincere person', her final act of literary self-projection; she was still not ready for a project on such a scale. Instead, persuaded by the generous remuneration offered, she wrote what she described as an 'absurd thriller story' for an American magazine[93] and satisfied a recent ambition. At the end of 1945, Stephen Tennant had encouraged Vita's desire to write a thriller: 'a detective story is the supreme relaxation and stimulant combined'.[94] *The Devil at Westease* occupied Vita for no more than a month and earned her a welcome £3,000. It was published by Doubleday & Co. in the States on 8 May 1947; correctly judging its quality, Vita was adamant that it should not be published in Britain. 'It is quite readable, and as I had completely forgotten it, I was able to read it quite objectively. But it is only a nonsense,' she told Harold on publication.[95] American reviewers agreed; and her story of a man intent on committing the perfect murder, who chose the vicar as his victim because he was 'small and weak and would easily be overwhelmed', failed to enhance her reputation. Vita's narrator, Roger Liddiard, a wealthy ex-RAF man with a taste for seclusion and the quiet life of a remote country village, suggests aspects of her usual role play. She complicates the reader's response to her story through her murderer's insistence that he escape punishment, 'since the work that I do is of importance to posterity'. The book was not reprinted, but appeared in several foreign language editions, proof of Vita's prominence and her ongoing marketability.

That prominence increased between the end of the war and Vita's death in 1962, despite her producing fewer books than at any other point in her life. It was largely the result of her *Observer* columns, and increasing acknowledgement of the importance and status of the garden at Sissinghurst. There were tokens of official recognition too. Vita attached little significance to her appointment as Companion of Honour in the New Year's Honours List in 1948 – Harold wrote that 'my own beloved is a nit-wit about such things'; how differently he would have embraced a peerage in the same list.[96] Her continuing unhappiness about the judgement of the Poetry Committee two years earlier diminished her pleasure in the 'passionate admiration for *The Land* of the Prime Minister Clement Attlee that lay behind the award. But she did agree to undertake overseas lecture tours for the British Council. As much as the formal decoration, they signalled her position as an Establishment lion.

Vita derived greater satisfaction from the letter she received on 15 November 1954, informing her that she had been awarded the Veitch Memorial Medal of the Royal Horticultural Society for services to horticulture. To Harold she described herself as 'rather pleased but even more astonished'; the only fly in the ointment was her surmise that she had received the medal on the unworthy basis of 'those beastly little *Observer* articles'.[97] Her astonishment was as unwarranted as her misgivings about her own worth. Two years earlier, at an RHS dinner at the Society's headquarters in Vincent Square, Vita had told Harold: 'I was made rather a fuss of; they made me speak – but you know, Hadji, *I don't like it*; I hate getting credit for the wrong things; and I felt that there I was, an amateur amongst real experts; and all because of my thin little *Observer* articles I had an undeserved reputation; and also because a lot of people in . . . the audience had been to the garden here. I felt a fraud.'[98] Chivalrously Harold swept aside all her misgivings: he pointed out to her that the award was 'like being made a Fellow of All Souls'.[99] Once the news had sunk in, Vita told a friend: 'I was rather pleased, but I was even more surprised than pleased as it generally goes to old gentlemen of over eighty, who have devoted the whole of their lives to horticulture.'[100]

Equally pleasurable was the visit to Sissinghurst of the recently widowed Queen Elizabeth the Queen Mother on 4 June 1952. The Queen Mother described it as 'all so simple and quiet': Vita wore a skirt in her honour; Harold served his best wine and truffles, having taken advice on etiquette from Diana Cooper.[101] Vita concealed from Harold a collapse brought on by heart trouble while she was deadheading lilacs only days ahead of the visit. Afterwards Vita responded to the Queen Mother's letter of thanks: 'May I be allowed to reply to Your Majesty's most charming letter, and say how great a pleasure (as well as an honour) it was to Harold and myself to welcome you to Sissinghurst. It had always been my dream . . . for if I may venture to say so Your Majesty can have no subject whose devotion and admiration has been deeper than mine for many years.'[102] Vita had dedicated *The Women's Land Army* to the Queen in her role as patron. A romantic engagement with the idea of royalty had formed part of Vita's psyche since her childhood encounter with the future Queen Alexandra at Knole and the appearance in her nursery of the beautiful Crown Princess of Romania, whom she later teased Virginia Woolf had first turned her thoughts to lesbianism. Royalty fitted Vita's 'pre-1792' philosophy. Earlier Sackvilles had enjoyed close personal relationships with the Crown; in the Chapel at Knole during Vita's childhood was the wooden Calvary that Mary, Queen of Scots presented to Thomas Sackville in gratitude for his tactful conveyance of news of her death sentence. The summer after the royal visit, moved by preparations for the Coronation and the spectacle of a beautiful young Queen, Vita wrote a poem for the *Times Literary Supplement*. In 'June 2nd, 1953', Vita concentrated on self-identity: 'How strange to be your Majesty/

How strange to wake in an ordinary bed/ And, half awake, to think "Now who am I?" . . ./ Am I Elizabeth or Lilibet?'

From courtiers, Harold heard that the Queen Mother had described herself as '"soothed" by the beauty and happy atmosphere' she found at Sissinghurst.[103] It was an atmosphere generated by the love lavished on their garden by its owners and their perception of their garden as a monument to that love. As Harold wrote to Vita in May 1955, 'What happiness you and I have derived from that garden – I mean real deep satisfaction and a feeling of success. It is an achievement – assuredly it is. And it is pleasant to feel that we have created a work of art. It is all your credit really. Mine was just rulers and bits of paper.'[104]

Harold had told Vita on 11 December 1947 that he had asked the King's private secretary Tommy Lascelles that the announcement of her award of the Companion of Honour be made in her maiden name rather than her married name. It was a measure of Harold's generosity of spirit and his accurate assessment of Vita's current state of mind. That summer Vita had finished work on proofs of the guidebook to Knole she had written for the National Trust, following her Uncle Charlie's handover of the house. It proved, predictably, a painful experience, which she likened to 'rodent teeth closing on one's wrist'.[105] She had refused to revisit Knole but wrote the book instead from memory, with a degree of accuracy indicative of the wholeheartedness of her continuing absorption. All her angry feelings of dispossession resurfaced. 'I wake to the truth, "This is *my* Knole, which I love more than anything in the world except Hadji", and then I can't bear to go on reading my own short little bare guide-book about my Knole which has been given over to someone else, not us.'[106] To Harold she confessed the irrational nature of her feelings and her inability to overcome them. 'I can't quite understand why I should care so dreadfully about Knole, but I do. I can't get it out of my system. Why should stones and rooms and shapes of courtyards matter so poignantly?'[107]

It was not a new debate, either for Vita or Harold. Two years earlier, Vita had told Harold that of the three things that mattered most in her life – Knole, poetry and him – Knole remained her strongest attachment; Harold had to make do with second place, which was better than it might have been. Vita never succeeded in disentangling her vision of herself from Knole. The identity she had forged in her childhood of herself as Knole's latest inheritor was too powerful. That vision had inspired *Orlando*; in time, unable to readjust her thinking, Vita had become Virginia's victim as much as her heroine. Lacking Knole, she clung instead to her name, wrote her family history, bought Sissinghurst, Wealden farmland, orchards and woods, flew the Sackville flag. In 1921, Vita had instructed Heinemann on publication of *Orchard and Vineyard* that for publicity purposes her name must always appear as 'V. Sackville-West', never 'The Hon. Mrs Harold Nicolson'. 'My name is mine,' she wrote in a diary poem, with a combination of defiance and self-importance; she called it 'My own my personal name,/ The name my ancestors gave to me' and insisted that she keep this name for herself.[108] Later, in the aftermath of Lionel's death and final exclusion from Knole, Vita attributed the same impulse to Rachel Godavary in her novella, *The Death of Noble Godavary*. Rachel refuses to change her name as it appears on her suitcase after her marriage. 'Godavary she had been born and Godavary she would remain; it wasn't an inheritance so readily thrown off.'[109]

Harold was tolerant. Soothingly he told Vita that 'Knole symbolises for you a great personal injustice'.[110] He had spent his married life in Knole's shadow, accepting this subservience as the price of Vita's love. Vita never shielded Harold from this passionate disloyalty. 'If only I had been Dada's son, instead of his daughter!' she wrote to him in December 1950, adding, with something approximating to an apology, 'I hoped that I had damped down the fire into embers, but the embers blow up into a flame in one breath, so easily.'[111] It was part of Harold's forbearance and his overwhelming devotion to Vita that he sympathised with every outburst; he was incapable of sustained criticism of Vita. James Lees-Milne recorded an incident during a ten-day tour of National Trust properties in the West Country which he made with Vita and Harold in the summer of 1947. In Wells, Vita left Harold for the post office. Harold watched her progress, crossing a quiet street. He gripped Lees-Milne's arm 'like a vice, turned his head away, and practically sobbing, cried out, "Oh, Viti, Viti, she's going to get run over. I know she'll be killed. Oh God! Oh God!" Vita glided across the street, upright and leisurely. Having despatched her telegram, she returned unruffled and unscathed . . . He really did at that particular moment, and on . . . thousands of similar moments, go through real agony lest she might come to harm.'[112] As remarkably, Vita's feelings matched Harold's. Their dependence, Lees-Milne concluded after ten days in their company, 'transcended the normal relationship between a husband and a wife'. As Harold recorded in his diary ahead of Vita's British Council lecture tour of Spain in 1949, 'Viti packs all day, and that saddens me. After all, she is only going off for three weeks, I have plenty to do and shall be busy, and it is childish to need her so much. But I know that I could not endure at my age to be separated from her for very long. I just could not bear it, and will not consent to it.'[113]

'No thinking man can be happy; all that we can hope for is to get through life with as much suppression of our misery as possible,' Vita wrote in 1953.[114] She attributed the sentiment to a character in her new novel, *The Easter Party*; it was characteristically her own (Harold described the Sackvilles as a 'gloomy melancholic breed'). More than a decade had passed since the publication of her previous novel, *Grand Canyon*. In contrast to her early novels, which she completed in months, *The Easter Party* took Vita two years to write. 'I have been writing all morning,' she told Harold on 4 January 1951. 'You know what ups and downs one has . . . One gets so easily dejected and then so readily elated, but the elation goes and the dejection returns.'[115] The great thing, she realised, was to be writing. Weeks earlier she had written to Harold to tell him how happy her writing made her. 'It makes the whole difference in life . . . I have been so miserable in the last two or three years, not being able to write; really worried I have been, thinking that it was gone from me for ever . . . It keeps me alive, living in an imaginary world which seems more real than the ordinary world. Of course I would rather write poetry. Perhaps that will also return to me one day.'[116] To an American correspondent she explained simply that, in writing, 'I really feel *myself*.'[17]

As ever, Vita's imaginary world was not wholly imaginary. The story of Walter and Rose Mortibois and their sexless marriage was a variant on Vita's own marriage; as always she endowed both Walter and Rose with aspects of her own character. She suggested too her ambivalence about the compromises her life had entailed. Rose forswears physical fulfilment in order to marry Walter, whose dominant characteristic is self-control; Walter is determined not to fall in love with Rose. In return for her agreement to Walter's conditions, Rose receives wealth, position, respectability and almost sublimates her desire. The unusually intense attachment of both Mortiboises to Walter's Alsatian dog 'Svend' mirrored Vita's own attachment to Martha, whose death inspired part of the novel's plot, and Martha's successor Rollo. Of Rose and Svend, Vita writes: 'They were happy together, quite simply with no complications, both of them so forgetful as to forget even Walter, just enjoying themselves in the big expanse of Anstey, the great green grass slopes going down towards the lake.'[118] Although Vita did not forget

Harold, absent in his Monday-to-Friday London world but alive for Vita in their daily exchange of letters, her diary records companionable solitary walks with her succession of Alsatians; Harold noted his misgivings about Vita's preference for a Sleeping Beauty world (his own words) in which only she, her dogs and a robin on her window ledge remained awake. *The Easter Party* is dominated by Walter's family home, Anstey, a red-brick Queen Anne house of assertive Englishness surrounded by gardens that, like Dottie's island in *The Land,* dazzle in the spring. The novel culminates with the house burning down, a dramatic set piece inspired by the destruction by fire five years earlier of Sissinghurst Place, the home of the Drummonds.

The Easter Party is the novel Vita wrote in the long shadow of her rejection by the Poetry Committee and her continuing wretchedness at the loss of Knole; it is shaped by her reluctance, and her inability, to confide her unhappiness to Harold. As Walter's brother Gilbert tells Rose: 'We are all egotists at heart; or, to put it less unkindly, our own sorrows are just about as much as we have the strength to take on.'[119] At first Vita's devastation in 1946 prevented her from writing at all; afterwards it exacerbated her long-held conviction that her writing arose from facility rather than talent. 'You know that I am not a good novelist – but at any rate it is exciting just doing it,' she wrote.[120] She had told Harold that writing kept her alive: deprived of Knole, out of love, Harold in London, her sons grown up, Virginia, Geoffrey, Hilda, and both her parents dead, she was not exaggerating. The novel ends with Walter Mortibois's reaction to Anstey's destruction. To Rose's amazement, Walter seems almost pleased: 'We have got the garden left, and I think that was what we both cared most about, at Anstey? Neither of us set much store by a large house, and parties?'[121] In her penultimate novel, Vita again succumbed to an element of wishful thinking.

*

Sales of *The Easter Party* were doubtless helped by the popularity of Vita's *Observer* columns. Despite a poor review in the *Observer* itself, Michael Joseph published five editions in the novel's first year, with sales at 13,000 within six months. With her customary level-headedness in business matters, Vita had refused to accept royalty payments of ten per cent: successfully she had insisted on fifteen per cent. She was intermittently concerned about money. The Sissinghurst wage bill, she explained to Harold, cost almost half her unearned income; she felt she needed her literary earnings. In 1950, she sold her emerald necklace. Happily, the number of Vita's 'shillingses' visiting Sissinghurst had risen steeply since the garden's first open days in 1938, with a corresponding rise in garden income: in 1954, entry fees amounted to the considerable sum of £1,394.[122]

Harold, too, had reason to celebrate. With initial misgivings he had accepted an invitation, on 3 June 1948, to write the official biography of George V. Vita encouraged him to accept the commission as long as he retained a free hand over his material. The book took him three years and effectively prevented any attempted return to public life. It was published in August 1952 to a chorus of praise and earned Harold £4,000 within its first fortnight. It also earned him a knighthood in the form of the KCVO (Knight Commander of the Royal Victorian Order), an honour both Harold and Vita were anxious that he should refuse. To the King's secretary Tommy Lascelles, Harold admitted 'there is snobbishness, whether inverted or perverted, in our attitude of disinclination'.[123] Accusations of snobbery have consistently dogged both Harold and Vita's posthumous reputations. Invariably their social outlook betrayed their generation and backgrounds; both remained 'Edwardian' in outlook and Vita exacerbated Ben's contempt as a result of what he regarded as her exaggerated concern with 'breeding'. In their disdain for Harold's knighthood, which they regarded as mediocre and middle class, were traces of their disappointment over the peerage he never got; Harold reasoned correctly that it would appear 'churlish, snobbish and conceited' to decline the sovereign's personal gift, but continued to prefer the prospect of a dozen bottles of Champagne or a Regency clock.[124] 'A knighthood is a pitiful business, putting me in the third eleven,' he wrote resignedly. A decade later he was still writing to Vita about a dream in which he found himself a peer: 'people bowed to me as I passed. I bowed back rather shyly.'[125] For her part, Vita forbad the servants at Sissinghurst to call her Lady Nicolson.

Both derived more pleasure from the marriages of their sons: Nigel in 1953 to Philippa Tennyson-d'Eyncourt; Ben in 1955 to Luisa Vertova, a Florentine art historian. Both marriages would end in divorce, in Nigel's case not until after the death of both his parents. In a letter written before they met, Harold told Philippa: 'You will find us shy, eccentric, untidy, but most benevolent. You will find Sissinghurst the strangest conglomeration of shapeless buildings that you ever saw, but it is an affectionate house and very mellow and English.'[126]

An American visitor to Sissinghurst in the summer of 1954 described her first impressions of Vita. 'Her hair . . . is now short, drab and uncared for – Her eyes are blue and rather prominent, her complexion ruddy – In her youth she must have been handsome, perhaps beautiful . . . I don't think I ever met a woman who cared less. She was dressed in a mustard-coloured blouse, brown skirt and dark red corduroy jacket. I might say that she was absolutely oblivious to her personal appearance, if it hadn't been for the fact that from time to time she pulled out an orange . . . lipstick and did her lips. She smokes . . . and the only touch of luxury about her was a thin gold cigarette case.'[127] Photographs of Vita taken in the fifties show ghost trails of former beauty, the darkness of the hooded Sackville eyes; stronger is the resemblance to her poet ancestor, Charles Sackville, 6th Earl of Dorset, painted by Kneller. Time imposed on Vita the sexlessness Virginia gave to Orlando. There is an iconic quality to Vita's appearance in old age, the result of her uniform of breeches, gaiters and the ever-present cigarette of Cypriot tobacco. The beauty of her soft, rich voice survives in radio recordings, which she continued to make sporadically until the year before her death. Of the smouldering physical beauty that, forty years earlier, inspired Violet Keppel with a species of madness, nothing remained.

Yet Vita was recognisably the same person. 'We know enough, I think, of her robust and ardent nature to argue that whatever she undertook she would not do by halves; no one who wrote with so vigorous a pen could be lethargic in the affairs of life,' she had claimed for Aphra Behn in 1927.[128] Vigorously Vita had devoted her middle age to gardening; she had gathered honours and awards; like her father before her she had embraced public service: the Committee for the Preservation of Rural Kent, local magistracy, even the Cranbrook Poetry Society; further afield she had lectured for the British Council. For a long time, Sissinghurst had consumed the bulk of her energies. Thanks to *The Garden*, her *Observer* 'sticklebacks' and Rose Mortibois's engagement with Anstey in *The Easter Party*, gardening had all but overwhelmed her writing too. Briefly displacing it, there would be one last love for Vita. Appropriately, the object of her last *béguin* was herself a gardener.

It was a relationship with some of the characteristics of old-fashioned drawing-room comedy. Alvilde Lees-Milne was married to James, Harold's former lover. Striking, chic and forceful, she was also a lesbian. Among her own former lovers was an ex-lover of Vita's ex-lover Violet Trefusis. Princess Edmond de Polignac was American sewing-machine heiress Winnaretta Singer, her wealth matched only by her ugliness. Parisian rumour dressed her in leather top boots and an ancient dressing gown and whis-pered of sado-masochism. Winnaretta de Polignac had been

Violet's literary patroness and purchaser of St Loup; she gave Alvilde a house too, at Jouy en Josas near Paris. Alvilde bought her own house in France, at Roquebrune, in the mountains between Menton and Monaco.

In June 1951, in Harold's absence, Vita entertained James and Alvilde to dinner at Sissinghurst. 'Alvilde baffles me: I can't find the key to her. I can't believe that marriage will, in the long run, be a happy one,' she reported to Harold.[129] Nevertheless, in November, Harold and Vita were witnesses at the Lees-Milnes' registry office wedding in London.

Four years later, Vita came closer to finding the key to Alvilde. Alvilde was one of a quartet of women friends who visited Vita regularly; unlike Bunny Drummond, Violet Pym and painter Edith Lamont, she did not live locally. Alvilde shared Vita's passion for gardening and would become in time a distinguished garden designer. Visiting Vita their friendship grew. As unpredictably as in the past, Vita found herself victim to one of her 'fancies'. Like erstwhile *béguins*, its duration would be finite. Her letters about Alvilde written to Harold later in the decade reveal the extent of Vita's subsequent withdrawal; in 1961 she described her as 'much improved – softened'.[130]

Yet while it lasted, it was every bit as exciting as earlier loves. Alvilde asked Vita to stay in Roquebrune; Vita resumed writing poetry; she described herself, in words reminiscent of those she had used repeatedly before, as 'head and heart in a whirl'. They discovered shared tastes, among them fast cars. Alvilde took pains to disguise their relationship from James; Vita worried about Harold and the proper focus of her loyalty. Once Harold had been entirely separate from her affairs; now Vita found that the thought of Harold affected her and governed her behaviour in a way she would previously have thought impossible. 'I have treated him badly enough in the past and must make it up to him now,' she told Alvilde.[131] Into her letters she poured all the writerly passion the women were mostly denied in the flesh. Vita declined Alvilde's invitation to France; instead she crossed the Channel with Harold. With Alvilde she travelled more prosaically to the Cotswolds. At home the letters resumed. Vita's desire for discretion matched Alvilde's. In the event, her customary caution was sharpened by a suspicion that her letters to Alvilde were being tampered with. Exposure terrified Vita. Not since the summer of 1919 had she wanted to rebel in public.

'Love as Evelyn saw it was an entire absorption of one lover into the other,' Vita had written in *Family History*.[132] She did not delude herself that her 'love' for Alvilde was more than a fleeting infatuation. It seemed as if she had moved beyond absorbing herself in anyone but Harold now: their love was too settled, too intimately bound up with every aspect of Vita's life. To Harold, on their forty-fourth wedding anniversary in October 1957, she wrote: '[I] love you even more now than I did then (which is saying a lot) and please forgive me all my trespasses.'[133] Vita had allowed herself one more trespass; she was anxious to make atonement. 'She is or *seems* absolutely devoted to Harold, but there is nothing whatever sexual between them,' Victoria had written in 1922. Time had proved Victoria right.

Vita and Harold's feelings for one another were coloured by their acute awareness of the passage of time and its depredations. 'My days are haunted by the thought of something happening to you. I simply couldn't bear you to be hurt,' Vita told Harold the winter before her death.[134] Harold had convinced himself he would die in 1956; both had been prey to health scares. At the relatively young age of sixty, Vita was already becoming bent with arthritis; Harold worried about his growing deafness and, in 1955, suffered a slight stroke. That winter, after an operation for an impacted wisdom tooth, Vita's recovery was sluggish; she caught flu, her temperature escalated, she was bedbound for weeks. She suffered a mild heart attack at the end of 1958; in April 1959 she was diagnosed with viral pneumonia. Again her recovery was frustratingly protracted. She and Harold did not much discuss their health. They concentrated on their writing and their garden. After minor disagreements, Jack Vass left Sissinghurst in January 1957 and was replaced as head gardener by Ronald Platt. At the end of Platt's two-year tenure, Vita employed two young women as joint head gardeners: she called them 'the *Mädchen*'. Pam Schwerdt and Sibylle Kreutzberger stayed at Sissinghurst for more than thirty years. The garden's visitor numbers hit 6,000 in 1959: they would continue to rise.

A birthday present to Harold decided the course of Harold and Vita's last six winters together. Quite unexpectedly, on 21 November 1956, Harold received a cheque for £1,370, a joint donation from 255 of his friends to celebrate his seventieth birthday. The decision to spend the money on a cruise was almost instantaneous; jointly Harold and Vita decided against a greenhouse. Instead they went to Indonesia on the *Willem Ruys*, a cruise liner noted for its luxury. They spent their days in separate cabins, reading and writing, joining one another for meals and shore visits. Harold described it as 'a halcyon existence'; at last Vita settled down to writing *Daughter of France*, the biography of La Grande Mademoiselle that she had vaguely intended to write for some time. More than forty years had passed since she had written to Harold telling him of a fancy dress ball at the Albert Hall in June 1913: 'I am in the Louis XIV court as La Grande Mademoiselle; such good clothes, orange velvet and black, a riding dress with high boots and a *cravache* [riding whip], and if you look in the illustrated papers you will find me probably.'[135] Something of those high spirits survives in *Daughter of France*. Vita considered it a bad book – 'I am not imagining this: I *know* it is bad,' she confided to Harold[136] – but her portrait of sincere self-delusion succeeds in capturing both Mademoiselle herself and something of Vita, too. 'What I really surmise,' she wrote, 'is that dear Mademoiselle was a bore, and it is worse to be a bore than to be a worry.' She labelled her a 'virginal, rough, boyish, generously unsophisticated witling'.[137]

Vita and Harold's cruises took them to Indonesia, the West Indies, the Far East, South Africa and South America. Vita paid, even if it meant plundering last remnants of Seery's splendid munificence: she sold £4,000 worth of silver from the rue Laffitte and bronze urns from the gardens at Bagatelle. On the journey to South Africa in 1960, she wrote her final novel, *No Signposts in the Sea*. It takes the form of a shipboard diary of a dying man, Edmund Carr. Edmund falls in love with Laura, who is Vita's only overt mouthpiece for lesbianism in her writing: Laura describes the 'concord' between two women in an ideal relationship as 'approaching perfection'. Edmund fails to realise that Laura nevertheless returns his love. Instead they engage in an extended dialogue about love and marriage, both unable to read between the lines. Laura tells Edmund: 'I have come to believe that even the strongest, the most self-sufficient, need one other person in their lives from whom nothing is concealed, neither the most important things nor the most trivial. Someone with whom at the end of the day one can sit over the fire and talk or be silent as the fancy moves one.'[138] It is the very picture she had once conjured in her poem 'Sometimes When Night . . .', that couple content to 'read, speak a little, read again'. Now, approaching the end, there is nothing to shatter their tranquillity.

Vita Sackville-West died of malignant abdominal cancer on 2 June 1962. She was seventy years old and failed to recover from an operation two months earlier. She lived long enough to hear of her Uncle Charlie's death on 8 May and the decision of her cousin Eddy to return to his Irish estate. 'Fancy inheriting Knole and leaving it!!!' she wrote to Harold.[139] That triplet of exclamation marks was a last huzzah of fighting spirit.

The order for her simple funeral service at Sissinghurst church included the best-known passage from *The Land*: 'She walks among the loveliness she made.'[140] Vita had written the lines a lifetime ago for Dorothy Wellesley, when the women were young and in love with flowers, gardens, poetry, one another; when Vita still believed in her gift for verse. They have become her own epitaph. Something of the loveliness she made survives today in her garden at Sissinghurst: Vita's younger son Nigel, to whom she left the estate, agreed its transfer to the National Trust on 17 April 1967, thereby safeguarding its continuance. Harold Nicolson died the year after Sissinghurst's transfer, on 1 May 1968. His diaries show that most of him died with Vita.

No Signposts in the Sea is a valedictory novel and Vita did not begin another. In the form of a quotation from a sixteenth-century sonnet, included in the text, Vita wrote her own fare-well. She did so characteristically, donning for one last time the well-worn mask of courtly swain:

Who so list, I know where is an hind,
But as for me, alas, I may no more.
The vain travail hath wearied me so sore
I am of them that farthest come behind.
Yet may I by no means my wearied mind
Draw from the Deer, but as she fleeth afore
Fainting I follow. I leave off therefore,
Since in a net I seek to hold the wind.[141]

The words belong to Sir Thomas Wyatt; the sentiments are wholly Vita's. She had chased the prize; she could run no further. But her travail had not been in vain and the effort of seeking to hold the wind in a net was, at moments, an heroic one.

ACKNOWLEDGEMENTS

AN AWARD FROM The Society of Authors assisted the writing of this book. To the Society, and particularly members of the distinguished judging panel, I express my thanks.

I acknowledge the gracious permission of Her Majesty the Queen to quote from material in The Royal Archives at Windsor Castle, and am grateful to Pamela Clark, senior archivist, for her help.

I am grateful to those individuals who offered information, advice and assistance during the research and writing of this book: Michael Bloch; Ellen Browne, House Steward, Sissinghurst Castle; Kate Butler, Archives Assistant, Hull History Centre; Brett Croft, The Condé Nast Library, London; Simon Houde (and Sir Timothy and Lady Clifford, Ivo and Pandora Curwen, who brought about our meeting); Susannah Mayor, House Steward, Smallhythe Place; Dr Joanna Meacock, Glasgow Museums; Mitzi Mina, Sotheby's, London; Geoffrey Munn, Wartski, London; Adam Nicolson; Heather Pisani, Glenn Horowitz Bookseller, Inc, New York; and Dr Amber Regis,

University of Sheffield. In New York, Susan Fox deserves special mention for her remarkable and unstinting efforts of my behalf.

Papers relating to Vita Sackville-West and her immediate family are scattered across the globe. I am particularly grateful to Cherry Dunham Williams of the Lilly Library of Indiana University in Bloomington, and to her staff, for their help and kindness during my visits to the library, as well as to the staffs of: the Berg Collection, New York Public Library; the Bodleian Library, Oxford; the Cushing Memorial Library & Archives, Texas A & M University Library; The London Library; the Neilson Library, Mortimer Rare Book Room, Smith College; the library of St John's College, Cambridge; the University of British Colombia Library, Rare Books and Special Collections; the University of Waterloo Library, Doris Lewis Rare Book Room; and Washington State University Libraries.

Immense thanks are due to my tremendous agent, Georgina Capel, my editor, Arabella Pike, and her colleagues at William Collins, Kate Tolley and Katherine Josselyn. My parents have been as wonderfully supportive as ever, and I am grateful, too, to my father-in-law. Above all, thanks are due to my beloved and beautiful wife Gráinne – for inspiration, encouragement, patience and so much love.

NOTES

Given Vita was christened Victoria Sackville-West, a name she shared with her mother until the latter became Victoria Sackville when Lionel Sackville-West succeeded his uncle as 3rd Baron Sackville in 1908, I have referred to Vita throughout these notes simply as 'Vita' or, in her role as author, 'V. Sackville-West', as she preferred; for these purposes her mother is 'Victoria Sackville'. In instances where annotation would simply reiterate information contained within the text, I have resisted annotating quotations from Vita's diaries held in the Lilly Library of Indiana University in Bloomington. Wherever possible where primary sources have been published – and many have, beginning with Nigel Nicolson's publication of Vita's confessional autobiography in *Portrait of a Marriage* – I have directed the reader towards the published source.

PREFACE

1   Vita to Harold, 30 July 1919, quoted in Nigel Nicolson, ed., *Vita & Harold: The Letters of Vita Sackville-West &*

Harold Nicolson 1910–1962 (Weidenfeld & Nicolson, London, 1992), p. 97.

2   Vita to Harold, 13 December 1928, quoted in ibid., p. 210.

3   V. Sackville-West, *The Garden* (Michael Joseph, London, 1946), p. 10.

4   V. Sackville-West, *In Your Garden* (Michael Joseph, London, 1951), p. 49.

5   Jane Brown, *Vita's Other World: A Gardening Biography of V. Sackville-West* (Viking, London, 1985), p. 87.

6   V. Sackville-West, *Grand Canyon* (Michael Joseph, London, 1942), p. 206.

7   Sackville-West/Evelyn Irons Archive, The Dobkin Collection of Feminism and Judaica, Dobkin Collection Item 4655540, Glenn Horowitz Bookseller, New York.

8   V. Sackville-West, *All Passion Spent* (The Hogarth Press, London, 1931), p. 268.

9   Victoria Glendinning, *Vita: The Life of V. Sackville-West* (Weidenfeld & Nicolson, London, 1983, repr. Penguin, London, 1984), p. 195.

10 Vita to Margaret Howard, undated, quoted in *Observer*, 13 July 2008.

11 Victoria Sackville diary, 27 June 1890, Lilly Library, Indiana University, Bloomington.

12 Harold to Vita, 12 May 1926 and 21 December 1944, quoted in Nicolson, ed., *Vita & Harold*, pp. 139, 360.

13 V. Sackville-West, *The Diary of Lady Anne Clifford* (William Heinemann, London, 1923), p. xxiv.

14 V. Sackville-West, *The Eagle and the Dove* (Michael Joseph, London, 1943), p. 22.

15 Ibid.

16 V. Sackville-West, 'Black Tarn', *Collected Poems: Volume One* (The Hogarth Press, London, 1933), p. 139.

PROLOGUE: HERITAGE

1   Calculation based on £5 in 1912 being equivalent to the purchasing power in 2014 of £330.

2   Susan Mary Alsop, *Lady Sackville: A Biography* (Weidenfeld & Nicolson, London, 1978), p. 147.

3   Violet Trefusis, *Don't Look Round* (Hutchinson, London, 1952), p. 43.

4   *The New York Times*, 27 June 1913.

5   Robert Sackville-West, *Inheritance: The Story of Knole and the Sackvilles* (Bloomsbury, London, 2010), p. 198.

6   Victoria Sackville, 'The Book of Happy Reminiscences for my Old Age, Started on my 61st Birthday, 23rd Sept. 1922', Lilly Library.

7   Alsop, *Lady Sackville*, p. 172.

8   Ibid.

9   Sackville-West, *Inheritance*, p. 212.

10 *The New York Times*, 27 June 1913.

11 Sue Fox and Sarah Funke, *Vita Sackville-West* (catalogue of manuscript material), Glenn Horowitz Bookseller (New York, 2004), p. 24.

12 Victoria Sackville diary, 17 June 1904, Lilly Library.

13 Victoria Sackville, 'Book of Happy Reminiscences', Lilly Library.

14 V. Sackville-West, *The Edwardians* (The Hogarth Press, London, 1930), p. 100.

15 Alsop, *Lady Sackville*, p. 160.

16 V. Sackville-West, *Pepita* (The Hogarth Press, London, 1937), p. 230.

17 V. Sackville-West, *The Death of Noble Godavary and Gottfried Künstler* (Ernest Benn, London, 1932), p. 148.

18 Mary Ann Caws, ed., *Vita Sackville-West: Selected Writings* (Palgrave, New York, 2002), p. 59.

19 Vita's diary, 7 July 1913, Lilly Library.

20 Glendinning, *Vita*, p. 124.

I THE EDWARDIANS

1   V. Sackville-West, *The Edwardians*, p. 9.

2   Ibid., pp. 9–10.

3   V. Sackville-West, *English Country Houses* (William Collins, London, 1941), p. 42.

4   V. Sackville-West, *The Heir: A Love Story* (William Heinemann, London, 1922; Virago repr. 1987), p. 52.

5   Victoria Sackville, 'Book of Happy Reminiscences', Lilly Library.

6   Ibid.

7   V. Sackville-West, 'Night', *Collected Poems*, p. 144.

8   V. Sackville-West, *The Edwardians*, p. 51.

9   V. Sackville-West, *Knole and the Sackvilles* (William Heinemann, London, 1922), p. 2.

10   Ibid., p. 20.

11   V. Sackville-West, 'April', *Collected Poems*, p. 150.

12   Victoria Sackville, 'Book of Happy Reminiscences', Lilly Library.

13   V. Sackville-West, *Knole and the Sackvilles*, p. 12.

14   Nigel Nicolson, *Portrait of a Marriage* (Weidenfeld & Nicolson, London, 1973, repr. 1990), p. 20.

15   V. Sackville-West, *Knole and the Sackvilles*, p. 11.

16   Victoria Sackville diary, 17 September 1894, Lilly Library.

17   Nicolson, *Portrait of a Marriage*, p. 17.

18   V. Sackville-West, *Pepita*, p. 181.

19   Alsop, *Lady Sackville*, p. 117.

20   V. Sackville-West, *The Easter Party* (Michael Joseph, London, 1953), p. 189.

21   Victoria Sackville diary, 9 March 1897, Lilly Library.

22   Victoria Sackville, 'Book of Happy Reminiscences', Lilly Library.

23   Trefusis, Violet, *Broderie Anglaise* (English trans., Methuen, London, 1986, repr. Minerva, London, 1992), p. 61.

24 Victoria Sackville diary, 9 March 1898, Lilly Library.

25 V. Sackville-West, *Pepita*, p. 210.

26 Victoria Sackville diary, 6 May 1903, Lilly Library.

27 V. Sackville-West, 'Beechwoods at Knole', *Collected Poems*, p. 142.

28 V. Sackville-West, *Pepita*, p. 201.

29 Nicolson, *Portrait of a Marriage*, p. 10.

30 Victoria Sackville diary, 20 February 1903, Lilly Library.

31 Nicolson, *Portrait of a Marriage*, p. 19.

32 Victoria Sackville diary, 1 August 1897, Lilly Library.

33 Diana Souhami, *Mrs Keppel and her Daughter* (HarperCollins, London, 1996, repr. Flamingo, London, 1997), p. 82.

34 Fox and Funke, *Vita Sackville-West*, p. 14.

35 Vita to Victoria Sackville, undated, Berg Collection (Album 1), New York Public Library.

36 V. Sackville-West, *The Dark Island* (The Hogarth Press, London, 1934), p. 42.

37 Victoria Sackville diary, 27 October 1897, Lilly Library.

38 Alsop, *Lady Sackville*, p. 139.

39 Nicolson, *Portrait of a Marriage*, p. 16.

40 Sackville-West, *Inheritance*, p. 184.

41 V. Sackville-West, *The Edwardians*, p. 11.

42 Trefusis, *Don't Look Round*, p. 42.

43 Michael Stevens, *V. Sackville-West* (Michael Joseph, London, 1973), p. 116.

44 Alsop, *Lady Sackville*, p. 120.

45 Sackville-West, *Inheritance*, p. 191.

46 V. Sackville-West, 'The Edwardians Below Stairs', *Vogue*, 25 November 1931, p. 55.

47 V. Sackville-West, *The Edwardians*, p. 24.

48 Ibid.

49 V. Sackville-West, 'To Knole'.

50 V. Sackville-West, *All Passion Spent*, p. 90.

51 V. Sackville-West, *The Heir*, p. 75.

52 Nicolson, *Portrait of a Marriage*, p. 14.

53 V. Sackville-West, 'To Knole'.

54 See Stevens, *V. Sackville-West*, p. 115.

55 V. Sackville-West, 'To Knole'.

56 Ibid.

57 V. Sackville-West, 'The Edwardians Below Stairs'.

58 V. Sackville-West, *Tale of a Cavalier*, quoted in Nicolson, *Portrait of a Marriage*, p. 63.

59 Sackville-West, *Inheritance*, p. 189.

60 Alsop, *Lady Sackville*, p. 142.

61 Trefusis, *Don't Look Round*, p. 70; Vita to Harold, 27 February 1912, quoted in Nicolson, ed., *Vita & Harold*, p. 23.

62 Brown, *Vita's Other World*, p. 26.

63 Vita's diary, 13 August 1907, Lilly Library.

64 Norman Rose, *Harold Nicolson* (Jonathan Cape, London, 2005), p. 42.

65 Trefusis, *Don't Look Round*, p. 42.

66 Alsop, *Lady Sackville*, p. 142.

67 Victoria Sackville diary, 21 August 1898, Lilly Library.

68 Victoria Sackville, 'Book of Happy Reminiscences', Lilly Library.

69 Nicolson, *Portrait of a Marriage*, p. 11.

70 V. Sackville-West, *Chatterton* (repr. The Through Leaves Press, 2002), p. 10.

71 Alan Pryce-Jones, Preface to *Little Innocents: Childhood Reminiscences* (Cobden-Sanderson Limited, London, 1932, repr. Oxford University Press, Oxford, 1986), p. 98.

72 Nicolson, *Portrait of a Marriage*, p. 11.

73 Vita's diary, 2 June 1909, Lilly Library.

74 *Saint Joan of Arc* (Cobden-Sanderson, London, 1936; Folio Society repr. 1995), p. 7.

NOTES

75 V. Sackville-West, *Solitude* (The Hogarth Press, London, 1938), p. 24.

76 V. Sackville-West, 'The Owl', *Collected Poems*, p. 125.

77 Nicolson, *Portrait of a Marriage*, p. 17.

78 V. Sackville-West, *The Eagle and the Dove*, p. 112.

79 Nicolson, *Portrait of a Marriage*, p. 17.

80 Sackville-West/Evelyn Irons Archive, The Dobkin Collection of Feminism and Judaica, Dobkin Collection Item 4655540, Glenn Horowitz Bookseller, New York.

81 V. Sackville-West, *The Diary of Lady Anne Clifford*, p. xxxix.

82 Nicolson, *Portrait of a Marriage*, pp. 14, 13; Souhami, *Mrs Keppel and her Daughter*, p. 84.

83 Glendinning, *Vita*, p. 22.

84 Virginia Woolf's diary, 23 January 1927.

85 Nicolson, *Portrait of a Marriage*, p. 82.

86 V. Sackville-West, *The Eagle and the Dove*, p. 16.

87 See Stevens, *V. Sackville-West*, p. 107.

88 Nicolson, *Portrait of a Marriage*, p. 24.

89 Ibid.

90 V. Sackville-West, *Aphra Behn* (Gerald Howe, London, 1927), p. 60.

91 Fox and Funke, *Vita Sackville-West*, p. 13.

92 See Stevens, *V. Sackville-West*, p. 26.

93 V. Sackville-West, *Aphra Behn*, p. 74.

94 V. Sackville-West, 'Turning Over New Leaves', *Vogue*, 10 July 1929, p. 43.

95 Nicolson, *Portrait of a Marriage*, p. 24.

96 Fox and Funke, *Vita Sackville-West*, p. 14.

97 Quoted in Nicolson, *Portrait of a Marriage*, p. 62.

98 Ibid.

99 See Glendinning, *Vita*, p. 25.

100 V. Sackville-West, 'Sissinghurst', *Collected Poems*, p. 113.

101 Sackville-West, *Inheritance*, p. 202.

102 Vita's diary, 18 July 1907, Lilly Library.

103 Ibid., 12 July 1907.

104 V. Sackville-West, *Pepita*, p. 230.

105 Glendinning, *Vita*, p. 41.

106 Victoria Sackville, 'Book of Happy Reminiscences', Lilly Library.

107 Victoria Sackville diary, 9 March 1905, Lilly Library.

108 Ibid.

109 Vita's diary, 24 July 1907, Lilly Library.

110 Nicolson, *Portrait of a Marriage*, p. 24.

111 Virginia Woolf, *Orlando* (The Hogarth Press, London, 1928, repr. Grafton Books, 1987), p. 52.

112 Nicolson, *Portrait of a Marriage*, p. 24.

113 Ibid., p. 180.

114 V. Sackville-West, *The Dark Island*, p. 14.

115 V. Sackville-West, *The Edwardians*, p. 89.

116 Stevens, *V. Sackville-West*, p. 117.

117 Trefusis, *Don't Look Round*, p. 43.

118 Trefusis, *Broderie Anglaise*, p. 26.

119 Ibid., p. 27

120 Nicolson, *Portrait of a Marriage*, p. 27.

121 Souhami, *Mrs Keppel and her Daughter*, p. 13.

122 V. Sackville-West, *Pepita*, p. 181.

123 V. Sackville-West, *Challenge* (William Collins, London, 1974), p. 129.

124 Trefusis, *Broderie Anglaise*, pp. 16, 99.

125 Souhami, *Mrs Keppel and her Daughter*, p. 74.

126 Nicolson, *Portrait of a Marriage*, p. 26.

127 Ibid., p. 25.

128 V. Sackville-West, *The Edwardians*, p. 246.

129 V. Sackville-West, *The Dragon in Shallow Waters* (William Collins, London, 1921), p. 231.

130 V. Sackville-West, *Passenger to Teheran* (The Hogarth Press,

London, 1926, repr. Cockbird Press, Heathfield, 1990), p. 148.

131 Nicolson, *Portrait of a Marriage*, p. 29.

132 Glendinning, *Vita*, p. 37.

133 Victoria Sackville diary, 5 March 1897, Lilly Library.

134 Ibid., 5 October 1905.

135 Sackville-West, *Inheritance*, p. 182.

136 Ibid., p. 185.

137 V. Sackville-West, *Family History* (The Hogarth Press, London, 1932), p. 147.

138 Nicolson, *Portrait of a Marriage*, p. 64.

139 V. Sackville-West, *The Dark Island*, p. 45.

140 Glendinning, *Vita*, p. 55.

141 Fox and Funke, *Vita Sackville*-West, p. 27.

142 V. Sackville-West, *Grand Canyon*, p. 167.

143 Vita to Hon. Irene Lawley, 22 March 1913, Hull History Centre (Hull University Archives U DDFA3/6/75).

144 Nicolson, *Portrait of a Marriage*, p. 36.

145 Glendinning, *Vita*, p. 37.

146 V. Sackville-West, *Grand Canyon*, p. 163.

147 V. Sackville-West, *Heritage* (William Collins, London, 1919, repr. Futura, 1975), p. 124.

148 Vita's diary, 22 March 1910, Lilly Library.

149 V. Sackville-West, *Heritage*, p. 8.

II CHALLENGE

1 Trefusis, *Don't Look Round*, p. 70.

2 Victoria Sackville, 'Book of Happy Reminiscences', Lilly Library.

3 V. Sackville-West, *Heritage*, p. 32.

4 V. Sackville-West, *The Dark Island*, p. 215.

5 Vita to Harold, 15 February 1913, quoted in Nicolson, ed., *Vita & Harold*, p. 34.

6   V. Sackville-West, *Chatterton*, p. 59.
7   Caws, ed., *Selected Writings*, p. 55.
8   V. Sackville-West, *Knole and the Sackvilles*, p. 28.
9   V. Sackville-West, 'The Bull', *Collected Poems*, p. 116.
10 Caws, ed., *Selected Writings*, p. 225.
11 V. Sackville-West, *Family History*, p. 274.
12 V. Sackville-West, *Challenge*, p. 46.
13 V. Sackville-West, *Seducers in Ecuador* (The Hogarth Press, London, 1924, repr. Virago, London, 1987), p. 6.
14 Vita's diary, 1 July 1910, Lilly Library.
15 Glendinning, *Vita*, p. 41.
16 Nicolson, *Portrait of a Marriage*, p. 82.
17 Mitchell A. Leaska, and John Phillips, eds, *Violet to Vita: The Letters of Violet Trefusis to Vita Sackville-West, 1910–1921* (Methuen, London, 1989), p. 61.
18 Nicolson, *Portrait of a Marriage*, p. 30.
19 V. Sackville-West, *Family History*, p. 159.
20 Nicolson, *Portrait of a Marriage*, p. 37.
21 Vita's diary, 15 May 1910, Lilly Library.
22 Vita to Harold, 29 May 1913, quoted in Nicolson, ed., *Vita & Harold*, p. 45.
23 V. Sackville-West, *Family History*, p. 40.
24 Vita to Harold, 10 April 1912, quoted in Nicolson, ed., *Vita & Harold*, p. 25.
25 Nicolson, *Portrait of a Marriage*, p. 77.
26 Richard Davenport-Hines, *Ettie: The Intimate Life and Dauntless Spirit of Lady Desborough* (Weidenfeld & Nicolson, London, 2008), p. 175.
27 Nicolson, *Portrait of a Marriage*, p. 31.
28 Vita to Harold, 21 February 1912, quoted in Nicolson, ed., *Vita & Harold*, p. 21.
29 Nicolson, *Portrait of a Marriage*, p. 32.
30 Ibid., p. 72.

31   Ibid., p. 35.

32   Leaska and Phillips, eds, *Violet to Vita*, p. 71.

33   Vita to Harold, (undated) March 1912, quoted in Nicolson, ed., *Vita & Harold*, p. 24.

34   Rose, *Harold Nicolson*, p. 45.

35   Glendinning, *Vita*, p. 68.

36   Nicolson, *Portrait of a Marriage*, p. 32.

37   Ibid., p. 23.

38   Ibid., p. 129.

39   Ibid.

40   V. Sackville-West, *The Death of Noble Godavary and Gottfried Künstler*, p. 124.

41   Nicolson, *Portrait of a Marriage*, p. 32.

42   Ibid.

43   Vita to Harold, 10 May 1912, Lilly Library.

44   Glendinning, *Vita*, p. 55.

45   Nicolson, *Portrait of a Marriage*, p. 32.

46   Quoted in David Cannadine, *Aspects of Aristocracy: Grandeur and Decline in Modern Britain* (Yale University Press, New Haven & London, 1994), p. 214.

47   Nicolson, *Portrait of a Marriage*, p. 83.

48   Harold Nicolson, 'The Desire to Please', 1943.

49   Cannadine, *Aspects of Aristocracy*, p. 256.

50   Glendinning, *Vita*, p. 49.

51   Nicolson, *Portrait of a Marriage*, p. 82.

52   Cannadine, *Aspects of Aristocracy*, p. 218; Rose, *Harold Nicolson*, p. 24.

53   Nicolson, *Portrait of a Marriage*, p. 84.

54   Vita to Harold, 23 July 1912, quoted in Nicolson, ed., *Vita & Harold*, p. 29.

55   Vita to Harold, 29 May 1913, quoted in ibid., p. 45.

56   Vita to Harold, 29 May 1912, Lilly Library.

57 Vita to Harold, 6 June 1912, quoted in Nicolson, ed., *Vita & Harold*, p. 26.

58 Michael Holroyd, *A Book of Secrets: Illegitimate Daughters, Absent Fathers* (Chatto & Windus, London, 2010), p. 179.

59 V. Sackville-West, 'Early Love', 1913, *Collected Poems*, p. 283.

60 Vita to Harold, 4 July 1912, quoted in Nicolson, ed., *Vita & Harold*, p. 27.

61 Glendinning, *Vita*, p. 78.

62 Ibid., p. 18.

63 Nicolson, *Portrait of a Marriage*, p. 33.

64 Ibid., p. 23.

65 Ibid.

66 Vita's diary, 29 August 1907, Lilly Library.

67 Glendinning, *Vita*, p. 22.

68 Ibid.

69 Vita to Harold, 8 April 1947, Lilly Library.

70 Victoria Sackville diary, 28 November 1890, Lilly Library.

71 Vita to Harold, 10 April 1912, quoted in Nicolson, ed., *Vita & Harold*, p. 24.

72 Sackville-West, *Inheritance*, p. 232.

73 V. Sackville-West, *All Passion Spent*, pp. 175–76.

74 V. Sackville-West, *Diary of Lady Anne Clifford*, p. 110.

75 Vita to Harold, 23 July 1912, quoted in Nicolson, ed., *Vita & Harold*, p. 29.

76 Vita's diary, 2 April 1912, Lilly Library.

77 Victoria Sackville scrapbook, Sissinghurst Castle.

78 Trefusis, *Don't Look Round*, p. 70.

79 V. Sackville-West, *Grey Wethers* (William Heinemann, London, 1923), p. 138.

80 V. Sackville-West, *Grand Canyon*, p. 173.

81 Vita to Harold, 2 April 1912, Lilly Library.

82 Vita's diary, 18 October 1908, Lilly Library.

83 Ibid., 7 March 1910.

84 Duff Hart-Davis, *Philip de László: His Life and Art* (Yale University Press, New Haven & London, 2010), p. 123.

85 Nicolson, *Portrait of a Marriage*, p. 30.

86 Leaska and Phillips, eds, *Violet to Vita*, p. 68.

87 Glendinning, *Vita*, p. 51.

88 Vita to Harold, 23 July 1912, quoted in Nicolson, ed., *Vita & Harold*, p. 28.

89 V. Sackville-West, *Chatterton*, p. 12.

90 Glendinning, *Vita*, p. 54.

91 V. Sackville-West, 'A Creed', *Poems of West and East* (John Lane, The Bodley Head, London, 1917).

92 V. Sackville-West, *The Dark Island*, p. 33.

93 V. Sackville-West, *Solitude*, p. 20.

94 V. Sackville-West, 'Sometimes When Night . . .', *Collected Poems*, p. 136.

95 V. Sackville-West, *The Eagle and the Dove*, p. 15.

96 V. Sackville-West, 'Night', *Collected Poems*, p. 145.

97 Harold to Vita, 28 July 1913, quoted in Nicolson, ed., *Vita & Harold*, p. 46.

98 Nicolson, *Portrait of a Marriage*, p. 80.

99 Fox and Funke, *Vita Sackville-West*, p. 24.

100 Glendinning, *Vita*, p. 52.

101 Quoted in 'Sotheby's English Literature, History, Fine Bindings, Private Press Books, Children's Books, Illustrated Books and Drawings', sale catalogue (10 July 2003), p. 101.

102 Vita to Hon. Irene Lawley, 9 November 1912, Hull History Centre (Hull University Archives U DDFA3/6/75).

103 Nicolson, *Portrait of a Marriage*, p. 82.

104 Vita to Harold, 23 July 1912, quoted in Nicolson, ed., *Vita & Harold*, pp. 29–30.

105 Vita to Victoria Sackville, 31 October 1912, Berg Collection, New York Public Library.

106 Vita to Harold, 29 May 1912, Lilly Library.

107 Vita to Harold, 2 April 1912, Lilly Library.

108 Harold to Vita, 18 June 1918, quoted in Nicolson, ed., *Vita & Harold*, p. 69.

109 V. Sackville-West, 'Fashions in Decoration', *Vogue*, April 1924, p. 61.

110 Nicolson, *Portrait of a Marriage*, p. 77.

111 Vita's diary, 14 August 1907, Lilly Library.

112 V. Sackville-West, *The Edwardians*, p. 14.

113 Vita to Harold, 23 January 1912, quoted in Nicolson, ed., *Vita & Harold*, p. 19.

114 See Stevens, *V. Sackville-West*, p. 114.

115 Harold to Vita, 10 March 1913, quoted in Nicolson, ed., *Vita & Harold*, p. 40.

116 Vita to Harold, 23 July 1912, quoted in ibid., p. 19.

117 Rose, *Harold Nicolson*, p. 51.

118 Nicolson, *Portrait of a Marriage*, p. 84.

119 Vita to Harold, 15 February 1913, quoted in Nicolson, ed., *Vita & Harold*, p. 35.

120 Harold to Vita, 19 May 1913, quoted in ibid., p. 42.

121 Vita's diary, 11 June 1913, Lilly Library.

122 Vita to Harold, 20 May 1913, quoted in Nicolson, ed., *Vita & Harold*, pp. 44–5.

123 Harold to Vita, 19 September 1913, quoted in ibid., p. 49.

124 Trefusis, *Don't Look Round*, pp. 70–1.

125 Nicolson, *Portrait of a Marriage*, p. 38.

126 Trefusis, *Don't Look Round*, p. 71.

127 Victoria Sackville scrapbook, Sissinghurst Castle.

128 Victoria Sackville diary, quoted in the *Guardian*, 29 April 2013.

129 Ibid.

130 Karyn Z. Sproles, *Desiring Women: The Partnership of Virginia Woolf and Vita Sackville-West* (University of Toronto Press, Toronto, 2006), p. 116.

131 Nicolson, *Portrait of a Marriage*, p. 39.

132 Woolf, *Orlando*, pp. 69–70.

133 Vita's diary, 1 October 1913, Lilly Library.

134 Trefusis, *Don't Look Round*, p. 156.

135 Fox and Funke, *Vita Sackville-West*, p. 24.

136 Nicolson, *Portrait of a Marriage*, p. 40.

137 Glendinning, *Vita*, p. 67.

138 V. Sackville-West, *Grey Wethers*, p. 203.

139 V. Sackville-West, *Seducers in Ecuador*, p. 1.

140 V. Sackville-West, *Passenger to Teheran*, p. 33.

141 V. Sackville-West, 'Morning in Constantinople', *Collected Poems*, p. 201.

142 Brown, *Vita's Other World*, p. 57.

143 V. Sackville-West, 'Dhji-Han-Ghir'.

144 V. Sackville-West, 'Retour en Songe'.

145 Rose, *Harold Nicolson*, p. 52.

146 Ibid., p. 53.

147 Nicolson, *Portrait of a Marriage*, p. 40.

148 Ibid.

149 Harold to Vita, 11 September 1914, quoted in Nicolson, ed., *Vita & Harold*, p. 55.

150 Nicolson, *Portrait of a Marriage*, p. 40.

151 Anne Sebba, *Enid Bagnold* (Weidenfeld & Nicolson, London, 1986), p. 138.

III INVITATION TO CAST OUT CARE

1   V. Sackville-West, 'Scorn', *Collected Poems*, p. 264.

2   V. Sackville-West, 'Gottfried Künstler', p. 133.

3   Elizabeth Pomeroy, 'Within Living Memory: Vita Sackville-West's Poems of Land and Garden', *Twentieth Century Literature*, 28 (Fall 1982), p. 283.

4   Vita to Harold, 1 June 1919, quoted in Nicolson, ed., *Vita & Harold*, p. 89.

5   Leaska and Phillips, eds, *Violet to Vita*, p. 61.

6   Vita to Harold, 9 July 1914, quoted in Nicolson, ed., *Vita & Harold*, p. 52.

7   Vita to Hon. Irene Lawley, 13 January 1913, Hull History Centre (Hull University Archives U DDFA3/6/75).

8   Trefusis, *Don't Look Round*, p. 70.

9   V. Sackville-West, *Family History*, p. 135.

10 Trefusis, *Don't Look Round*, p. 76.

11 Alsop, *Lady Sackville*, p. 142.

12 V. Sackville-West, *The Dark Island*, p. 167.

13 Vita to Harold, November 1915, quoted in Nicolson, ed., *Vita & Harold*, p. 56.

14 V. Sackville-West, *Grey Wethers*, p. 208.

15 Vita's diary, 7 February 1916, Lilly Library.

16 See Brown, *Vita's Other World*, p. 64.

17 Ibid.

18 V. Sackville-West, 'The Garden', 1915.

19 Brown, *Vita's Other World*, p. 67.

20 Anne Olivier Bell, ed., *The Diary of Virginia Woolf, Volume 3, 1925–30* (5 volumes, Penguin, London, 1979–85), pp. 145–46.

21 V. Sackville-West, *Heritage*, pp. 11–12.

22 V. Sackville-West, 'Fashions in Decoration', p. 61.

23 Vita to Harold, February 1917, quoted in Nicolson, ed., *Vita & Harold*, p. 58.

24 V. Sackville-West, 'Song: Let Us Go Back', 1915.

25 Nicolson, *Portrait of a Marriage*, p. 42.

26 Vita to Harold, August 1917, quoted in Nicolson, ed., *Vita & Harold*, p. 59.

27 Souhami, *Mrs Keppel and her Daughter*, p. 115.

28 V. Sackville-West, 'A Fallen Soldier', *Collected Poems*, p. 158.

29 Vita's diary, 2 October 1917, Lilly Library.

NOTES

30 Algernon Charles Swinburne, 'The Oblation'.

31 Vita's diary, 28 January 1917, Lilly Library.

32 Ibid., 31 December 1916.

33 V. Sackville-West, 'A censor for the tiny tots', *Spectator*, 2 February 1954.

34 Robert Cross and Ann Ravenscroft-Hulme, *Vita Sackville-West: A Bibliography* (St Paul's Bibliographies, Winchester, 1999), p. 86.

35 Vita's diary, 5 February 1917, Lilly Library.

36 Brown, *Vita's Other World*, p. 62.

37 See Sotheby's, p. 197.

38 Fox and Funke, *Vita Sackville-West*, p. 25.

39 Caws, ed., *Selected Writings*, p. 56.

40 V. Sackville-West, *Heritage*, pp. 236–37.

41 Nicolson, *Portrait of a Marriage*, p. 41.

42 Ibid.

43 V. Sackville-West, 'One Day', *Collected Poems*, pp. 147–48.

44 Harold to Vita, 11 September 1914, quoted in Nicolson, ed., *Vita & Harold*, p. 54.

45 Glendinning, *Vita*, p. 218.

46 Trefusis, *Don't Look Round*, p. 71.

47 Leaska and Phillips, eds, *Violet to Vita*, p. 102.

48 Vita to Harold, 11 September 1914, quoted in Nicolson, ed., *Vita & Harold*, p. 54.

49 Ibid., p. 67.

50 Nicolson, *Portrait of a Marriage*, p. 100.

51 Ibid., p. 134

52 V. Sackville-West, *Heritage*, pp. 20–1.

53 Leaska and Phillips, eds, *Violet to Vita*, p. 74.

54 Harold to Vita, 7 November 1917, quoted in Nicolson, ed., *Vita & Harold*, p. 60.

55 Glendinning, *Vita*, p. 88.

56 V. Sackville-West, *Heritage*.

57   Vita's diary, 18 November 1917, Lilly Library.

58   Vita to Harold, 11 May 1918, quoted in Nicolson, ed., *Vita & Harold*, p. 66.

59   Vita to Harold, 9 June 1919, quoted in ibid., p. 90.

60   Victoria Sackville, 'Book of Happy Reminiscences', Lilly Library.

61   Harold to Vita, 9 September 1918, quoted in Nicolson, ed., *Vita & Harold*, p. 70.

62   Leaska and Phillips, eds, *Violet to Vita*, p. 92.

63   V. Sackville-West, *Challenge*, p. 243.

64   Leaska and Phillips, eds, *Violet to Vita*, p. 87.

65   Souhami, *Mrs Keppel and her Daughter*, p. 243.

66   Leaska and Phillips, eds, *Violet to Vita*, p. 89.

67   See Rose, *Harold Nicolson*, p. 142.

68   V. Sackville-West, *Aphra Behn*, p. 12.

69   Leaska and Phillips, eds, *Violet to Vita*, p. 74.

70   Vita's diary, 14 March 1918, Lilly Library.

71   Nicolson, *Portrait of a Marriage*, p. 99.

72   Ibid.

73   V. Sackville-West, *The Land* (Spring), *Collected Poems*, p. 60.

74   Nicolson, *Portrait of a Marriage*, p. 99.

75   Ibid., pp. 100, 102.

76   Woolf, *Orlando*, p. 25.

77   Vita's diary, 18 April 1918, Lilly Library.

78   Leaska and Phillips, eds, *Violet to Vita*, p. 78.

79   Harold to Vita, 28 April 1918, quoted in Nicolson, ed., *Vita & Harold*, p. 65.

80   Vita to Victoria Sackville, 29 April 1918, Berg Collection, New York Public Library.

81   Souhami, *Mrs Keppel and her Daughter*, p. 129.

82   Victoria Sackville diary, quoted in the *Guardian*, 29 April 2013.

83 Harold to Vita, 18 June 1918, quoted in Nicolson, ed., *Vita & Harold*, p. 68.

84 Adam Nicolson, *Sissinghurst: An Unfinished History* (HarperCollins, London, 2008), p. 291.

85 Glendinning, *Vita*, p. 405.

86 Nicolson, *Portrait of a Marriage*, p. 103.

87 Trefusis, *Don't Look Round*, p. 7.

88 Leaska and Phillips, eds, *Violet to Vita*, p. 108.

89 Harold to Vita, 2 September 1918, quoted in Nicolson, ed., *Vita & Harold*, p. 69.

90 Leaska and Phillips, eds, *Violet to Vita*, p. 90.

91 Vita's diary, 11 October 1918, Lilly Library.

92 V. Sackville-West, *Passenger to Teheran*, p. 29.

93 V. Sackville-West, *Gottfried Künstler*, p. 124.

94 Leaska and Phillips, eds, *Violet to Vita*, p. 108.

95 Alsop, *Lady Sackville*, p. 209.

96 V. Sackville-West, 'Dissonance', *Collected Poems*, p. 289.

97 V. Sackville-West, 'Eve', 'Eve in Tears', *Collected Poems*, pp. 262, 263.

98 Vita to Harold, 1 February 1920, quoted in Nicolson, ed., *Vita & Harold*, p. 105.

99 Souhami, *Mrs Keppel and her Daughter*, p. 148.

100 Vita to Harold, 20 March 1919, and Harold to Vita, 26 March 1919, quoted in Nicolson, ed., *Vita & Harold*, p. 81.

101 Glendinning, *Vita*, p. 106.

102 Leaska and Phillips, eds, *Violet to Vita*, p. 101.

103 Vita to Harold, 1 June 1919, quoted in Nicolson, ed., *Vita & Harold*, p. 88.

104 Nicolson, *Portrait of a Marriage*, p. 108.

105 V. Sackville-West, *Grey Wethers*, p. 202.

106 Brown, *Vita's Other World*, p. 90.

107 Vita to Harold, July 1919, quoted in Nicolson, ed., *Vita & Harold*, p. 96.

108 Brown, *Vita's Other World*, p. 73.

109 V. Sackville-West, *Grey Wethers*, p. 69.

110 Nicolson, *Portrait of a Marriage*, p. 110.

111 Vita to Harold, 1 February 1920, quoted in Nicolson, ed., *Vita & Harold*, p. 104.

112 V. Sackville-West, *The Dragon in Shallow Waters* (William Collins, London, 1921), p. 254.

113 Vita to Harold, 9 February 1920, quoted in Nicolson, ed., *Vita & Harold*, p. 108.

114 Nicolson, *Portrait of a Marriage*, p. 159.

115 Vita's diary, 10 February 1920, Lilly Library.

116 Ibid.

117 Vita's diary, 14 February 1920, Lilly Library.

118 Vita's diary, 19 February 1920, Lilly Library.

119 Vita's diary, 15 March 1920, Lilly Library.

120 Vita's diary, 23 September 1920, Lilly Library.

121 V. Sackville-West, 'To Any M.F.H.', *Collected Poems*, p. 123.

122 Vita's diary, 17 April 1920, Lilly Library.

123 Ibid., 30 April 1920.

124 Ibid., 7 May 1920.

125 Ibid., 12 October 1920.

126 V. Sackville-West, *The Dragon in Shallow Waters*, pp. 5–6.

127 Ibid., p. 232.

128 V. Sackville-West, *Diary of Lady Anne Clifford*, p. 60.

129 Nicolson, *Portrait of a Marriage*, p. 128.

130 Harold to Vita, 8 February 1921, quoted in Nicolson, ed., *Vita & Harold*, p. 113.

131 V. Sackville-West, 'Before and After', *Collected Poems*, p. 284.

132 Souhami, *Mrs Keppel and her Daughter*, p. 199.

133 V. Sackville-West, 'Memory – bad and good', *Spectator*, 29 July 1932, p. 8.

134 Nicolson, *Sissinghurst*, p. 271.

135 Nicolson, *Portrait of a Marriage*, p. 167.

136 V. Sackville-West, 'Night', *Collected Poems*, p. 145.
137 Robert Sackville-West, *Inheritance*, p. 237.
138 V. Sackville-West, 'Night', *Collected Poems*, p. 144.
139 V. Sackville-West, *The Land* (Winter), *Collected Poems*, p. 17.
140 Pomeroy, 'Within Living Memory', p. 274.
141 V. Sackville-West, *The Land* (Spring), *Collected Poems*, p. 63.
142 Cross and Ravenscroft-Hulme, *Vita Sackville-West: A Bibliography*, p. 209.

IV ORLANDO

1   V. Sackville-West, 'Sometimes When Night . . .', *Collected Poems*, p. 136.
2   V. Sackville-West, *The Easter Party*, p. 76.
3   Vita to Harold, 8 December 1922, quoted in Nicolson, ed., *Vita & Harold*, p. 117.
4   Vita's diary, 22 February 1924, Lilly Library.
5   V. Sackville-West, *Passenger to Teheran*, p. 91.
6   V. Sackville-West, *Aphra Behn*, p. 50.
7   Ibid.
8   Glendinning, *Vita*, p. 238.
9   V. Sackville-West, *Solitude*, p. 30.
10 Vita to Harold, 31 May 1926, quoted in Nicolson, ed., *Vita & Harold*, p. 145.
11 Glendinning, *Vita*, p. 113.
12 Jane Wellesley, *Wellington: A Journey Through My Family* (Weidenfeld & Nicolson, London, 2008), p. 277.
13 Vita's diary, 28 August 1920, Lilly Library.
14 Ibid., 20 September 1921.
15 Brown, *Vita's Other World*, p. 96.
16 Souhami, *Mrs Keppel and her Daughter*, p. 220.
17 V. Sackville-West, 'Penn-y-Pass', *Collected Poems*, p. 141.
18 Wellesley, *Wellington*, p. 272.

19 Ibid., p. 308.

20 James Lees-Milne, *Harold Nicolson: A Biography, Volume 1* (Hamish Hamilton paperback reprint, London, 1988), p. 179.

21 Glendinning, *Vita*, p. 129.

22 Leonard Woolf, *Downhill All the Way: An Autobiography of the Years 1919 to 1939* (The Hogarth Press, London, 1967), pp. 111–12.

23 Caws, ed., *Selected Writings*, p. 235.

24 Victoria Sackville, 'Book of Happy Reminiscences', Lilly Library.

25 Ronald Firbank, *The Flower Beneath the Foot*, (1923 repr. *The Complete Firbank*, Picador Classics, London, 1988), p. 541.

26 Caws, ed., *Selected Writings*, p. 235.

27 Vita's diary, 10 January 1924, Lilly Library.

28 Ibid., 15 January 1924.

29 Ibid., 1 February 1924.

30 Ibid., 4 February 1924.

31 Ibid., 3 December 1926.

32 Lees-Milne, *Harold Nicolson, Vol. 1*, p. 238.

33 Alsop, *Lady Sackville*, p. 204.

34 Glendinning, *Vita*, p. 143.

35 V. Sackville-West, *Grand Canyon*, p. 194.

36 Vita's diary, 30 September 1925, Lilly Library.

37 Vita's diary, 14 October 1925, Lilly Library.

38 Vita to Harold, 29 December 1925, quoted in Nicolson, ed., *Vita & Harold*, p. 136.

39 Vita to Harold, 28 June 1926, quoted in ibid., p. 149.

40 Vita's diary, 3 January 1924, Lilly Library.

41 Souhami, *Mrs Keppel and her Daughter*, p. 214.

42 Leaska and Phillips, eds, *Violet to Vita*, p. 292.

43 Souhami, *Mrs Keppel and her Daughter*, p. 220.

44 Ibid., p. 121.

45 Leaska and Phillips, eds, *Violet to Vita*, p. 282.

46 Souhami, *Mrs Keppel and her Daughter*, p. 209.

47 Ibid., p. 215.

48 Ibid., p. 219.

49 Glendinning, *Vita*, p. 126.

50 Souhami, *Mrs Keppel and her Daughter*, p. 218.

51 V. Sackville-West, 'Black Tarn', *Collected Poems*, pp. 137–39.

52 Souhami, *Mrs Keppel and her Daughter*, p. 218.

53 Vita's diary, 3 January 1924, Lilly Library.

54 Ibid.

55 Souhami, *Mrs Keppel and her Daughter*, p. 217.

56 Ibid., pp. 219–20.

57 Ibid., p. 220.

58 Ibid., p. 219.

59 Vita's diary, 8 March 1924, Lilly Library.

60 Quoted in the *Guardian*, 13 July 2008.

61 Louise DeSalvo and Mitchell A. Leaska, eds, *The Letters of Vita Sackville-West to Virginia Woolf* (Hutchinson & Co., London, 1984, repr. Virago, 1992), p. 61.

62 Nicolson, *Portrait of a Marriage*, p. 187.

63 Bell, ed., *Diary of Virginia Woolf, Vol. 2*, p. 239.

64 Vita's diary, 17 August 1926, Lilly Library.

65 Bell, ed., *Diary of Virginia Woolf, Vol. 2*, p. 235.

66 Sproles, *Desiring Women*, p. 49.

67 V. Sackville-West, 'Self-Epitaph, Composed by an Honest Sensualist', *Collected Poems*, p. 253.

68 Woolf, Virginia, *Between the Acts* (The Hogarth Press, London, 1941, repr. Oxford World Classics, 1998), p. 107.

69 Bell, ed., *Diary of Virginia Woolf, Vol. 3*, p. 203.

70 Woolf, *Orlando*, pp. 20, 70.

71 Bell, ed., *Diary of Virginia Woolf*, Vol. 2, p. 307.

72 Ibid., pp. 216–17.

73 Ibid., p. 225.

74 Vita to Harold, 19 December 1922, Lilly Library.

75 Bell, ed., *Diary of Virginia Woolf, Vol. 3*, p. 52.

76 DeSalvo and Leaska, eds, *Vita Sackville-West to Virginia Woolf*, p. 56.

77 Vita to Harold, 30 November 1926, Lilly Library.

78 See Cross and Ravenscroft-Hulme, *Vita Sackville-West: A Bibliography*, p. 86.

79 Vita to Enid Bagnold (Jones), 15 September 1933, Manuscripts, Archives and Special Collections, Washington State University Library, collection number: Cage 4688.

80 DeSalvo and Leaska, eds, *Vita Sackville-West to Virginia Woolf*, p. 53.

81 Cross and Ravenscroft-Hulme, *Vita Sackville-West: A Bibliography*, p. 30.

82 Bell, ed., *Diary of Virginia Woolf, Vol. 2*, p. 313.

83 Ibid., *Vol. 5*, p. 328.

84 Ibid., *Vol. 2*, p. 313.

85 Hermione Lee, *Virginia Woolf* (Chatto & Windus, London, 1996, repr. Vintage, London, 1997), p. 517.

86 Glendinning, *Vita*, p. 140.

87 Lee, *Virginia Woolf*, p. 499.

88 DeSalvo and Leaska, eds, *Vita Sackville-West to Virginia Woolf*, p. 54.

89 Bell, ed., *Diary of Virginia Woolf, Vol. 3*, p. 52.

90 Harold to Vita, 8 January 1926, quoted in Nicolson, ed., *Vita & Harold*, p. 149.

91 DeSalvo and Leaska, eds, *Vita Sackville-West to Virginia Woolf*, p. 318.

92 Rose, *Harold Nicolson*, p. 136.

93 Vita to Harold, 12 July 1928, quoted in Nicolson, ed., *Vita & Harold*, p. 198.

94 Vita to Harold, 13 December 1928, quoted in ibid.

95 Vita to Harold, 16 November 1922, quoted in ibid., p. 114.
96 V. Sackville-West, 'Bitterness', *Collected Poems*, pp. 290–91.
97 V. Sackville-West, *The Heir*, p. 109.
98 V. Sackville-West, *Grey Wethers*, p. 64.
99 Harold to Vita, 2 September 1923, quoted in Nicolson, ed., *Vita & Harold*, p. 123.
100 V. Sackville-West, *Grey Wethers*, p. 306.
101 Harold to Vita, 18 September 1921, quoted in Nicolson, ed., *Vita & Harold*, p. 113.
102 Glendinning, *Vita*, p. 103.
103 V. Sackville-West, *Pepita*, p. 258.
104 Alsop, *Lady Sackville*, pp. 206, 208.
105 Bell, ed., *Diary of Virginia Woolf, Vol. 3*, p. 57.
106 V. Sackville-West, *Passenger to Teheran*, p. 115.
107 V. Sackville-West, 'Persia', *Collected Poems*, p. 173.
108 V. Sackville-West, 'At Rhey [Rhages]', *Collected Poems*, p. 177.
109 V. Sackville-West, *Passenger to Teheran*, p. 61.
110 DeSalvo and Leaska, eds, *Vita Sackville-West to Virginia Woolf*, p. 120.
111 Ibid., p. 197.
112 Ibid., p. 127.
113 V. Sackville-West, *Passenger to Teheran*, p. 129.
114 DeSalvo and Leaska, eds, *Vita Sackville-West to Virginia Woolf*, p. 133.
115 V. Sackville-West, 'Madame Dieulafoy', *Vogue*, June 1926, p. 77.
116 DeSalvo and Leaska, eds, *Vita Sackville-West to Virginia Woolf*, p. 131.
117 V. Sackville-West, *The Land* (Spring), *Collected Poems*, p. 56.
118 John Drinkwater, *Observer*, 2 January 1927.
119 Vita's diary, 10 October 1926, Lilly Library.
120 Quoted in Lee, *Virginia Woolf*, p. 502 (1 March 1926).

121 DeSalvo and Leaska, eds, *Vita Sackville-West to Virginia Woolf*, p. 162.

122 V. Sackville-West, 'Year's End', *Collected Poems*, pp. 168–69.

123 V. Sackville-West, 'A Bowl of Blue Beads', *Collected Poems*, p. 178.

124 Nicolson, *Sissinghurst*, p. 292.

125 See Cressida Connolly, *The Rare and the Beautiful: The Lives of the Garmans* (Fourth Estate, London, 2004), p. 70.

126 Bell, ed., *Diary of Virginia Woolf, Vol. 3*, p. 188.

127 Connolly, *The Rare and the Beautiful*, p. 71.

128 Victoria Sackville, 'Book of Happy Reminiscences', Lilly Library.

129 Vita to Harold, 17 August 1926, quoted in Nicolson, ed., *Vita & Harold*, p. 159.

130 Nicolson, *Portrait of a Marriage*, p. 189.

131 Vita's diary, 'Memoranda', February 1927, Lilly Library.

132 Rose, *Harold Nicolson*, p. 148.

133 Ibid., p. 149.

134 Vita's diary, 3 September 1927, Lilly Library.

135 V. Sackville-West, *King's Daughter* (The Hogarth Press, London, 1929), p. 35.

136 Ibid., p. 37.

137 Connolly, *The Rare and the Beautiful*, p. 75.

138 Glendinning, *Vita*, p. 180.

139 Connolly, *The Rare and the Beautiful*, p. 75.

140 Vita to Harold, 7 November 1927, quoted in Nicolson, ed., *Vita & Harold*, p. 187.

141 Connolly, *The Rare and the Beautiful*, p. 78.

142 Harold to Vita, 23 October 1927, quoted in Nicolson, ed., *Vita & Harold*, p. 184.

143 Roy Campbell, *The Georgiad* (Boriswood Ltd, London, 1931).

144 DeSalvo and Leaska, eds, *Vita Sackville-West to Virginia Woolf*, p. 256.

145 Ibid., p. 252.

146 Glendinning, *Vita*, p. 183.

147 Ibid., p. 186.

148 Campbell, *The Georgiad.*

149 Ibid.

150 Vita to Harold, 15 January 1952, Lilly Library.

151 Vita's diary, 19 December 1927, Lilly Library.

152 Caws, ed., *Selected Writings*, p. 68.

153 DeSalvo and Leaska, eds, *Vita Sackville-West to Virginia Woolf*, p. 265; *Montreal Gazette*, 15 August 1955.

154 Robert Sackville-West, *Inheritance*, p. 231.

155 Bell, ed., *Diary of Virginia Woolf, Vol. 3*, p. 175.

156 Ibid., p. 191.

157 Ibid., p. 174.

158 Glendinning, *Vita*, p. 205.

159 Vita to Harold, 11 October 1928, quoted in Nicolson, ed., *Vita & Harold*, p. 206.

160 Radclyffe Hall to Vita, 16 December 1928, Dobkin Collection, Glenn Horowitz, New York.

161 Glendinning, *Vita*, pp. 205–06.

162 V. Sackville-West, *King's Daughter*, p. 36.

163 Vita to Harold, 18 April 1928, quoted in Nicolson, ed., *Vita & Harold*, p. 193.

164 Bell, ed., *Diary of Virginia Woolf, Vol. 3*, p. 180.

165 Hilda Matheson to Vita, 15 January 1929 and 6 February 1929, quoted in Michael Carney, *Stoker: The Life of Hilda Matheson OBE 1888–1940* (Published by the author, Llangynog, 1999), p. 57.

166 Ibid., p. 49; Glendinning, *Vita*, p. 213.

167 Vita to Harold, 24 June 1928, quoted in Nicolson, ed., *Vita & Harold*, p. 196.

168 Carney, *Stoker*, p. 44.

169 Ibid., p. 49.

170 Ibid.

171 Ibid., p. 51.

172 Bell, ed., *Diary of Virginia Woolf, Vol. 3*, p. 239.

173 Nicolson, ed., *The Letters of Virginia Woolf, Vol. IV* (repr. Hogarth Press, London, 1994), p. 110.

174 Bell, ed., *Diary of Virginia Woolf, Vol. 3*, p. 267.

175 Vita's diary, 25 July 1929, Lilly Library.

176 1 August 1929, ibid.

177 DeSalvo and Leaska, eds, *Vita Sackville-West to Virginia Woolf*, p. 359.

178 Rose, *Harold Nicolson*, p. 162.

179 Vita's diary, 1928, Memorandum, Lilly Library.

180 Rose, *Harold Nicolson*, p. 163.

181 DeSalvo and Leaska, eds, *Vita Sackville-West to Virginia Woolf*, p. 361.

182 Carney, *Stoker*, p. 55.

183 Ibid., p. 90.

184 V. Sackville-West, *Gottfried Künstler*, p. 143.

V THE LAND AND THE GARDEN

1 V. Sackville-West, 'Sissinghurst Castle', *House & Garden*, October/November 1950, p. 55.

2 Caws, ed., *Selected Writings*, p. 201.

3 Stevens, *V. Sackville-West*, p. 117.

4 V. Sackville-West, *Family History*, p. 194.

5 Brown, *Vita's Other World*, p. 109.

6 V. Sackville-West, *King's Daughter*, p. 35.

7 V. Sackville-West, *The Edwardians*, p. 247.

8 DeSalvo and Leaska, eds, *Vita Sackville-West to Virginia Woolf*, p. 345.

9 Sackville-West, *Inheritance*, p. 239.

10 V. Sackville-West, *The Edwardians*, pp. 121–22.

11 V. Sackville-West, 'Knole', *Spectator*, 14 October 1943, p. 8.

12 V. Sackville-West, *The Garden*, p. 14.

13 V. Sackville-West, 'Sissinghurst Castle'.

14 Nicolson, *Sissinghurst*, p. 272.

15 Vita to Harold, 23 October 1920, quoted in Nicolson, ed., *Vita & Harold*, p. 228.

16 V. Sackville-West, 'Sissinghurst Castle'.

17 Brown, *Vita's Other World*, p. 111.

18 Ibid.

19 Woolf, *Downhill All the Way*, p. 112.

20 Anne Scott-James, *Sissinghurst: The Making of a Garden* (Michael Joseph, London, 1974, repr. 1981), p. 53; Bell, ed., *Diary of Virginia Woolf, Vol. 4*, p. 87.

21 V. Sackville-West, 'Sissinghurst', *Collected Poems*, p. 111.

22 V. Sackville-West, *The Heir*, p. 65.

23 V. Sackville-West, *Knole and the Sackvilles*, p. 35.

24 Harold to Vita, 24 April 1930, quoted in Nicolson, ed., *Vita & Harold*, p. 227–28.

25 Glendinning, *Vita*, p. 224.

26 V. Sackville-West, 'Absence', *Collected Poems*, p. 254.

27 V. Sackville-West, 'Sissinghurst', *Collected Poems*, p. 111.

28 V. Sackville-West, *Daughter of France* (Michael Joseph, London, 1959), p. 199.

29 V. Sackville-West, *No Signposts in the Sea* (Michael Joseph, London, 1961), p. 87.

30 Nigel Nicolson, *Long Life: Memoirs* (Weidenfeld & Nicolson, London, 1997), p. 209.

31 Ibid., p. 210.

32 Scott-James, *The Making of a Garden*, p. 67.

33 Bell, ed., *Diary of Virginia Woolf, Vol. 4*, p. 87.

34 Vita to Harold, 27 February 1912, quoted in Nicolson, ed., *Vita & Harold*, p. 22.

35 Scott-James, *The Making of a Garden*, p. 67.

36 V. Sackville-West, 'Sissinghurst', *Collected Poems*, p. 111.

37 V. Sackville-West, *Family History*, p. 193.
38 V. Sackville-West, *All Passion Spent*, p. 160.
39 V. Sackville-West, *Passenger to Teheran*, p. 111.
40 V. Sackville-West, *All Passion Spent*, pp. 58–9.
41 V. Sackville-West, 'Sissinghurst Castle'.
42 Vita to Harold, 23 October 1930, quoted in Nicolson, ed., *Vita & Harold*, p. 228.
43 Nicolson, *Sissinghurst*, p. 291.
44 Nancy MacKnight, *Dearest Andrew: Letters from V. Sackville-West to Andrew Reiber, 1951–1962* (Michael Joseph, London, 1980), p. 83.
45 Philip Hoare, *Serious Pleasures: The Life of Stephen Tennant* (Hamish Hamilton, London, 1990), p. 279.
46 Brown, *Vita's Other World*, p. 94.
47 Scott-James, *The Making of a Garden*, pp. 57–60; V. Sackville-West, *Passenger to Teheran*, p. 77.
48 Glendinning, *Vita*, p. 403.
49 Brown, *Vita's Other World*, p. 228.
50 Harold Nicolson's diary, 26 December 1943.
51 V. Sackville-West, 'Sissinghurst Castle', p. 92.
52 Rose, *Harold Nicolson*, p. 173.
53 V. Sackville-West, 'Sharawadji', *Spectator*, 13 January 1944, p. 9.
54 Zoob, Caroline, *Virginia Woolf's Garden* (Jacqui Small, London, 2013).
55 Clive Bell to Lyn Newman, 13 August 1931, Lyn Newman papers, St John's College, Cambridge.
56 V. Sackville-West, 'The Lake', *Country Notes* (Michael Joseph, London, 1939).
57 Harold Nicolson's diary, 20 March 1932.
58 Nigel Nicolson, *Long Life*, p. 69.
59 Trefusis, *Broderie Anglaise*, pp. 49–50.
60 V. Sackville-West, *Family History*, p. 99.

61 DeSalvo and Leaska, eds, *Vita Sackville-West to Virginia Woolf*, p. 384.

62 Glendinning, *Vita*, p. 241.

63 Brown, *Vita's Other World*, p. 116.

64 V. Sackville-West, *Aphra Behn*, p. 12.

65 Vita to Harold, 26 November 1919, quoted in Nicolson, ed., *Vita & Harold*, p. 101.

66 Quoted in *Kent & Sussex Courier*, 21 June 2013.

67 *Spectator*, 21 January 1922.

68 Stevens, *V. Sackville-West*, p. 48.

69 V. Sackville-West, 'Tess', *Collected Poems*, p. 249.

70 Rose, *Harold Nicolson*, p. 186.

71 V. Sackville-West, *The Garden*, p. 29.

72 Vita to Nancy Noyes, 9 May 1930, Manuscripts, Archives and Special Collections, Washington State University Library, collection number: Cage 4688.

73 Review of *Twelve Days*, *Daily Telegraph*, undated, 1928.

74 V. Sackville-West, *Country Notes*, p. 70; Pomeroy, p. 288.

75 V. Sackville-West, *Passenger to Teheran*, p. 52.

76 Woolf, *Downhill All the Way*, p. 158.

77 Bell, ed., *Diary of Virginia Woolf*, Vol. 4, p. 39.

78 V. Sackville-West, *Andrew Marvell* (Faber & Faber, London, 1929), p. 27.

79 Bell, ed., *Diary of Virginia Woolf*, Vol. 3, p. 306.

80 Glendinning, *Vita*, p. 268.

81 Ibid., p. 177.

82 Bell, ed., *Diary of Virginia Woolf*, Vol. 4, p. 7.

83 Stevens, *V. Sackville-West*, p. 36.

84 Pomeroy, p. 285.

85 Bell, ed., *Diary of Virginia Woolf*, Vol. 3, p. 330.

86 V. Sackville-West, *Passenger to Teheran*, p. 28.

87 Bell, ed., *Diary of Virginia Woolf*, Vol. 4, p. 134.

88 James Lees-Milne, *Harold Nicolson*, Vol. 2, pp. 33–4.

89 Glendinning, *Vita*, p. 257.

90 Vita to Harold, 14 February 1933, quoted in Nicolson, ed., *Vita & Harold*, p. 238.

91 DeSalvo and Leaska, eds, *Vita Sackville-West to Virginia Woolf*, p. 388.

92 Vita's diary, 15 February 1933, Lilly Library.

93 Glendinning, *Vita*, p. 255.

94 Vita's diary, 4 February 1933, Lilly Library.

95 Vita to Harold, 14 February 1933, quoted in Nicolson, ed., *Vita & Harold*, p. 238.

96 Vita's diary, 28 January 1933, Lilly Library.

97 Vita's diary, 7 February 1933, Lilly Library.

98 Rose, *Harold Nicolson*, p. 175.

99 Vita's diary, 21 February 1933, Lilly Library.

100 Ibid., 20 February 1933.

101 Lees-Milne, *Harold Nicolson, Vol. 2*, p. 38.

102 V. Sackville-West, 'In New England', *Collected Poems*, p. 212.

103 DeSalvo and Leaska, eds, *Vita Sackville-West to Virginia Woolf*, p. 394.

104 Vita's diary, 27 February 1933, Lilly Library.

105 DeSalvo and Leaska, eds, *Vita Sackville-West to Virginia Woolf*, p. 391.

106 Lees-Milne, *Harold Nicolson, Vol. 2*, p. 38.

107 Harold to Vita, 23 February 1933, quoted in Nicolson, ed., *Vita & Harold*, p. 238.

108 Rose, *Harold Nicolson*, p. 178; Lees-Milne, *Harold Nicolson, Vol. 2*, p. 39.

109 Glendinning, *Vita*, p. 238.

110 V. Sackville-West, 'Valediction', *Collected Poems*, p. 298.

111 Bell, ed., *Diary of Virginia Woolf, Vol. 4*, p. 7.

112 V. Sackville-West, *Chatterton*, p. 34.

113 Lees-Milne, *Harold Nicolson, Vol. 2*, p. 3.

114 Stanley Olson, ed., *Harold Nicolson Diaries and Letters 1930–1964* (Penguin, London, 1984), p. 40.

115 V. Sackville-West, *Family History*, p. 159.

116 V. Sackville-West, 'Warning', *Collected Poems*, p. 297.

117 V. Sackville-West, *Family History*, p. 75.

118 Ibid., p. 197.

119 V. Sackville-West, 'Provence', *Collected Poems*, p. 205.

120 Glendinning, *Vita*, p. 249.

121 DeSalvo and Leaska, eds, *Vita Sackville-West to Virginia Woolf*, p. 382.

122 V. Sackville-West, 'Tess', *Collected Poems*, p. 249.

123 V. Sackville-West, 'Valediction', *Collected Poems*, p. 298.

124 Vita to Harold, 25 September 1934, quoted in Nicolson, ed., *Vita & Harold*, p. 255.

125 Scott-James, *The Making of a Garden*, p. 49.

126 Olson, ed., *Harold Nicolson Diaries and Letters*, p. 55.

127 Diary poem, 16 May 1933, quoted in Glendinning, *Vita*, p. 280.

128 V. Sackville-West, *The Dark Island*, p. 33.

129 V. Sackville-West, *Passenger to Teheran*, p. 82.

130 Vita to Harold, 30 January 1913, quoted in Nicolson, ed., *Vita & Harold*, p. 33; DeSalvo and Leaska, eds, *Vita Sackville-West to Virginia Woolf*, pp. 138–39.

131 Virginia Woolf to Vita, 28 April 1931.

132 Lees-Milne, *Harold Nicolson, Vol. 2*, p. 25.

133 Olson, ed., *Harold Nicolson Diaries and Letters*, p. 33.

134 Ibid., p. 27.

135 DeSalvo and Leaska, eds, *Vita Sackville-West to Virginia Woolf*, p. 401.

136 Olson, ed., *Harold Nicolson Diaries and Letters*, pp. 39–40.

137 Ibid.

138 V. Sackville-West, 'Sissinghurst Castle', p. 92.

139 V. Sackville-West, *Even More for Your Garden* (Michael

Joseph, London, 1958, repr. Frances Lincoln, London, 2004), p. 122.

140 V. Sackville-West, *The Women's Land Army* (Michael Joseph, London, 1944), p. 23.

141 Olson, ed., *Harold Nicolson Diaries and Letters*, p. 31.

142 Harold to Vita, 1 October 1934, quoted in Nicolson, ed., *Vita & Harold*, p. 260.

143 Glendinning, *Vita*, p. 246.

144 Cross and Ravenscroft-Hulme, *Vita Sackville-West: A Bibliography*, p. 88.

145 V. Sackville-West, *The Dark Island*, pp. 34, 128.

146 Ibid., p. 147.

147 Ibid., p. 30.

148 Bell, ed., *Diary of Virginia Woolf, Vol. 4*, p. 226.

149 V. Sackville-West, *The Dark Island*, p. 215.

150 Ibid., p. 206.

151 DeSalvo and Leaska, eds, *Vita Sackville-West to Virginia Woolf*, p. 406.

152 Ibid.

153 Lees-Milne, *Harold Nicolson, Vol. 2*, p. 43.

154 Olson, ed., *Harold Nicolson Diaries and Letters*, p. 60.

155 Elizabeth von Arnim, *The Enchanted April* (Macmillan, London, 1922), p. 1.

156 Ibid., p. 7.

157 St Aubyn, Gwen, *Towards a Pattern* (Longmans, London, 1940), p. 49; see Raitt, Suzanne, *Vita and Virginia: The Work and Friendship of V. Sackville-West and Virginia Woolf* (Clarendon Press, Oxford, 1993), p. 133.

158 V. Sackville-West, *The Dark Island*, p. 171.

159 V. Sackville-West, *Solitude*, p. 5.

160 V. Sackville-West, 'Reddín', *Collected Poems*, p. 231.

161 Ibid., p. 232.

162 Vita to Harold, 23 July 1912, quoted in Nicolson, ed., *Vita & Harold*, p. 29.

163 V. Sackville-West, *Saint Joan of Arc* (Cobden-Sanderson, London, 1936, repr. The Folio Society, London, 1995), p. 7.

164 Scott-James, *The Making of a Garden*, p. 51; Glendinning, *Vita*, p. 283.

165 Olson, ed., *Harold Nicolson Diaries and Letters*, p. 92.

166 Lees-Milne, *Harold Nicolson, Vol. 2*, p. 74.

167 V. Sackville-West, *Pepita*, pp. 281–82.

168 Ibid., p. 19.

169 Cross and Ravenscroft-Hulme, *Vita Sackville-West: A Bibliography*, p. 101.

170 V. Sackville-West, *Pepita*, p. 267.

171 V. Sackville-West, *Some Flowers* (The Hogarth Press, London, 1937).

172 Harold to Vita, 8 June 1937, Lilly Library.

173 Brown, *Vita's Other World*, pp. 70–1.

174 Fox and Funke, *Vita Sackville-West*, p. 42.

175 Vita's diary, 24 March 1939, Lilly Library.

176 MacKnight, *Dearest Andrew*, p. 94.

VI ALL PASSION SPENT?

1 Stevens, *V. Sackville-West*, p. 117.

2 V. Sackville-West, *Solitude*, p. 30.

3 V. Sackville-West, *The Garden*, p. 111.

4 Woolf, *Downhill All the Way*, p. 113.

5 Harold to Vita, 9 March 1938, quoted in Nicolson, ed., *Vita & Harold*, p. 298.

6 V. Sackville-West, 'Sissinghurst', *Collected Poems*, p. 111.

7 V. Sackville-West, *The Garden*, p. 127.

8 Dorothy Wellesley, *The Annual*, with an Introduction by V. Sackville-West (Cobden-Sanderson, London, 1930), p. vi.

9 Vita to Harold, 19 December 1944, quoted in Nicolson, ed., *Vita & Harold*, p. 359.

10 Vita to Margaret Smyth, 22 August 1945, Norman Colbeck Collection, Rare Books and Special Collections, University of British Columbia Library.

11 Glendinning, *Vita*, p. 288; Vita to Harold, 19 December 1944, quoted in Nicolson, ed., *Vita & Harold*, p. 359.

12 V. Sackville-West, *Solitude*, p. 5.

13 V. Sackville-West, 'The Touch of Nature', *Vogue*, late February 1924, p. 49.

14 V. Sackville-West, *The Land* (William Heinemann, London, 1926).

15 V. Sackville-West, *Solitude*, p. 53.

16 V. Sackville-West, 'Country Notes', *New Statesman*, 18 February 1939.

17 V. Sackville-West, *The Land* (Winter), *Collected Poems*, p. 19.

18 Cross and Ravenscroft-Hulme, *Vita Sackville-West: A Bibliography*, p. 223.

19 V. Sackville-West, 'Country Notes' ('Buying a Farm')

20 Stevens, *V. Sackville-West*, p. 116.

21 V. Sackville-West, *The Women's Land Army*, p. 20.

22 Vita to Harold, 4 June 1941, quoted in Nicolson, ed., *Vita & Harold*, p. 339.

23 Ibid.

24 Nigel Nicolson, ed., *Harold Nicolson Diaries and Letters 1930–39* (William Collins Sons & Co., London, 1966), p. 83.

25 Vita to Harold, 28 October 1935, quoted in Nicolson, ed., *Vita & Harold*, p. 278.

26 Vita to Harold, 26 August 1943, quoted in ibid., p. 353.

27 Rose, *Harold Nicolson*, p. 190.

28 Nigel Nicolson, ed., *Harold Nicolson: The Later Years 1945–*

1962 (William Collins Sons & Co., London, 1968), p. 52.

29   Vita to Harold, 7 February 1945, quoted in Nicolson, ed., *Vita & Harold*, p. 361.

30   Vita's diary, 3 June 1926, Lilly Library.

31   Ibid., 11 June 1926.

32   Nigel Nicolson, ed., *The Letters of Virginia Woolf, Vol. V* (repr. Hogarth Press, London, 1994), p. 291.

33   Bell, ed., *Diary of Virginia Woolf, Vol. 5*, p. 121.

34   Quoted in Glendinning, *Vita*, p. 286.

35   Vita to Harold, 14 November 1938, quoted in Nicolson, ed., *Vita & Harold*, p. 308.

36   Glendinning, *Vita*, p. 299.

37   Vita to Harold, 29 May 1913, quoted in Nicolson, ed., *Vita & Harold*, p. 45.

38   V. Sackville-West, *Knole and the Sackvilles*, p. 11.

39   V. Sackville-West, *Grand Canyon*, p. 191.

40   Ibid., p. 167.

41   Scott-James, *The Making of a Garden*, p. 94; p. 8.

42   V. Sackville-West, 'Sissinghurst Castle', p. 92.

43   Ibid.

44   V. Sackville-West, *Grand Canyon*, p. 93.

45   Brown, *Vita's Other World*, p. 142.

46   V. Sackville-West, *The Garden*, p. 15.

47   Tony Lord, *Gardening at Sissinghurst* (Frances Lincoln, London, 1995), p. 129.

48   V. Sackville-West, *Knole and the Sackvilles*, p. 18.

49   Jane Brown, *Sissinghurst: Portrait of a Garden* (Weidenfeld & Nicolson, London, 1990), p. 12.

50   Vita to Harold, 12 December 1939, quoted in Nicolson, ed., *Vita & Harold*, p. 318.

51   Vita to Shane Leslie, 15 January 1946, Manuscripts, Archives and Special Collections, Washington State University Libraries, Collection Number: Cage 4934.

52 Robert Sackville-West, *The Disinherited: A Story of Family, Love and Betrayal* (Bloomsbury, London, 2014).

53 V. Sackville-West, *The Garden*, p. 9.

54 Vita to Harold, 16 February 1944, quoted in Nicolson, ed., *Vita & Harold*, p. 357; Cross and Ravenscroft-Hulme, *Vita Sackville-West: A Bibliography*, p. 227.

55 Vita to Harold, 19 December 1944, quoted in Nicolson, ed., *Vita & Harold*, p. 359.

56 Glendinning, *Vita*, p. 326.

57 V. Sackville-West, *The Eagle and the Dove*, p. 133.

58 Ibid., p. 158.

59 Vita to Harold, 28 August 1940, quoted in Nicolson, ed., *Vita & Harold*, p. 328.

60 Brown, *Vita's Other World*, p. 154.

61 Quoted in Stevens, *V. Sackville-West*, p. 25.

62 Harold to Vita, 31 March 1941, quoted in Nicolson, ed., *Vita & Harold*, p. 336.

63 Trefusis, *Don't Look Round*, p. 97.

64 Vita to Harold, 28 August 1940, quoted in Nicolson, ed., *Vita & Harold*, p. 328.

65 Souhami, *Mrs Keppel and her Daughter*, p. 274.

66 Ibid., p. 273.

67 Ibid., p. 276.

68 Leaska and Phillips, eds, *Violet to Vita*, p. 51.

69 Glendinning, *Vita*, p. 324.

70 Souhami, *Mrs Keppel and her Daughter*, p. 282.

71 Leaska and Phillips, eds, *Violet to Vita*, p. 52.

72 Vita to Harold, 8 January 1952, Lilly Library.

73 Vita to Margaret Smyth, 21 April 1945, Norman Colbeck Collection, Rare Books and Special Collections, University of British Columbia Library.

74 Brown, *Vita's Other World*, p. 177.

NOTES

75 Nicolson, ed., *Harold Nicolson Diaries and Letters 1945–62*, p. 31.

76 Lees-Milne, *Harold Nicolson, Vol. 2*, p. 187.

77 Rose, *Harold Nicolson*, p. 268.

78 V. Sackville-West, *All Passion Spent*, p. 168.

79 Lees-Milne, *Harold Nicolson, Vol. 2*, p. 178.

80 Vita to Harold, 26 August 1943, quoted in Nicolson, ed., *Vita & Harold*, p. 353.

81 *The Sunday Times*, 15 January 1970.

82 Glendinning, *Vita*, p. 342.

83 Barber, Elizabeth, *Author by Profession* (Volume 2): Denys Kilham Roberts Papers, University of Iowa Special Collections MsC0828, University of Iowa Libraries.

84 Greene, Richard, *Edith Sitwell: Avant-Garde Poet, English Genius* (Virago, London, 2011), p. 286.

85 *The Times*, 15 May 1946.

86 Harold to Vita, 15 May 1946, quoted in Nicolson, ed., *Vita & Harold*, p. 368.

87 Stevens, *V. Sackville-West*, p. 25.

88 Vita to Harold, 2 June 1954, quoted in Nicolson, ed., *Vita & Harold*, p. 412.

89 V. Sackville-West, *In Your Garden* (Michael Joseph, London, 1951, repr. Frances Lincoln, London, 2004), p. 49.

90 Lord, *Gardening at Sissinghurst*, p. 130.

91 V. Sackville-West, *Observer*, 21 April 1957.

92 Nicolson, ed., *Harold Nicolson, The Later Years*, p. 88.

93 Vita to Harold, 5 June 1947, quoted in Nicolson, ed., *Vita & Harold*, p. 372.

94 Philip Hoare, *Serious Pleasures: The Life of Stephen Tennant*, p. 279.

95 Vita to Harold, 5 June 1947, quoted in Nicolson, ed., *Vita & Harold*, pp. 372–73.

96 Harold to Vita, 11 December 1947, quoted in ibid., p. 375.

97 Brown, *Vita's Other World*, p. 203.

98 Vita to Harold, 27 February 1952, Lilly Library.

99 Harold to Vita, 16 November 1955, quoted in Nicolson, ed., *Vita & Harold*, p. 416.

100 MacKnight, *Dearest Andrew*, p. 69.

101 Harold to Vita, 11 June 1952, Lilly Library.

102 Vita to HM Queen Elizabeth the Queen Mother, 16 June 1952, Royal Archives RA QUQM/PRIV/PAL: 16 June 1952.

103 Harold to Vita, 11 June 1952, Lilly Library.

104 Harold to Vita, 24 May 1955, quoted in Nicolson, ed., *Vita & Harold*, p. 416.

105 Nicolson, ed., *Harold Nicolson: The Later Years*, p. 110.

106 Ibid.

107 Ibid.

108 Stevens, *V. Sackville-West*, p. 115.

109 V. Sackville-West, *The Death of Noble Godavary*, p. 47.

110 Nicolson, ed., *Harold Nicolson: The Later Years*, p. 110.

111 Ibid., p. 196.

112 Lees-Milne, *Harold Nicolson, Vol. 2*, p. 210.

113 Olson, ed., *Harold Nicolson Diaries and Letters*, pp. 338–39.

114 V. Sackville-West, *The Easter Party*, p. 84.

115 Vita to Harold, 4 January 1951, quoted in Nicolson, ed., *Vita & Harold*, p. 398.

116 Nicolson, ed., *Harold Nicolson: The Later Years*, pp. 195–96.

117 MacKnight, *Dearest Andrew*, p. 61.

118 V. Sackville-West, *The Easter Party*, p. 27.

119 Ibid., p. 140.

120 Nicolson, ed., *Harold Nicolson, The Later Years*, pp. 195–96.

121 V. Sackville-West, *The Easter Party*, p. 235.

122 Glendinning, *Vita*, p. 380.

123 Lees-Milne, *Harold Nicolson, Vol. 2*, p. 262.

124 Harold to Vita, 4 September 1952, quoted in Nicolson, ed., *Vita & Harold*, p. 407.

125 Harold to Vita, 23 May 1961, Lilly Library.

126 Nicolson, ed., *Harold Nicolson: The Later Years*, p. 239.

127 MacKnight, *Dearest Andrew*, pp. 53–4.

128 V. Sackville-West, *Aphra Behn*, p. 41.

129 Vita to Harold, 20 June 1951, Lilly Library.

130 Vita to Harold, 19 May 1961, Lilly Library.

131 Glendinning, *Vita*, p. 383.

132 V. Sackville-West, *Family History*, p. 274.

133 Vita to Harold, 1 October 1957, Lilly Library.

134 Vita to Harold, 13 November 1961, Lilly Library.

135 Vita to Harold, 29 May 1913, quoted in Nicolson, ed., *Vita & Harold*, pp. 45–6.

136 Vita to Harold, 26 February 1958, quoted in ibid., p. 424.

137 V. Sackville-West, *Daughter of France*, p. 196.

138 V. Sackville-West, *No Signposts in the Sea*, p. 135.

139 Vita to Harold, 17 May 1962, Lilly Library.

140 V. Sackville-West, *The Land* (Spring), *Collected Poems*, p. 54.

141 V. Sackville-West, *No Signposts in the Sea*, p. 121.

BIBLIOGRAPHY

MORE THAN FIFTY years have passed since Vita's death. During that period, many of her personal papers, once housed at Sissinghurst Castle in Kent, have been dispersed in collections across the globe. A list of those collections of sorts can be found in the Acknowledgements. All primary source material used is credited to its donor organisation in the Endnotes.

SECONDARY SOURCES

Alsop, Susan Mary, *Lady Sackville: A Biography* (Weidenfeld & Nicolson, London, 1978)

Amory, Mark, *Lord Berners: The Last Eccentric* (Chatto & Windus, London, 1998)

Bell, Anne Olivier, ed., *The Diary of Virginia Woolf*, 5 Volumes (Penguin, London, 1979–85)

Blanch, Sophie, 'Contested Wills: Reclaiming the Daughter's Inheritance in V. Sackville-West's *The Edwardians*', Critical Survey 2007, Volume 19, Issue 1

Bradford, Sarah, *Sacheverell Sitwell: Splendours and Miseries* (Sinclair-Stevenson, London, 1993)

Brown, Jane, *Vita's Other World: A Gardening Biography of V. Sackville-West* (Viking, London, 1985)

————*Sissinghurst: Portrait of a Garden* (Weidenfeld & Nicolson, London, 1990)

Cannadine, David, *Aspects of Aristocracy: Grandeur and Decline in Modern Britain* (Yale University Press, New Haven & London, 1994)

Carney, Michael, *Stoker: The Life of Hilda Matheson OBE 1888–1940* (Published by the author, Llangynog, 1999)

Caws, Mary Ann, ed., *Vita Sackville-West: Selected Writings* (Palgrave, New York, 2002)

Connolly, Cressida, *The Rare and the Beautiful: The Lives of the Garmans* (Fourth Estate, London, 2004)

Cross, Robert, and Ravenscroft-Hulme, Ann, *Vita Sackville-West: A Bibliography* (St Paul's Bibliographies, Winchester, 1999)

Davenport-Hines, Richard, *Ettie: The Intimate Life and Dauntless Spirit of Lady Desborough* (Weidenfeld & Nicolson, London, 2008)

David, Hugh, *Stephen Spender: A Portrait with Background* (Heinemann, London, 1992)

DeSalvo, Louise, and Leaska, Mitchell A., eds, *The Letters of Vita Sackville-West to Virginia Woolf* (Hutchinson & Co., London, 1984, repr. Virago, 1992)

————*The Letters of Violet Trefusis to Vita Sackville-West, 1910–1921* (Methuen, London, 1989)

Dowson, Jane, ed., *Women's Poetry of the 1930s: A Critical Anthology* (Routledge, London & New York, 1996)

Fox, Sue, and Funke, Sarah, *Vita Sackville-West*, catalogue, Glenn Horowitz Bookseller (New York, 2004)

Glendinning, Victoria, *Vita: The Life of V. Sackville-West* (Weidenfeld & Nicolson, London, 1983, repr. Penguin, London, 1984)

———*Rebecca West: A Life* (Weidenfeld & Nicolson, London, 1987)

Greene, Richard, *Edith Sitwell: Avant-Garde Poet, English Genius* (Virago, London, 2011)

Harris, Alexandra, *Virginia Woolf* (Thames & Hudson paperback, London, 2013)

Hart-Davis, Duff, *Philip de László: His Life and Art* (Yale University Press, New Haven & London, 2010)

Hoare, Philip, *Serious Pleasures: The Life of Stephen Tennant* (Hamish Hamilton, London, 1990)

Holroyd, Michael, *A Strange Eventful History: The Dramatic Lives of Ellen Terry, Henry Irving and their Remarkable Families* (Chatto & Windus, London, 2008)

———*A Book of Secrets: Illegitimate Daughters, Absent Fathers* (Chatto & Windus, London, 2010)

Humm, Maggie, *Snapshots of Bloomsbury: The Private Lives of Virginia Woolf and Vanessa Bell* (Rutgers University Press, New Brunswick, New Jersey, 2006)

Jebb, Miles, ed., *The Diaries of Cynthia Gladwyn* (Constable, London, 1995)

Keppel, Sonia, *Edwardian Daughter* (Hamish Hamilton, London, 1958)

Leaska, Mitchell A. and Phillips, John, eds, *Violet to Vita: The Letters of Violet Trefusis to Vita Sackville-West, 1910–1921* (Methuen, London, 1989)

Lee, Hermione, *Virginia Woolf* (Chatto & Windus, London, 1996, repr. Vintage, London, 1997)

Lees-Milne, James, *Harold Nicolson: A Biography*, 2 Volumes (Hamish Hamilton paperback reprint, London, 1988)

———*Fourteen Friends* (John Murray, London, 1996)

————*Holy Dread Diaries, 1982–1984* (John Murray, London, 2001)

————*Diaries, 1942–1954* (John Murray, London, 2006)

————*Diaries, 1984–1997* (John Murray, London, 2008)

Lees-Milne, Alvilde, and Verey, Rosemary, *The Englishwoman's Garden* (Chatto & Windus, London, 1980)

Lehmann, John, *Virginia Woolf* (Thames & Hudson, London, 1975)

Lord, Tony, *Gardening at Sissinghurst* (Frances Lincoln, London, 1995)

Mackenzie, Norman and Jeanne, eds, *The Diaries of Beatrice Webb* (Virago Press, London, 2000)

MacKnight, Nancy, *Dearest Andrew: Letters from V. Sackville-West to Andrew Reiber, 1951–1962* (Michael Joseph, London, 1980)

Middelboe, Penelope, *Edith Olivier: from her Journals 1924–48* (Weidenfeld & Nicolson, London, 1989)

Nagel, Rebecca, 'The Classical Tradition in Vita Sackville-West's *Solitude*', International Journal of the Classical Tradition, September 2008, Volume 15, Issue 3

Nicolson, Adam, *Sissinghurst: An Unfinished History* (HarperCollins, London, 2008)

Nicolson, Nigel, ed., *Harold Nicolson Diaries and Letters 1930–39* (William Collins Sons & Co., London, 1966)

————*Harold Nicolson Diaries and Letters 1939–45* (William Collins Sons & Co., London, 1967)

————*Harold Nicolson: The Later Years 1945–1962* (William Collins Sons & Co., London, 1968)

————*Vita & Harold: The Letters of Vita Sackville-West & Harold Nicolson 1910–1962* (Weidenfeld & Nicolson, London, 1992)

————*The Letters of Virginia Woolf*, Volumes III to VI (repr. Hogarth Press, London, 1994)

Nicolson, Nigel, *Portrait of a Marriage* (Weidenfeld & Nicolson, London, 1973, repr. 1990)

————*Long Life: Memoirs* (Weidenfeld & Nicolson, London, 1997)

Olson, Stanley, ed., *Harold Nicolson Diaries and Letters 1930–1964* (Penguin, London, 1984)

Pearce, Joseph, *Bloomsbury and Beyond: The Friends and Enemies of Roy Campbell* (HarperCollins, London, 2002)

Pomeroy, Elizabeth, 'Within Living Memory: Vita Sackville-West's Poems of Land and Garden', *Twentieth Century Literature*, 28 (Fall 1982)

Pryce-Jones, Alan, Preface to *Little Innocents: Childhood Reminiscences* (Cobden-Sanderson Limited, London, 1932, repr. Oxford University Press, Oxford, 1986)

Raitt, Suzanne, *Vita and Virginia: The Work and Friendship of V. Sackville-West and Virginia Woolf* (Clarendon Press, Oxford, 1993)

Regis, Amber, 'Competing Life Narratives: Portraits of Vita Sackville-West', *Life Writing*, 8:3, pp. 287–300

————'Performance Anxiety and Costume Drama: Lesbian Sex on the BBC', in *Television, Sex and Society: Analysing Contemporary Representations*, eds James Aston, Basil Glyn and Beth Johnson (Continuum, London, 2012)

Rose, Norman, *Harold Nicolson* (Jonathan Cape, London, 2005)

Sackville-West, Robert, *Knole, Kent* (National Trust, London, 1998)

————*Inheritance: The Story of Knole and the Sackvilles* (Bloomsbury, London, 2010)

————*The Disinherited: A Story of Family, Love and Betrayal* (Bloomsbury, London, 2014)

Sackville-West, Vita, and Raven, Sarah, *Vita Sackville-West's Sissinghurst: The Creation of a Garden* (Virago, London, 2014)

Scott-James, Anne, *Sissinghurst: The Making of a Garden* (Michael Joseph, London, 1974, repr. 1981)

Sebba, Anne, *Enid Bagnold* (Weidenfeld & Nicolson, London, 1986)

Sharpe, Henrietta, *A Solitary Woman: A Life of Violet Trefusis* (Constable, London, 1981)

Sitwell, Osbert, *Great Morning* (Macmillan, London), 1947

Sitwell, Osbert, *Laughter in the Next Room* (Macmillan, London), 1949

Souhami, Diana, *Mrs Keppel and her Daughter* (HarperCollins, London, 1996, repr. Flamingo, London, 1997)

Sproles, Karyn Z., *Desiring Women: The Partnership of Virginia Woolf and Vita Sackville-West* (University of Toronto Press, Toronto, 2006)

Stevens, Michael, *V. Sackville-West* (Michael Joseph, London, 1973)

Trefusis, Violet, *Don't Look Round* (Hutchinson, London, 1952)

Wellesley, Jane, *Wellington: A Journey Through My Family* (Weidenfeld & Nicolson, London, 2008)

Woolf, Leonard, *Downhill All the Way: An Autobiography of the Years 1919 to 1939* (The Hogarth Press, London, 1967)

WORKS BY V. SACKVILLE-WEST

Chatterton (privately printed: J. Salmon, High Street, Sevenoaks), 1909

Constantinople (privately printed: The Complete Press, London), 1915

Poems of West and East (John Lane, The Bodley Head, London), 1917

Heritage (William Collins, London), 1919

The Dragon in Shallow Waters (William Collins, London), 1921

Orchard and Vineyard (John Lane, The Bodley Head, London), 1921

The Heir: A Love Story (William Heinemann, London), 1922

Knole and the Sackvilles (William Heinemann, London), 1922

BIBLIOGRAPHY

Grey Wethers (William Heinemann, London), 1923

The Diary of Lady Anne Clifford (William Heinemann, London), 1923

Seducers in Ecuador (The Hogarth Press, London), 1924

The Land (William Heinemann, London), 1926

Passenger to Teheran (The Hogarth Press, London), 1926

Aphra Behn (Gerald Howe, London), 1927

Twelve Days (The Hogarth Press, London), 1928

Andrew Marvell (Faber & Faber, London), 1929

King's Daughter (The Hogarth Press, London), 1929

The Edwardians (The Hogarth Press, London), 1930

All Passion Spent (The Hogarth Press, London), 1931

Sissinghurst (The Hogarth Press, London), 1931

Invitation to Cast Out Care (Faber & Faber, London), 1931

The Augustan Books of Poetry: V. Sackville-West (Ernest Benn, London), 1931

Duineser Elegien: Elegies from the Castle of Duino (The Hogarth Press, London), 1931

Thirty Clocks Strike the Hour (Doubleday, Doran & Company, New York), 1932

The Death of Noble Godavary and Gottfried Künstler (Ernest Benn, London), 1932

Family History (The Hogarth Press, London), 1932

Collected Poems: Volume One (The Hogarth Press, London), 1933

The Dark Island (The Hogarth Press, London), 1934

Saint Joan of Arc (Cobden-Sanderson, London), 1936

Pepita (The Hogarth Press, London), 1937

Some Flowers (The Hogarth Press, London), 1937

Solitude (The Hogarth Press, London), 1937

Country Notes (Michael Joseph, London), 1939

Country Notes in Wartime (Michael Joseph, London), 1940

Selected Poems (The Hogarth Press, London), 1941

English Country Houses (William Collins, London), 1941

Grand Canyon (Michael Joseph, London), 1942

The Eagle and the Dove (Michael Joseph, London), 1943

The Women's Land Army (Michael Joseph, London), 1944

The Garden (Michael Joseph, London), 1946

Nursery Rhymes (The Dropmore Press, London), 1947

Devil at Westease (Doubleday & Company, New York), 1947

Knole, Kent (Country Life for The National Trust, London), 1948

In Your Garden (Michael Joseph, London), 1951

Hidcote Manor Garden (Country Life for The National Trust, London), 1952

The Easter Party (Michael Joseph, London), 1953

In Your Garden Again (Michael Joseph, London), 1953

More for Your Garden (Michael Joseph, London), 1955

Berkeley Castle (English Life Publications, Derby), 1956

Even More for Your Garden (Michael Joseph, London), 1958

Daughter of France (Michael Joseph, London), 1959

No Signposts in the Sea (Michael Joseph, London), 1961

Faces (The Hogarth Press, London), 1961

Challenge (William Collins, London), 1974

INDEX

INDEX

INDEX

INDEX

INDEX

INDEX

BEHIND THE MASK